ON EATING INSECTS

ESSAYS, STORIES AND RECIPES

A grasshopper

ON EATING INSECTS

Josh Evans, Roberto Flore, Michael Bom Frøst and Nordic Food Lab

The beginning of Nordic Food Lab's Insect Project – the long journey detailed in the pages of this book – can be told through three short stories.

The beginning of Nordic Food Lab

It was sometime in 2006. I don't remember when – I only remember the bitter cold and howling, freezing winds that raged against my face and hands as I biked down winding streets, racing towards Noma. When I finally got to the restaurant, I began defrosting my hands and feet in the kitchen while I waited for the others to arrive.

The meeting we held that night was crucial to our future. It was still in the very early stages of Noma, at a time when we couldn't seem to figure out anything about the cuisine we wanted to cook. We were fumbling our way through every day, trying to do some creative work in between all the prep, and lunch and dinner services. In the few spare moments we had, we wondered what we were doing. What was it that defined a cuisine? Was it the ingredients or the technique, or both? Was it based on traditional ideas, or could you invent your own? With these questions (and more) in mind, we delved into books exploring food cultures of the past and looked at chefs from other countries for inspiration. It seemed that we were ready to explode with new ideas at any moment.

Some of these ideas were very bold and required much more attention than we could give them. We did whatever we could to stay afloat back in those early days. We ran a café that sold coffee, breakfast, pastries and sandwiches. On weekends we did weddings, and on Mondays we served scores of cruise-ship guests. So there was rarely enough time for proper experimentation. Back then Copenhagen was already rumbling with talent. I remember having the feeling that something amazing was about to happen, but the story in every kitchen across town was the same: they were all short-staffed and too overworked to really delve into these sorts of projects.

So, on that cold evening, I explained to the other chefs gathered my idea of a new, collaborative and experimental kitchen, where science, academia and cooking could all meet. It would operate with the sole objective of answering the questions we lacked the time to consider. It would take on research that rose from the Noma kitchen, and distil the culinary zeitgeist into tangible projects. It would be a place dedicated to fresh and bold ideas – a place for change that would share everything openly and freely. I thought that this could not only help Noma move forward, but could also act as a real boost for the whole city's dining scene. It took some time to make things official, but in 2008, we opened Nordic Food Lab as a non-profit foundation.

The beginning of the MAD Symposium

By 2010, we at Noma had been talking for some time about creating a meeting space for the restaurant trade. We didn't know how it would shape up, but we knew that it was time to connect with other professionals from around the world. We had felt it coming: the questions asked of our trade by both the media and our guests had started to change dramatically. No longer were they questions about the vinaigrette recipe for the turbot, or 'How on earth is this malt soufflé so light and fluffy?' The Spanish kitchen revolution had swept through the world and with that came a new dialogue between science and cooking, one that warped the idea of the traditional chef. Now we were asked: 'Are there hydrocolloids in your sauce?' 'Do you care about sustainability?' And even, 'How will you influence everyday people to take part in this new kitchen phenomenon?' In hindsight, it seems weird that these questions were so surprising to hear, but only because of how commonplace they are today. Back in those days, cooking school didn't teach you much about life outside the kitchen.

We wanted to discover the many ways in which meals influence cultures and societies across the world. That is how the MAD Symposium came into being, as a place to learn and experience new things. For the inaugural year, our theme was the plant kingdom. I thought it was a great moment to focus on vegetables, as they were starting to step into the limelight within the cooking community. Around the world, chefs were starting to see them not only as a 'side *Gemüse*' but as valuable and tasty – as exciting as a piece of foie gras!

As a teasing element of this symposium, we wanted to throw insects into the mix. Here was a genre of food so taboo in the West that it bordered on 'impossible to serve'. For that topic, we invited Alex Atala to speak. Alex was, and still is, a culinary mastermind and an authority on insects in food. He was the first to really get me into bugs, with a big fat ant from the Amazon that tasted like the best lemongrass you could ever imagine. I was sure that he had fed it something. That 'aha!' moment is what we wanted everybody at the symposium to experience.

The beginning of the Insect Project

In 2011, a couple of short months after Alex's presentation, I was sitting by my computer, dreading the necessary task of reading my emails. It's something I've always disliked, and ever since 2010, when we became a well-regarded restaurant, my daily intake of emails had exploded. It had become a super pain in the ass, and most of the time I just skimmed through a third of what was there. I'm sure I missed out on meeting a lot of great people as well as a lot of great conversations and opportunities during those years.

For some reason, though, one email luckily escaped my 'filter' that day. Interestingly, it was one of those painstakingly long emails (I later found out that Mark writes the longest of emails to describe the shortest of things), yet it was full of enthusiasm; it was from a young Dane, Mark Emil Hermansen, an anthropologist at the University of Oxford, eagerly explaining his master's thesis. It was called 'Creating Terroir: An Anthropological Perspective on New Nordic Cuisine as an Expression of Nordic Identity'. It had really grabbed the attention of his professors, and he had used Noma and our story as the basis for his research. It was fascinating to read a case study on the work that happens every day. It was enlightening and motivating at the same time. We quickly got Mark to intern at Nordic Food Lab. We didn't have any specific role or job for him – I just really wanted him to be part of the team, and I hoped something would crop up along the way that would enable us to keep him on permanently.

At the time, Nordic Food Lab was dabbling quite a bit in fermentation. It was more intuitive – which is how a chef works – but with Mark coming on board, it gave us the opportunity to do something more structured, something longer term. The only question we were waiting to answer was: what would that opportunity be? And then, out of the blue – I don't know where it came from, but it was like a sudden flash – all the dots were connected: our new fascination with insects through what we had just experienced at MAD; having a space like Nordic Food Lab, devoted to research; and a person who could actually do in-depth work. So I picked up the phone, got Mark on the line and asked him, 'Why don't we eat insects in the Western world?' That was my question, and from there the Insect Project was born. It has resulted in an incredible journey around the world, countless hours of research and an understanding of bugs and their potential. It also resulted in the hiring of some of the brightest people I've ever come across to conduct this exploration, and thus the very pages of this book.

Wild flowers from a Danish summer

This book has a few main parts. First are some introductory **Essays**, which tie together lessons and insights from over the course of the project. There is a bit of background on Nordic Food Lab and our Insect Project, and some things we think it is useful to keep in mind when working with and thinking about insects: how we form food preferences; how we talk about eating habits and cultural appropriateness; and who produces within, and controls and benefits from, emerging sections of the food system – such as that of insects.

Then there is the meat of the matter – the **Stories**. The stories from the field explore how we learned about insect gastronomy in cultures around the world through our fieldwork, and each one focuses on a certain species and the particular world it occupies. The first few field stories from Denmark are more general, as they are based on experiences from throughout the project; the others are from specific episodes during our fieldwork. The stories are organized chronologically, and list the date, location and participating team members, to help keep track.

Finally, there are the **Recipes**. They span the early stages of our research all the way to the moment of compiling this book, and as such they also illustrate our own learning process in the kitchen and the field. Many relate to our fieldwork trips, or were inspired by the background of a team member, or both; many were also created or recreated as part of a menu for a significant event or occasion. They reflect the dynamic space of the lab and the constantly changing roster of colleagues and collaborators that make the place what it is. Taken together, they show our vision for cooking, serving and eating insects in a gastronomic way.

Speaking of the team, you will notice a few recurring names throughout the book. The main ones are: **Ben Reade**, a chef from Scotland, who studied gastronomic sciences in Italy and who was part of the team as an intern from September to December 2011 and as head of culinary research and development from July 2012 to June 2014; **Josh Evans**, an academic from Canada, who studied humanities and sustainable agriculture in America and who was part of the team from June 2012 as an intern and then as researcher and project manager for the Insect Project from June 2013 to May 2016; **Roberto Flore**, a chef from Sardinia, who studied agronomy on his home isle and who became an intern with the team in February 2014, then head of culinary research and development from June of that year; and **Andreas Johnsen**, an independent documentary filmmaker who came with us on our fieldwork and made a documentary about the project, entitled *Bugs*. These four formed the core team, with many other collaborators joining in for specific parts of the project, at and beyond the Lab. One example is **Mark Bomford**, director of the Yale Sustainable Food Program and a member of our project advisory board, who has written the introduction for this book. Other key people include **Michael Bom Frøst**, a sensory scientist and director of Nordic Food Lab since the start of 2012 (see his essay on food preference formation on p.39), and **Mark Emil Hermansen**, an anthropologist with the lab from February to October 2012 who, as **René Redzepi** mentions in his foreword, helped conceive the project and initiated the process of seeking funding.

The book closes with a short conclusion, some tasting notes about the insects from our fieldwork, a glossary of terms, references with directions for further reading and recipe notes. This work is of course the fruit of many people's collective effort, whom we attempt to list as wholly as possible in the acknowledgements.

As a final note, at some points in the text, you will see parenthetical page numbers. These will point you to another part of the book with a direct connection to your current one. You may be led from one field story to another or from a moment in the field to the recipe that it inspired. Consider it an option to read the book choose-your-own-adventure-style – to stumble on things in an order that might yield unexpected surprises. Otherwise, good old chronology will work just fine.

On the Internet, insects always win. Choose any foodish enviro-metric you like: gallons of water, CO_2 equivalents of greenhouse gases, acres of land, feed-conversion-ratio comparisons, you name it. Truth, as interpreted and disseminated by infographics, will declare the unequivocal superiority of insects over any other animal we could choose to eat. Compare beef and crickets, for instance, and you'll see that per unit of water and feed input, a cricket always brings far more edible protein to the table than beef. If an insect and a cow get into a metrics fight, it doesn't matter if it's about saving the planet or going paleo – the insect always triumphs.

Despite insects' status as the most successful class of animals ever to have walked, flown, squirmed, hopped and swarmed about the planet, humans have not been generous in bestowing superlatives upon them. In western food traditions, insects are never the heroes and always the villains: pestilent forces of famine, disease and contamination. The current wave of gastronomic interest in insects casts such traditions into sharp cultural relief, rendering the contemptible creatures as infographic messiahs. Insects might be the best solution we have to the superlative problem of how to feed the world.

Messiahs notwithstanding, I've also seen the infographics about planetary resource depletion. Juxtaposing insects with cows is rather different from juxtaposing insects with the disheartening projections of the damage we are doing to our planet. When I do the latter, I am left asking: will eating insects be enough? Is it enough to aspire to a wholesale switch from eating cattle to eating insects, or can we do better?

Possessing the entrepreneurial spirit and disruptive proclivities that come with high-speed Internet and a decent Science, Technology, Engineering and Mathematics (STEM) education, I am keenly driven by the need to outclass the insects-as-food proposal. Instead of fewer greenhouse-gas emissions, how about zero greenhouse-gas emissions? Instead of minimal land use, how about no land at all? Instead of reduced freshwater consumption, how about removing the need for freshwater altogether? And instead of an ethical calculus that feels marginally less desultory when applied to insects than cows, how about an ethics that imbues the provision of food with forethought and beneficence?

I believe we already have a food source that not only meets the zero-impact criteria just outlined, it also – from a standpoint of calculated utilitarian ethics – is significantly more ethical than eating insects. I entreat you: bear with me while I make the case for eating whales.

The vast majority of the solar-energy resource that arrives on the planet every day is wasted. It does not reach our terrestrial crops but, rather, falls upon our oceans, where it is photosynthesized by highly nutritious but effectively inedible plants. A literal ocean of environmentally efficient food just out of our reach, these primary producers are too small and too dispersed, and we lack any practical harvesting technology to reap their benefits. Or do we? Consider the whale: an advanced biotechnology capable of autonomous navigation, collection, concentration and transformation of this untapped resource into human-edible form. Consider its sophistication: it is self-repairing, auto-reproducing, sentient and strategic. It roams oceans inhospitable to human life, employing a harvesting algorithm perfected over generations to concentrate dispersed marine photosynthesis into the most calorie-dense discrete food package of which we might conceive.

According to data helpfully provided in the US Department of Agriculture's *National Nutrient Database for Standard Reference Release 28*, 25 grams of bowhead-whale blubber provides almost 250 calories, meaning that a full day's worth of energy is contained in just 280 grams of the beast's flesh. If an adult blue whale weighs 420,000 pounds that adds up to nearly two billion calories in each archetypal whale unit. Info.gram suggests that one human, at an average burn rate of 2,470 calories per day, needs to assimilate 60,403,850 calories to complete a statistically average life. This means that 33.33 satiated human lives can be obtained for the outlay of just a single whale life. Granted that whale consciousness is ontologically opaque, I feel entirely justified in rounding up to fifty human lives for the purposes of this illustration. Further, seeing that these assumptions are for an adult whale who has already lived a rich and rewarding life in a natural environment, we might be able to prorate the value of its life fixated on that single, unfortunate day of harvest. As a blue whale might live 30,000 days, we arrive at only 0.00000333 lost whale lives per individual harvest, leading to an astonishing 1.5 million human lives gained for each whale life lost.

Compare all this to crickets: 100 grams of cricket meal contains 121 calories, but from the data provided on openbugfarm.com, I know it takes 470 crickets to yield 11 grams of meal, hence only 0.01934 calories per cricket life taken. Returning to our statistically average value of caloric nutrition needed to sustain a human life, a life subsisting on crickets would require three billion cricket lives per single human life. Since these figures are for crickets reared in captivity, unable to freely live up to their natural and inherent cricket capabilities, we will not prorate their lives in the manner that was appropriate for our hypothetical self-actualized adult wild whale nearing life's end. The lives of those 1.5 million humans who might be sustained through this single, quality-adjusted whale life would, by contrast, require the loss of four quadrillion cricket lives, if sustained through entomophagy alone. If you believe that the needs of the many outweigh the needs of the few, you can conclude that cetaphagy is more ethical than entomophagy by fifteen orders of magnitude.

I could continue in this inhumane style of argument ad infinitum, but it would only serve the same simple plea: be careful with the metrics you choose to assess the sustainability of food systems. Food systems are diverse and complex webs of life, and will elude capture by any single metric, model, frame of reference, narrative or way of knowing. Food-system problems – especially those that presume to forecast long-term sustainability – are 'wicked problems', which are defined in part by their unsolvability, at least using conventional methods of rational enquiry.

Five years ago, I created a colourful chart that compared the feed-conversion efficiencies of crickets with cows, chickens and pigs. I excitedly shared this information with Josh Evans, who was graduating from Yale University just as I arrived to lead its Sustainable Food Program. We were soon both caught up in a globe-spanning, three-year project that proposed to 'explore the deliciousness of edible insects' – Josh immersed full time as the lead researcher, and me offering sidebar commentary at annual advisory meetings. The project rested upon the assumption of the environmental superiority of insects and, by extension, the assumption that it would be a very good thing to eat more of them. First, though, we had to figure out how to make them delicious to people who currently preferred to eat cows, chickens or pigs. To do this, we had to learn what made insects delicious to some of the two billion people who find them delicious today – and to do that, Josh and crew had to set boots on the ground, watch, listen and learn. It became clear that insects, like all foods, were much more than the sum of terrific-looking feed-conversion ratios or carbon footprints on a triple-bottom-line spreadsheet. Insects were land, life, culture, ecology, meaning and mystery.

I still believe that it would be good if more people ate more insects. I no longer believe that this dietary shift will cause the planet to stand and applaud, subduing its rising oceans or recharging its depleted aquifers in gratitude. Why bother, then? Because eating insects is provocative. To eat a novel food – especially one that elicits initial fear or disgust – is the essence of eating mindfully. You have to ask questions, to satisfy trust in its provenance and, in doing so, begin to situate yourself in a place. To then ask further about how you are situated in this place, and the life (and lives) that ended only to be assimilated into your own – that's the beginning of thinking about what it means to belong and to sustain. I applaud the Nordic Food Lab team for this book that deftly avoids the 'edible insects save the world' hype trap. Like all hype, it will pass, and we'll be left with the longer-term questions of finding meaning as a moderately successful social animal with a poor feed-conversion ratio.

Ants and distillate used to make Anty Gin (p.222)

NORDIC FOOD LAB

_____

Nordic Food Lab is a non-profit, open-source organization that investigates food diversity and deliciousness. Established in 2008, we combine scientific and humanistic approaches with culinary techniques from around the world to explore the edible potential of the Nordic region. We work to broaden our taste, generating and adapting practical ideas and methods for those who make food and those who enjoy eating.

That's our mission statement; but there's more to the story. Before zooming in on insects, it might be useful to start at the beginning.

HISTORY

Nordic Food Lab was founded by René Redzepi and Claus Meyer, the chef and entrepreneur who started the restaurant Noma together in 2003, with the purpose of exploring food in the Nordic region – what it was, and what it could be.

The origin story may be apocryphal, but it's a good one, and goes something like this:

René was working on a dish with wild horseradish. Every time the foragers brought in some new horseradish to work with, it would taste completely different: sometimes sweet, sometimes delicate and aromatic, sometimes face-burningly pungent. At first, the variety was exciting; but when making a dish for a menu, to be replicated to exacting standards over and over again, such a broad variation in a primary ingredient just doesn't cut it. René was frustrated, and eventually shared his woes with a Danish naturalist, who told him something like, 'Well, of course you're getting different tastes each time – there are over 100 different varieties of wild horseradish in Denmark alone.' Something clicked: René realized that, as a chef, this was exactly the kind of knowledge he needed to have to develop the kinds of dishes he wanted to make. Yet he also realized that this investigation could not be undertaken in the restaurant kitchen alone.

Thus the idea for the Lab was born: a space where cooks, historians, foragers, scientists, producers and others who work with and research food could come together to investigate raw materials, traditional processes and modern techniques more deeply than the pressure of daily service would allow. They would pose gastronomic questions to the Nordic region, see how it responded, and share the open-source results with the region and the world.

The Lab was founded as a non-profit foundation at the end of 2008, and, at the beginning of 2009, gained a physical space on a refitted houseboat moored just outside the restaurant, on Copenhagen's main harbour. It resided there until November 2014, when it moved onto land as part of a collaboration with the Department of Food Science at the University of Copenhagen, and has been based there since.

———

METHODOLOGY

The Lab's primary driving force is the pursuit of deliciousness: if it's not delicious yet, experiment and play with it until something emerges – then iterate.

We cannot explore deliciousness with just one method. Food is complex, and requires multiple modes of investigation to come to know it best. By integrating the humanities, science and arts with the applied and tacit knowledge of the kitchen, we attempt to dissolve the arbitrary divide between 'theoretical' and 'practical' knowledge, and recognize that both are always involved when we try to make sense of food and eating. Biochemical knowledge can help us make better bread, for example, just as baking can recast the principles and nuances of biochemistry in a new light.

We have many interests and are experts in few of them. We will never know as much about vegetables as a farmer, or about microbes as a microbiologist – so we seek to put these approaches and their experts in dialogue, using modern and traditional methods to combine craft and science for delicious results. This cross-pollination gives rise to many interesting directions for research and cooking.

Examples

So what does this approach look and taste like, and what sorts of things does it yield?

Foraging for wild plants is nothing new. Yet the range of flavours is still astounding: the spiciness of cresses, the tonka-bean-like aroma of sweet clover (*Melilotus officinalis*), wood avens' (*Geum urbanum*) clove-like root, roseroot's (*Rhodiola rosea*) floral intensity, the acidities of sorrels and unripe plums. The list unfurls quickly. What further expands their gastronomic potency, however, are the different techniques we can

Local plants both wild and cultivated

use to bring out their different characteristics and fix them for longer periods of time. Understanding how temperature, solubility, hydrophilia and hydrophobia affect extraction of different compounds allows us to make infusions, oils, tinctures, enfleurages and absolutes, as appropriate to the material and the purpose. Indeed, many of these techniques come from other crafts – perfumery, distillation and traditional medicine, for example. They also expand our gastronomic toolkit in both novel and useful ways.

As far as culinary techniques go, fermentation is one of the most diverse and exciting. It is not a coincidence that much of our research has focused on different ways of using fermentation to unlock deeper flavours in Nordic ingredients. Lactic fermentations, like those used for pickled vegetables, cheese, butter and sourdough; acetic fermentations, as with vinegar; and symbiotic fermentations, involving yeasts and bacteria in kombucha, all enable us to produce different sources of acidity, which are essential in the kitchen, and mean a lot in an area where the growing season is quite short. Focusing on yeasts opens up new possibilities for brewing beer, mead and other alcoholic beverages, as well as baking bread. Collaborating with multicellular fungi has led to projects on curing meat, fermenting tea and working with *kōji* (*Aspergillus oryzae*), an enzymatic powerhouse we can use for fermenting other proteinous substrates. *Kōji* is the backbone of many of our misos, garums (see p.214–15), and other fermented, umami things: when fresh it is like a sweet cake with aromas of tropical fruits, and when roasted it becomes chocolatey, malty and even more complex. And while some of the substrates we use may be new to these processes, all of the techniques themselves are very old.

Umami is a constant fascination, and is not only found in fermented sources. Investigating the gastronomic potential of Nordic seaweeds was one of the Lab's first projects, a big part of which focused on developing sources of umami from the region's raw materials. Many algae are enjoyed in other cultures, notably in Japan, where *kombu*, or aged Japanese kelp (*Saccharina japonica*), is simmered with shaved *katsuobushi* – a hard, dried, smoked, multi-fermented bonito product – to make dashi, an umami broth that forms part of the foundation of Japanese cooking. Our interest in umami also led to the creation of a 'pork-bushi' or *butabushi*, a porcine version of *katsuobushi*, which we used in trials with regional algae such as Danish kelp (*Saccharina latissima*) and dulse (*Palmaria palmata*) to make our own dashi. These trials also led us to collaborate with chemists and sensory scientists to publish a paper on the synergistic effects of glutamate and certain 5'-ribonucleotides in enhancing the perception of umami taste (see References, p.320).

Exploring the food of this specific region does not preclude looking beyond it for inspiration. We have a perennial interest in learning from other cultures' foodways and how we can translate a technique or mode of preparation into our own geography, which dictates the materials we have to work with. Beyond many of the fermentation techniques outlined above, other examples include cooking with acid in the style of ceviche, alkalizing grains and pulses using nixtamalization, facilitating the enzymatic transformation of black garlic and many more.

Examples of the above undergird the recipes in this book. Ultimately, it is about cultivating an edible consciousness: strengthening the gastronomic response upon encountering a wild plant, an alga, a novel ferment or insect, so it is not one of disgust, but rather of appetite.

——

DELICIOUSNESS, DIVERSITY, RESILIENCE

What exactly is 'deliciousness', and why does it matter?

Far from positing it as an objective, discoverable property inherent in foods, we understand deliciousness as a contextual, relational phenomenon that varies across cultures, individuals and, for each of them, over time. We discover and develop our own tastes by eating, making, tasting and sharing.

While individual concepts of deliciousness may vary or not wholly coincide, few are the deliciousnesses that are satisfied with a single food. Many of us certainly have one favourite food, yet were it to become the sole food we ate for every meal of every day for the rest of our life, sooner or later most of us would tire of it. In some circles, this concept is called 'the boredom effect'; in others, it might simply be called getting sick of the same old. Yet what it indicates is clear: humans are omnivorous. Generally, we require, and thrive on, multiple sources of food.

Yet infinite choice can be paralyzing. By acknowledging geography as the foundation of gastronomy – of all knowledge that relates to eating – we gain a constraint that in return gives us freedom to experiment and play. Exploring our edible surroundings lets us discover and rediscover the diversity that is particular to this part of the world – and it gives us the opportunity to create foods that, at their best, speak truly of their birthplace and their future.

In this way diversity becomes our goal, as well as our starting point. It forms a loop of feedback mediated by ecology, necessity and appetite. There is no single food that can nourish us on its own. The pursuit of good food is also the pursuit of biocultural diversity – the pursuit of a future where everyone can not only eat, but eat well. Diversity – of autochthonous genetic material, of organisms, of cultural practices, of ideas – is what keeps our world at its most resilient and robust. Much research on food systems, conservation and agroecology, as well as traditional practices of cultures worldwide, support this notion. Diversity is the foundation of resilience; it is the cloth that weaves our fates together, and upon which we share our meals. It also often happens to help everything taste its best.

WORKING WITH INSECTS

WHY INSECTS

This insect madness all started for the Lab at the first MAD Symposium, a now-annual symposium for chefs and food professionals, in July 2011. Alex Atala, chef of the restaurant D.O.M. in São Paulo, gave a talk entitled 'Plants and Insects: Together for Life' and served an Amazonian ant that tasted of lemongrass, which blew the minds of everyone willing to try it (p.7). René then posed the question to the Lab team of why he couldn't serve insects on his menu. That question evolved into a multi-year research project into insect gastronomy, which gave rise to the stories and recipes in this book.

Why should we want to eat insects in the first place? And who is 'we'? From the beginning of the project, the primary reason was taste, and the primary 'we' was who we will call 'newcomers' – those eating an insect for the first time. Our mission is to look to the Nordic landscape as a source of flavours, some rediscovered and some tasted and investigated for the first time. It is part of our work to explore the gastronomic potential of all the organisms that comprise our biome: the algae, wild plants, game animals, sea creatures, fungi and microbes of all sorts. Yet it was only when confronted with such a tasty, lemongrass-y arthropod that we realized we had been overlooking a huge swathe of this edible diversity, simply because it was not already part of the culturally concurred edible domain.

Then, as we wrote the grant application for the funding that allowed us to carry out the research, it also became about many other things: sustainability, nutrition, legislation and food politics. Indeed, compared to conventional livestock animals, many insect species require fewer resources to grow, such as land, water, feed and energy; have less environmental impact; contain high proportions of protein, fats, vitamins and minerals; and are harmless to ingest. For these reasons and more, edible insects have rapidly become a popular topic in sustainable food discourse over the last few years. The United Nations Food and Agriculture Organization's (FAO) 2013 publication *Edible insects: Future prospects for food and feed security*, for example, is by far the most-downloaded publication in the organization's entire history.

Yet what kinds of sustainability and food security do certain insects contribute to, and when? How do, and can, certain insects fit into agroecological systems of food production? What are the relationships between traditional knowledge and scientific knowledge in supporting diverse diets of nourishing foods? And what is the role of taste and gastronomy in cultivating the kind of food systems that let life flourish?

Our project began with an enquiry into how certain insects taste and who eats them – where, how and why. It has also become necessary, as part of this enquiry, to grapple with the larger questions.

—

THE EDIBLE AND THE DELICIOUS

At the outset, these ingredients – grasshoppers, wax moths, bee larvae, local ants – were completely new to the Lab team. The work quickly began to engage with and question the concept of edibility itself.

When we say that something is 'edible', often we mean that it won't kill us. Sometimes, in a more humorous sense, we mean that the thing doesn't offend our senses so much that we would refuse to eat it. Yet toxicity is a matter of degree – almost anything in a high enough dose can kill – and of processing. Many ingredients are benign in one form, but harmful in another: elderberries (*Sambucus nigra*), for example, or fly agaric mushrooms (*Amanita muscaria*). Edibility is not a natural property of organisms, but a function of amount, technique and – especially – cultural convention. We set out to understand this last property more deeply, in the hope of using this conceptual clarity to make insects not merely 'edible', but genuinely enjoyable for us newcomers.

If you will indulge us, we present a brief, and basic, theory of the relationship between the delicious and the edible. Every individual possesses a set of things they find edible and a set of things they find delicious, which overlap like this:

Edible and delicious, a diagram showing overlap

In the middle, where the two sets overlap, are all the things this person eats and thinks are, or can be made, delicious. This is the category we call 'food'. In the remainder of the 'edible' set are things like plants that don't immediately taste that good to this person, but also won't kill them in a commonly ingestible amount – for example, this person knows you can eat dandelion greens, but they find them totally unpalatable. On the other side, in the remainder of the 'delicious' set, are things that *could* taste good to them, but which they do not immediately consider edible – let's say *kvass* ('It's rotten!'), or really aged butter ('It's rancid!'), or giant water bugs ('It's a bug!'). In this case, deliciousness becomes a potential property: not just something a food has already, but also something it *could* have under different circumstances.

So just as there are things that are in one sense edible before they are delicious, there are also things that are delicious before they are edible – which is to say, before they are *considered* edible. With insects or anything else, we try, through cooking and other methods, to make the edible things delicious and the delicious things edible for the palates of our region, expanding and diversifying its set of foods in both directions.

For most of us newcomers, few insects fall into the former group – perceived as edible but not enjoyed. On the contrary, most insects fall into the latter group, as their perceived edibility is almost entirely due to cultural appropriateness. Many of us simply do not know how tasty certain insects can be. To really understand this group of organisms well enough to steer their delicious potential towards newcomer palates, we had to look to the cultures where they are already celebrated and deeply known.

———

WORKING IN THE FIELD

One does not simply make up a cuisine from scratch, however 'new' it may aspire to be. In order to have any chance at cooking insects in a culturally appropriate way, we needed to understand some of the existing techniques – and the best way to learn technique is to absorb it firsthand, in its cultural and geographical context.

We could read about digging for Lepidoptera larvae in acacia roots in the Australian outback (pp.142–4). But books wouldn't tell us how critically their availability depends on season and rainfall; nor could they

Specimen samples from fieldwork in Australia

show us how to detect the presence of grubs from signs in the trees and soil, or how long and where to cook them in the ash of a fire.

We could interview locals in central Mexico about *escamoles* (pp.150–58). But interviews alone would not give us the thirst, from trekking in the dust to find a hive to harvest, fit only for the *escamol* collectors' pulque to quench; or get us stung by the ants that swarmed our bodies as we harvested their eggs; or let us smell the singular, beguiling smell from the hole in the earth beneath the maguey cactus.

We could find a *casu marzu* from Sardinia (pp.92–4), the pecorino or *casizolu* cheese colonized by the *Piophila casei* fly and nurtured to ripeness, and have it sent to Copenhagen. But we would not see how closely the farmers work with their special breeds of cows and sheep; how they warm and stretch the curd, pulling it into a bundle and indenting their mark into the crown with a finger; how, when the flies emerge by glorious accident, the producers keep it that way; and how the men – for it is mainly men who love it – smear it on thin *pane carasau* and eat it with a glass of thick red wine.

Even on our home turf of Denmark we encountered profound surprises in the field. An expedition to the isle of Livø, yielding a much lower haul of cockchafers (*Melolontha melolontha*) than we had hoped for, returned us to an initial question of this project: why don't we already eat insects in Denmark, or even, shall we say, in 'the West'? People propose different answers to this question – temperate climate, religious taboo, shibboleth and more – but one of the biggest reasons might be because nowadays, there really aren't that many around. Multiple historical records show immense numbers of *Melolontha* taking over fields in Denmark, Germany, France and other European countries, as late as the nineteenth and early twentieth centuries. In many of these places, there were also published recipes for how to use them, and they were seen as delicacies by many; *Maikäfersuppe* (May-beetle soup) in Germany, for example, was a soup made with the cockchafer adults, served with veal liver and toast, and is reported to have tasted like crab. Yet the cockchafer was, and is still, seen primarily as an agricultural pest. Along with many other insects in European landscapes it has been pushed out of the ecology with the rise of industrial agriculture and concomitant and widespread use of synthetic pesticides, especially from the mid-twentieth century onwards. There is still quite high species diversity in Denmark; there just aren't such high numbers, even if there used to be. We chose high-seed-yielding grasses over the insects that compete with us for them. Could we make a system where we can have both? Do such systems already exist?

To be sure, in each of these cases we did our preparatory reading, conducted interviews with locals and brought samples back with us (preserved in ethanol, for reference). Yet important as these efforts are, they merely supplement the core of this kind of research, which is personal, sensory and embodied. This is part of the purpose of this book: to share some of these stories and sensations and their potency for us, as well and as luminously as we are able.

In his talk at MAD1, Alex described his excitement over 'discovering' these 'new' flavours. They may indeed be new for many of us newcomers; yet the more we learn, the clearer it is that, in their own contexts, they are anything but new. Learning about these ingredients and techniques is not 'discovery' – which is to say, coming into knowledge of something for the first time anywhere; rather, it involves a gradual initiation into what is already vastly known, and a reckoning with how limited our awareness has been up to now. Many of these flavours and techniques are very old. They are known by societies around the world and it is likely we all consumed them at some point as part of our ancestral primate diet. Sometimes, the best way to access the most delicious versions of the present and the future is to look for what is already there.

———

TASTE DIVERSITY

No one eats all insects. In fact, a recurring theme in our fieldwork was that such questions as, 'Do you eat insects?' and, 'Which insects do you eat?' are rarely the best ones to ask. And often among the people in the world (and there are many) who eat some kind or kinds of insects, for every species they do eat, there are many more in their surroundings that they do not. From these observations, it quickly became clear that we cannot talk about eating 'insects' per se, as if they were a homogeneous category, but that we must talk about specific kinds of insects – certain species, developmental stages, sexes, and specific parts. This is what it means to have and develop gastronomic knowledge. We would rarely, if ever, talk about eating 'mammals' or 'birds'. It just doesn't make sense.

Similarly, what became abundantly clear on our fieldwork trips was that many of these insects, far from being foods of famine or desperation, were real delicacies. In many situations they were valued more highly than the meat of other local animals, for their particular tastes and often also for their nutritional richness.

With this goal of gastronomic specificity in mind, when we began working with insects in our own region, it was clear that different species had potential to serve very different gastronomic functions. Ants (pp.84–6) were of primary interest for their sour taste and distinct aromas, useful more as a spice or seasoning than for substance; meatier varieties like adult grasshoppers held the most umami potential, through fermentative breakdown into savoury sauces (pp.214–15); and bee brood (pp.87–9), the immature metamorphic stages before they hatch into adult bees, had a versatile flavour and texture that could be used variously in different contexts.

We also had to develop greater sensitivity to how flavours and textures changed depending on the season and the insects' developmental stages (as with bee brood, for example); when it makes sense to use them whole and celebrate their form, or use them less visibly as a supporting player; and when to keep them intact or remove legs, wings and/or other parts. For many newcomers, the hard part is not the taste, but rather the texture, paired with the psychological factor of consuming an entire organism, whole, in its immediate, unabstracted form. This is where the ingenuity of cooking comes into play. What are all the ways we can cook with insects, beyond putting a whole one on the plate? We hope to offer some illustrative examples.

For the whole adult insect, especially in older instars (phases of hemimetabolous insects, which moult as they grow), the crunchy exoskeleton can pose a challenge; we can either remove it, render it crisp or break it down. Though in many cases, we can also think of it as we do the thin shell of small crustaceans, or the bones of smaller fish – parts of those animals that, in many cuisines, are eaten along with the flesh. People in many cultures toast, roast or fry insects whole, crisping the crunchy, chitinous exoskeleton, composed of structural proteins and long polysaccharide chains, into something that shards and dissolves in the mouth. Fermentation provides another strategy for dealing with the exoskeleton: instead of cooking or removing it, we can break it down physically, enzymatically and metabolically, along with the flesh, to gain aroma and taste while alleviating the difficult texture. This is another goal of the fermented sauces (pp.214–15): to enhance umami taste and develop complex flavour, while sidestepping the exoskeleton entirely.

Many more examples of culinary considerations fill this book. Suffice it to say for now that whenever we encountered a novel culinary challenge, most of the time we were able to draw on an experience from the field to use as a starting point. Our lessons and techniques learned in the field deeply informed our culinary research at the Lab, and for this we are grateful to everyone who helped us learn.

FOOD SECURITY

We are investigating insect gastronomy and the potential of insects in Nordic cuisine, but we should be clear that investigating is not the same as promoting. Certainly there are many cases in which bringing insects into our kitchens doesn't make sense – when it means importing large numbers of insects from halfway around the world, for example. Culinary knowledge, on the other hand, is transferable and fertile; this is why our fieldwork focuses on technique.

The recent surge of global interest in edible insects might make them seem like a panacea for world hunger and a slew of environmental problems. What is more likely is that no organism is inherently sustainable – no one species can create sustainable food systems, just as no single food can nourish and delight us for every meal of our lives. There seems to be a similar narrative arising around insects that has arisen before around other foods. Consider soy products: a few decades ago, in the 1960s and 1970s, nutritionists and food activists alike seemed in broad agreement that soy was going to save the world. High in protein, cheap to produce, easily transportable and amenable to being processed into many different products, soy seemed an obvious cornerstone of the imminent utopian food system. Moreover, as a traditional food in many cultures, soy brought with it ample and well-developed knowledge about how best to prepare and eat it.

Today, of course, what we see is far from what the first soy supporters supposed. More than four million hectares of forest in South America alone are destroyed each year for soy production, and at least 80 per cent of this soy goes to cheap feed for industrially raised animals, the meat of which is then shipped around the world. Mass deforestation, paired with mass-produced, artificially cheap and bland meat, is not a food system at its most delicious or its most robust. And industrial soy, like industrial corn, is a far cry from the varieties grown and eaten in East Asia, which are processed and prepared to make it nourishing and delicious.

The same may well be happening with insects right now. One of our biggest fears, despite our best intentions and caution about the possible implications, is that our and others' research will be used to reinforce the established industrial paradigm of monocultural mass production, instead of challenging and reconfiguring it. This pattern is already emerging with insects, and it is a path that rarely ends well – not for taste, not for ecological resilience and not for biocultural diversity.

One widely quoted FAO statistic says that the world population will increase to nine billion by 2050, and that meeting this demand will require increasing food production by 70 per cent. Yet this figure is mainly used to reinforce prior ideological commitments to modes of food production that are demonstrably destructive to the Earth and its systems, rather than opening up space for alternative ones (see the Tomlinson paper in References, p.320). Furthermore, the UN World Food Programme (WFP), on the other hand, states that there is already enough food on the planet to feed the global population. Increasing industrial mass production makes sense only if we intend to perpetuate the existing system of overabundant yet poor food, monstrous food waste and lack of food accessibility, as well as the cycles of poverty, hunger and malnutrition. 'Insects', in the discourse of global food security, seem more and more to be another swapping strategy – changing an input within a stagnant system. The input is trivial when the whole system is broken.

––

THE IN-BETWEEN

The anthropologist Claude Lévi-Strauss famously used cooking as an analogy for mediation between the realms of the 'natural' (the raw) and the 'socialized' or 'civilized' (the cooked). This binary is clearly outmoded. Alex Atala has proposed an interesting reinterpretation of this distinction. He notes that in Brazil – incidentally the country where Lévi-Strauss conducted much of his research on structuralizing tribal mythologies – many cultures distinguish the natural material from the cultured one not through cooking, but through fermentation: a process that occurs constantly, without human input or intervention, some aspects of which we have tinkered with and now also use for our own purposes. This third category, fermentation, presents something in between, something that is neither quite 'nature' nor 'culture'. Western colonists' obliviousness to this understanding of 'cooking', Alex posits, has been part of the reason why they for so long regarded these cultures as 'savage'.

This in-between space not only breaks down the binary, but also reveals the ambiguity of the categories in general – an ambiguity that has huge implications for how we interact with diverse methods of food production and preparation. For example, 'the wild' and 'the cultivated' can be seen as analogous to the raw and the cooked, yet many of the most delicious things often spring from the space in between: the semi-cul-

Outback landscape around Yuendumu, Australia

tivated, the replanted, the opportunism of organisms. Bees are one of the most immediate examples. Honeybees and humans have co-evolved with one another – indeed, in many regions of the world, such as northern Europe, one is unable to exist without the other. Yet honeybees are neither fully domesticated nor fully wild (whatever either term may mean). There is a preponderance of similar examples of how humans have interacted with the insect class: tending to *escamol* nests to safeguard their survival from overharvesting (pp.150–58); felling dead or dying palm trees to facilitate the life cycle of palm weevil larvae in their pith (pp.125–9); or growing plants in dense polyculture to create ideal habitats for giant tobacco crickets (pp.116–19). We can see further examples of the in-between in our interactions with the plant kingdom: taking wild plants and replanting them in our fields, without selecting for seed; or the wild plants growing in profusion in disturbed and marginal areas, like hedgerows, roadsides and rewilded industrial land. We are not growing these plants directly, but are advertently or inadvertently creating conditions of which they take advantage.

Even if we do not realize it, we change 'nature' and cook the 'raw' simply by existing and doing what we can to perpetuate ourselves. Australian honey ants (pp.137–41) emerge in the desert landscape because they serve the function of storing energy for the hive during unpredictable periods of dryness. The Australian desert landscape itself emerged with the rise, and decline, of methodical burning to manage the landscape and stimulate diverse, consistent, predictable food production – a sophisticated land-management strategy developed by aboriginal peoples over the last 40,000 years, across the entire continent. Now, even the seemingly simple act of digging up a honey ant and sucking out its concentrated nectar is not a purely 'natural' act; there are thousands of years and layers of cultural phenomena and knowledge that have made that moment possible.

As cooks and as eaters, we are not grand mediators, but rather just a few of the many players in a messy natural-cultural system that gives rise to the diversity and deliciousness in our diets. Recipes are but one of many means to this end; kitchens are but one of many areas where this endlessly complex set of processes plays out. Let us recognize and celebrate all the rest.

FOOD FOR EVERYONE

We do not believe that everyone in the world should eat any one insect, or even insects in general. We do not believe that everyone in the world should eat any one thing – that is probably not the way to make tasty, nourishing, diverse, culturally appropriate food available to everyone. It also smacks of imperialism and dystopia! Though where and when it makes sense – where and when specific insects can help cultivate more diverse, resilient local and regional food systems – it may be an idea worth pursuing, for the same reasons that we should investigate the edible potential of our entire surroundings, wherever we live in the world. And who gets to decide 'what makes sense'? It is an ongoing question throughout this book, and one we hope to begin to address.

Nor does accepting insects as food necessarily entail eating them. Western cultures have quite a bit of normative power in the world, and if they were to dismantle the stigma they perpetuate and acknowledge the ecological, cultural, nutritional and culinary value of diverse insects to many people around the world, it could help reverse the perception of eating insects as inferior and inappropriate and disgusting. It could help slow or stop the destruction of biocultural diversity in the places where insect-eating traditions are both most historically robust and most rapidly being given up, often with serious consequences for human nutrition. Instead, it could help continue the development of these rich culinary traditions and, crucially, the ecological stewardship, biocultural diversity and food security that go along with them. This principle applies not just to insects, but to the world's many traditional foods in general.

What do you eat, and what do you not eat, and why? These are the questions at the core of this book. Our hope is that it helps us begin to answer them, and to listen to the answers of others with open hearts and mouths.

INSECTS: AN ACQUIRED TASTE

MY FIRST TASTE OF INSECTS

By Michael Bom Frøst

There's a first for everything, and my first time intentionally eating insects[1] was a unique situation. Through tasting them, I learned why we should eat them. It happened at the first MAD in July 2011, a symposium in an unusual location: a remote corner of Copenhagen, in a place that was lying fallow called Refshaleøen. For that weekend, it had been turned into a food event called MAD Food Camp. In the furthest corner of it, MAD Symposium took place – a meeting place for chefs, artists and scientists. The audience was limited to who could fit in a small circus tent, and it was clear that this was different from the festival ambience that characterized the surrounding Food Camp. As the seasoned academic that I am, it was clear that the organizers – although enthusiastic and determined – had little experience in arranging symposia. Instead, the ambience had the hustle and bustle of kitchen and restaurant scenes. But this was clearly intentional, and it was a refreshing place to share knowledge and visions. As the event rolled out and speakers delivered their presentations, I had what I would best describe as a religious experience. The organizers, presenters and the audience shared a great passion for food and a belief in food as fundamental to our lives. There was a shared belief that food can, and should, be used to make our future more delicious.

There were many good ideas shared in that symposium. My favourite talk, and the one that changed both my mindset and those of many other people, was Alex Atala's: 'Insects and Plants: Together for Life'. In it, he presented thoughts and ideas behind his use of various ingredients and raw materials from the Amazon rainforest. It was an amazing line-up of exotic products and mind-blowing foods, and for each one, he explained his vision and elaborated on its background. Alex is not a native English speaker, and he is famed for his food, not his talent as a public speaker. But despite the difficulties we non-native speakers have – or perhaps even because of them – he mesmerized the audience with his bold ideas about why indigenous ingredients from the Amazon have a significant role in the cuisine at his restaurant, D.O.M. A few tasters were distributed among the audience during the presentation, while Alex showed more examples on-screen and to the camera. The ambience reached a crescendo when a type of ant from the Amazon was distributed, trapped in a soft gelatin gel and encased in a clear plastic wrap. Alex described it as having a distinct flavour similar to lemongrass and ginger. That description built up my anticipation as I unwrapped it. The soft, slightly cold but completely flavourless gel met my mouth first; as I crushed it with my molars, I was surprised by the intensity and singularity of the refreshing flavour. We were all relieved by its deliciousness and its familiarity, with its resemblance to lemongrass and ginger. The audience burst out laughing when Alex told us how, when Amazonians were introduced to the flavour we know as ginger, their reply was, 'It tastes just like ants!' Culture is indeed a determinant for what we like and how we perceive food.

Eating an Amazonian ant in this setting was, at the time, the paragon of an exotic taste experience for me. It was mind-changing – not just the flavour, but the flavour in combination with a powerful narrative about indigenous products. Alex presented a number of good reasons to eat insects: they're a good protein source, doing so preserves indigenous peoples' foodways and it's fun! Alex strengthened the sensory experience with his arguments, with the punchline that it was a piece of the Amazon in your mouth – a stunning example of how place is important for cuisine. D.O.M.'s valorization of Amazonian foodways helps to preserve them. To preserve tradition, you must eat it.

Now I don't see an ant as a particularly exotic food. Through my work at Nordic Food Lab, ants have become part of my food preferences – the food that I know, like and have a sensory library for. I readily admit to not eating insects every day. But how did this change in my preferences happen? I'll try and explain how we at the lab utilize the underlying principles for the formation of food preferences to direct the general public's interest towards the diverse tastes of insects, which are treasured by the people who eat them.

The theoretical framework that we apply to get a comprehensive understanding of what good food is was inspired by design theory. It provides a useful direction for factors that anyone who wants to make delicious food can use. The experience we have with a product or object occurs at three distinct levels: first, the basic, immediate sensory level is determined by how our senses are hardwired to transform the physical and chemical properties of food into a sensory experience. Second, food has the basic biological function of nourishing us. Last, food has meaning to us, and that meaning is a large part of our appreciation of the food. It may be that we like the methods by which the food is produced, or we admire a particular dish for its innovative content and its creative process. This reflective level is where the narratives work. Good narratives around the food we try are what have the potential to change our food behaviours.

The idea of three distinct levels of interaction with food guides us in the creation of new foods and dishes. We have repeatedly experienced that when a food excels on all three levels, it is irresistible. A short description of how a food or dish builds on tradition, or applies ancient techniques in novel ways, can provide a powerful weapon for those who seek to change the foodways of the world. A word of warning to those who apply storytelling to food without transparency about the ways the food is produced: this is sure to backfire if the story behind the food is not really what it is made to seem.

In essence, good food is good for the senses, the body and the mind. Deliciousness extends beyond the bodily pleasures a food provides.

———

CULTURE IS A DETERMINANT FOR OUR FOOD PREFERENCES

Humans are omnivores. That is the main reason for our success in our all-encompassing settlement of the planet. We shape our environment to suit the imperative of getting enough calories year-round. The procurement of food has probably shaped much of our cultured world all the way back to the dawn of humankind, but it was first adequately documented in Mesopotamia, in the Fertile Crescent. From a biological perspective, we can sustain ourselves on a very broad range of nutrient compositions. If it makes us feel satiated, and we do not immediately become sick from it, there are neural feedback mechanisms that teach us that this object has value as food. Learning to appreciate insects is a special case in the general topic of how we come to like the foods we eat. We have a way of scanning what we taste that is located not only in our taste buds, but in all of the sensory systems we use to make sense of the world around us.

There are a few predetermined taste preferences that we use to guide us in our search for nutrients. We are hardwired to like the three macronutrients: carbohydrates, lipids and easily digestible protein. They possess distinct, unique taste sensations for us – sweet, fat and umami, respectively. Our innate likes prepare us for our first food, breast milk, which is rich in these three taste sensations. In opposition to our innate likes, we have an inborn dislike for bitter tastes. The innate dislike for bitter tastes prevents us from eating foods that contain poisonous compounds. These compounds are often bitter, and our taste receptors contain a battery of around twenty-five different bitter receptors, so we can detect a very broad array of potential toxins. Yet there are also many bitter compounds that we can come to like, despite our initial negative feelings about their taste. Some of the most popular beverages in the world – such as coffee and beer – contain bitter-tasting compounds. Our preference for these particular bitter tastes is due to their link to the positive effects that these compounds have on our bodily and mental states – a conditioned response. Does the name Pavlov ring a bell? The stimulating effect of caffeine teaches us that coffee is something positive; with enough exposure, people can come to appreciate its bitter taste. The stimulating and intoxicating effect of alcohol is coupled with the bitter taste of hops in beer, and so, with exposure, we come to appreciate that bitterness. However, the power of alcohol can also backfire; if we drink too much and become intoxicated to the point of getting sick and vomiting, it is common to develop an instant aversion to the particular type of alcohol we were drinking. This is commonly known as the alcohol binge aversion – very often experienced with tequila, after taking too many shots in too short a time for the alcohol to show its full effect.

So there are the few innate likes and dislikes for basic tastes. In addition, there are a few textures and consistencies that people generally do not like – slimy, gummy and stringy – most likely because they signal the decay of food, or because they make it more difficult to be in command of the food in your mouth. Everything else we like or dislike is learned via exposure, and the consequences that exposure has for our bodily state. From a narrow, sensory point of view, a liking for new food starts by pairing its sensory properties (flavour, texture, taste, etc.) with a feeling of satiety and an absence of short-term negative consequences, such as sickness or discomfort. This principle is known as flavour-nutrient learning. Also, we come to associate the positive, basic sensations of sweet, fatty and umami, as well as the flavours that often co-occur with these taste sensations, to satiety and pleasurable bodily states. Once this has been learned, it is enough to pair these sensations with unknown flavours (such as the nutty, raw-corn flavour of bee larvae) for us to develop a preference for those new properties. This is known as flavour-flavour learning. However, for those two principles to have an effect, the requirement is that we do have to eat the food.

Our experience of a food starts prior to when we actually taste it. The two distance senses – sight and smell – allow us to assess foods without being in direct contact with them. The appearance and smell of a food will create many expectations for its other sensory properties: its tastes, flavours and textures. For us to leap into tasting a food, we must be confident enough that it is something safe to eat, and something that we will like. Since we are omnivores, the palette of foods that are safe and liked by at least some people is enormous. That is our dilemma whenever we make food choices.

DISGUSTING INSECTS!

The word disgust originates from Latin, and its original meaning is 'bad taste'. Although its broader definition encompasses domains other than food, disgust is something that plays a central role in what we reject eating. The psychologist Paul Rozin has studied disgust for many years and has produced several seminal insights in the field. Disgust is a powerful feeling that has a basic, universal facial expression connected to it. The muscles that are most active in that expression are the ones utilized to get rid of the substance causing the feeling of disgust: the nostrils close, the mouth gapes and the tongue often extends out of the mouth. The internalization of foods is a critical control point; we must make sure that what we're eating is good, and if it isn't, then we must rid ourselves of the foul object by all means. The main reasons for disgust for a food are distaste, danger and inappropriateness. It is imperative that we protect ourselves from dangerous foods. This could include dangerous decay – such as pathogenic microorganisms that would cause us harm or great intestinal discomfort – so immediate rejection is required. It could also be contaminated with dangerous matter, harmful bitter compounds or, for example, faeces or dirt.

Some of the quintessential animals associated with faeces, dirt and decaying matter are insects: cockroaches, blowflies, black soldier flies and dung beetles. They are connected to the foulest things around us. How, then, can we overcome the barrier against eating insects? At the lab, we use all the tricks of the gastronomic trade, as well as insights from psychology and food preference formation, to convey the message that insects are safe to eat. The ideational barriers about insects being unfit for us Westerners to eat can be met with good storytelling, and by creating food that brings out all the beauty of these novel ingredients.

When a diner trusts him or herself to a restaurant's tasting menu, an implicit contract is made: the diner trusts the chef to have selected foods that will be delicious and not make him or her sick. However, in the fine-dining temples of the world, part of the entertainment is to deliver something more risky than crowd-pleasing. At Noma's ten-day pop-up restaurant at Claridge's in London, put on in connection with the Olympic Games in August 2012, they served ants on a piece of cabbage leaf, dressed with crème fraîche. This was a clear-cut dare from Noma, and it naturally made headlines all over the gastronomic world as people discussed the topic. Undeniably, whenever Nordic Food Lab serves insects to insect-eating novices, we also push the boundaries of what they want to eat. The key is to do it in a way that is compelling and inviting – not pushy.

Mise en place for Whead and Weed (pp.248–9)

BALANCE IS THE KEY TO SUCCESS FOR NEW FOODS

The omnivore's dilemma consists of two elements, contained in our relationships to familiarity[2] and novelty[3]. We like what we know: the familiar foods and flavours of our culture and our childhood. Yet too much of the same is not pleasurable; familiarity breeds contempt. So we do like familiarity in our foods, but too much of the same is boring and unpleasant. We also like to try novel flavours and eat novel foods. Because they are unknown to us, they have the potential to provide us with diversity in both macro- and micronutrients, as well as delightful, new experiences. However, exactly because they are unknown, they may also be unsafe to eat. Less severely, but more immediately, they may just be unpleasant or distasteful. This is the second element of the dilemma: we both like and fear novel foods and flavours. We each like and pursue novelty and variety in our food in different amounts. This is known as variety-seeking behaviour, and it is a basic psychological trait. Some have a voracious appetite for new flavours, while others are devastated when their favourite staple food is discontinued by the producer.

For anyone who wants to introduce new foods to the world, a balance between familiarity and novelty is central to success[4]. This is relatively new knowledge in relation to food. It was first demonstrated in craft beer, but it appears to be a sound principle that extends to other consumables. Interestingly, experienced novelty and familiarity are not necessarily inversely correlated; rather, they can be completely uncorrelated – a food can be experienced by the eater as both highly familiar and highly novel. A food that strikes a sound chord of recognition, yet still gives the eater the excitement of trying something new, is a sure success.

Each food experience is an interplay between the person eating, the food and the context in which the food is consumed. The diner's background and experience have a major influence on what the experience will be for that person in that situation. However, the immediate context exerts a sound influence on the experience as well. In their book *The Perfect Meal: The Multisensory Science of Food and Dining*, the experimental psychologists Charles Spence and his protégé Betina Piqueras-Fiszman stick their necks out and estimate that up to a good half of the dining experience is controlled by the context in which the food is eaten. So to a very large extent, those who cook and serve the food can shape the food experience of the eater by controlling the context. Consider the desire to make people – insect debutants – open to eating insects, probably overstepping the boundary of what they think is edible: here, it is beneficial to create situations in which insect debutants feel open to new experiences, and in which the whole setting seduces the eater into being adventurous.

There's only one first time for every food experience. The only way we can come close to re-experiencing this virgin tasting is by inviting someone else to join in and observing their first experience. In recent years, sharing these experiences with others online, through images and words, has become part of the escalating self-representation of ourselves as diners. Sadly, for the well-versed diners of the world's fine restaurants, it has become almost impossible to experience a fine-dining meal without explicit expectations about signature dishes. With exposure and experience, our perception of novelty and familiarity of a particular food changes. When diners repeat an eating experience, part of the experience is also the memory of previous experiences: how they felt about it, and how this exact food experience compares with others. The memory extends beyond the memory of the food to encompass the setting and the narrative that surrounded an eating experience, and that narrative is reinvigorated every time they talk about it. That is why the narrative around a food is such a powerful tool: a story about food can travel much faster and wider than can the food itself or the experience of eating it.

———

APPROPRIATE BEHAVIOUR – FOR GOODNESS' SAKE!

Although I do love a good beer, there are very few instances when I have had it for breakfast. Even if at the time it seemed like an appropriate beverage, beer is generally highly inappropriate at that time of day. The principle of appropriateness is a strong determinant for the food and drinks we will have in a given situation. The time of day, season and place all give strong indications for which foods we want and like to eat. This goes far in determining the proper foods for different situations. The day is divided by the meals we have, and in most Western cultures it is easy to classify a meal according to time of day just by glancing at its constituents. There are also implicit guidelines for what we can serve guests and family, and what we can eat alone. These are examples of how appropriateness determines which food to make and eat for different situations. In the darker seasons, for me, a drop in temperature induces a desire for soup. In summer, a few days of sunshine begs for *koldskål* [5]. The rise of local and New Nordic Cuisine is evidence of how strong a role time and place play in the creation of a unique experience. This is skilfully utilized by restaurants such as Noma and Fäviken, which are heralded for their local and regional cuisines.

Some of the recent research on consumer responses to insect foods in Western countries has investigated the role of appropriateness in the acceptance of insects. Grace Tan, a talented young researcher at Wageningen University, executed a careful study in which she modified burger patties with various raw materials, leading people to think that some of them contained insects. The result was that the eaters did like the taste of the modified beef patties when they believed it to be because of insects, but they still found the patties inappropriate to eat. This indicates that there is resistance when trying to convert Western consumers from curious tasters to regular eaters of insect foods. This may be due to slowness in our recategorization of novel foods as they are introduced to us. It takes many exposures for us to understand their place in our cuisine and in our everyday diet. However, I think that globalization speeds up the pace of recategorization. Sushi is one example of a food that has won over many Westerners, turning them into loyal eaters in recent decades. It is also my belief that our likelihood of perceiving novel foods as appropriate is higher when we possess good intercultural competence.

——

DESIGNING FOODS THAT WILL CONVERT PEOPLE TO EATING INSECTS

Cooking delicious food with insects relies on choosing the right elements for all parts of its appeal – to the senses, to the body and to the mind. We have been going at this task, humbled by the implications it could have on the world's food habits if we and others with the same mission succeed in convincing the Western world to eat insects. Recent research has demonstrated that if foods or ingredients are experienced as unfamiliar, they are considered appropriate for fewer eating occasions than are familiar foods. The typical Western diner surely sees insects as unfamiliar, and the eating situations in which they can imagine eating them are limited. The skilled chefs and the interdisciplinary team of students and researchers who have been involved in the lab's project have met the challenge of introducing eaters to insects for the first time. Over the years we have had many memorable moments when people from all walks of life have eaten insects for the first time. In my memory, there is one story that exemplifies what we have had to overcome, and what we have achieved. It was in connection with our first real insect event, held at the Wellcome Collection in London in April 2013 for a festival called Pestival. We had invited several chefs from our head chef, Ben Reade's, network to work with us and contribute to the development of the menu. Nurdin Topham was one of them. When we started out, the first insects Nurdin tasted were simple, pan-roasted mealworms.

He literally shook his head in disgust and jumped back from the stove, screaming inarticulately in a shrill voice, but managed to not spit them out. This was not a pleasant experience for him! But he ate them, stayed on and made wonderful contributions to the menu and its execution.

One of the initial questions that we needed to answer was whether the appearance of insects was detrimental to the appreciation of dishes containing them. Others have found that the strategy of adding insects to food without making them visible has increased the acceptance of those foods. However, two of the eclectic examples of this include burger patties made with ground crickets and meatballs made with mealworm flour; the foods were served without telling the eaters that they contained insects. Stealth introduction of insects is not a strategy that we at Nordic Food Lab endorse, and we needed to investigate that systematically. Is it really the sight of insects that will make you like a food less?

In November 2012, Josh created a Bee Brood Granola (pp.220–21)[6]. The granola can be designed without visible insects, yet it has the distinct flavour of roasted bee larvae. To the uninitiated, it will be characterized by the dark colours of the granola – the product of the Maillard reaction, caused by heat and the presence of proteins and many carbohydrates at the same time. The granola had lots of roasted aromas: nutty and toasted, with slight notes of popcorn. However, to those in the know, it clearly had the flavour of bee larvae. In addition, we had discovered that if we dried the bee larvae in a dehydrator, they turned slightly crunchy and quite savoury. They are the perfect bar snack. In a systematic sensory test, Line Elgård, for her bachelor's degree project, created three versions of the granola: one with visible dehydrated bee larvae; one without visible bee larvae; and one traditional granola. Line invited ordinary consumers in two shopping centres to taste the granola, making it explicit that some of it contained bee larvae.

Much to our surprise, it was not difficult to find subjects who would volunteer to taste the granola. However, the study also showed that those most likely to try the granola were people who had low food neophobia – people who were generally interested in trying new foods. The experiment showed that visible bee larvae had no detrimental effect on people's liking for the granola, nor were the bee-larvae granolas liked less than the version with oil and honey. Later in the project, in early 2014, Jonas Astrup Pedersen, a former staff member at Nordic Food Lab, carried out a similar study while he was a student with us. He tested how bee larvae fared in a creamy, wintry vegetable soup[7]. He developed a set of three soup recipes with bee larvae – both with visible and invisible bee larvae, as well as one without bee larvae which only contained vegetables. The results showed that the soup with visible bee larvae was less liked than the other versions, but the version with invisible bee larvae was not less liked than the version with only vegetables. Similar to the granola experiment, the people who were more interested in new food experiences also liked the food containing insects much more.

The take-home message of these systematic sensory studies is that yes, we can create foods where the visibility of the insect ingredient is not a drawback. If the insect ingredient can be made to fit the context, ordinary people will not like it less. The dehydrated bee larvae fit snugly into the context of granola; the pale bee larvae in the creamy soup, less so. Tactful incorporations of insects that bring out their beauty is necessary.

A good strategy for familiarizing and engaging people with new ingredients is to make them cook with them. Marco Ortiz Sanchez, then a student of interactive design at the Technical University in Delft, worked with the lab to investigate how to break down barriers to eating insects. He carried out an experiment to collect data on people's emotions when manipulating, cooking and tasting insects – research that had never been done before. Although it was a small study, it showed interesting results that advocate transparency. The participants preferred to eat versions of insects when they could see what they were eating – meaning insect flour was less appreciated than whole insects. As part of the cooking, participants were invited to remove the legs and wings of locusts. This did give the subjects intensive negative emotions of frustration and disgust, but it also made them realize that those body parts were less delicious, and gave them a feeling of being adventurous. In many situations where we have invited larger groups of people to eat food that pushes the boundaries of what they think they will like, we notice an increase in the loudness of the conversation, as if crossing this boundary together has created a bond between the eaters; after tasting the insects, they feel courageous and connected through the act of eating insects together. In conclusion, we see that we can lower the barriers for insect-eating debutants by serving them thoughtful creations, in situations where it is appropriate to do so – yet there are still considerable barriers for people who are not generally intrigued by unfamiliar foods.

One of the purposes of the lab's global fieldwork was to study how insects are incorporated into local cuisines. This fed into the development of systematic tasting experiments and the development of dishes for many different types of eating situations. The collected knowledge about global insect foodways has been utilized to find strategies that will make insects look like a well-adapted and familiar part of the food we have created. Many of the foods and dishes we have developed over the years embody the knowledge gained during fieldwork. Please read for yourself, and let yourself be enticed to eat insects.

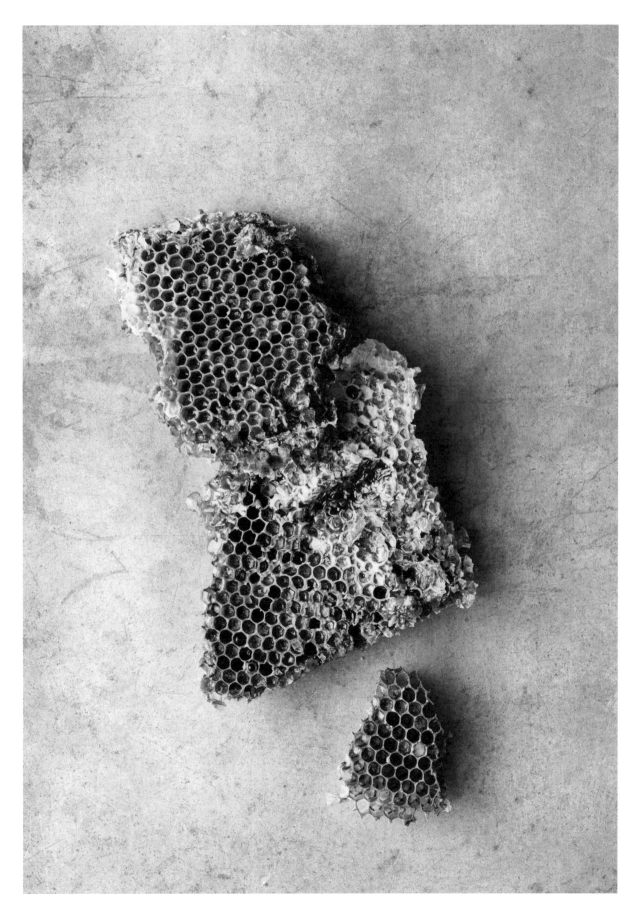

Honeycomb home to the bee brood (p.32)

TERMS: BUGS, INSECTS AND ENTOMOPHAGY

_____

This chapter has been condensed by Josh Evans from its original form, an academic paper entitled "'Entomophagy': an evolving terminology in need of review' by Josh Evans, Mohammed Hussen Alemu, Roberto Flore, Michael Bom Frøst, Afton Halloran, Gabriela Maciel-Vergara, Annette Bruun Jensen, Christopher Münke-Svendsen, Søren Bøye Olsen, Caroline Payne, Nanna Roos, Paul Rozin, Hui Shan Grace Tan, Arnold van Huis, Paul Vantomme and Jørgen Eilenberg, published under a Creative Commons licence in 2015 by the Journal of Insects for Food and Feed (full citation in references).

What is an insect, and what is not? Is 'entomophagy' an apt concept to describe eating insects? Why does it matter? Get ready for a rather nerdy chapter on words, their histories, meanings and ambiguities.

The construction of entomophagy as a practice uniting otherwise diverse groups has brought attention to the widespread normality of eating insects in many parts of the world. Yet the words and concepts many of us newcomers use to describe these organisms and the human practices that surround them are still rudimentary – especially compared with the diversity of the organisms themselves, and the complexity of the practices the terms aim to describe. Here is a brief, non-comprehensive historical review of insect-eating as described by certain Western cultural sources, an exploration of some of the taxonomic ambiguities and challenges surrounding the 'insects' category, and an argument for more precise and contextual terminology in this traditional and rapidly developing field.

———

PREHISTORIC AND HISTORICAL ACCOUNTS OF INSECT-EATING IN WESTERN CIVILIZATIONS

The practice of eating insects is ancient and widespread among many organisms, and is particularly common among our primate ancestors. Insects are nutritionally significant for all primates, and based on chimpanzees' (our closest living non-human relatives) enjoyment of certain insects, many researchers believe insects played a key role in our own evolution.

One of the oldest written accounts describing insects as food is found in the Old Testament (Leviticus 11.20–23) and permits the edible use of 'the locust of any kind, the bald locust of any kind, the cricket of any kind and the grasshopper of any kind'. Insects are also mentioned in the New Testament (Matthew 3:1,4), when John the Baptist is 'preaching in the wilderness of Judea', wearing 'a garment of camel hair and a leather belt around his waist' and eating 'locusts and wild honey'. Later Western accounts include Aristotle's description in the fourth century BCE of cicadas – the nymphs in particular – as a delicacy in ancient Greece (*The History of Animals* V.30), a sentiment echoed by Athenaeus of Alexandria in the early third century CE (*Deipnosophistae* IV.133b), as well as Pliny the Elder's account in the first century CE, of Romans fattening 'cossus' larvae on flour and wine (*Natural History* XVII.37). Émile Bergier (1941, p.19–23) and Shimon Fritz Bodenheimer (1951, pp.42–3) each present a satisfying deduction of the identity of the 'cossus' (see their works in References, pp.320–22). Yet for our purposes, the first recorded encounters by newcomers or outsiders may be more pertinent. This may be Herodotus of Halicarnassus in the fifth century BCE, when he describes the Nasamonians, who, along with gathering palm dates, 'hunt the wingless locusts, and they dry them in the sun and then pound them up, and after that they sprinkle them upon milk and drink them' (*The Histories* IV.172). Later on, in the early third century CE, Aelian of Rome describes a dessert of larvae from the tawny palm, served by a king of India to a group of Greek visitors; the Greeks, apparently, did not like it (Bodenheimer, 1951, p.43).

Even from these few historical sources, we see that the evidence for humans eating and delighting in certain insect species extends back at least a couple of millennia, and that each practice described had its particular context, species and conditions of appropriateness.

———

ORIGINS OF THE TERM 'ENTOMOPHAGY'

The term 'entomophagy' itself, at least in English and some other European languages, is rather new. Even the Italian naturalist Ulisse Aldrovandi's *De animalibus insectis libri septem, cum singulorum iconibus ad viuum expressis* from the beginning of the seventeenth century, which includes information on insects' uses for food and signals the start of the 'new age of entomology', does not contain the term. The Oxford English Dictionary has an entry for it, though no record of its coinage. Google Ngram, a word-tracking tool that searches all works published online for a given term, currently dates the first published mention of 'entomophagy' in English to 1871, when it was used in a volume entitled *Sixth Annual Report on the Noxious, Beneficial and Other Insects of the*

State of Missouri by Charles V. Riley, state entomologist. This book refers to a paper by one W. R. Gerard entitled 'Entomophagy' that 'in the same year … ha[d] brought together all the facts [known of the practice and was] read before the Poughkeepsie Society of Natural History.' (Riley, 1871; alas we were unable to find the paper by Gerard itself).

Published records of the term continue to appear throughout the 1870s and 1880s – including the notable publication of Vincent Holt's *Why Not Eat Insects?*, arguably the first document to bring the notion of entomophagy to the wider English public. It drops off for a few decades, then returns around 1934 and steadily increases until today. The first published mention of the term (according to Google Ngram – which, while broad, is not a complete record of every document ever published) in French (*entomophagie*) seems to be by one J. J. Virey in 1810, and in Spanish (*entomofagia*) by an anonymous writer in 1919.

The beginning of this twentieth-century resurgence coincides with a boom in the fields of anthropology and ethnology – and, in particular, ethnoentomology and cultural entomology. The meaning of 'entomophagy' at this time seems to have been slightly different from that of today, as evidenced by Bodenheimer's implication that honey consumption also constituted a kind of entomophagy. This position might seem somewhat strange today, though it is analogous to categorizing the consumption of animals and their products together – as would a vegan, for example.

'Insectivory' is a complementary term to 'entomophagy', often used in English to distinguish between insect consumption by any organism (the former), and by humans in particular (the latter). Some of the publications from this period, however, do not seem to distinguish between the two. The distinction may also not necessarily exist beyond English, even within the Romance languages; French, for example, seems to have used the words interchangeably, even in light of the recent addition of *entomophagie* to the dictionary Le Petit Robert in 2015.

Even current definitions of 'entomophagy' do not necessarily make such a clear distinction. While Oxford Dictionaries Online defines the term as 'the practice of eating insects, especially by people', the more discipline-specific Dictionary of Entomology lists 'entomophagy' as 'consumption of insects by other organisms'. There is an ambiguity here, as 'other organisms' could be taken to mean the set of all organisms, including *or* excluding insects. The same book defines 'insectivore' as 'an organism which eats insects', which could still include consumption by all organisms, including other insects; it defines 'insectivorous' as 'insect-eating; pertaining to organisms *subsisting* on insects' (italics

A hornet, part of the order Hymenoptera (p.59)

added). This is the only time it hints at a firmer distinction between 'entomophagy' and 'insectivory', where the former could describe a behaviour of eating insects in a specific situation, and the latter a behavioural pattern or habit of eating primarily or only insects, as a rule. This distinction might also be generalized to other eaten substances that have both '-phagy' and '-vory'-suffixed words. We can compare 'insectivory', in this sense, with other terms of similar construction ('herbivory', 'carnivory', 'omnivory') that describe general dietary patterns more than they do specific instances of food choice.

We also found an interesting pattern when looking into the Web of Science search engine, using 'entomophagy' as a search term for scientific papers in English over time. From 1900 to 1980, only two articles were found (published in 1930 and 1938), and in both cases the studies were about insects practising 'entomophagy' (that is, insectivory). From 1981 to 1990, there was one article published: an evaluation of a book about human consumption of insects among Aboriginals in Australia. From 1991 to 2000, and from 2001 to 2010, there are fifteen and sixteen articles, respectively, that use the term 'entomophagy', with some using the definition of 'human consumption of insects' and others using that of 'insect consumption by other animals' (insectivory). The number of papers has since multiplied: between 2011 and mid-2015, there have been forty-nine entries, most of which deal with human consumption of insects, and many with a focus on traditional foraging of insects (ethnoentomology).

> Anthropologists ... expressed puzzlement at the apparent health and vigor of peoples whose food sources seemed to lack essential amino acids, vitamins and minerals. It took many years before some realized these nutrients were supplied through entomophagy. Even today relatively few studies of cultural foodways include recognition of entomophagy, and this lack is attributed more to the bias of the researchers than the infrequency of the practice. We also find it telling that Western researchers give the practice of eating insects a distinctive term – entomophagy – that to our students in class sounds more like a disease than a descriptor, and that an important anthropological article on entomophagy is published in a collection entitled *Consuming the Inedible*. (Looy et al. 2014)

'Entomophagy' has become increasingly used by largely non-insect-eating researchers to denote an eating habit that is not appropriate in their own cultures. The title of Bergier's 1941 work, *Peuples entomophages et insects comestibles* (Entomophagous people and edible insects), for example, clearly illustrates this perspective. His work cites examples of human insect-eating from all over the world, while his chapter on Europe (his home continent) deals mainly with the ancient history of the Greeks and Romans – distant enough in time, apparently, to qualify as different enough cultures. The word thus changed from a general to a primarily anthropological term, associated with humans eating insects in 'other' countries and cultural groups. This fact is now evolving – and with it, so must our understanding and use of the term.

———

'INSECTS' AND 'INSECTA': A TAXONOMIC ISSUE

Before we can fully address the terminology issues of 'entomophagy' itself, we must first examine those organisms with which the term is concerned: insects. The main issue is one of taxonomy. The term is used in different contexts: both for different taxa in scientific classification, and for different categories in lay or folk classification.

The simplest and most technical way to define insects is by direct correspondence to the Linnaean class Insecta. The taxon, part of the phylum Arthropoda, comprises over one million species described, and around five million total species estimated. It is thus one of the most diverse classes of animals on the planet, and represents more than half of all known living, multicellular eukaryotes (organisms with cellular nuclei). Insecta includes many orders, of which the most common and speciose (rich in species) are: Coleoptera (beetles), Lepidoptera (butterflies and moths), Diptera (true flies), Hymenoptera (bees, ants and wasps), Orthoptera (grasshoppers and crickets) and Hemiptera (true bugs, cicadas and aphids). There are about twenty-three others.

Yet this technical definition of 'insect', used by many specialists, differs from the informal, vernacular meaning in English of 'any small invertebrate animal' (Oxford Dictionaries Online), which can be employed both loosely and with significant variation between speakers. This broader and more fluid category of 'insect' – sometimes but not always analogous to the word 'bug' – has different layered subsets that build on the core group of Insecta, as laid out in Figure 1 (p.60). Taxonomy is being constantly renegotiated as we learn more about species' evolutionary histories from genomic sequencing, and the currently most accepted arrangement is what follows. The subphylum Hexapoda contains the Ectognatha, those six-legged arthropods with external mouths (that is, Insecta), as well as the Entognatha, six-legged arthropods with internal mouths (the Collembola, also called 'springtails', the Diplura and the Protura, all of which lie outside Insecta). Beyond the Hexapoda come other Arthropoda, including those of the Arachnida (spiders, scorpions and mites), Myriapoda (centipedes and millipedes) and Crustacea (woodlice and crabs) – a vernacular relation particularly divergent from scientific taxonomy, in light of the recent suggestion that Insecta are actually much more closely related to Crustacea than other subphyla.

At this point, a taxonomist might be impelled to snap the vernacular English category back to technical rigour, with the descriptor 'terrestrial arthropods' – that is, all members of the Arthropoda that live on land. But this definition then excludes all the various aquatic 'insects' that are eaten (and there are a lot), as well as certain other organisms sometimes included in the vernacular category, such as earthworms (Annelida) and snails and slugs (Gastropoda, of the phylum Mollusca – not even an Arthropod!). And in some places, languages and cultures – for example, in parts of South America – the 'insect' category might extend even further, to include vertebrates such as snakes, toads, lizards and others.

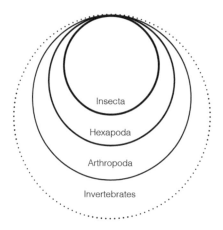

FIGURE 1. Relative subsets of the vernacular category 'insect', also sometimes analogous with 'bug'. Other possible configurations exist.

So, it's complicated!

Furthermore, even if many entomologists subscribe to a strict definition of Insecta in principle, few employ such a narrow category in their own practice: a brief and non-systematic survey of scientific entomological journals and conferences, for example, quickly shows it to be common to also include Arachnida and Myriapoda in the professional 'insect' category.

DIVERSE INSECT-EATING PRACTICES

Not all insect-eaters eat all insects, just as not all meat-eaters eat all types of meat from all animals. In cultures where certain insects are food, there are clear and localized norms regarding which species are considered to be edible, and how they are most appropriately prepared and consumed. While this book contains many examples from our own fieldwork, here we feel it is prudent also to give a few examples from the literature.

In sub-Saharan Africa, different, often neighbouring, ethnic groups have varying preferences and prohibitions. The Mofu-Gudur in Cameroon, for example, eat a number of grasshopper species that are not eaten by the Hausa in Niger, and vice versa. There are also many examples of prohibitions against eating specific insects within ethnic groups: certain Pygmy peoples eat the larvae and nymphs of the goliath beetle, but do not eat the adult, as it is sacred to them. More examples can be found in van Huis (2003) and Bergier (1941).

In a recent sensory and consumer study, Tan et al. (2015) examined the consumer perceptions and acceptance of insects in the Netherlands and Thailand, where the degree and nature of experiences regarding insects as food differ greatly. Dutch participants were mainly concerned with sustainability, while Thai participants were mainly concerned with taste and culinary familiarity. The Thai had a strong preference for ant larvae, grasshoppers and giant water bugs (familiar species in Thai cuisines), and were strongly repulsed by mealworms, mopane worms and witchetty grubs, which bear no resemblance to food insects in Thai cooking and are associated most closely with rotting food. The Dutch, on the other hand, were familiar with mealworms as a potential 'sustainable' food source, due to their recent availability on the market and offerings at public events, and were thus more willing to try them.

Furthermore, in cultures where certain insect species are part of the traditional diet, identifying the practice may not even be part of the vocabulary. For example, one of the co-authors of the paper from which this chapter draws, Gabriela Maciel-Vergara, is from Mexico, and she described how they do not use the term 'entomophagy' at all in their vocabulary, nor do they distinguish between those who choose to eat insects and those who don't. It is considered a matter of personal preference, influenced by exposure during childhood and regional custom.

Food selection is a complex process involving genetic, environmental, behavioural and cultural factors. Insects are far from the only nutritive organisms that some humans reject, and humans are far from the only species to exhibit such selectivity about what to eat. Human communities in some regions of Africa, for example, have in the past rejected fish as food, and many wild plant species considered edible in some regions of Europe are regarded as pest species in others. Wild chimpanzee communities are also selective in their food choices: protein-rich oil palm nuts, for example, are ignored by chimpanzees in western Uganda, yet are a valued food item among a well-studied group of chimpanzees in Guinea. In chimpanzees, as in humans, patterns of food cultures – and, indeed, insectivory – cannot be explained solely by material, environmental or genetic factors. In human cultures, food taboos are complicated and symbolic, and those involving insect species are no exception.

———

CLASSIFICATION DISCREPANCIES IN CULTURAL CONTEXT

Discrepancies in practice between 'insects' and 'Insecta' abound, and not only within English-speaking communities. The range of vernacular versions of 'insects' that extend beyond 'Insecta' is broad, and can vary significantly between different human cultures.

In western Kenya, many members of the Luo and Luhya tribes eat lake flies, termites and black ants (pp.95–112). Yet most Luo and Luhya we interviewed during our fieldwork did not assign their Dipteran, Ephemeropteran, Isopteran or Hymenopteran delicacies to the category 'insect' at all; they used this descriptor solely for the terrestrial arthropods they did *not* eat, particularly pests such as the species of termite that are not eaten.

Japanese insect-eating cultures exhibit their own notable distinctions. The Japanese language uses two terms: *konchū* (昆虫) and *mushi* (虫). *Konchū* refers to the order Insecta, while *mushi* is a more colloquial term that is often extended, particularly among older generations, to include snails, slugs, millipedes, scorpions and even frogs and snakes. The characters that refer to these animals are often compounds containing the character for *mushi* (虫): for example, snake is *hebi*, or 蛇. Yet, similarly to the Kenyan example above, when insects *are* of the eaten variety – Japanese wasps, for example (pp.187–92) – they often cease to be part of the *mushi* category.

Distinguishing between simply 'insects' and 'edible insects', 'eaten insects' or 'food insects', makes a significant difference.

Specimen samples from fieldwork in Japan

'STRANGE' EATING HABITS

It is no coincidence that the term and concept of 'entomophagy' are conspicuously absent from the lexica of most cultures where insects are eaten. Exceptions, of course, include cultures with precolonial insect-eating and the subsequent use of entomophagy-containing colonial languages – Spanish in Central and South America, for example. As a parallel, there is no analogous term in Europe among European languages for 'the eating of crustaceans' (crustaceaphagy?), the mostly aquatic arthropods whose terrestrial cousins we call 'insects'. From a historical perspective, this asymmetry makes sense: 'crustaceaphagous' European cultures have no need for a word to describe the practice of eating crustaceans. Eating shellfish has been normal in European cultures for quite some time, while these same cultures have only relatively recently started paying more attention to cultures where insect-eating is analogously commonplace.

Closer analysis of other 'phagy'-suffixed words reveals further nuances. Common lists of such words also containing 'entomophagy' (such as can be found on Wikipedia) are often titled along such lines as 'Lists of *Feeding Behaviours*' (italics added), in which terms like entomophagy are in such predominant company as 'hyalophagy', the eating of glass – a habit generally regarded as inappropriate or even pathological in many cultures (Western and otherwise) – and 'adelphophagy', the eating of one embryo by another in utero, a term used almost exclusively in relation to certain amphibians, sharks and fish. The few other terms on these lists whose corresponding practices are considered appropriate in some human cultural contexts more often denote eating habits – or shall we say 'feeding behaviours' – of animals: these include 'acridophagy' (the eating of grasshoppers and locusts), 'encephalophagy' (the eating of brain), 'geophagy' (the eating of earth, soil or clay), 'hemotophagy' (the eating of blood), 'hippophagy' (the eating of horse), 'myrmecophagy' (the eating of ants), 'ophiophagy' (the eating of snakes) or 'placentophagy' (the eating of placentae). Even if English-speakers do not intend it, and even if there do exist technical terms of 'insectivory' and 'entomophagy' to differentiate between animal and human behaviour (regardless of how rigorously they are deployed), employing the latter to describe human eating habits also automatically deploys this historical and cultural baggage – such as the association of a classical etymological formation with animal or pathological behaviours, and a correspondingly diagnostic tone.

In other words, it makes the eater sound insane, animalistic or both.

Term	Meaning
Acridophagy	Eating of grasshoppers or locusts
Anthropophagy	Eating of humans
Adelphophagy	Eating of one embryo by another in utero
Arachnophagy	Eating of spiders
Coprophagy	Eating of faeces
Encephalophagy	Eating of brains
Entomophagy	Eating of insects
Geophagy	Eating of earth, chalk or clay
Hemotophagy	Eating of blood
Hippophagy	Eating of horse
Hyalophagy	Eating of glass
Myrmecophagy	Eating of ants
Necrophagy	Eating of dead or decaying flesh
Ophiophagy	Eating of snakes
Oophagy	Eating of eggs or embryos
Placentophagy	Eating of placentae

TABLE 1. A selection of English words ending in '-phagy', their meanings and associations (from Wikipedia and Wiktionary).

Such issues are not only present in English. In German, for example, the term 'Entomophagie' only begins to appear in relatively recent publications, yet previous work from 1955 and 1968, based on travel diaries from the eighteenth century, use the pejorative terms '*Insekt-fresser*' and '*Insektesser*' to describe people eating or 'feeding' (*fressen*) on insects. Similarly, in Dutch, the closest analogue to 'entomophagy' is 'eulipotyphla', used for both humans and other animals. It's a word that describes the now-defunct taxonomic order Insectivora (literally, 'insect-eaters') that used to include hedgehogs, moles, shrews and other mammals that did not fit easily into earlier existing taxa. The parallels in both of these terms to animal feeding behaviour are clear indeed.

Certainly, every culture finds ways to describe cultures that differ from their own. Yet our concern here is that committing to a universal concept that frames eating insects as inappropriate, paired with the dominance and pervasiveness of Western cultural values, is contributing to at least two detrimental processes: a growing rejection in many insect-eating cultures of important and locally advantageous foodways to conform to Western cultural norms, and to the unnecessary, if less obvious, impediments that the same term – because of the inappropriateness it implies – may pose to newcomers.

———

WHY THE TERMS MATTER

Taxonomy and classification

Scientific taxonomy is not always the most accurate or most precise classification of organisms, and in many lay classifications 'insect' is not only, or even primarily, a morphological or phylogenetic category – it's also an affective, ideological and ethnological one. In some contexts, insects are classified according to their behavioural similarities (that is, one name may be used for both the flea and the jumping spider, or a collective name for all insects drawn to light at night), their importance as food (that is, larval instars, adult males and adult females of the same scientific species with different terms) and their importance as harmful creatures, as distinguished from less harmful insects. Different configurations of the lay category 'insect' are also regularly used by researchers for practical purposes, prioritizing descriptive power over taxonomic precision. Failure to recognize different approaches to classification obstructs crucial exchange of knowledge, and it can further marginalize cultures where insects are not only eaten, but classified differently.

Basic and applied entomological research

The current estimate of insect species eaten worldwide is 2,037, and there are likely more species eaten and edible. This species diversity covers a broad range of geographical distributions, ecological roles, environmental impacts and nutritional profiles – by species, life stage, processing method, similarity to and suitability as 'livestock' and status as food within and across cultures. The precision, accuracy and applicability of basic research are only as good as the precision of the terms and concepts we use to carry it out.

Gastronomy

Different insects have different physico-chemical compositions, tastes and textures, which is why they are prepared in different manners by those who already eat them. Familiarity with a food breeds distinction within the category; yet the terms 'insects' and 'entomophagy' place the foods' key differences as secondary. For newcomers, the use of a single, homogenizing term constrains the process of differentiation that is part of developing culturally appropriate cuisine.

> Insects [should] not just be seen as one item to be placed under an existing familiar food category, such as meat. Trying to extend an existing food category to include insects misses the fact that the real challenge is category distinction, and not category extension: people's initial single category of insects has to allow for a distinction to be made between inedible and edible insects, and the latter set has then to be seen as a source of rich variety, open for distinct food experiences, and pleasures. (Deroy et al. 2015)

Many insect species, due to their size and physiology, pose challenges to more conventional concepts of 'meat' and 'livestock'. 'Meat' can range in meaning from only skeletal muscular tissue, to internal organs such as the heart, lungs, liver and kidneys, to other parts such as tendons and marrow. Depending on the insect species, its developmental stage and other factors, different people eat different parts, including or excluding parts of the cuticle, legs and wings. Perhaps different insects may even demand their own concepts of 'meat'?

The general concept of 'eating insects' can be a first step, but certainly not the last. We understand 'fish' as a general category, but when we cook and eat, we do so with cod or sardines, monkfish or salmon – and sometimes even Norwegian or Baltic salmon, or coho, sockeye or spring, early or late in the season, at different distances from their spawning river and so on. In this same way, we must also develop progressively more specific knowledge and tastes when it comes to insects and their roles in different cuisines. Actively engaging in this co-evolution of available foods and the language we use to describe them is a crucial step in developing the gastronomic knowledge between different species, developmental stages, anatomical parts, times of year and other factors necessary to make these differences palatable, meaningful and celebrated.

Regulatory policy

Paul Vantomme, the former director of the United Nations Food and Agriculture Organization's (FAO) Non-wood forest products section, explained to us how the FAO's use of the term 'entomophagy' in its official reports since 2012 may well have helped to spread the message about the usefulness of insects for food. Yet the term also leads to simplification of the many issues in the sector. This phenomenon can be compared with what happened when the term 'non-timber/wood forest products' was introduced in the early 1990s. While this term had a great impact in drawing attention to funding, policy, legal frameworks and development for parts of the forest sector other than timber, after twenty-five years, the term has lost relevance. Preference has shifted to using the names of specific products, such as honey, berries, mushrooms, game or tree grubs. We can learn from this general terminology experience: it helps, during a launching period, to draw attention to something with a general term – but once attention has been gained, then more specific wording becomes necessary.

At the time of writing, the legislative situation in the EU is in a transitional moment. The current novel food legislation from 1997 does not address edible insects explicitly, and as such, member states exhibit a wide range of attitudes towards this legislative grey area (pp.175, 210–11). In November 2015, however, new novel food legislation that does address insects as food was adopted by the European Parliament, and will come into effect in all member states by the beginning of 2018.

In some cultures where insects have traditionally been consumed and specific terminology for the practice is lacking, such as in Thailand, they are treated no differently than other types of food in terms of food-safety standards. This normality approach also seems to be how the US Food and Drug Administration is currently treating frozen crickets: as any other food-grade, frozen product. This approach, paired with more specific terminology, could also help build constructive legislation.

———

CONCLUSION

Compared with the long history and prehistory of humans eating insects, the term 'entomophagy' is relatively new. The term's meaning in at least a few European languages has shifted even over the course of its short life, becoming less synonymous with the general eating of Insecta and several other arthropods by *any* organism, and more specifically referring to human insect-eating practices. This shift does not, however, lessen the term's implicit judgement of human insect-eating from a Western, non-insect-eating paradigm, as an animalistic, inappropriate, or even pathological eating or 'feeding' behaviour – an attitude that may be contributing to the atrophy of normal insect-eating in certain regions of the world.

Use of the term can continue to alienate members of insect-eating cultures and homogenize their diverse practices. Different cultural traditions engage with different registers of the category 'insect' in different contexts, which inform different approaches not only to classification, but also to edibility and cultural appropriateness of foods.

What is an 'insect' and who is an 'insect-eater'? And who gets to decide: the eater, the non-eating observer, or both, in a process of constant cultural negotiation? The questions raised here go beyond just names and categories; they are also about how individuals and groups build and maintain identities, interact with companion species and negotiate the structures of power that inform and react to these practices.

Precision, diversity, consideration: these are the goals we must pursue – in research, cooking and eating.

POLITICS AND POWER

This chapter has been condensed and revised by Josh Evans from its original form, an academic paper entitled 'Entomophagy and Power' by Andrew Müller, Joshua Evans, Charlotte Payne and Rebecca Roberts, published under a Creative Commons licence in 2016 by the Journal of Insects for Food and Feed (full citation in references).

Edible insects are being framed as a panacea for health, resource and climate challenges, and the 'entomophagy movement' is growing rapidly. Yet as the insect 'solution' is scaled up, there is a greater focus on technical innovation and less on the structural inequalities that govern who produces within, who controls and who benefits from the edible insect trade. So we find it important to ask: to what extent is the promotion of 'entomophagy' challenging or reproducing power relations in global food systems?

ACADEMIA

Using a systematic review of the academic literature on insects as food, we posed the following questions of insect research in academia:

- Who is speaking, and whose voices are being heard?
- What is the status (farmed or wild) of the insects being researched?
- Which areas of the world are most represented?
- Who is funding this emerging field?

And here are some of our main findings:

- There is a clear rise in the number of papers published between 2000 and 2015: of 118 articles, nine were published between 2000 and 2005, twenty-four between 2005 and 2010, and eighty-five between 2010 and 2015.
- It is only in the latter half of this period that articles about farmed insects have been published.
- There are more researchers based in North America, Europe and Asia than there is research conducted in these areas; the opposite is true for Africa. South America and Australasia are notably underrepresented for both authors and research.
- Over half of all articles do not declare their source of funding. Of those that do, the majority were fully funded by public money.

INDUSTRY

Using a systematic review of companies selling insect products online, we posed the following questions of the edible insects industry:

- Which edible insect products are easily available online in the West?
- What are the features of these products and their respective companies, with regard to how and where they procure their insects and market their products?
- How are they produced, traded and consumed?

And here are some of our main findings:

- The majority of companies were based in North America or Europe, and owned by North Americans or Europeans.
- We could only determine the geographical origin of just over half of the products, the majority of which were sourced in North America, Asia and Europe.
- Over half of the products did not state whether the insects were farmed or wild-harvested. Of those that did, almost all were farmed.
- The majority of products were sold in a ready-to-eat form as snacks, with a few marketed as potential meal supplements, such as protein shakes and breakfast cereals.
- About one-fifth of the products were dehydrated or freeze-dried, and a similar number were sold as an unseasoned ingredient that required further processing before consumption – for example, in flour or powder form.
- The mean price of products was US$20.90, and nearly half of all products were sold at prices exceeding US$10.00. For those with adequate information about the weight of the product, the mean price per serving of 30 grams was US$25.30.
- The majority of marketing claims were about health and wellness, and over half specifically referenced 'protein' and 'meat alternatives'.
- Environment-related claims were the third most popular marketing category.

CASE STUDY: REGIONAL INSECT TRADE IN SOUTH EAST ASIA

One of our collaborators and co-authors of the paper, Andrew Müller, conducted fieldwork in Thailand – recognized as a global edible insects hot spot – to investigate how these flows of power were shaping economies and livelihoods on the ground. There are long traditions of eating many kinds of insects in Thailand, especially in rural areas – though there is also a resurgence of insect-eating in cities, which likely began in the wake of Thailand's economic and industrial boom in the 1980s and 1990s, when many people from rural areas left their agricultural backgrounds and moved to the cities to find work. Here are some of Andrew's main findings:

- In urban areas, many people who eat insects came from Isan – a rural region with a pronounced culture of using certain insects as food. 'When I left Bangkok for the US in the Seventies, you'd never come across insects, and now you can buy them everywhere!' (Male, early sixties, Thai, Bangkok.) This new trend is mainly driven by young people: 'They are tasty, and full of protein and vitamins – very healthy!' (A group of males, late teens, Thai, central Bangkok.)
- In the countryside, insects are procured by wild harvest or trade at local markets, and eaten as elements of main meals. Diversity of eaten species is high, and depends on local custom and seasonal and regional availability.
- In urban areas, many insects are available year-round due to cold storage and deep-freezing, but the range of species is limited, and some are increasingly farmed rather than wild-harvested. They are usually purchased from street vendors or market stalls as ready-to-eat evening snacks.
- The Thai insect industry is becoming increasingly supraregional and organized, and already encompasses a considerable business network of collectors, farmers, middlemen, wholesalers, street vendors, superstores and other entrepreneurial actors. Some have been reported to earn up to 100 million baht (approx. US$2.8 million) or even 600 to 700 million baht (approx. US$17 to 20 million) per year.
- While interviewees' and informants' general replies often varied according to demographic parameters and social status, virtually everybody shared the opinion that the insect trade would continue to grow – though not everyone is thrilled about it:

'I think selling insects as snacks in Bangkok is a bad idea. If it becomes popular there, what does that mean for the future of our children here in Isan? If those businesses need a lot of raw material, maybe they will buy many insects from the local people, and then the future generations will not have enough to eat any more. Nowadays, all kinds of natural resources are decreasing because people are collecting them for sale. If demand for insects increases like that as well, this would add to the destruction of ecosystems and burden the local people here.' (Female, early fifties, Thai, Ban Sarng Sang.)

A snapshot of Talad Rong Kluea, insect megamarket

Talad Rong Kluea is a large market on the Thai side of the Cambodian–Thai border, in the province of Sa Kaeo. It contains a hall built around 2009 specifically to serve the growing insect trade. The market shifts thousands of tonnes of insects each year, forming a hub of the international insect trade. Large quantities of different insect species are imported into Thailand every year from neighbouring countries such as Myanmar, Laos and Cambodia, where they are mainly collected in the wild. Most wholesalers are Thai.

One Cambodian wholesaler reported, 'It is becoming increasingly difficult to enter higher positions without considerable starting capital, contacts and know-how. When I started in 2000 [as a labourer], 20,000 baht [approx. US$570] was all I had, but nowadays you need at least 200,000 baht [approx. US$5,700] to get started. It's an unstable business, and if you don't know the right people, you have to pay a lot extra to get involved. And that is only if you manage to get a compartment, since the market [which is privately owned by a rich family] is fully hired out' (male, early fifties, Cambodian). He employs around fifteen day labourers for his business, and their number fluctuates seasonally. This was true for most people transporting, washing, processing and shelving the insects at Talad Rong Kluea. According to the same wholesaler, 'Ninety per cent of [the workers] are Cambodian, because it's cheaper to hire migrants, and also they tend to negotiate less and work harder.' The labourers were paid at most 300 baht (approx. US$8.57) per day, and had no employment contract or social security.

Behind the main insect hall at Talad Rong Kluea is a large cold-storage room, used to freeze and store wild insects from Cambodia. A supervisor reported, 'I'm officially employed, with a salary of 10,000 baht per month [approx. US$280], including social welfare. The other staff are Cambodians who get 200 baht [approx. US$5.71] per day, plus food and accommodation, without social security or anything like that. But if they get ill we organize medical treatment – because we need their labour. That rarely happens though, because they are incredibly resilient, while Thais couldn't and wouldn't want to do this kind of hard, unrespected work, involving extreme temperature fluctuations. Poor Thais prefer to work in factories where they have more security, rights and at least some social welfare. But these Cambodians here don't have much choice – and 200 baht is not bad for them' (female, late thirties, Thai).

There was also a site at the end of the vast market area, which seemed less visible and less official, and was used as a workplace for the seasonal processing of fish, frogs and insects. In July 2012, dozens of Cambodian women and children were processing locusts manually by pulling off their wings. They were seasonal day labourers paid according to the amount of insects they managed to process: 5 to 6 baht (US$0.14 to 0.17) per kilogram, on average 100 baht (US$2.85) per day. One of the women said, 'We are glad about the job – it is not too hard physical work, and we get the money straight after work' (thirties, Cambodian). Many of the workers had small wounds on their hands, which came from the monotonous motion of de-winging the locusts. A girl with plasters on her hands explained, 'It's a bit painful and annoying, especially for writing at school' (twelve, Cambodian). Not all of the children attended school – especially not during the locust season. Usually, they work from 5.00 a.m. to 5.00 p.m. A woman explained, 'Where we come from, there isn't any work at all, so it's better than nothing' (forties, Cambodian). A mid-level employee at the same site said that 'the insect trade really is big business – my [female] boss has made 25 million baht [approx. US$714,960] or so in three years, and the turnover will probably continue to increase' (male, early forties, Thai). An officer of the district office in charge of hygiene and safety at Talad Rong Kluea said, 'The insect trade has grown very fast, and some people are becoming rich. The profit margin is extremely high and they have organized the business efficiently. For example, insects are sold within franchise structures in many cities in Thailand. The entrepreneurs invest in a large number of carts, organize fresh insects from Rong Kluea market every day and employ retailers who get 500 baht [approx. US$14.29] per working day [minimum wage for Thai citizens]. These people are usually seasonal workers from agricultural backgrounds' (male, forties, Thai).

While Talad Rong Kluea may be the biggest insect-trading spot in Thailand, there are other hubs as well. One of them is Talad Thai, a huge agricultural market near Bangkok. A young man employed there at an insect business owned by his mother earned a fixed monthly salary of 60,000 baht (approx. US$1,715). He said, 'I'm very happy with this job – it's a good, stable income. Currently, we make about 100,000 baht [approx. US$2,859] per day, and we expect that to increase further' (early thirties, Thai).

Giant water bugs

One reason for the expected growth of the insect sector is the continuous demand and rising prices of popular insects. Many species reach remarkably high prices, exceeding those of pork or beef many times over. Giant water bugs (*Lethocerus indicus*), for example, are valued because of the special aroma the males produce, and their market price has steadily been increasing, up to 25 baht (approx. US$0.71) per specimen. Most giant water bugs are still collected in the wild, but they have become relatively rare. Demand is not sufficiently met, because of the bugs' decreasing natural occurrence in Thailand – which many informants explained was due to pesticide use in agriculture.

As a result of the decline in wild populations, imports from other countries are increasing, artificial aroma is being produced, and interest in farming potential is growing. Breeding giant water bugs is a difficult and complicated procedure. The high-school teacher Chatree Patisol (male, sixties, Thai) was one of the first to develop a successful small-scale farming procedure, and he shares his knowledge with anybody who is interested: 'Giant water bugs are predators, and need lots of fresh, live prey. I usually feed them small frogs or fish, which we also breed ourselves'. While commercial interest in such knowledge could grow in the future, Mr. Chatree does not see water bug farming primarily as a business idea, but rather as an activity integrated into the sustainable-agricultural learning centre he runs. It is also a social project that aims to be inclusive and give underprivileged children the chance to gain knowledge in a safe environment. The pupils participate in the whole process of agricultural production and learn to sell the products they make. They are allowed to keep the money they earn, in order to support their further education and as a basis for a better life.

––––

DISCUSSION

Though these findings have their limitations – they are by no means comprehensive across all times, geographies, languages or levels of access to resources and information – and may also, to some degree, reproduce the very power structures we critique, there are some important political implications that arise from working with insects as food.

Global inequalities, technical problems and apolitical solutions

The emphasis in both academia and business is on apolitical solutions, without adequately considering local social contexts. The literature review confirms that there has been a shift towards a more technical view of insects as food, with an emphasis on farmed insects, global environmental impact, consumer acceptance, nutritional properties and the priority of scaling up production. Notably, the global distribution of authors working on edible insects is starkly different from the global distribution of insect-eating practices. The growing interest in insects as food is not empowering those with a culture of insect consumption as much as it could, and world regions without a tradition of eating insects dominate the current discourse.

Questions of structural inequalities, justice, access and distribution are rarely considered. Even when these social and political factors are acknowledged, they tend not to be included in empirical research. Earlier publications, by comparison, did tend to address contextual and social concerns, as well as the historically rooted, Eurocentric biases against eating insects. Instead of further developing these perspectives, contemporary literature shows a less critical, more universalizing tendency.

The predominant marketing strategies of many companies rely heavily on an abstract, politically neutral solution narrative. This narrative presumes that all 'solutions' work the same way everywhere, and that current food challenges are due to a global lack of food rather than structural inequalities of power, distribution, availability and access. Overall, edible insects are marketed in a way that homogenizes their diversity, frequently omits their geographical and ecological origin and frames them as a meat alternative – yet in terms of both price and composition, they cannot be considered as such. Furthermore, most products are presented in a snack context, providing supplement to a diet that, at least in the West, is already oversaturated with protein.

The disjunction between where insects are being produced and procured, and where they are increasingly being sold and eaten, suggests resource extraction that may not necessarily be benefiting the people most threatened by food insecurity. Control of value is also shifting, as reflected by the marketing focus on what Western cultures perceive as tasty, healthy and safe to eat. While the market is certainly an important arena for implementing the potential of edible insects, there is little detailed information on the distribution of gains from the edible insect trade. To assume that the global market is universally constructive and mutually advantageous is to dangerously neglect the power asymmetries that influence who actually benefits from trade of insects as food.

These critiques do not even take into account the problems that arise from the lack of transparency and accountability that comes as a result of inaccessible information on funding and financial drivers of research, traceability and origin of food products, and their production conditions.

Universalized 'sustainability'

The idea that every insect species is universally sustainable is deceptive. Firstly, the means of procurement is not always sustainable.

In some cases, wild-harvesting may lead to overexploitation of insects – a threat feared by the Thai villagers quoted above. Secondly, not enough is known about the environmental impact of insect farming, and it appears to be much more complex than suggested by the 'solution narrative'. For instance, farmed insects may be fed on a substrate with its own complicated sustainability status – shown by the example of the giant water bug in Thailand, which requires additional resource use for the farming of its amphibian prey. The same issue applies to more commonly farmed insects, which tend to be fed with cultivated grain that adds to the insects' environmental footprint, so that scaled-up production may be no more sustainable than conventional protein sources (see Lundy and Parrella 2015). Thirdly, farmed insects for a consumer market require processing for preservation and to meet consumer preference. When this is done on a large scale, common methods include grinding and freeze-drying, which use significant energy.

Overall, the realities of rearing insects on different substrates and on a large scale are yet to be fully understood, and may bring with them hidden or unforeseen environmental costs. The same certainly applies to the environmental costs of processing methods that tend to stay unmentioned in the marketing of insect products.

The arguments outlined above show the complexity regarding the sustainability of edible insects – yet all largely ignore the human dimension of sustainability. An approach such as Chatree Patisol's may provide a more holistic answer to how edible insects can be sustainable. In his position both as a teacher and as an insect farmer, he gives local underprivileged youth the chance to gain income and education. So far not even adequately measurable in the most complex multi-dimensional life-cycle assessments, these social components may be given less recognition, but are highly relevant to implementing insects' full democratic potential as sustainable food.

Inequalities within the Thai insect trade

As edible insects are commercialized, they become more and more subject to conventional market forces, which involve both new opportunities, but also the reproduction of existing inequalities. The Thai edible insect market is still relatively open and accessible, and in some cases facilitates upward social mobility. But those who benefit – who are regularly employed, successfully run small to medium-size businesses and/ or make a considerable annual profit – usually enjoy certain privileges to begin with: for example, being Thai, a man, from a well-off family, or having the right contacts, know-how and/or capital. The industrialization of the insect trade is increasingly accompanied by a reinforcement of existing power relations. Labourers in the insect industry are subject to the same structural inequalities faced by workers in other sectors in South East Asia: many reside illegally, and are subject to highly precarious working conditions. The women and children who pull off locusts' wings at Rong Kluea market, for example, work in a place where illegal migration, child labour, human trafficking and child prostitution are common. Their wage is vanishingly small, relative to the turnover of the industry and the profits made by their supervisors.

These working conditions reproduce, more than they challenge, social and economic inequalities. Even if the day labourers at Talad Rong Kluea state to be 'happy' about their jobs, they also know they don't really have a choice. It is highly unlikely that their role in the insect trade will substantially alter their position in society, while others retain their superior social status, partly through benefiting from the growing insect business. Thailand also profits from insects imported from neighbouring countries (Myanmar, Laos and Cambodia), which have higher rates of malnutrition. From a food security perspective, it might make more sense if these insects were eaten locally where they are collected, rather than being further concentrated in the regional centre of economic power. Whether insects' commercialization empowers the underprivileged will largely depend on the distribution of benefits within the trade chain. Currently, the popularity of insects among the affluent urban culture in Thailand, and the subsequently rising prices, mean that people who are used to enjoying certain insects as normal food can no longer afford them. Overall, the Thai insect trade creates opportunities for some, but is increasingly reproducing social inequalities.

CONCLUSION

The promotion of 'entomophagy' may at the same time challenge and reproduce existing power relations. Whether or not edible insects are 'doing good' is therefore impossible to answer universally. But it is important and fruitful to ask: what are the general trends and the effects in specific contexts, and, above all, who benefits from them?

On the one hand, the potential of insects as food remains. The informal local use of edible insects already contributes to food security in various ways. Growing markets for edible insects offer new, low-threshold opportunities for innovative entrepreneurs and small companies that could challenge current power structures, offer cheaper and more accessible insect food products that may eventually be successfully marketed as meat alternatives, and facilitate trade that benefits the underprivileged. The increasing prominence of the topic in academia may also offer researchers in 'less-developed' countries an opportunity to publish research that is internationally recognized.

However, these hopes and claims may not align with the current practices of the expanding edible insect trade and discourse. There is a dominance of 'developed' regions over structurally marginalized ones, both in academia and business. These patterns of social exclusion are also evident on a regional level in the Thai insect trade. These findings suggest that the current activities of the edible insects movement do not significantly benefit those whom it claims to empower, and this tendency may intensify with time.

How do we move forward? In short: power-awareness.

- We must acknowledge that deep structural inequalities and power imbalances exist, and that they can, and should, be challenged.
- We must critically consider who produces, who controls and who benefits, at the outset of, and throughout, business and research initiatives.
- We must do detailed, multidisciplinary research on the relationship between entomophagy and power in other regions, languages and contexts.
- We must demand accountability and transparency in research, governance and trade.
- And we must fight for the inclusion of marginalized voices in research, business and governance: not just speaking about people, but letting them speak for themselves.

STORIES FROM THE FIELD

ANTS

They may have been the very first insect we started working with. After Alex's Amazonian lemongrass and ginger ant sparked our enquiry at the first MAD symposium (p.40), Nordic ants seemed a viable first direction to pursue.

Many ants produce formic acid for defence, which makes them taste sour. Formic acid even takes its name from the ant family (Formicidae), as it was first distilled into its pure form by English naturalist John Ray in 1671 from the red wood ant (*Formica rufa*) – widespread throughout Europe and, incidentally, an ant common in Danish forests. In the spring and summer, at the height of its aromatic power, the wood ant has a straight and sharp acidity with the aroma of caramelized lemon rind. Meanwhile, the smelling carpenter ant (*Lasius fuliginosus*), another ant we work with, has a gentler acidity and a pronounced aroma of Kaffir lime. Different species, populations and perhaps even castes within the same colony can express different aromas. This aromatic diversity arises from the pheromones ants use to communicate within and between species. It just so happens that humans perceive these same volatile molecules as aroma – and across a broad range of smells such as citrus, pine, coriander, leather, cinnamon, peach, wintergreen, vanilla and more.

I will always remember the moment when this discovery sprung into being. It was on the Lab's houseboat (known simply as 'the boat'), in the summer of 2012; Lars Williams, then head of research and development and, since July 2012, head of the test kitchen at Noma, was reading the Morgan paper on ant pheromones, 'Chemical sorcery for sociality' (2009; see References), which is riddled with molecular diagrams; Arielle Johnson, then a PhD student in flavour chemistry and part of the Lab team for the summer (later heading up research at MAD), walked by and said, 'Oh, what's that?', and began rattling off all the smells she saw on the page. The connection would not have been made unless Lars, a chef, and Arielle, a scientist, were sharing a space to investigate together.

Because of their big taste and small size, we use ants as a spice or seasoning. An early example is the Chimp Stick (pp.230–31); another is Anty Gin (p.222), in which we use distillate of common wood ant for their citrusy notes. This approach to working with certain insects may be more similar to, say, how Thai people use the giant water bug (*Lethocerus indicus*) in the chilli paste *nam prik maeng da* (p.185): for flavour more than substance. Not all insects need be a 'protein source' to be worth eating.

Barely a week after I came to Nordic Food Lab in June 2012, I was on my first ant-harvesting expedition. Lars and Mark Emil Hermansen – the Lab's anthropologist at the time and, from October 2012, part of the MAD team – were presenting our insect work thus far at MAD2 (the second MAD Symposium) and we needed to prep ants for the audience of 600. Arielle, Trevor Moran (then-forager at Noma), and I drove to Hareskoven, a forest just northwest of Copenhagen. Trevor led us briskly across the forest floor, a thick carpet of pine needles. Just off the path rose a mound, perhaps one metre (about three feet) high, that seemed to shimmer. The ants were active. As soon as we began to harvest, a miasma of volatile acid lifted into the air around the mound. We had read old stories of Swedish woodsmen seasoning their bread by holding it over an anthill; I suddenly understood why.

There are different methods of harvesting. The fastest is to scoop up a bit of the mound – pine needles, ants and all – into a plastic bin. This is possible with small amounts from large mounds, done infrequently and only in a pinch, but is probably not ideal. I wonder if one could dig a hole into a mound, and fill it with bark and other natural debris to keep it open, similar to the *escamoleros'* technique we observed in Mexico (pp.154–5). Another way, not for those faint of heart or hand, is to place your hands on the surface of the mound, let the ants crawl all over and then shake off the load into a plastic tub. (A similar technique can be used with a sheet of paper or plastic, if you want to be high-tech.) Yet another involves a simple homemade suction device – two lengths of tubing, one end of each stuck into the lid of a jar or container, the cracks sealed – with which one may then suck through one free end while using the other free end to catch ants: a kind of human-powered vacuum cleaner. This tool can be useful with the smelling carpenter ants, which are smaller and tend to build nests in old trees and stumps, rather than large, conspicuous mounds.

There has arisen one potential food-safety concern. The lancet liver fluke (*Dicrocoelium dendriticum*) is a trematode parasite that inhabits the bile duct of its terminal host, normally a grazing animal such as a cow or sheep. Yet to fulfil its life cycle, it needs to complete its developmental stages in intermediate hosts: first terrestrial snails, then ants. Infected ants don't usually die from the infection per se, but the parasite does change the ant's behaviour to its own ends. During the day, the ant behaves normally; but come dusk, the parasite directs the ant to climb up a piece of vegetation, such as a blade of grass, and to bite into it with its mandibles. In this position, the ant is more likely to be eaten by a grazing animal, and thus allow the parasite to pass to its final host. Once there, the fluke feeds on the animal's liver and lays eggs in its bile duct, which are then shed in the animal's faeces – and the cycle starts again: snails feed on the faeces and ingest the eggs, which are passed to ants when they feed on the snails' trails of slime.

Humans are not the lancet liver fluke's intended host, but there are some rare reported cases of human infection, possibly from eating infected animal liver. Thus, the possibility of acquiring the parasite from eating raw ants does exist, however low. Luckily, freezing the ants, which we do anyway after harvesting to preserve them, kills any potential parasites – a technique tested and confirmed by our collaborator Annette Bruun Jensen, an insect pathologist and apiologist at the University of Copenhagen. In general, eating anything involves some degree of risk, so it is important not to blow the lancet liver fluke out of proportion. Nonetheless, it remains a fascinating and fearsome example of the evolutionary intricacy of many parasite life cycles.

All this said, I have eaten raw ants many times while foraging. It is something you do at your own risk, like eating fresh sashimi, despite the official edict of many to freeze the flesh first to kill any potential parasites.

Though we have been working with them now for years, there is still quite a bit of mystery for me around the ants. In July 2015, for example, I was up in northern Norway visiting a good friend who dives for sea urchins and other shellfish, and who also has a farm. His property has multiple colonies of what are likely red wood ants. Sometimes we would taste them and they would taste of nothing; other times, it would zing like sucking half a lemon. Was it the different colonies? The caste? The time of day, or weather? Or did we, perhaps, happen to pick ones that had already sprayed all their formic acid, or were low on pheromones? There are many more questions to address in developing this knowledge. In the meantime, we'll use our senses.

—Written by Josh Evans

BEE BROOD

I remember the first time clearly. It was a hot day at the end of June 2012 (for Copenhagen, at least, it was hot), and I biked south from the boat to Amager, a large island neighbourhood in the southeast of the city. Bybi, or 'city bee' in Danish, is an organization that builds and keeps beehives on roofs across the city, as well as training homeless and unemployed people to keep bees as a job. The organization's work enriches the social and environmental landscape of the city. We had begun experimenting with their bee brood the month before.

That afternoon, Oliver Maxwell, the founder and director of Bybi, was going to show me how they harvested the brood from the hives they kept at their own office. We donned white, lightweight tops with drum-like hoods and mesh over the eyes, and joined a couple of employees in the green space behind the building. The harvest was already in progress. Oliver explained to me some of the hows and whys of drone removal, while the last hive boxes were opened, harvested and resealed.

Starting with what Oliver shared with me that day, and developed through talks with beekeepers and entomologists and books I've read since, here is what I've been able to learn: increasingly, many beekeepers remove drone brood, the developing male honeybees (*Apis mellifera*), as a way to reduce the population of varroa mites (*Varroa destructor*) in a hive. The mite attaches to the bee and sucks its haemolymph (its blood-like vital fluid), causing wounds that do not fully heal, exposing the bee's circulatory system to the environment and making it suscep-

tible to viral attack. There is no complete cure for varroa mites, just a battery of strategies beekeepers can use to mitigate its presence once detected. Varroa mites are thus thought to be a prominent factor contributing to colony collapse disorder, a phenomenon in which the majority of a colony's worker bees disappear, in many places around the world.

The mites prefer to reproduce on drone brood (developing males) over worker brood (developing females), as the former have a longer developmental period than the latter: it takes about twenty-four days for a drone to grow from egg to adult, and only twenty-one days for a worker. Hence varroa mites' higher reproductive success in drone cells (2.2 to 2.6 mites per cell) than in worker cells (1.3 to 1.4 mites per cell). Beekeepers and researchers have noticed this preference, and trapping the mites in drone brood frames once the cells are capped as the brood begin to pupate has become generally recognized as one of the more sustainable practices for combating varroa mites – compared with using pesticides, miticides and other invasive techniques, which can end up harming the bees as well.

In Denmark, many beekeepers use this so-called 'safe strategy', which involves removing one-third of a comb frame of drone brood per week during the drone brood season, from May to July, to reduce the mite population for the rest of the year. As a result of this practice, many tonnes of drone brood comb are removed every year in Denmark alone. Some beekeepers feed this removed brood to chickens or other animals, but many, especially those in urban areas, have no use for it, and it goes to waste – a casualty, and untapped by-product.

Honeybee drone brood also happens to be very nutritionally rich. It averages 20 per cent protein and 50 per cent fat by dry weight, and this composition does not seem to be adversely affected by varroa infestation. The mite poses no threat to species other than the honeybee, and of the many thousands of drones laid in a season, only a few are involved in inseminating the queen for the following year.

During the season, there are piles of drone brood waiting and wanting to be used. And especially in the Nordic region, where the temperate climate and, in certain areas, many decades of intensive agriculture have dramatically reduced the population density of many insect species, bee brood is one of the most accessible and readily available sources of tasty, locally produced insects to eat. Indeed, direct local use of drone brood could be one of the more viable ways of realizing the common claims of insects' positive potential.

But first we need to learn how to cook with, and eat, it. Our first trials started simply: mayonnaise, using larvae instead of chicken eggs; granola (pp.220–21), which we served at a pop-up we held for International Restaurant Day in November 2012, called 'Bee Breakfast Club'; and others. The recipes have become more complex as we have learned more about brood's taste, variations and responses to cooking. It has proven versatile; many of our recipes made at the Lab use bee brood in some way.

Perhaps the most involved part of working with bee brood is separating the brood from the comb. We have found freezing to be the most efficient method – ideally with liquid nitrogen, which freezes

the lot to a brittle –197°C (–322.6°F), allowing the comb to be smashed to smithereens, while the individual larvae and pupae themselves stay intact. At this point the brood can be sifted from the waxen debris, rubbed in a clean cloth (almost like removing skins from roasted nuts) and sorted into larvae and pupae by hand, removing any that are too developed. (We tend not to use pupae whose eyes have begun to turn purple, as this signals they are becoming adults, and the taste becomes quite bitter and unpleasant.) We then seal the larvae and pupae separately in vacuum bags to prevent oxidation, on a 50 per cent vacuum seal, so that only half the air has been removed and they do not clump together but remain loose. Stored in this way, they can be kept in the freezer for many months.

Once thawed, the brood is more delicate than when fresh, and must be treated gently. If ruptured, it will begin to oxidize, and, if left, after a while will turn black and gain an unpleasant taste. This is important to keep in mind with recipes where the larvae are ruptured before being cooked, such as in the Chawanmushi (pp.237–9), or ruptured and not cooked at all.

We have also conducted a more structured sensory analysis of the drone brood, to begin to more systematically understand how factors such as developmental stage, local forage and genetics may impact taste in different ways. One main finding from the study, aside from the range of words used to describe the samples, was that the developmental stage – the difference between larvae and pupae – is the main factor accounting for variation in taste. The second was the impact of location, likely as a result of differences in local forage. ('A descriptive sensory analysis of honeybee drone brood from Denmark and Norway', 2016; see References.)

The batch Oliver and his team had harvested that day in June was large: kilos of brood, still warm in the comb. I hefted the big blue plastic bag to check that I could carry it across a shoulder. It was sticky, and clung to my arm and back. With the taste of the honey strong in my mouth and its smell hovering about me in a cloud, I pedalled my bike quickly to gain momentum, and prayed to the traffic gods for a green wave back.

Three or four blocks in, I felt a sting on my forearm. Not all the workers, it seemed, had left their kin.

Back at the Lab, on the boat's foredeck in the sun, I slung off the bag and let it lie open for any remaining adults to fly away. Then, I peeled off a section of comb and, with a finger, gently brushed out a plump, white larva, and put it in my mouth. Its skin burst delicately on the tongue. It was smooth and fatty, with faint flavours of honeydew melon, raw hazelnuts, avocado. A slight sweetness, and lingering savouries. The texture was bewildering: it had a kind of luxury. I ate another, slowly, as the sun's light and heat bled through my closed eyelids.

—Written by Josh Evans

BEE BREAD

——

We first got it into the Lab in April 2012. We were putting together a dessert for our menu for an event called Pestival at the Wellcome Collection in London, based on the different components of the beehive beyond honey (The Whole Hive pp.224–6). We had tasted bee pollen before, and thought we knew its range of flavours and textures. That was until we tasted bee bread. We fell in love and have been working with it ever since. Here is what I've been able to learn about it, from a bit of background research.

Honeybees (*Apis mellifera*) have mastered feats of chemical engineering as various as they are alchemical. Their best-known substances are honey (their concentrated, stable, hive-warming energy source) and beeswax (their pliable, moisture-proof structural material). Yet there are others which, nowadays, are known primarily only to beekeepers and practitioners of traditional medicines. Propolis, or 'bee glue', is used as a structural sealant and potent antimicrobial agent within the hive, and carries a beautiful, resinous aroma. Royal jelly is what all brood – the immature larvae and pupae – are first fed before being weaned onto honey (unlike the future queen, who is fed only royal jelly); it has remarkable moisturizing, emulsifying and stabilizing properties. Even the brood are used as food in many cultures and have a delicate savouriness, with hints of raw nuts or avocado (pp.87–9).

Each substance is fascinating in its own right, though the pollen is particularly notable for the transformation it undergoes between its collection and storage. While bees use honey as their primary energy source, pollen is where they find the rest of their nourishment: proteins, vitamins and other vital nutrients. At first glance, bee pollen seems like quite a straightforward product. In the course of pollinating thousands of flowers every day, worker bees are repeatedly showered with grains of pollen, some of which accumulate into granules on the hairs of their hind legs. This is the pollen most commonly available – largely because it is relatively easy to gather, often by using a small device attached to the hive door that knocks the pollen off the returning bees' legs as they enter.

But the bees do not consume their pollen fresh. Instead, they take it into the hive and pack the granules into empty comb cells, mixing them with nectar and digestive fluids and sealing the cell with a drop of honey. Once processed in this way, the pollen remains stable indefinitely. Beekeepers call this form of pollen 'perga' or 'bee bread'.

Fresh pollen is high in moisture and protein and, especially when brought into the hive – which stays around an internal temperature of 37°C (98.6°F) – becomes an ideal substrate for mould growth. The bees' digestive fluids, however, are rich with lactic acid bacteria (LAB), which come to dominate the pollen substrate when it is packed together and sealed from the air with honey. The bacteria metabolize sugars in the pollen, producing lactic acid and lowering the pH from 4.8 to around 4.1 – well below the generally recognized threshold for pathogenic microbial growth of 4.6.

The LAB come predominantly from the bees themselves, rather than, for example, from the plants from which they forage. The difference in microbial ecology of fresh pollen versus stored is great. Furthermore, many of the genera that come to dominate fermented pollen are also some of those most common in fermented food products made by humans: *Oenococcus*, *Paralactobacillus* and particularly *Bifidobacterium*, a known probiotic genus whose activity in beehives has also been correlated with lower counts of pathogenic microbes in the colony. Beneficial yeasts and fungi have also been documented. Many of these beneficial fungi are susceptible to fungicides in the environment, often applied to plant crops. Greater microbial diversity of beneficial microbes in bee colonies has also been correlated with greater genetic diversity of the bees themselves, and this symbiosis between bees and their microbes, as in humans, is becoming increasingly studied as likely a key part of overall hive health.

In addition to preservation, the fermentation process of the pollen also renders its nutrients more available. Some proteins are broken down into amino acids, starches are metabolized into simple sugars and vitamins become more bioavailable – that is, they are more easily taken up by the body. In this sense, bee bread is even more health-giving than the more commonly available fresh bee pollen.

Yet the sensory transformation of the bee pollen into bee bread might be the most remarkable. The floral and herbal notes of individual granules become enhanced; the powdery, sandy texture becomes firmer and moister; the acidity from the lactic acid brightens the flavour and balances possible bitterness; and the fermentation produces secondary aromas that generate new flavours of fruit – some, for example, gain the distinct taste of mango. The particularities of the fresh pollen, depending on the season and its plant sources, become enhanced, and new qualities are revealed.

We have used the bee bread in different recipes: Peas 'n' Bees (pp.288–9); The Whole Hive (pp.224–6); or Rhubarb and Roseroot (pp.227–9). The potent bacterial activity of the bee bread also makes it a fantastic inoculum, or microbial starter, for a robust start to lactic fermentation of cream into crème fraîche, especially for making butter (pp.232–3).

Our interaction with *Apis mellifera* is one of the oldest co-evolutionary relationships between insects and humans – and yet there is still so much we don't know about them. For example, despite the current explosion of interest among scientists in studying the complex microbiota of bees, we still do not know exactly which species of microbes are driving this transformation of pollen into bee bread, or exactly how.

As fascinating, delicious and versatile as bee bread is, my favourite part about it might be the realization that we humans are not the only ones who ferment our food. In fact, we are likely not the first to have stumbled upon, and learned to collaborate with, the vast world of beneficial microbes that transmute some of our most valued gastronomic products; *Apis mellifera* probably got there long before.

—Written by Josh Evans

FROM SARDINIA TO THE NORDIC FOOD LAB

'How is it possible that, with all those strong traditions and such incredibly tasty food, an Italian could fall in love with edible insects?'

This is one of the most frequent questions that curious observers and chefs ask me. Many of these people are unaware of my Sardinian roots, and equally as unaware that engaging with one of these kinds of foods changed my life forever.

My gastronomic dogmas were shaped when I was very young. I grew up in a social context where self-sufficiency characterized most of the elements of the food we consumed. The methods that I use today to explore the potential of the edible landscape are a part of the fundamental life lessons granted to me by my late grandmother. I recognize her contribution to the development of the person I am today with great gratitude.

I grew up eating ingredients which are recognizable as prehistoric foods: *sa cordula*, the long intestines of a sheep; *su sambene*, blood; *cazu de crabittu*, a cheese made inside the stomach of a suckling goat; and *casu marzu*, the famous cheese infested with fly larvae.

Sardinia is the second largest island in the Mediterranean Sea. Its human history – dating back to somewhere around 13,000 BCE – is characterized by an impressive list of traditional foods and their associated methods of preparation and preservation. For millennia, at any given epoch, Sardinia has been mixing and mingling with cultures from all corners of the world.

I come from a culture where repulsion for some kinds of foods was not an option. Preventing food waste through the development of delicious recipes for products that might otherwise be wasted is a part of the foundation of Sardinian gastronomy, and consequentially a part of my family heritage. In my romantic vision of edible insects, I can easily conceive the image of the *casu marzu* as a symbol of the struggle against food waste.

Over time, our world has become defined by legislation and policy that is increasingly disconnected from human knowledge about how to interact with food. The ability to recognize whether something has spoiled by inspecting its smell, colour and texture is, for me, a celebration of cultural know-how. Sadly, these skills are slowly being lost.

Known also as *casu saddi saddi*, *casu fattu a cazu* or *casu giampigattu* in some other Sardinian dialects, *casu marzu* literally means 'rotten cheese'. This raw-milk cheese is generally produced with sheep's or cow's milk, and is naturally the meal of choice of the *Piophila casei* fly.

Under the right environmental conditions, usually occurring during the Sardinian spring and summer, the larvae of this species, also known as the cheese skipper, are able to transform an entire piece of hard cheese into a highly potent and pungent cream in a matter of a few weeks. The cream is readily consumed as a thick smear on a piece of bread. For many people in Sardinia, *casu marzu* is considered a natural aphrodisiac.

Banned from trade within the European Union and perceived by many as dangerous and disgusting, this product was commonly found throughout Sardinia until only a few years ago. Today *casu marzu* has become exclusively symbolic, interconnected with the impenetrable world of the Sardinian shepherd.

Imagine a shepherd discovering that, after months of hard work, his cheese is completely infested with maggots. His stomach and his skills offer him a choice. He asks himself the inevitable question: taste it – or waste it? I love entertaining the idea that this is how the deliciousness of *casu marzu* was first discovered.

Even as a young child, the practice of eating insects was part of my gastronomic imprint, and I can still vividly remember my very first experience with this controversial product. It was summer, and I was probably eight years old. Together with my family, I was enjoying a celebration in the middle of the mountains looming behind my hometown, Seneghe.

I can still clearly recall the moment when a friend gently placed an *istredzu,* a rounded, terracotta pot, on the basalt-slab table at the end of lunch. A cloud of small flies lazily circled around the lid of the pot, while others entered and exited from a small hole in the top.

ABOVE: sheep grazing in Sardinia

At that moment, I noticed some people who were conscious of what was going on start to smile, a sparkle in their eyes.

Like the opening of Pandora's box, another plume of small, dark flies abandoned the pot as my friend opened it, and I witnessed the entire piece of *casu marzu* that lay inside. It was the first time that I had seen a product like this: a cheese with many tiny, white maggots jumping around inside.

Some of the people present that day were elated to see the cheese and each gathered around the pot with their personal *leppa*, a traditional Sardinian pocketknife. They started to dig their long blades into the creamy mass, taking big portions and spreading both the cheese and wiggling larvae together on top of some fresh, homemade bread. This primordial delicacy was served with a dark red wine in some small glasses. I still remember my friends and family's happy faces. Their cheerful voices were a clear expression of pleasure. The special seasonal delicacy revealed from the magical pot was maintaining the invisible strings of connection between this group of people – a web that I was fascinated by, and proud to be a part of.

Overcome with curiosity, I decided to try the cheese. It was an extremely delicious experience. Nobody at that moment even considered the fact that we were eating insects. For us, the *casu marzu* was just a food.

Even before I started working with insects, I always felt it was inappropriate and culturally disrespectful to use a sensationalistic approach and describe these products as 'unusual'. In fact, *casu marzu* is often found on lists of the top ten most disgusting foods in the world, alongside other contenders such as *balut* (fertilized avian eggs) from the Philippines and Thailand, or *kæstur hákarl* (fermented shark) from Iceland. But the people placing such a label on these traditional foods are most likely those who live in places where the paradigm of industrialized food systems is predominant.

My appetite for delivering authentic food experiences drove my interest in trying to eliminate the barriers and repulsion related to certain foods, even before coming to the Lab. The idea of celebrating culture and valorizing the food behind it, creating a more complex definition of food diversity and promoting the diffusion of knowledge, is – and has always been – one of the main reasons why I am so intrigued by the argument for eating insects.

Outside of Sardinia, insects as a source of food have been steadily emerging in Europe. In 2013, as the Sardinian spring was vibrantly announcing its arrival, a message appeared on my phone: 'Hey, our common friend Viola told me that you are the person I have to contact if I want a piece of *casu marzu*! When will it be ready? I will jump on an aeroplane, just to find this marvellous piece of cheese! Let me know. Ben.'

I replied: 'Hey Ben, I'm happy to find a piece of *casu marzu* for you, maybe I can get two, but it won't be ready until August. I'll call the shepherd tomorrow and ask him to keep one aside for you. I know from Viola that you are the head of research and development at Nordic Food Lab. I would like to come join you on the boat. Will that be possible?'

'Yeah, of course. Let's talk about it,' Ben wrote back.

And so my adventure with Nordic Food Lab began.

—Written by Roberto Flore
with Afton Halloran

TERMITE SAGA

'We cook chicken to order. I can have one from death to table in forty-five minutes. My mom was very strict – you might say she was a disciplinarian. She was hard, but it certainly taught me to cook.' Pamela Muyeshi sits with us in the covered, open-air dining room, overlooking a green hill sloping down to a stream. She is the founder and owner of the restaurant Amaica in Nairobi.

'So you would like to know about the white ants,' she continues. 'We use 20 kilograms a week. I have two groups of women around Kenya, around fifty in total. It is their responsibility to send us our supply. It is the fastest-moving starter on the menu.'

'I can see why,' Ben says, snacking on the termites from the calabash, a hollowed-out gourd, on the table.

'The cuisines of west Kenya and from the coast tend to be the most elaborate,' Pamela tells us. 'We serve two versions of the white ants: toasted and seasoned with ash water the traditional way, and the other with chilli powder and lemon juice added. Most traditional Kenyan food is simple, without spices – except for the cuisine near the coast, where there is a lot of influence from India, from when the English brought Indians over to build the railroads. That's where the ginger and garlic come from, and the biryanis, curries, chapatis and pilau. In fact, maybe people who come to the restaurant prefer the spicy ones.

'Our goal is to keep the Kenyan culinary traditions of all the regions alive. I want to build a cultural connection among Kenyans, especially young Kenyans, so they know what these foods are, what they taste like, how they are prepared. Some of the dishes we serve are almost extinct. Even thirty years ago, many were almost extinct already. So we are also starting demonstrations and workshops in January.

'It is expensive and becoming more difficult to find many traditional ingredients, like the termites. Their habitats are being disturbed and there are more pesticides being used, so there has to be a deliberate effort to conserve them and their habitats.

'A large part of my project here is also economic empowerment for women. I work with many women farmers. I find them more reliable.'

Pamela stands, tall and lithe, her patterned dress in black and red flowing with new folds. 'Come into the kitchen, and my cooks will show you how we make the termites.' Her staff follow her every move.

'We have both professionally trained cooks and traditional recipe experts in the kitchen. Many of the trained cooks are young men – they know hygiene and storage, and they have good habits, but they do not know the traditional techniques. This is why the recipe experts are so important. Most of them are women who have cooked their whole lives and know the recipes, and they teach the cooks. In my experience, men like to do shortcuts; women will do the details better.

Here, everybody learns something from everyone else.'

In the kitchen today, there are four traditional recipe experts (all female) and three professionally trained cooks (all male). 'Here, meet Esther Mutambi, Millicent Muhavi and Alex Murangi,' says Pamela. 'Esther and Millicent will show you. Alex,' she addresses the young cook. 'You may help them.' She turns back to us. 'All the best cooks – and women – are from western Kenya! So you are in good hands. I must take a call.' She disappears back into the dining room.

'First, we must make the ash water,' Esther tells us. 'It is called *omunyu* or *omusherekha*. It is one of the important parts of Kenyan cuisine. You make ash by burning dry banana skins. There are a few other plants you can use also. Mix it with the same amount of water, and let it filter. We use this special clay filter pot called *olusherekho*. Traditionally one can filter through banana leaves, though we also use filter paper nowadays. Then we use the liquid to cook with. It is salty and also makes foods more tender. You can evaporate the water to get the salt. It is popular with diabetics.'

We taste a little of the ash water on its own. It is salty, bitter, slightly sweet and alkaline.

CLOCKWISE FROM TOP LEFT: 1. Building termite traps from clay in Onyurnyur **2.** Shellan's termite queen **3.** Lunch spread at Epang'a Valley **4.** One of many daytime termite traps, in Kakamega

'Wash the termites and drain them. Dry them in a hot pan for thirty seconds. Once they are dry, add the *omusherekha*, about a teaspoon, and stir and heat until it dries. Remove when the wings have come off and they look dry. If you are making the spicy ones, add the chilli powder with the *omusherekha*,' Esther says, stirring the termites on the heat until they dry again. 'Then add two teaspoons lemon juice, heat and stir for two minutes, and remove. Like this.'

We taste them soon after they come off the pan. 'They're really nice warm!' says Ben.

'And with tea with milk,' Millicent says, handing us two cups.

'Gentlemen, if you're ready,' says Pamela, popping her head back inside the kitchen. We thank Esther, Millicent and Alex and rejoin Pamela at our table in the open dining room. We ask her further about Kenyan indigenous wild plants, and fermentation techniques. She also tells us about large mushrooms that grow from some termite mounds, in May, June and July. We scribble to absorb the rapid flow. I look up and her eyes are on us. 'I will put you in contact with one of my termite women in Kakamega. She will take you to catch some.' She pauses. '*Pole pole*, boys,' she says. 'Go slowly.'

'How do you say "thank you very much" in Swahili?' I ask her.

'*Asante sana*.'

'*Asante sana*.'

She smiles winningly. 'I never told you where "Amaica" comes from.' She pauses. 'The three cooking stones we use to hold the pot over the fire. Look out for it as you head west. The *amaica* is the heart of Kenya.'

The common handshake here, between males, begins and ends with gripped palms; in between, the hands swing inward towards the other's body, and then back, hinged at the thumbs. It is thus that Thomsen Ole Tenges, already a friend of a friend, introduces us to Sylvester Kipkebut and his friend Elijah Kapkiyai at Lake Baringo in the Great Rift Valley.

Sylvester talks charismatically and a lot. 'There is not much here, ehh. The lake is nice though.' It glitters below us at the end of the road, shards of mirror pooled in the dip of the arid Rift. 'Tourists like it. They come for it.'

'We came for insects,' Ben says.

'So let's go!' And with that, Sylvester leads us off the road, away from the lake. He shows us around the dry landscape, describing how they collect termites from different kinds of mounds. Then, after a while, Elijah invites us back to his village. 'You should meet my elder.'

We walk up from the dry scrubland and gain a bit of elevation. Cacti and shrubs give way to steeper slopes and a lush canopy overhead.

Chebii Cheptoo is Tuken, a sub-tribe of the Kalenjin, and speaks only the Tuken language. He is eighty-five, has been married twice and has fathered twelve children – all of whom, he tells us, have jobs. He has lived here in Chebarsiat his whole life.

'People take termites from the mound closest to where they live,' he tells us, through Elijah. 'Mine is right behind my home. I will show you.' He takes us just behind his woodpile to show us. This one has only a slight mound, and the curved sticks for his daytime harvests are in the ground. 'If I see one termite flying around, I know to check to see if it is time to harvest.

Usually during the rainy period, when the rain is not there.

'This is how I prepare them: I dry-fry them to kill, and I burn this *kokchan* wood and stir them with it as it smokes.' He ignites one end of the wood in the fire to show us: it smells of melon rind, tomato leaf, limonene and coriander. 'Then sun-dry, and pound them in this wooden bowl with this wooden mallet. Then I add honey, around 1 kilogram honey to 20 kilograms termites. Then I put it in this wooden pot with this lid and a leather cover to store. It keeps this way for a long time, maybe two or three years – but it never lasts that long,' he says, his eyes lit. 'We call this *kunen* in Tuken. It is what I give my guests when they come. It also builds the body strong, good for health. I am very sorry I do not have any now, the season is just beginning. I will have some soon.'

We did not get to taste it, but what a great recipe. I would have liked to make the *kunen* with Chebii.

We head to Eldoret that evening. The car climbs steep switchbacks out of the Great Rift Valley, the sunset colours rich and tinged with murk.

'I have been here at the University of Eldoret since it began twenty-three years ago,' Dr Raphael Ochieng tells us. 'I am an entomologist. I can tell you what I know about termites in western Kenya.

'The first thing to know is that there are many kinds. Many. They have different names, and multiple names. Most termites people eat belong to the Macrotermitinae subfamily, and most commonly eaten are the winged reproductives, or alates – what are often called 'white ants'. Generally there are two seasons – one in November and December, before the small rainy season, and in April, before the big rainy season.

'I don't know if anyone knows their way completely around it all. But we will try. I will try in Luhya.' He runs through three or four types, their characteristics and behaviours off the top of his head, as well as a couple of species that are not eaten, and the *Termitomyces* spp., the termite mound mushrooms.

'You know,' he tells us, 'as you are here, I think we should visit my colleague, Professor Wanjala. He might be able to add some more.'

We walk down the hallway to Professor Frederick Wanjala's office.

'Hello! Come in. Termites! Yes, ha, I think maybe we can help. What do you have so far?'

He looks at our notes, adds his own list of terms to the mix, then breaks into drumming on his desk to show us the song used to draw some kinds out of their mounds.

'It sounds like you like termites,' Ben ventures.

'Like them? Between termites and meat, both prepared well, I would take termites.'

'Oh, yes, so would I,' Dr Ochieng concurs.

'They are more expensive though. One thousand shillings [approx. US$9.85] per kilogram is normal, whereas beef you can get for 300 to 340 shillings [US$2.95 to 3.35] per kilogram.

'Here is the process. Boil them casually, then dry them out in the sun intimately, and remove the wings. These can be preserved. To cook, add salt, no fat – they are already fatty – and never spices. Eat with *ugali* [a stiff, sticky Kenyan staple of boiled maize flour]. Very sweet,' Wanjala affirms, staring out the window.

'Here, taste this,' Ferdinand Wafula says. It is a fresh groundnut: the flesh is bright white, crunchy and fresh, with a clear, deep pea flavour. 'And these,' he says, offering us a bag of termites, warm from the sun. The oil is more present, and stays on our fingers. 'Sometimes I will eat them on a piece of bread, and that is all I need for lunch.'

Ferdinand walks us around his garden. It is dense, diverse, productive.

'I founded Bio-Gardening Innovations in 2009, to create a space to train farmers on sustainable farming, indigenous seeds, permaculture, planting food forests. I want to revalorize traditional farming practices and crops. Rising disease is bringing back consciousness of what we eat. Official medical guidelines are coming back to our indigenous foods. So we need to help each other relearn.

'What can I tell you about insects? There is a lot to say.

'Conventional agriculture sees termites as a pest. They destroy buildings! So people kill them with pesticides. But then they are also destroying part of the ecosystem, that also brings something good for the organic farmer: the termites degrade wood and other organic materials, increasing biomass in the soil.

'The presence of mushrooms, especially the edible ones like *Termitomyces*, is a good indicator of soil health. And they have been decreasing, especially where there is heavy use of synthetic chemicals for maize production.

'But let's talk more over at Epang'a Valley. But before we go, I have a request.'

'Of course,' I say.

'I ask every guest to plant a plant here in the garden at BioGI.' His colleague Rechael Eyauma brings over two seedlings. 'And I ask them to plant it with a certain thought in mind.

'Here is a young orange for you, Ben. And this one, Josh, is a young *Sesbania* sp. It is an excellent nitrogen-fixer.' He points to the patches of soil where we can plant them.

'May their roots grow deep,' I say, as Ferdinand rinses our hands and waters the newly planted trees from a metal can.

'Let us go to Epang'a. There is more there to see.'

A short walk brings us to Epang'a Valley. It is a community of a few dozen adults and children. It is calm throughout.

'It is not a big piece of land – just a half acre – but it is productive,' says Ferdinand. We walk past compact, sturdy houses interspersed with small diverse plots, trees at different heights, compost pits, wells and sinkholes to hold water.

'Most who live here are Abanyole, a Luhya subtribe,' says Ferdinand, after introducing us. 'So they are associated with chicken. We keep indigenous breeds here, they will be able to tell you.' He smiles around at people we pass.

A man comes right over. 'Hello, I am Naaman,' he says. 'Let me show you.' He takes us over to a sheaf of straw stuck in the earth. 'We trap the termites, called *amache*, to feed our chickens. They love the termites, and the chickens fed with termites taste better. We take a bunch of dry grass, put it in the termite hole, cover it with soil and leave it overnight. In the morning, remove the cover and there will be many soldiers. You can feed them to the chickens right away, live, or dry and store them for later. It is endless chicken feed. Drying them makes it safer for the chicks to eat, and it makes them sellable. We also feed the termites to our quails.

'We eat only the winged ones, called *chisua*, which come at different times of year. When it rains, you see where they come up. We build a little cover over the holes, and put transparent plastic at one end to let in light. We put a container in a pit near the hole, lined with banana leaves – so they slide down and can't get out – and open the plastic so they come into the pot.

'Some people use a stick to make a path, so that they follow each other into the container. Everyone has different techniques and tricks, different styles.'

'Is it possible to overharvest termites?' Ben asks.

'No, not with these techniques.'

'The winged ones are said to be a kind of aphrodisiac,' adds Ferdinand. 'It does make some sense, as some are rich in zinc, and zinc is needed to produce testosterone. There are also many expressions in local languages about love and termites: people "love each other like termites", or, you "walk together like termites", after the winged termites' pairing behaviour. Mating winged pairs will start a small nest – and if it grows, they will become the queen and king.'

'We sometimes eat the queen as well, for longevity,' says Naaman. 'She is called *lianangina*. She can be thirty to fifty years old. The bigger she is, the older. Some Luhya also slice her and feed it to cattle – it makes them grow big and fast.'

'And we were discussing the mushrooms before,' Ferdinand recalls. 'We still find them here, from April to June, at the onset of the big rain. Though they have become smaller. People used to harvest very big ones! This year, we started seeing more of them. It is a sign that the soil is remediating. The Permaculture Research Institute Kenya is conducting more research into the *Termitomyces*. We hope to collaborate with them.'

Ferdinand leads us down the slope, coming out to a pool dug just above the riverbank. 'Here we have built a modified oxygen–nitrogen aquaculture system, with catfish and tilapia. The two fish keep each other in balance, and the water is pumped back up the hill to use as fertilizer for the plants.'

We pick our way on winding paths back up the slope. At a large gathering table, some of the women are making clay pots. Ben asks if he can try. The women laugh and pass him some clay.

Jerusa, one of the women, sits with me. 'Can you tell me more about the termites you eat?' I ask her. She proceeds to tell me about many different kinds, their names and behaviours and preparations.

'The wings are a personal preference. The pan should be slightly hot – enough to kill, but not enough to cook or rupture or burn. The tradition is that we do not add anything to them to season them, because then we have killed them and no more will come out of the mound. We eat them simply with *ugali* or tea.'

By this point we have received at least three or four distinct folk classifications. It is unclear how, or even whether, they interact.

I have little more time to mull on names, which is probably for the best. Rosemary, another woman, takes me to her kitchen. 'We are going to cook the quail for lunch.'

She takes a few quail from a pen next to her house, and gently but swiftly breaks their necks. They fall limp. She takes them inside, and her daughter plucks them while she fans the coals. When the coals are hot, she places the quail on them to singe off any vestiges of down and sear the skin, then puts them on a grate just above the wood embers to finish, whole. 'These *jikos*' – a kind of ceramic stove – 'keep the heat when we cook, and reduce firewood use by more than 50 per cent. We are starting to use solar cooking too.'

When the quail are done, we put them in a dish and return to the others. The table has been laid with many things: *ugali*, winged termites, whole tiny chillies, beef stew and many different greens – colewort, kale, nightshade, jute, cowpea, pumpkin leaves, amaranth and spider herb. The quail's head is remarkable. The chillies are beautiful – very hot, and very fragrant, like flowers.

It is finally at this lunch that we learn how to eat *ugali* properly. You have to shape it in your hand: take a bit and massage it until smooth, then make an indent with your thumb and use it sort of like a spoon. It is quite amusing for everyone when we finally get it. Eating the beef stew with termites now makes much more sense.

The tastes on the round table emerge directly from the dense biodiversity that surrounds us. I sit back and follow the vines into the trellis overhead. Air potatoes (*maruku*) hang within reach, their bulbous, starchy fruits sweeter than potatoes. The children love them. February to March is air-potato season, Ferdinand tells me, and by that time they can grow quite large – 100 to 200 grams each.

I become aware of the birdsong that has been there the whole time, more of it than I can keep track of. The songs fade across each other, to the background and to the fore, different sounds across minutes and different times of the day – so various in dynamic, tone, suppleness. Some seem to pair off, with a quarter-tone difference in pitch.

Lunch ends with a ceremony of thanks. Everyone stands and sings a song in a round: the words 'To whom does it belong' resonate in a slow spiral beneath the canopy.

We are up at dawn, to work before the day gets too warm. We are on Rusinga Island, hosted by Evans Owuor Odula, the founder of Badilisha Eco Village. We are staying on the land of his father Michael Odula, where Evans lives along with his siblings and their families. A termite colony (*Macrotermes subhyalinus*, or *biye* in Luo) has been building a nest in an exposed embankment a few metres from Michael's house. The morning's task is to remove it.

'There are many ways to do it,' Evans tells us. 'Some people use poison, or gasoline, or even water to flood them out. But instead of those, today we will find the queen.'

We begin digging, and take turns swinging the pickaxe and moving soil away from the hole with shovels. A couple of the older children have joined us to help.

'Where is she likely to be?' Ben asks.

'The queen follows the moon. So over here,' Evans says. I think on this, and wonder at how it might work.

We have gotten deeper into the colony. The compound's clutch of chicks and chickens pick through the debris for soldiers and workers. From the gravelly, silty soil emerge fascinating pieces of the hive structure: involuted forms, light in weight and colour, covered with tiny, white termite nymphs. And suddenly, something different: a hefty, layered piece of harder-looking, packed earth. Evans signals to us to stop, and pulls the piece from the exposure. Carefully, he picks off some dirt, and turns the cavity around.

Inside is a creature the likes of which I have never seen before. It is the closest I suppose I have come to an alien encounter. The head and thorax are slightly larger than a termite soldier, but still proportionate to each other. The light brown abdomen, however, extends for maybe 8 cm (3 inches), punctuated with pairs of dark-brown dots at even distances. I am most in awe of the queen's movements. Her abdomen seems liquid – it undulates, engorges, constricts in what must be patterns but ones so complex I can only behold it as an eerie, shatteringly beautiful whole. It is mesmerizing. I could gaze at it for hours.

Evans brings her over into the shade of the house and drops her softly onto some waxy leaves. Michael's mother, vivacious and commanding and the clear matriarch of the household, will cook it. We bring it into the cooking house, and she places it onto a searing pan. It cooks quickly, the proteins firming, the enfolded tissue puffing up. She takes it off the heat, and we slice it into pieces at each pair of dots. Some of the family have never tasted it before either. Occasionally, it is administered as a medicine to children and infants – raw, squeezed down the throat.

The taste is, and I do not exaggerate, sublime. It is nutty, fragrant, with a texture somewhere between poached sweetbreads and foie gras – in short, it is majorly delicious. From its taste, it is no surprise it is a delicacy. The labour, skill and knowledge involved in obtaining one makes it only more rare and special.

Monica Ayieko is associate professor of consumer science at Jaramogi Oginga Odinga University of Science at Technology (JOOUST) in Bondo. She and her assistant Jackline Oloo meet with us to share their efforts to integrate certain insects – both those traditionally eaten in the region, such as lake flies, black ants and termites, and those that are not, such as crickets – into new foods.

'I love the termites because they have such a strong flavour,' Monica says. 'We have used them in cookies, muffins, sausages, meatloaf, samosas, rolls and wraps. Many with good acceptance. We have also experimented with big light traps to catch them at night. A lot of potential, yes.'

We tell Monica and Jackline about the queen we tasted.

'The termite queen – oh, you are lucky. Finding it is often a diversion for active children. Which is great, because it is also full of polyunsaturated fatty acids.

'When you take the queen, the colony will move, identify a new queen and re-establish. Winged reproductives might also take off and establish new hives. It will never re-establish in the same place – after it is associated with danger.'

I ask Monica about the moon. 'No, the queen does not move. She stays in her chamber.' I wonder where the impression of her lunar movement comes from.

'We have tried with some colleagues in Nairobi to farm termites, but we have not yet succeeded,' she tells us. 'We still do not know enough about how to raise queens and kings.

'Tomorrow, I will introduce you to some farmers. They might take you digging.'

Monica has introduced us to Osewre Joseph Oketch and Patrick Onyango Puye, two local farmers who also run the Fab Lab at the Agricultural Resource Centre in Majiwa, a village near Bondo. The Fab Lab (short for fabrication laboratory) idea began at Massachusetts Institute of Technology (MIT), and now comprises a global network of small-scale, open-source workshops that aim to help people 'make almost anything', especially their own machines.

We sit and eat mangoes in Joseph's yard. They have thick skin, large stones and bewilderingly aromatic flesh, sour and sweet. A large shrub of *onyalobiro* or *atek* (*Lantana camara*) blooms nearby, small flowers bursting out astrally in a gradient of gold, tangerine and fuchsia. They emit an enlivening scent, akin to guava.

'So, you are looking for termite queens!' Joseph says. 'Great, I have a few mounds I need to move.'

We follow him on a path that comes out to an enormous mound, built right into his field. We have also attracted quite a large gaggle of kids who want to watch. Joseph begins to swing his pickaxe into the dense surface. 'Termite soil is hard to dig, but is good for housebuilding,' he says between a grunt, a heave and another swing. Joseph, Ben and I take turns with the digging. 'Where should we focus our digging?' I ask Joseph. 'In the centre,' he says. 'Until we find the small ones, and follow them to the queen.'

'I'm afraid that after one of these swings, it's going to come up with half a queen dangling from the end,' I joke. 'I really don't want that to happen.'

We keep digging, switching off when we need a break. After a particularly wet thud by Joseph, the blunt end of the pickaxe blade stays firmly in the ground and he moves in to investigate. He pulls a piece of well-packed earth from the rubble, and lifts the top layer to reveal a large moist mark of squelch. A couple tiny workers tend to the squelch frantically.

'Oh no,' says Ben.

'Mm, *pole pole*,' Joseph mutters. 'Once in the nest, we must go slowly.'

'Well, at least you got rid of this mound here,' I say with a crestfallen smile.

'Hm. I have another hive.' Joseph moves on.

'It would be like running over a foie gras duck,' pipes Ben, in comic agony.

'Except, it would have to be, like, a subterranean duck you have to dig out first,' I say.

'Yeah, like you just spent five hours digging, and then it ran out, and a truck ran over it.' We snigger to keep our spirits.

We walk a couple of hundred metres along Joseph's field until we reach another mound, this one lower but still quite wide, and nearer to his home on the edge of another field of younger maize.

We go more slowly this time, excavating the mound in what we think is a methodical way. After half an hour, no queen. Nor after one hour – not even a sign of the royal chamber. We are beginning to think we've lost it in the debris, or inadvertently and blindly crushed it without a trace, when Joseph's son Shellan appears from across the field with a few smaller boys in his retinue.

'What have you got there?' shouts Ben when Shellan is some metres away. He comes up to us holding a familiar, dense, layered piece of earth. He lifts a broad leaf and reveals a queen, her belly dancing its perpetual dance in the crevice.

'Where did you find that?!' exclaims Ben.

'I just dig. Not too deep.'

High fives are had all around, and Shellan is the hero of the day.

Back in Joseph's yard, we start a fire under the shade of a tree. Patrick, who lives nearby, has his son run off to boil some maize. Ben and I get to work.

'Joseph, I'd like to cook this queen for you,' Ben says. 'I'd like to use one of your delicious mangoes. And maybe something from your garden?' Joseph takes us over to a vegetable patch near his house. We pluck some young cabbage shoots, some sweet pea leaves (*umbulu*) and some tiny wild sorrel flowers (*awayo*) growing around the plot. The pea leaves are used for coughs, Joseph tells us, and the wild sorrel leaves draw off fluid from boils.

Back under the tree, the fire has grown. While the flames erode the wood, Ben blanches some sweet young cabbage leaves in a small pot of water, slices the mango (*mawembe*) and cuts out circles of it with the plastic sealing ring off a water bottle. I pick sweet pea leaves and wild sorrel flowers from the stem. The children watch us silently, eating mangoes.

Ben arranges three stones, places a cast-iron pan on them and lets it heat up. When it is hot enough, he places the queen gently onto the surface. 'What a privilege to cook this,' he murmurs. 'It's an honour,' I say quietly. We cook it more slowly, letting it puff up gently without taking very much colour. Ben removes it from the heat to rest. After a few minutes, he slices it into rounds. The inner structure is revealed: two lobes run the length of the abdomen.

We place a couple blanched cabbage leaves on a plate, and a few rings of mango in a loose stack, followed by the segments of queen, and garnished with the flowers. 'Queen with mango,' says Ben, offering the plate to Joseph, who sits watching all this from a chair next to the tree.

'Very, very sweet. Very nice,' Joseph says. Patrick takes a piece, and Shellan.

I can't say Ben and I don't feel a little silly, sitting here making this fancy dish, placing tiny white blossoms just so. But it is also fun, and our hosts seem to enjoy it.

'What is the queen called, Joseph?' I ask.

'*Nyailiel*. We say *nyailiel*.'

Patrick's son brings over the huge plate of corn on the cob, unshucked and still steaming. The kernels are enormous, plump and pale yellow, almost white.

It is delicious. '*Nyailiel*,' I say, rolling the sounds around in my mouth before taking another bite.

Benjamin Mwene is twenty-two and the cook at the Anyoun Cultural Hotel and Educational Centre, established in 2011. He makes traditional 'ancient' foods. 'It's a wake-up for the community!' he says with zeal. 'We make our own ghee. Taste.' He hands us two spoons. 'Boiled from milk of *zebu*, traditional cattle. It also gets better with time.

'And we make our own soured milk, called *teso*.' It is the most sour milk ever – like sucking a lemon.

'Today we are going to make dishes with termites,' says Benjamin. 'Termites are flying vegetables! Very healthy – and a medicine. Termites with soured milk, termite mushrooms with termites and ash water. And rat stew with groundnut sauce. And brown *ugali*, of course. Let's go.' He takes us out behind the restaurant, where there is an open yard and two *jikos*, with fires already started. A calf sleeps in the corner.

'So let's start with the *ugali*, because it must cool.' Benjamin places an enormous *sufuria* (pot) on the *jiko*, the largest we have seen yet, and fills it with water.

'And now, while we wait, I will show you the *elumuci*, winged termites cooked with sour milk.' He grinds some alates in a mortar, adds them to a pot with a bit of water and lets it reduce. '*Elumuci* is the technique of using soured milk. One can make *elumuci* with many things. Same with *elirina*, which uses soured milk and blood. Though we have no blood today.' He adds some soured milk, and also lets it reduce. 'There, easy!' says Benjamin. 'Eat with brown *ugali*. Very sweet.'

The huge pot is almost to the boil. Benjamin's assistant takes a calabash and heaps scoop after scoop of finger-millet flour from a plastic carboy into the pot. It floats on the water like a raft. He takes a huge wooden paddle and stirs it back and forth until all the flour is wet, and then until it begins to incorporate. He keeps stirring until the flour has absorbed all the water and begins to come together in a slick mass. And then he turns the whole thing over itself, like a massive thick dough. It takes some serious endurance. He is hardly fazed.

'So, let's make the rat,' Benjamin says. The paddle stands upright in the *ugali* pot. 'Maybe it is not a rat. We call it *ameldeng*, or *emekeleng*. It is big. The most traditional. We hunt it in the forest. Some kind of rodent, yes. We will call it "rat".' The rat has been dried whole. Benjamin breaks off the tail and the body into quarters, and sets them into a pot. 'We will add some water to soak. Then this is what we will do: boil it for ten minutes, wash it, add salt, leave for thirty minutes, add soured milk, let boil five minutes, and add groundnuts ground into groundnut paste. Yes?'

'Benjamin, I'd like to try cooking these termite mushrooms. Can I do it?' Ben asks.

'OK, how do you want to do that?'

'Well, I was thinking of simmering them in water with the termites, then adding some groundnut paste.'

'Oh, no, not groundnut with *ebale*. We cook the mushroom with ash water, and eat with *ugali*.'

'Right, I understand. Let's definitely do that too. I'd also like to try my idea.'

Here perhaps is the staunch rigour of traditional regional cooking: there is one way, and anything else is wrong. Perhaps it is more what is *not* allowed that defines

a way of cooking, than what is. And how does this approach interact with the 'beef/goat/chicken/fish × steamed/boiled/wet-fry/dry-fry + *ugali*/chapati/rice' decision matrix we have eaten from Nairobi to here? Is it because that is how restaurants in particular cook? Is it because we are *muzungu* – white people?

'OK,' says Benjamin. 'Here is a pot.'

While the cooks cook their mushrooms, I watch Benjamin's assistant turn the *ugali* out into an equally huge dish to let it cool. A thin layer of residual *ugali* sticks to the hot, emptied pot. Already it is beginning to dry. I have an idea for dessert.

'Guys, I'm going to get something from the hotel,' I say. 'I'll be back soon.'

I run down the road to the hotel, grab a jar of Ogiek honey – given to us when we were in the village of Mariashoni in the Molo Forest visiting Ogiek beekeepers – and rush back to Anyoun.

When I return, Benjamin has taken some dried mushrooms – they smell strong and deep, most like a boletus – and let them soak for some minutes, rinsed them to remove dirt and placed them in a clay pot on the fire. He is showing Ben a big stone with a kind of layered crystal pattern. 'This is *onagardi*. Ash stone salt. We grate a little and use like *abalang* or *aserot*, the ash water. We use it much with vegetables.' He holds up a piece and grates some into the pot. Ben follows suit. Foam starts to rise up inside the narrow neck of the clay pot.

The *ugali* pot has cooled, and the layer of *ugali* has dried. It now fractures easily, into flat shards. I chisel off a few and take them to the front of the restaurant. I spread them with some of the forest honey, salt them and top them with the toasted soldier termites Benjamin served us when we arrived.

In the small bowl, their large, shiny heads look like polished stones.

Back in the backyard, Benjamin has reduced his water and added the *ikong*, the dried winged termites. Ben is reducing the water in his wider pot. He adds some winged termites, stirs through some groundnut paste and simmers to warm and thicken.

Benjamin and his assistant are placing everything into dishes and bringing it to the small outdoor area in front of the restaurant, on Amagoro's wide main street. We sit down to a very tasty lunch with many flavours, in browns of many shades.

Afterwards, I share my simple dessert. 'Benjamin, do people ever eat the crispy parts from the *ugali* pot? Does it have a name?'

'Ehh, *imudud*. It is strange to eat!'

Neither of them take much. Andreas and I do some damage.

Some hours later, in the late afternoon, we have found ourselves on a small hill in a field in Onyurnyur, near the Ugandan border. Our recent acquaintance David Idewa heard we've been wanting to collect termites (*Odontotermes kibarensis*) with the singing technique, which is a tradition from this area of Kenya. He pulled together some local boys to make it happen. Now we're a crowd of men, women and children, a few dozen strong, piled on the hill.

The teenage boys lead the effort. There are four or five of them. They spot where the eyes are – this species makes small holes at the surface of the mound, which local people call 'eyes' – and mark them with leaves. They pour water down to make the termites think it's raining. They take clay (*elupe*) from the nearby river to block most of the eyes. Over the

remaining few, they build a tunnel leading to a clay-walled pot. Some connect tunnels from multiple nearby eyes into one central collection pot. They cover the tops of the pots with waxy leaves (*ebechel*), some with a slit so they can see inside.

'This is a special skill,' says David. 'Only a few do it, and only men. The women eat!'

David explains how they work together for the drumming, and each can keep what he collects from his own tunnel. It seems to become a display of skill and prowess.

The boys have begun drumming, each holding a stick beneath one foot and hitting the stick with two others as they kneel. The sound mimics the rain, which rouses the winged termites to fly. The boys have many rhythms and polyrhythms, which they switch in and out of as they sing songs. The first goes '*Kurus kurus toma, chakari toma*', sung in descending triad, occasionally modulating up and down, punctuated with a rapid, high-pitched cry of '*kurus kurus kurus kurus*!'. It means 'Let them come in plenty, so they come and fill this pot'. Another is '*mengere*', the local name for these white ants, chanted in a continuous stream, as if to draw them up out of the earth. There are others.

Some lift off their leaves every so often to check if the torrent has begun. Some soldiers and workers have emerged to clear the way for the alates.

It may be a competition, but more boys also join and switch out on each others' drums, so overall the tone is of a game. The sun drops lower, and the winds come up. It's almost a race to see who can get the winged ones to come first.

A man kneels down, removes a leaf blocking an eye and blows cigarette smoke into the hole. 'They get high from the smoke,' says David. 'It lowers inhibitions, makes them brave.' He smiles. 'Tobacco is fine, *bang* [marijuana] is better.'

At some point, winged termites appear in the air as if from nowhere. They flutter around the circle, some sticking in the mud, others flying out and over our heads. Some of the boys keep drumming while others check their pots, and then they switch. They all have some, not too many. They keep singing. The sun dips to the level of the crops, casting the fields in green-gold. The guava smell of the *onyalobiro* hangs thick in the dusk.

Two days ago, we crossed the border into Uganda. We stayed on at the head of the Nile for one day, the mornings covering the wide water in mist. Now, we have come to Kampala.

'I started a project in 2006 on school gardens, while a student at Makerere University. Now I work with traditional foods more and more.' Edie Mukiibi is Ben's friend, and our guide while we are in Uganda. Edie's friend Rogers Sserunjogi joins us while we are in Kampala. 'Rogers knows a lot about the insects in particular. He wants to keep the traditions alive.

'I eat the day ants [termites],' Edie continues, 'but I am allergic to the ones that come at night. I get itchy.'

'The *nsenene* [katydids, pp.120–24] are most popular anyway,' says Rogers. 'But even they aren't eaten by everyone. Many people see it as a totem.'

'Totem?' I ask.

'There are fifty-three clans in Uganda: one royal clan and fifty-two others,' explains Edie. 'Each clan has a totem. The totems began a thousand years ago. Many of the totems are foods – plants or animals, domesticated or wild. One of the clan's totem is the *nsenene*. So people who are part of that clan tend not to eat them.'

'What clan are you?'

'We are both Lugave,' says Edie. 'Our totem is the pangolin.'

Yesterday we returned to Kampala from Masaka and the Ssese Islands in the south-west, where we were researching *nsenene* and palm weevil larvae (pp.125-9). We crossed the equator on the drive up, and took a photo with a bottle of grasshopper garum perched on the monument at the line.

Today, Rogers takes us to visit his friends Tom and Rita Lubeba, farmers in Banda Kyandazza.

Coffee flowers bloom around Tom and Rita's house. Tom emerges in a cobalt-blue boiler suit. 'Hello! White ants! Let's go.' He takes us out to a stand of pine trees over a ridge behind his home.

'We also eat the soldiers. Some believe you will gain wisdom if you eat the soldiers' heads,' he says, as he digs effectively into a small mound. The light colour of the porous internal structure contrasts sharply with the red soil. Within five minutes he has opened up the nest and plucks out the royal cavity, a curved red mass, smoother than the rest. We ask him how he knew where it was so easily. 'They follow the sun,' he says.

'There are many types,' Tom adds. He leads us out of the pine copse to his maize fields. 'Some need rain, some need rain then dry, some fly at midnight, some fly at 4:00 or 5:00 a.m. There are some that open and close holes for air regulation. Small animals can nest in the holes.

'Watch for the fresh holes, fresh soil – this is a sign they will come up, that the workers have made the holes ready.

When you find a mound like this, clean off the brush, dig a pit near the base around 6.00 p.m, line the pit with leaves and put a light on sticks over the pit. Here, you can see how I've made it here.' He points to the pit with an oil lamp perched on a stick across it. It seems ready for immediate action. 'At big mounds, you can make multiple pits. Sometimes, like with this big hill' – he pats a mound that rises taller than him out of the red earth – 'I can get 50 kilograms of termites in one night. If you know how to do it, you can harvest from many termite hills in one night.'

'Right. I wonder how that much food compares to another farmer who might remove all his termite mounds so he can plant a full field of just maize,' muses Ben. 'Sounds like he'd be missing out …'

Tom takes us walking through the field, and we stop near a large pit. 'When mounds get old and big, they can also become hazardous. I once found a calf that had dropped down into a mound. But the mound holes are good – very good soil. I have planted jackfruit trees in old termite holes. But the mushrooms come only when the colony is alive. And different termites give different mushrooms. There are the *empawu* termites (*Macrotermes bellicosus*) – they are smaller, and the mound has flat eyes. They come at 4:00 a.m. There are also the *nsejere* (*Macrotermes subhyalinus*) – they are bigger, and more tasty. They make curved eyes in their mound and they come at 12:00 a.m. And their soldiers are less violent.

'You can blow into the holes to draw the termites out. When we were children, we would open up an eye, blow in, place clothes there and wait. The soldiers would bite the clothes, then we would bite the soldiers! A snack on the way home from school.'

He leans back. 'And if you want to move a colony without killing, you can cut off the top during rain – it will move.

'Come, there is something else to show you.' He walks down the slope, around the pine ridge to the lower part of his property. We round a bend and there stands one of the largest termitaria (termite nests) we've seen.

We move over to it and Tom beckons to us to come close. He points to a small brown funnel poking out of the mound. He says nothing. He begins to dig, gently. After a few minutes he exhumes something different from what we've seen before. Inside the small cavity is a darker brown mass which, upon closer inspection, reveals a highly organized structure.

'Is this the African stingless bee?' Ben exclaims in astonishment. 'I'm just going to reach in there and …' He takes a cell of honey to his lips and reels in ecstasy. We place the hive on banana leaves and move in. The honey is like nothing else. It is like wine and all the best fruit. It carries a persistent but not overwhelming sourness. Sometimes, it tastes like lemongrass. It is ambrosial.

'It's like Sauternes with all of the good bits and none of the shit!' Ben is beside himself.

The hive itself is different from kept beehives I have seen. The wax (or what seems analogous to the wax I know) is brown and sticky and pliant; the honey is suspended in small waxen pods, which hang together in a network. The pollen is also held in the pods; it is a vivid, neon orange, mottled with pink and white, and it is soft and very bitter. It tastes like grapefruit, the flesh and the pith, and has the aroma of the white coffee blossoms near Tom's house. Deeper in, I can see the brood in hexagonal combs, themselves arranged in hexagons, and here and there, the tiny, liminal bees.

We are all very much stuck into this honey. 'The glory of it is, they don't sting you!' Ben squeals, swinging around to Andreas. 'How can any species that makes something so delicious not have a sting?' he cries gleefully, squeezing honey pods into his mouth.

I come back over to Tom, who has unearthed a second hive from the mound. 'The *kadoma* always build their nest in a termite mound. Usually, there is only one. This one must be lucky.' He then points to a trail of large, black ants descending into the mound through another hole. 'The ants also live here, but we won't harvest them today.'

Termites, ants, bees, mushrooms – all these things living in one mound. It is not just a hill, or a single-species hive. It is a multispecies habitat. The termites clear the forest of dead debris; the bees pollinate flowers around the farm and further. The mound will enrich the soil when the colony moves or dies. It is riotously fertile, the collaboration inextricably interconnected. Everyone is on the menu.

We carry the remains of the hives back to Tom's house on the banana leaves. Rita prepares us some termites before we go. 'This is just one way I make them,' she says. She heats some pork fat in a pan on the fire, and adds in some chopped white onion. When it gets translucent, she adds some diced tomato and lets it all thicken and adhere to itself. Then, last, she adds toasted winged termites, stirs and spoons it into a bowl. It is simple and tastes vividly of what it is: onion, tomato, termite, pork fat.

'Sometimes, I scramble them in eggs. Sometimes, with *posho* [a variant of *ugali*] cut into small pieces.'

We thank Rita for the dish, and both of them for having us. As we leave, I notice a square, yellow plastic carboy container sawed in half. It is filled with coffee cherries. As we drive away, I can think only of the bursting white coffee blossoms, and the neon pollen to which they gave their flavour, bitter and floral in the brown wax. The bees' sting stayed in.

— Fieldwork Team: Josh Evans, Andreas Johnsen, Ben Reade. Guides: John Shikhu, Pamla Muyeshi, Jane Karanja, Ferdinand Wafula, Evans Owuor Odula, Monica Ayieko, Rogers Sserunjogi. Written by Josh Evans.

SAM

It is late afternoon by the time we arrive from the mainland. Evans Owuor Odula is hosting us at Badilisha Eco Village for a few days to show us how termites fit into the island's ecology (pp.101–2). Tomorrow, we will start fresh. Right now, I sit with his father, Michael, outside his home. We gaze across his gently sloping land, past the houses of his children and their families, to the lake – wide and shoreless as the sea, hugged by a hazy sky.

'I ate the lake flies much when I was young,' Michael tells us. 'My mother and her mother collected them when they came to land, right down here at the island's shore. You could see the column from kilometres away, a pillar of food from the lake.' I nod silently, listening intently. 'They had a special basket with a pointed end, which they swung through the thick air when they came,' he continues. 'The flies came together into a paste. Then they would flatten them into round sheets, and dry them on the roof in the sun. They would keep for up to a month. We call this *sam*. We would save them for guests and special occasions. My mother and her mother would cook them in a little water on the fire, until soft, and serve like a chapati – a black chapati, with ghee. We would eat them with *ugali*. Very sweet.

'Now, people don't really gather them much – the women no longer run down to the shore. Maybe one or two.'

'Have they come this season?' I ask.

'Yes, they have come.'

We rest. I study the bougainvilleas strewn across the ground, the pattern of the lowering sun across the corrugated roofs.

'Traditionally, all knowledge – not just about our foods – is passed down through established gender roles. But, there does not necessarily have to be a tension between traditional knowledge and gender equality. Now, some boys are learning to cook, for example. There is a returning interest in traditional foods. Perhaps some of them will learn to harvest the lake flies,' says Michael. His expression is avuncular, with an elegiac tinge – or maybe it is only how I read it. 'Evans will show you more tomorrow.'

Michael's uncle, Otieno Nundu, is seventy-seven years old. He has lived on Rusinga Island his whole life. After a long day of termite-digging (pp.101–2), we (Michael, Evans, Ben, Andreas and I) join him on his porch, up the gentle slope from Michael's land.

'Termites. Yes, I heard you down there earlier. *Ngwon*, we call them. They come after two or three days rain. I pull off the wings, fry dry, no salt, nothing else. Eat with *ugali*. They can keep for a few days, not months or years. If you dry them they can. It must be a specific pattern of wet and dry for them to come.'

'And what about the *sam* – can you tell us about it?' Ben asks.

'Yes. The *sam* can also be a medicine, for strength. It adds more blood into the body. The women use a big dish and catch as many as they can. They press them together, add salt, sometimes milk, and boil them in cakes. Like this, they can keep for a few days, but if dried, they will keep longer.

'The flies come here to Rusinga often because we are in the water. Though it depends entirely on the wind, whether they come to shore. They come in November, and again in March or April.

'Many of the children today don't know about it. We are missing the old foods – the flies, the different kinds of millet, the groundnuts. There were also the ants, big ants, which we ate, without salt. They lived around the lake. But now most of them are gone. The insect foods – we did not put them in a bag to sell. They are something we put on the table then, to enjoy. I wonder if we will regain them.'

The dusk comes, and lights flicker on in the eaves of shops in the village below.

'Otieno, I have a question,' I say. 'I have heard many Kenyans use the word "sweet" to describe foods that taste good. I know "sweet" to be the taste of sugar, or honey. Is it different here?'

Evans translates into Luo, the local language, and they smile a small smile.

'Ha. In Kiswahili, we say *tamu*, which means "sweet" and "delicious",' says Otieno. 'There is no distinction. So, that must be why many Kenyans say "sweet".'

We sit, mesmerized by the flat line of the living lake. 'Thank you for sharing with us, Otieno,' I say.

'You are welcome. I am also grateful.'

During our meeting with Monica and Jackline at Jaramogi Oginga Odinga University of Science and Technology (JOOUST; p.102), we discuss their work with lake flies.

'The last rain was around two weeks ago,' says Monica 'The lake flies have a very fast life cycle – most hatch, live and die within twenty-four hours. There are many species. In Africa we call them 'lake flies' because they tend to emerge around lakes. Other ones in Europe are often called 'mayflies' because they emerge in May. They are members of the orders Ephemeroptera ['short-lived wings'] and Diptera ['two wings']. Often the ones we have here are the *Chaoborus* and *Chironomus* species. The taxonomy is a challenge.

'Not all the insects we have are seen as edible. And even many people in the interior and around rivers don't consider the lake flies edible! Even though they may eat other ones, like termites.

'There is the black ant – called *onyoso* in the local langauge, *Carebara vidua* in Latin – which many lake-dwellers also eat. Though they have become harder to find, as many of the wetland habitats around the lake have been spoiled. Here, try it,' Monica says, opening a plastic bag from the freezer. They have a strong taste: fatty, a little bitter, and perhaps a little rancid from being kept in contact with air. I wonder what they taste like fresh – whether this comes from storage or is part of the taste. These are often roasted, which makes the nutrients more available and leaves less chitin.

'And here, you should taste the lake flies too!' Monica exclaims, pulling a large sack to the centre of the bench. 'We harvested these when they came a few weeks ago. Sometimes, when there are many and the conditions are right, I hire a speedboat with a huge net on the mast. It is very efficient, but expensive – it takes four to six strong men to do it well. We keep the netted ones loose and frozen so we can use them in different recipes.

'With the biscuits and muffins, for example, we use puffed amaranth and lake flies, add eggs, sugar and flour, and bake at 200°C [392°F] for ten to fifteen minutes. They are really a hit. We also make some with termites and have done consumer tests. We cannot do blind public sensory tests in Kenya, though. But that would be interesting.'

The lake flies on their own tend to have a fish-like taste – which makes sense, given their habitat.

'We also make *sam*, which is more traditional. We use around 95 per cent flies, a little egg and flour to hold it together well. Traditionally, the *sam* is dried, boiled and dried again so it keeps for a long time,' Monica adds.

The *sam* is a little fishy, and a little bitter. The texture is hard and compact, and thus the flavour is very concentrated. It reminds me and Ben of the dried tiny fish one can find in Japan and South East Asia: small but with potent flavour. It seems like the sort of thing that could also work well in a supporting role in a dish.

Monica agrees. 'Yes, some people also do that – using the *sam* in a sauce, or making a soup, like a fish stock. It is really a taste of the lake tribe – the Luo are the main ones who eat it, and even then only some. But they are very healthy. They are also used to remove diarrhoea in children. And they are over 69 per cent protein by dry weight. We should eat more of them.'

'What do you think, Monica?' Ben asks. 'Do people prefer eating the lake flies as *sam*, or in muffins, or both?'

'Yes,' she replies. 'Maybe it is strange to put our traditional foods into these colonial recipes. Especially because all this flour and sugar is not so good for us. But maybe they can also be a way to have the lake flies be seen as not strange. My main interest is to encourage chil-

dren, especially, to embrace edible insects. I am also interested to hear what you and others are doing with them. Maybe these products can help keep the tradition, at least for now. Maybe we can have both.'

Monica gives us a bag of lake flies to take with us. When we return to our hotel down the road, Ben asks the kitchen team if they might keep them for us in their freezer. They give us quizzical and amused looks, but they agree.

Later that evening, they serve us a splayed roast chicken for dinner. It is good. We get along. They ask us what we are doing in Bondo, and we tell them about the insects. They think it is hilarious. 'Shall I show you how to make *sam*?' the chef asks. We need little further bidding and follow him into the kitchen.

There are few other guests in the hotel at the moment, and it is late, so the kitchen has time. The chef shows us his *sam* technique: he thaws the flies in a pan, and pats them into thin cakes. 'Let's also make some spicy *sam*!' Ben says excitedly, channelling our earlier discussion with Monica. 'Chef, where are your spices?' The chef shows Ben a cupboard. We pound some garlic, ginger and bird's-eye chillies in a mortar, chop some spring (green) onions and mix these in with some of the lake flies. 'Things are getting experimental!' Ben says. Chef and Ben place the flattened *sam* of two types on tinfoil, and place them on top of the oven to dry. 'Looking forward to using that in a soup,' Ben muses, gears already turning. We cook on into the night.

— Fieldwork Team: Josh Evans, Andreas Johnsen, Ben Reade. Guide: Evans Owuor Odula. Written by Josh Evans.

FARMING CRICKETS

———

We return to JOOUST to learn about Monica's work on cricket farming.

'Crickets are not so traditional to eat in Kenya, compared with termites [pp.95–109], lake flies [pp.110–12] or black ants,' says Monica. 'In Kisii, for example, it is believed that witches keep crickets. So I joke about that when I show them how. I try to let them know it's OK.

'I will also say that I am not an entomologist!' she adds with an honest smile. 'My background is in consumer science and social work.'

'So how did you come into working with insects for food?' I ask her.

'Well, I used to work on the coast, on coconut production and insect pest control. There were beetle larvae that would live in the palm fronds, and they would just spray them, even though they were actually food. On the coast, there are some people who eat one species of a beetle larvae that lives in cow dung. But they do not eat the palm beetle larvae. It is not part of their tribal identity. So I started noticing these patterns there.

'And now I raise crickets and teach others how to do it too,' Monica says with a laugh. 'We have tried it with different species. *Gryllus assimilis* takes so long to rear, and *Gryllus bimaculatus* tastes horrible! So we are mainly working with *Acheta domesticus*, the common house cricket. It is popular to rear in other places too, like in Thailand and Europe.

'We also tried to raise these,' she says, pulling a giant cricket out of a bag from the freezer. It is the biggest cricket I have ever seen – at least as large as my thumb. 'These are plump and sweet! We all love it. The genus is called *Brachytrupes*.'

'That's a proper meal right there!' exclaims Ben.

'And they are a pest – they dig big holes in my garden,' says Jackline.

'Now that you could put on a stick and roast,' I suggest to Monica with a smile.

'Yes,' she replies. 'We had high hopes for it, but even with our singing and dancing, it refused to survive in our cage.'

'The person who can figure it out will make millions,' muses Ben.

'Oh, yes – whoever figures out how to rear this one will be a millionaire, overnight,' she says thoughtfully. I watch Jackline look past Monica into Andreas' camera; her face, almost inscrutable, shows glints of something melancholy. 'They will be a millionaire,' Monica repeats slowly, the giant cricket yielding a film of frost as it thaws in her palm.

Monica and Jackline lead us out of their laboratory into the shaded colonnades of the university buildings. We pass a gate, cross a red-dirt road and head for an unassuming shed nestled among trees and bushes. 'Here is where we rear our crickets for our research,' says Monica.

Inside it is humid and warm. 'We try to keep them at a consistent 36°C [96.8°F], with ideally 65 per cent relative humidity,' says Monica. 'They need fresh water and fresh vegetables every two days. We give them two petri dishes: one with water for drinking, with rocks so they do not drown, and one with damp cotton for the females to lay their eggs. For feed, we use cabbage leaves and chicken feed. Next year, we will have funding from DANIDA [Denmark's Ministry of Foreign Affairs]. Part of the work is research on feed for the crickets. In the future, we would like to see if feeding them different things can give different tastes.'

'And are you also looking into them for animal feed, or primarily for human consumption?' Ben asks.

'Right now we are looking solely into human food, which is our main concern here in Kenya. And it is not just about protein and macronutrients.

Zinc, selenium and other minerals are all found in certain insects. And micronutrient deficiencies are some of the most pressing problems we have, especially among young children. These insects can be a big help. But other people might be interested in them for livestock feed also.'

'And with a set-up like this, how many can you produce?' Ben asks.

'Well, we can produce 4 kilograms per bucket per rearing cycle, and there are sixteen buckets here,' says Jackline. 'It takes about eight weeks per rearing cycle. So, if everything goes well, 64 kilograms every eight weeks.'

CLOCKWISE FROM TOP LEFT: 1. Monica's giant cricket 2. Florence's varieties of finger millet 3. Fallen jacaranda flowers 4. Jacaranda tree

'That's quite a bit,' I say. 'What are some of your challenges?'

'Well, the biggest challenge is predators – rats and other things,' says Monica. 'That is why we must use these containers with lids, and keep them in a closed building. We have not had any diseases yet, and we hope we will not. Other than that, funding can be a challenge. When you put in a request for funding to rear edible insects, people don't take you very seriously. I hope that is starting to change.

'The crickets in particular have many advantages. They are relatively easy to rear, and people can start doing it at home quite easily. Even kids can do it. We are doing a project with a local primary school and they love it.

'As for having some escape, that is another good thing about working with *Acheta domesticus*: it is already in the wild in most places, including here, so there is no risk of introducing it unintentionally.

'I have been teaching some local farmers to rear crickets – there are two nearby. Would you like to meet them?' Monica asks us. We nod eagerly. 'Here,' she goes on, 'publications do not sit on the shelf. Once you produce, you are encouraged to take it out!'

A ten-minute car ride later, we are standing with Florence Awuor beneath her flowering jacaranda trees. The purple blossoms carpet the cracked earth. She is sitting on a blanket when we arrive, loosening colourful finger millet from its stalks. She shows us her small cricket-rearing operation in a hut nearby. 'I am pleased that Monica has shown me how to rear crickets,' she says, softly but proudly. 'I can do it by myself. It is very empowering.' We sit a while longer with Florence and talk about her life. I admire her finger millet, in hues of cel-adon, crimson and ochre. 'It is beautiful,' I tell her. 'Yes,' she says. 'It has a good taste.'

Another short ride and we meet Beatrice Ngesa. 'Come, I will show you,' she says, leading us behind her home to a covered concrete pen. 'I like to rear them, and my children like them too. And if I want to, I can sell a few on the side. It helps when there is a break in the crops.'

'And do you eat other insects as well, Beatrice?' we ask.

'Ehh,' she replies. 'The white ants, the black ants, some grasshoppers,' she says. '*Ngwen*, *onyoso*, *dede*, in Luo, my language. And many kinds of termites.'

'The local Agricultural Resource Centre is working with nine others like Florence and Beatrice,' says Monica. 'There is a kind of informal cricket-rearing cooperative forming. We hope there will be only more over time.'

'Ehh, I think so,' says Beatrice.

'Soon, Kenya will have to wake up to edible insects, because the rest of the world is,' Monica notes. 'A difference is that the resistance here is not to *insects* – it is to certain types, species and stages. The Westerners, for a long time, would say none of them were food. But not all that the Westerners do is correct.' We laugh. 'People here are waking up and saying, "Hey, our foods were better, they didn't have all these chemicals." People are rediscovering their traditional foods: local plants and insects. And maybe we can help these traditions develop and grow.'

— Fieldwork Team: Josh Evans, Andreas Johnsen, Ben Reade. Guide: Monica Ayieko. Written by Josh Evans

MAYENJE

——

Mzee John Ssentongo and our friend and guide in Uganda Edie Mukiibi share an extended, songlike greeting, Edie kneeling briefly, Mzee humming as if (it seems to me, lulled by their melody) in repeated assent, all of which makes it even more surprising when Mzee shoves the enamel teapot abruptly under our noses. 'Look, look,' he says, pointing in. He is a spry man with silver hair and scruff, eyes glinting with mirth and mischief. We are meeting him in December in his garden in Lukindu, in the hills of south-west Uganda. There is a persistent scratching from inside the patterned pot that intensifies when he moves it about. 'Four, five, six – so many! Haha! I asked my grandchildren – five, I have five – they caught them for you this morning.'

We peer inside. Huge crickets the size of my thumb scamper against each other and the sides of the pot. They are called *jjenje* (singular) and *mayenje* (plural) in Luganda, the main language of central and south Uganda. Ben and I stare in, but Mzee has already moved on, laughing all the while and pulling us along to see the garden, a series of plots linked by paths lined with vines and hedges, anchored by compost sinkholes that hold moisture in and return nutrients to the soil, trees twisting umbriferously overhead. This is robust and productive land. Mzee plucks herbs and flowers for us to smell and taste: indigenous greens, pea aubergines (eggplants), air potatoes ('*Ekobe!*'), rare banana varieties, coffee flowers and fruit. The place pulses with a green, incessant health.

He brings us inside and serves us watermelon in the dark room. It is warm, crunchy, juicy, with no grain and the flavour of demerara sugar. Next, he says, he will show us how to find the crickets.

We head to another area of the garden. Mzee's friend and collaborator in the garden, Gerald Gyagenda, plucks green mangoes (*miyembe*) on the way. They are full of mango flavour, more sour than sweet, and lightly astringent, with a resin (*masanda*) on the skin. Gerald tells us a tree will grow wherever we throw the stone. I don't doubt it. I also don't want to put a tree where it's not suited. He tells us that, once they sprout and take root, he digs them up and transplants them to a more suitable location within the garden. Eating grows the garden further.

We walk along a path between a patch of maize and land left to grow as it will, flowers and scents I have not smelled or seen bursting from the green. A tall bush with aromatic fronds grows into the path. Mzee tells me it is a kind of marigold (*Tagetes minuta*, originally from Peru where it is known as *wakatay*, and which we used at our jam in Lima, pp.170-74), known locally as *kawunyira*. He uses it in various forms, a pest repellant and medicinal plant. I am lost in its spicy scent.

'Here!' Mzee says, finding a hole in the reddish earth on the other edge of the path. 'This is where we dig!' He begins chopping into the low bank, revealing a tunnel in receding cross sections, sloping down. 'This is where the *jjenje* lives. It makes two chambers: one for eating which is above, one for laying eggs and sleeping, which is below. It is very clean.' Mzee cuts further, and comes to a dead end. 'It's trying to trick us! Haha!' he says, backtracking to the fork and digging down the other way. 'Sometimes it makes more tunnels, to fool us.' And then the bottom of the pit erupts in a violent buzzing. The cricket is filling a cavity under its wings with air, vibrating in loud resistance. Mzee grabs it gingerly from behind and holds it up for us to see. Then he pops it into the teapot and we're off searching for the next.

After a few more, we return to the house to cook. We have nine in total. We take two for samples (one female, one male) and begin preparing the rest. They are still vigorous, some of the males buzzing indignantly. Gerald takes them from the teapot one by one, plucking off the wings and the legs at the lower joint. The remaining upper parts flail. He takes the head and pulls it forward, inserting a small twig at the top of the neck to lift out the digestive tract – two small, connected sacs. When he has done them all, he puts them into a pail of water to clean them. They die.

While Gerald has been cleaning the crickets, Ben and I have sliced some tomatoes, green peppers and chillies. Mzee has

CLOCKWISE FROM TOP LEFT: 1. Mzee John Ssentongo 2. Jackfruit 3. *Mayenje* ready for cooking, with spring (green) onion 4. Live *mayenje*

chopped some spring (green) onion and has the stove prepared. We bring the crickets and onion into the cooking house. Mzee pours a few drops of oil into the hot pan and fries the crickets whole, tossing in the onions after a few minutes, along with a pinch of salt. He cooks them for about seven minutes over a medium flame. The cooking house fills with a distinct and savoury aroma.

We bring them outside to eat. Mzee has arranged a mat on the grass. We lay out the crickets and the raw vegetables. 'No, we must wait,' Mzee says, when Ben asks if we can try them. 'They should be eaten a little cooled.' The tomatoes are sweet, sour and full, the peppers fresh and bitter. The chillies are intensely floral.

The crickets are delicious. They are large enough that we can taste different properties in different parts. The thighs are thick, with a crisp shell and a concentrated flavour of chicken, which leads us to consider our comparative lack of descriptors for animal flavours compared to those we have for, say, plants. The head is bursting with fat and umami juices, silky and reminiscent of lamb brains. The body is milder, creamy and slightly sweet.

Yet this is but one course of many on the menu of the day. After the crickets are scooped up and the last of the tomatoes and peppers are eaten, Mzee brings over an immense jackfruit ('Ffené!'), lays it on some banana leaves and slices it open with a machete. Sticky white sap begins to ooze from the pale yellow flesh. He shows us how to wipe it away repeatedly with aubergine (eggplant) leaves (the fuzzy, rough surface is good for catching the gum) until it stops and we can then remove the fleshy, succulent hearts from the anemone-like pith. The fruit has the iconic aroma of tutti-frutti or bubblegum (for which, apparently,

jackfruit was the inspiration). From the solvency whiff of ethyl acetate, you can tell that this one is just a tad overripe, and delicious nonetheless.

Half the jackfruit picked apart, the knobbly green skin and fragments of pith strewn over the banana leaves, we follow Mzee with sticky hands and faces over to the edge of the garden. 'Here!' he says, plucking deep-red nasturtium flowers and pulling slender carrots straight from the ground. 'Here! Taste!' he says again, cutting leaves of adult rocket (arugula) as long as my forearm. They are not tough, but crisp and eye-watering and aromatic as they only are in the first half-minute of being picked.

The flavours in this garden are intense, and seeing how things are grown, with a wide range of intercropped species, it is clear that this diversity underlies both such healthy land and such incredible taste. Forget the Paleo diet; this 'primate diet' – fruits, greens and bugs – leaves us refreshed, eager and alive.

We want to know more about these crickets! Mzee tells us, 'Previously, you could get a lot, a lot. Now it is more scarce. Maybe because of the weather, maybe because people burn the bushes. Before, it was only the men who ate them; that was the culture. Now, women eat them too. The same with the *nsenene*, the grass-hoppers [pp.120–24].

'They don't just eat anything. They eat only plants with soft leaves, like beans, groundnuts and others. So they live in gardens and some wild land.' These must have been the same crickets – the *Brachytrupes* sp. – that Monica showed us, and that dug big holes in Jackline's garden in Bondo, Kenya (pp.113–5). Pests indeed – however big and tasty.

We ask him if he thinks they could be farmed. 'Yes, maybe, but only in a garden!

You would need a big garden with lots of things, like this. And they can also fly away at night.' We discuss maybe lining a garden with a net. 'Yes, you could, but then, why not just keep the garden?' he says. The point is clear: if the garden is diverse and healthy, it is attractive not only to humans, but also to many other species. The crickets are one of many food sources – and if they aren't to be found one day, there is always something else to eat.

This experience contrasts with other farming communities we have visited, where a diversity of crops, short supply chains and circular agroecologies and economies had been given up or destabilized, in favour of various editions of miracle maize that were meant to generate income and create food security. Yet the problems of monocropping were evident: if the crop failed for various reasons, there was nothing to be done, and if it grew well, then everyone's high-yield maize came to market at the same time, deflating the price so much that many farmers couldn't make nearly enough to pay back the loans they had taken for the new seeds, and would be forced to give up their property to the bank. Such is the ruthless paradox of a bumper harvest in a food system that relies too heavily on one crop and one taste.

Meanwhile, Gerald digs up radishes and Mzee plucks a sprig of rosemary for us to take. Aromatic herbs like this are rare in the cuisine we've tasted here, but Mzee is not a purist for indigeneity in his garden. He has also taken some of the jackfruit seeds, big brown things the size of a Brazil nut, and wrapped them in dry banana leaves – 'You can use it instead of ash water!' (p.96) – and tied the small packages with a length of fibre. He loads us up with the gifts. He is coming with us into town, but he thanks us

anyway for coming and we say goodbye to Gerald, a man of fewer words but no less presence.

The smell of the rosemary fills the car as it trundles down the stony road. The package of jackfruit seeds sits loosely in my hand. The tree won't grow back home in Denmark, but the knowledge from Mzee's garden has already taken root. It matters less the specific animal, vegetable or fungus – what matters is cultivating the ecology out of which gastronomy emerges. We could try and farm these crickets back home, but what would it achieve? It is useful to know that an insect is eaten at all, and how it is cooked, but the real gain is knowing why. The *mayenje* are eaten not just because they are delicious, but because they are a part of this rich ecology; their presence is part of the earth they build their nest in, the bean and potato leaves they eat and the birds and people that eat them.

How do we make something delicious for which we have no cultural context, no tradition of eating and no gastronomic knowledge? We begin at ground level and work our way up. If we, as cooks and growers and eaters, want a specific ingredient, our common method is to try to breed, raise and grow it directly. Yet sometimes it is both more effective and more delicious – and more interesting – to build a system out of which the desired food can emerge. Gastronomy begins in ecology: we want to eat what is around us, and if insects are part of this diversity, so much the better.

— Fieldwork Team: Josh Evans, Andreas Johnsen, Ben Reade. Guide: Edie Mukiibi. Written by Josh Evans.

NSENENE

The first time I tasted *nsenene* was when we were driving down from Kampala to Masaka. The bus hawkers wait at common bus stops and sell all sorts of things: grilled chicken, grilled beef, grilled *matoke* (starchy plantain), grilled *gonja* (smaller, tart plantain). Edie bought us a bag of salted fried katydids through the window of his car.

Now we are staying in Masaka. We leave town at dusk and drive to the outskirts. When we arrive, men are standing long sheets of corrugated metal upright into old metal drums. The metal curves slightly from the lip of the drum. Wires hang above in an intricate rigging, and a main cord traces back to the road, spliced off from the power line. When all the metal is set up, more men come and we stand, waiting for the dark to arrive.

'To be a real man here, he has a plot of land, and ten kids in shoes,' Edie's friend tells us, who runs the trap. 'I began collecting the *nsenene* in 2000, to send my children to school. On a good day, this trap can catch 200 sacks. The *nsenene* will swarm, hit the metal and slide into the barrels. They cannot get out. They come in November and December, and April and May – the two rainy seasons.

'I have four men who all work from 7:00 p.m. to 7:00 a.m. There is no particular time the *nsenene* come, so you have to be ready. It depends on the wind direction, and the strong lights. This season has been not so good so far.'

The darkness begins to fall, and one of his men moves over to the electricity box to set the wires. He pulls the plastic casing off the end of a new wire with his teeth, and bends it into a hook; a blue arc flies and crackles as he brings it close and sets it to the live, conducting metal. 'Before the lights,' Edie's friend tells us, 'people gathered them in the early morning, when the dew held them down in the grass. In the old days, when the swarms landed on tree branches, they could break them.'

'Now,' Edie adds, 'the lights in the city attract them from the country, and the rural people have to buy them back from the city people.'

'Is anyone studying where they are increasing and decreasing?' I ask Edie. It seems not.

'I sell only to wholesalers and retailers,' Edie's friend continues. 'They prepare them, take off the legs and wings, repackage and sell like that. Sometimes, they cook them and sell them. Some in Nyendo add salt, chilli, onion, tomato. Yes, it is a community – I have many friends who hunt the *nsenene*. The number of hunters is rising. There is even an assocation now.'

'And how much can you make? It sounds like a pretty organized industry,' Ben says.

'Oh, the price per sack can range from 20,000 Ugandan shillings [approx. US$6], if there is a lot during the peak of the season, to around 80,000 [approx. US$23] if there are few. Right now, market price is 70,000 to 80,000, because so far this season is low-supply, high-demand.

'Our main cost is the light: I pay 700,000 [approx. US$200] for the whole season, for eight 400-watt lights, so that's 3.2 kilowatts.'

'That's a lot of electricity,' I say. Ben and I both have our sunglasses on – strange at night but necessary. The men wear their caps low and stay in the shadows of the curved metal pans.

'The electricity does sometimes short-circuit. But we have never had any accidents, yet.'

The men sit and wait. Some of them play cards.

'We also call them *jjanzi* for one, *mayanzi* for many,' Edie's friend continues. 'There are other insects also drawn to the light – black crickets, big crickets, flying termites, especially at the beginning of the seasons. We pick them out of the drums by hand – black in green, they are pretty easy to see. The *nsenene* come in many colours: green is common, but also yellow-brown like dried banana leaf, purple and terracotta. We do not sort them.

'Nobody knows where they come from. Some people think they fly from across the Indian Ocean. There is also a myth that they come from a sack from a man in the sky.'

'Where do they lay their eggs? What do they eat?' I ask.

CLOCKWISE FROM LEFT: 1. Gathering *nsenene* by hand 2. Raw *nsenene*, de-winged and de-legged 3. Deep-frying *nsenene* 4. Deep-fried *nsenene*

'I don't know. Maybe they drink the dew on the morning plants. They do not destroy the crops.'

Hypotheses abound. We hunker down with the men and wait.

Some hours go by. No crickets arrive. Some of the men have left. A boy has joined the company. His name is Ronny. He sits with us, and we talk. Around 3:00 a.m., he takes us to check the traps. We walk through the floodlit rows, careful to avoid the wires, and peer down into the barrels. We find two or three green ones, alone and still, at the bottom of the barrels.

'Do you think any more will come tonight?' Ben asks Ronny.

'No, don't think,' Ronny replies slowly, looking away.

'Do you ever find these lights hurt your eyes?'

'Yeah.'

'Yeah. Well, thanks man,' Ben says.

'Thank you for showing us, Ronny,' I say.

We drive back to our hotel, and arrive famished. The cook is awake, but there is no power. Ben, Andreas, Edie and I sit down at a table in the dark and listen to the night sounds. The cook comes out with a small electric light and puts it on the table. After a few minutes, despite its dimness, it starts to irritate our eyes. Somehow the cook manages to make food with no light and no power. We eat and retire, exhausted.

I wake a few hours later to searing pain. I need to shut the blinds. I lurch over and somehow get them down. I cannot open my eyes more than a fluttering slit without a deluge of involuntary tears and the impression that I am peeling back my own corneas; nor can I keep them closed and still without letting demons dance upon them. I discover sensory distraction: I move my eyes around ceaselessly, press into them to create patterns and coloured starbursts. I begin to sing to myself, forcing more auditory processing onto my cognitive load. I pace the room, counting steps, noticing kinaesthetic shifts in weight, inertia, response time. I do not know how long it goes on. I am a beast driven by a single pain-reduction impulse.

At some point there is a knock on the door, and a voice says, 'Josh.' It's Ben. I go to the door, and open it.

'I can't open my eyes,' I say.

'Me neither. Edie slept through the collection in the car last night, so he's slightly better. He's gone to get a doctor.'

'OK. Thanks. Yeah.' I leave the door open, stagger back to my bed and writhe in the sheets.

What I know next is there are two men above me. I hear Edie's voice. They hold my eyes open and it is a form of loving torture. The other man drops two drops into each eye. Almost immediately comes the flooding of the world, the barbed demonic feet swept away. There is pain still where their weapons stay lodged, but now at least they lie inert. 'Josh, take these for the inflammation,' Edie says, holding up two white pills and a cup of water. I down them. The doctor holds a cold compress to my eyes. 'Sleep,' he says. 'We will come back in a few hours.'

It has been two days. We now know we had photokeratitis, severe snow blindness, from the lights at the trap. Is it just we who are weak? Apparently, when Edie went to the clinic to get a doctor, there was a line of young men waiting, all with the same.

The day after, we travelled to Kalangala Island. The sun still tingled and ached on the wide water, but I could keep my eyes open and see.

Early this morning, before dawn, on our way to harvest palm weevil larvae (pp.125–9), we drive by a meadow. Women, children and men are scattered throughout, moving slowly in looping paths, at points bending down. Birds circle overhead in the overcast sky. It is a striking scene. We stop to look, and notice clouds of winged things flitting in front of the humans as they walk. We clamber up to the misted field from the road for a better look. Edie launches himself in. '*Nsenene!*' he stage-whispers back at us. We have time.

We see the greens, the sandy yellows, the striped purples. The katydids all behave differently, with different grasses: the greens land on the tall stalks of green grasses; the yellows burrow down vertically into the dead brush near the ground; the green ones with the purple stripe align themselves along the purple spine of another grass.

A young boy in a brown shirt comes close, adept, his hands full of katydids tucked within his fists. I point to the camera and ask if I can take his portrait. He stands still, calmly, in assent. Then he comes to show me.

Edie has stuffed his catch inside a plastic water bottle. They make a distinctive scratching noise against the surface. We have something to bring our host.

Tonight we have returned to Masaka. From the stairwell of our hostel, we watch the compound next door: a man tends a wide, shallow iron cauldron, in which he deep-fries *nsenene* by the bucketful; children run between doorways across the yard.

'I have an idea,' says Ben.

We go out to the street. The main intersection of town is just down the road, and populated mainly with vendors under coloured umbrellas selling *nsenene*, fresh and fried. A few people sit behind each stall, pulling off legs and wings. The ground is littered with the thin white things. They collect in piles at the curb, like a kind of plant refuse, an abstracted debris repeated en masse. 'Two cups, six thousand [US$1.77],' our vendor cites with slow sibilance when we ask. We buy a big bag of fresh ones. Edie buys a small bag of cooked ones too, to snack on. They are tasty: crisp, salty, with the taste of prawns (shrimp) minus the sea.

'Let's go to the market,' Ben says, leading the way. We pick up tomatoes, garlic, shallots, red chilli pepper, wheat flour and salt.

Back up the road, we pass the gate of the hostel and turn into the neighbouring one, a collection of doors built around a central yard. Ben talks with the man frying *nsenene*. We share a few laughs. 'I would like to cook for you,' says Ben, 'but we don't have a kitchen in our hostel. Do you think we can cook here?'

'Eh!' the man laughs. 'Ehh, talk to the woman in that door over there.' Soon, we are set up in the courtyard with a *jiko* full of roaring coals, a worktable, a couple of pots, some water – and a growing crowd of curious neighbours.

'Right, gents, we don't have much light left, so let's get this show on the go,' Ben shouts briskly. 'Edie, I need you to dice those tomatoes. Josh, you take care of the garlic and shallots. I'll start the dough.'

Ben pulls over a small stool, makes a wide crater of flour, pours in some water and starts to incorporate them. 'Josh, can you start frying the garlic, shallots and chilli in that pot right there,' he says.

'Yes, chef!' I reply, jumping to it. The kids look on curiously, tittering, hiding behind each other when we look over. Some of the braver ones peer into the pot as the ingredients go in.

Meanwhile, Ben is rolling out the dough, copious flour coating the stool, his hands and his rolling pin, which turns out to be a spray-can of insecticide. 'The only appropriately-sized cylinder I could find,' he says with a chuckle.

'Right – Edie, can you get those tomatoes into the pot? Let's start simmering down the sauce,' Ben says as he rolls the floured dough and slices it into even widths. 'Josh, can you check on the pot of water please?'

'Almost at the boil.'

'Right, when it comes up, salt it. Edie, toss those *nsenene* into the sauce, would you?'

The courtyard is filled with cooking smells as the light begins to fall. Despite the countless eyes upon it, the water comes up quick, and Ben shakes in the noodles in a dramatic cloud of flour. After a few minutes, 'al dente!' is confirmed, and the pot is drained. Ben stirs the pasta into the simmered sauce, tastes, adds a bit of cooking liquid. 'Gentlemen, I give you "Linguine all'Ugandese"'! Right – can we get some forks? Lots of forks!' He scoops the noodles into three bowls, and passes them around, twirling some left in the pot onto a fork. The kids go crazy. We all have smears of sauce on our faces and hands. The bowls are empty in a matter of minutes. It is satisfying.

After cleaning up and exchanging jovial goodbyes, we climb the brick staircase at our hostel. From the top, I can see the hills of the city in silhouette, flooded with 400-watt, washed-out light. The night is not black, but a claustrophobic grey. I wonder how many young men will show up at the clinic tomorrow, temporarily blind. Or worse, how many will not.

On our last day in Uganda, we visit Philip Nyeko, professor of entomology at Makerere University in Kampala.

'The *nsenene* are often identified, wrongly, as *Ruspolia nitidula*,' he says. 'In fact, most *nsenene* caught in Uganda are *Ruspolia differens*. These are the ones that swarm. There are also other Ruspolia species, which live especially in Uganda's more remote areas. In the wild they eat grasses and leaves, generally, and also sometimes cereals like rice and sorghum.

'Yes, you suspected right – the variation in morphology that you saw was polymorphism among one species, not different species. They all begin green and then change over the course of the season, according to surrounding vegetation.

'These ones that I am rearing, as you see, stay green,' he concludes. 'I am doing research on rearing them for their full life cycle – we might understand more about how they live in the wild, and also, perhaps we might raise them in captivity for food. The demand for them is only increasing, and we don't know how much longer the wild populations will stay.'

— Fieldwork Team: Josh Evans, Andreas Johnsen, Ben Reade. Guide: Edie Mukiibi. Written by Josh Evans.

MASIINYA

A section of the landscape from Masaka to the coast is flat and full of termitaria as far as the eye can see. 'There's your termite queen export industry,' I joke to Ben, pointing out the car window with my thumb.

At the terminal, we drive Edie's car on board the ferry, and sit on the open deck above. There are a few islands in sight, luminously green on the lake. 'These are the Ssese Islands,' Edie says. 'In the 1800s, there was an outbreak of sleeping sickness, from the tsetse fly. It killed a lot people. Some were evacuated to the mainland.

'People across the whole island group eat the *masiinya* [palm weevil larvae], and also some on the mainland facing them, near Masaka and Entebbe – probably the descendents of those who were evacuated. In the 1940s, the colonial government started spraying for the tsetse fly. After that, people started to return to the islands in the 1960s – four generations after the evacuation. They found that the palms had grown very much.

'I will take you to one who has lived here all his life. His name is Paul Mugerwa.'

We get to land and drive down the road. Edie pulls over in a village called Kagulube, near a few buildings off the road. Paul comes out to greet us.

'Hey, Edie,' he says, 'You come for *masiinya*. Let's go to the tree, we talk there.' He jumps in his car, and the jungle closes over us as we follow him further down the road.

Some minutes later, the cars are pulled over to the side and we stand around a huge felled palm. Paul digs around near the base of the trunk, opened from the felling, and soon comes up with two larvae, wriggling vigorously in his palm, trying to undulate away at every opportunity: *Rhynchophorus phoenicis*, the African palm weevil.

'I take care of the forest,' Paul tells us, through Edie. 'The *masiinya* come only after that. More and more of the forest is being razed to plant *binazi*, the oil palm. *Mpalanda*, the adult beetle, lays its eggs in palm trees. Of the wild palm, *kibo*, there are female and male trees; the male joints are very close, and have harder bark, while the female joints are further apart and have a softer core, so the females attract many more worms. You can find the *masiinya* in the *kibo* and the *binazi*. But the ones from the *kibo* taste better.

'The price is the same though. Minimum for one *ssiinya* is 200 shillings [approx. US$0.06]. We can also use them for trading for other things: 100 *masiinya* for a chicken, 200 for a goat.

'When a wild palm grows, it produces fruit once, dies and begins to dry. Then the beetles come in the cool dusk to lay their eggs. So once we see a palm drying, we cut the tree down – we help it return to the forest faster. We help the beetles lay their eggs and we can also make sure it doesn't fall in an unpredictable way, onto a house or field or road.

'The larvae will start to come one week after felling the tree. After three weeks is the largest number, the peak. The liquid that comes from the *masiinya* – this is the sign to cut into the tree. No one cuts before. You can also find them in the leaf stalk,' he says, cutting open a nearby leaf and pulling a small larva out. 'We also use the *kibo* leaves for their fibre, and some people use the fruits as a necklace.

'The sun and drought have a big effect on the growth; the larvae need moisture and humidity to grow, which is why the trunk is their ideal habitat. So there are often fewer when it is dry.'

'How often do you collect them, Paul?' I ask.

'Hm, when I feel like it, or when one of my family feels like it – maybe six or seven times per month. Sometimes I take the children; sometimes multiple families go together to share our knowledge and whatever we find. If half a trunk is eaten up, we can fill a 20-litre [5-gallon] bucket sometimes. Alone, it might take me from 7:00 a.m. to 1:00 p.m. for the whole tree; with the children, it's faster.' By this time, a few children from nearby houses have joined us, sitting on the trunk, watching, listening.

'They are a food for celebrations, especially in the past. And when a good family friend comes to visit, it is the first

CLOCKWISE FROM TOP LEFT: 1. Using wooden stakes to pry open the palm **2.** Gutting and cleaning the *masiinya* **3.** Cooking the *masiinya* **4.** Fruits of the palm tree

thing they must eat. They would also be given for gifts at weddings: the ultimate gift, always given last, often as part of a male dowry – a challenge for male suitors. Now, though, the practice is less.'

'And why is that?' I ask Paul.

'Dowries are becoming less common as awareness around human rights grows,' Edie explains.

'Most people collect for themselves, but some people are also commissioned by higher-class people who love the taste but don't want to go into the forest. There are certain people who are known as collectors. People who really love them will seek out someone, an elder, to teach them how to collect. And the children are becoming more and more interested in eating and collecting them. There are about 370 people in our village, and twenty to thirty collectors.

'Tomorrow, we can harvest this tree. Meet me at my house, 8:00 a.m.'

It has rained in the night. The dense earth in front of the guesthouse is wet and littered with flower petals – no, white wings.

'Termites,' Edie says, as he gets in the car.

We arrive at Paul's just before 8:00 a.m., after stopping at the meadow with the *nsenene* (pp.120–24). He comes out and leads us in his car back to yesterday's tree. 'This trunk might be ready,' he says, pulling an axe from the back seat.

A couple of men meet us here, and more than a couple of children. Paul begins swinging the axe in high, full arcs, marking two lines along the top side of the trunk. The axe blade makes a dull thud at each impact, wet but hard. Paul grimaces slightly. Paul's friend, Benezet Alozias, and Edie have whittled stakes of

harder wood from nearby branches, and have come to insert them in the cracks with a mallet. It helps to widen the gap, but the trunk still resists. Eventually, with the axe and many hands prying the section up, the trunk emits an arduous shudder as its outer casing peels back from its inner core. The inside looks like rough pencil shading done in wood: a tangle of thick, cross-hatched fibres. The smell is like nothing else: resin and strong cheese, boozy, solvent. To me, it has a distinct note of white pepper, and of body odour.

Hands are already pulling through the fibres to find *masiinya*. A few turn up in the rotting pulp. 'The core is not soft enough yet,' Paul notes. 'We could wait a bit more time for this trunk.' We find a few larvae, but because the inside is still quite tough, the wrigglers have an advantage, boring back up through their existing tunnels where human fingers cannot follow. The men confer. 'Come, Benezet knows another one close by. We will go to there,' Paul says, leading us across the road. We walk along a path, past a few houses and through a field of maize surrounded by the forest.

This trunk looks slightly older. It is darker, with a drier-looking exterior; the cut edge exudes a dark wet. The axe swings again and with a sonorous difference, immediately palpable. It enters with less resistance; the sound is broad and hollow. The men make quick work of the first section of the trunk and it lifts up almost with relief, breathing its cheesy, peppery stench into the company. The inside is all pulp. Several larvae, longer and wider than the ones we have already found, move quickly up the trunk, away from the sounds and exposure, but are plucked and put into our green plastic bucket. I dig down into the pulp. Liquid has pooled at the bottom. 'Find the bubbles,' Paul instructs. I feel wriggling skin, and lift my hands up. Two larvae surface, and within an instant they have already reoriented and are boring downward. They are fast! I pluck them by their back ends before they get away. They can handle a good pinch.

The children come and help us pan the pulp. The men are already up, chopping the next section of trunk away. Edie pulls up a small ovoid of wound fibre, with a larva-sized cavity inside. It looks like where a larva might pupate.

It is not a long tree, as it seems that part of it had already been cut away to clear the path. It takes us between one and two hours to clear the whole thing. Our pail is full of worms wriggling over one another. Paul gives some to Benezet and the other men who helped, and the man whose property the trunk was on. We walk back to the road and drive back to Paul's place to cook the rest.

One of Paul's elder sons shows us how to clean them. They are first rinsed in clean water to remove any residual pulp. He has two *sufurias*, one full of the larvae in clean water, the other empty. The larvae writhe through the water, like a lake teeming with fish.

'You squeeze the body like this – tuck the head so it can't bite you – and pierce the neck like this, with a long wire or needle.' His movements have a practised ease. Cream-coloured flesh erupts from the hole along with a thin brown coil, the digestive tract. 'Pull this out,' he says, gingerly lifting the brown coil out of the body. In addition to removing the intestine, one must pierce the larvae so that, when cooked, they do not expand and explode.

He lets me and Ben try. By the end we've managed to develop a basic degree of competence, which means we can pierce the flesh and lift out the tract without getting bitten, though we are still slow and inconsistently accurate.

Paul's son takes the pierced larvae and returns them to the pot of clean water to remove the brown liquid, careful not to lose any of the fatty flesh. The digestive juices that remain in the other pot can be used as a herbicide. 'It prevents weeds for up to one month,' he informs us.

Meanwhile, Paul has readied the coals. He splits the larvae into two portions, and places the first in the *sufuria* between three stones over the fire. I think of Pamela at Amaica in Nairobi (p.97).

He squeezes the larvae gently with a spoon to help the fat leave the bodies and render. After about five to seven minutes over the hot embers, the larvae soften and release a dark liquid. He drains it off. 'You can use it as cooking fat,' his son explains, 'for cooking other things. Delicious. *Butto wa masiinya*, the oil is called. Even people who don't eat the worms love food cooked in the oil.'

A wonderful aroma has filled the kitchen: strong and peppery like the rotting palm, but gentler, sweeter and caramelizing. Now drained, the larvae are crackling away merrily in their own fat. 'When we cook the *masiinya*, the smell fills the village. Usually others will come by for a taste,' Paul says. By now the larvae have browned well, and any remaining liquid has reduced to a crackly crisp. Paul scrapes the pot with a fork, salts them lightly and tumbles them out into a bowl.

They are, in fact, the ultimate gift. The outer skin is taut, slicked in its own fat, and the insides are tender. They are coated in crisp bits of their innards, fragrant and sweet. 'We mainly eat it just like this. It is best alone, as a snack, not a full meal, though sometimes people eat it with potatoes or cassava. The aroma is very strong, it doesn't need other things. It is complete.

'We eat them for the taste. In most cases, it is the women who cook them, but the men and children also can and do. In the past, only the men were allowed to eat the *masiinya*, same with pork and crickets. But now, everyone eats them. The husband still eats the most,' Paul says, with a rare, furtive wink.

'Paul,' Ben says. 'Do you think we could try cooking the other ones for you? I'd like to try something out.'

'Yes, you are welcome. And you can use anything in the garden.'

We head out back past the pig pen (labelled 'Animals Farm' with a painted sign), pluck some chilli peppers and tomatoes and lift a leek and a couple of small shallots from the soil. Paul also asks us if we'd like a bit of ginger, and hands us a small knob.

'Josh, can you get on with chopping those?' Ben says to me, and starts cooking the remaining larvae following Paul's method. He proceeds in the same way until after decanting the fat, and adds in the chopped ginger, shallot, leek and chilli pepper. We cook them until the larvae are tender, then add in the tomatoes for a few minutes, and let everything simmer and get to know each other. He seasons the dish and takes it off the heat, spooning it into a bowl.

We let it cool a little, and Paul tastes. He holds the bowl out for one of his younger daughters, who comes over and scoops a whole one into her mouth with a long smile. She takes the plate outside to the backyard, where the other children are peeling *nsenene*. 'Ah, we have some too!' I remember, and Edie pulls the plastic bottle from his jacket pocket. We open it up, add ours to the pile and help peel. Meanwhile, everyone has a taste of the *masiinya*, and another, and soon the plate is empty. 'Very good,' Paul says, bringing out the crisp ones to share, with a few neighbours in his wake.

We finish peeling the *nsenene* together and play hide-and-seek with the children around the yard. 'Paul, we have to leave soon to catch the boat, but before we go, can I take your photo all together?' I ask him. He gathers his family in front of his home. Ben and Andreas join.

'Thank you, Paul,' I say.

'Yes. *Webale* – thank you.'

In the car to the ferry dock, I hold the *masiinya* smell in my mind. It is neither a farmed smell, nor a wild one, exactly. The larvae decompose the tree; the humans facilitate. The pulp returns to the ground. And for each larvae caught, I wonder how many wriggle back into the dark, weave their pupal homes, hatch and start the cycle over.

— Fieldwork Team: Josh Evans, Andreas Johnsen, Ben Reade. Guide: Edie Mukiibi. Written by Josh Evans.

BOGONG MOTH

I head down to Australia a week before we begin our fieldwork, to make some final preparations. I stay in Melbourne with my friend Kelly Donati, a lecturer in gastronomy and food studies.

'So, you're going to Canberra,' she says. 'Do you know what the parliament has been doing, year after year, during the summer? They spray the entire parliament grounds with pesticides, to kill the aestivating moths. It's not enough that the country's agricultural industry already kills and poisons many of them, all the way up the coast, even up into Queensland. The ones that do make it to the mountains, as they have for thousands of years, have to be systematically poisoned on the very land that the present nation declares its capital, because they are considered to be "a nuisance". How painfully symbolic of this country's relationship with the land and the land's first people.

'These are the questions I would think about when you are in Canberra. How has colonial history shaped the landscape in very particular ways? What kind of agencies – human agencies, insect agencies and others – are involved? How is your relationship with the moths refigured by a city like Canberra? And the biggest one: what represents hope to aboriginal communities? You may not find an answer, but it is maybe the most important question to ask.'

I know I may not even be able to ask it right away, or expect a response I understand immediately, or even any response at all. It will likely require a deeper context that unfolds over time. But this is where I start.

Through the grapevine, I've managed to contact Tyronne and Wally Bell, brothers and people of the Ngunawal, on whose land lies Canberra (though like many aboriginal land claims, this one is, and has been, disputed). 'We say it like "NOO-na-wahl",' Tyronne says when I ask. He has invited us to meet him and Wally at a cultural event they are holding at the National Arboretum, a beautiful piece of territory laid out over rolling hills with the city in the distance.

'Yeah, it's a shame, the moths [*Agrotis infusa*] have come and just gone,' he says. He hands me a jar with holes pierced in the lid. 'This one I found outside my window last night, trying to get in to the light. It didn't live. I kept it for you, though.

'When I was young, my dad would squeeze them out onto his steak. He liked that. Nowadays, even when they come, we eat them less, because they are said to have arsenic, from all the pesticides they use in Queensland.

'I know that in earlier times, the people would scoop them up out of the rock, or use a stick to move them and smoke to sedate them, dump them on the coals and pull them out. The wings would singe off and the bodies cooked like that. They would pound them into a paste, pack it into cakes. They could mix in herbs, acacias, wattleseed, or pound seeds into flour and mix with the moth paste, then cook in the coals. They were a food, and a medicine. Not so much anymore, though.

'But there is still a Bogong festival in September, when the season starts and all seven groups of the region come together.

'But, hey, I have to give this presentation now,' he says. 'Maybe come listen, and we can talk more after.'

Tyronne and Wally have laid a table full of artefacts. The wooden benches fill with people, families and children. We learn much about Ngunawal history, which may not be about the moths directly, but also is.

'Ngunawal land is about 15,000 km² [18,000 yd²],' Tyronne tells us. 'Land was marked in different ways. There were rock markers. They were known not with writing but by the way they were placed. And there were scar trees – bark was removed to mark the tree, and then was used for burials, marking trails, making canoes. Between borders, people here left spaces that belonged to neither group, where they could meet and trade.

'There was strong trade across the country. We know this because we find artefacts from different places around the country – for example, artefacts from the Kimberley [in the north-west] found down in New South Wales [in the southeast]. These are some of these artefacts.' Tyronne passes around a spear whose barb is held to the shaft with kangaroo tendon. 'Boomerangs – there are different styles for different uses. Hunting ones were shorter; longer ones were for fighting, and could be thrown or held. Some people began adding designs on them to turn them into objects for trading. So nowadays you find these' – he gestures towards a smooth, symmetrical one, painted with a garish butterfly – 'for a white man.' We laugh with Wally and Tyronne. Is it a twinge of irony that passes across Tyronne's face?

'And stone axes. They have a smooth bottom edge where they have been used, and a groove for carrying. And river rocks for cooking. Some persist, only the ones that work. There are some restaurants that still use the method. This round stone was

LEFT TO RIGHT: 1. Aboriginal stone artefacts 2. The Australian Parliament in Canberra

for games. Some scientist guy wanted to cut it up and see what it's made of – well, no!' he says with a chuckle. It is more important to Tyronne and Wally that the stones are intact and artefactual than split and known as material. 'I probably have more stone axes than the museum,' he says with a smile. 'Though I still need a permit to keep my own people's artefacts.

'And there are many objects with post-contact materials: blades made of glass, with serrated edges, or porcelain, or ceramic. Some people would chip off ceramic insulators from electrical poles and use them to make tools.'

Tyronne passes these objects around and lets us hold them, feel the heft and grip and the arcs of movement they draw from the body.

After their talk, we hang out around the table.

'We are trying to reconstruct our history through artefacts rather than through the written history of the white man,' Tyronne says. 'Dad used to give me hints, but never told me everything, because in our culture we need to work things out for ourselves too.' In a context without external threats to this kind of cultural transmission, I can see how this wisdom is well-suited to developing complex relationships with each other and the land over time. Yet, since the advent of colonialism after 'the First Fleet' arrived in Australia in 1788, I wonder whether these traditions also impede their own survival – practices that become challenged because everything around them changes, how time works, how knowledge is disseminated.

'The burden of proof is always on the minority – to prove our presence at certain points in the past,' says Tryonne. 'These artefacts are our best shot at "evidence", to help us keep our sense of place.

It is important. To go back out to country, on what are now national parks for example, I still need permission. *Permission* to go out and practise your own culture!'

We fall silent, in thought, looking out to the land. Centuries of English explorers and surveyors could not believe their eyes at how well-tended the landscape appeared, across the entire country. 'Just like a gentleman's park in England' is a phrase that repeats throughout every single logbook. Some began to make the connection that this landscape was not found, but made – a continent-wide mosaic of sophisticated collaborations involving associations of specific plants, animals and geographies, built with fire. But not enough of them, and then not quickly enough, made the small but important leap from 'like a park' to 'is a park'. Colonialism has dismantled these complex systems of land stewardship and food production, in the beginning without even knowing it; now, but traces remain.

'So, you are going north,' says Tyronne finally.

'Yes, to Warlpiri country.'

'OK.'

'Anything that is good to know?' I ask.

'Men traditionally do the hunting; women gather seeds and plants,' Wally responds. 'One hunts for the clan – usually around thirty people, or more, previously. Everything is shared, depending on what is gotten.'

Tyronne nods. 'Different places have different histories and customs. The central landscape in some ways has a different history from the coastal regions, especially around here in the south-east. The inhospitability of the central landscape was its greatest defence against missions. They still had them, of course, but maybe not as strong as here.'

'Thank you, Wally. Thank you, Tyronne.'

'Here, take this hat,' Tyronne says, handing me a black cap with 'TS' embossed in white thread on the front. 'You'll need it in the desert.'

'What is "TS"?'

'"Thunderstone". I was down in Cotter Dam; there was a storm coming; I found a cracked stone on cracked earth. It was part of what I had to figure out for myself. Thunderstone.'

'We've grown out of the rock,' says Wally.

'We come up out of the rock.'

I leave Tyronne and Wally thinking about the questions Kelly gave me. What represents hope for Wally and Tyronne? What ideal future do they envision, and what determines which versions of that future are attainable, for the Ngunawal?

Our fieldwork presupposes that traditional knowledge is valuable and important to preserve and help flourish. But that is our assumption. What about indigenous communities? Tyronne and Wally and the other aboriginal people we will come to know over our time here – do they think the same way? Do we want the same thing? Sharing one's ancient knowledge with outsiders – relatives of the descendants of the people who contributed to their demise, no less – to help keep it alive may come at the expense of giving up its stewardship, and risks, if not guarantees, its appropriation. But not sharing it, to preserve the integrity of traditional knowledge-sharing practice, almost certainly also means having the knowledge eventually die. It is an ultimatum whose depth is unfathomable to me. It is like a Zen koan: impossible to answer, and nonetheless demanding one.

The dialogue in my head goes like this: I take for granted that it is good for knowledge and practices that exist to persist. Yes, they always change, evolve and die. But right now it seems like they are coming to a mass extinction, different in degree from what we have known before. Could that not also be the result of being more aware of the diversity of what exists, so that the more aware we are of its existence, the more aware we are when it dies?

It is easy for me to think knowledge is good, full stop, when I am a beneficiary of structures of power that let me make that call – that give a sense of entitlement to decide so for myself and others.

The best I can do is care, stay with the trouble, and try my best to come to grips with it. The best I can do is listen when I am told, respect the silence when I am not, and wait, if I may, for it may not yet be time.

We never did taste the Bogong moth, but hearing of it – dreaming of it – was more significant for me than just knowing how it tastes. And if I had to choose, I would rather leave with a hard question on my mind than a taste, however nice, on my tongue.

— Fieldwork Team: Josh Evans, Andreas Johnsen, Ben Reade. Guide: Tyronne Bell, Wally Bell. Written by Josh Evans.

LERP

The desert heat as we step off the plane is a tentative kind of embrace, sizing us up, warm enough to be pleasant and hot enough, too, to let us know it gets hotter.

Luckily for us, Gloria is in town for a couple of days, and will take us with her this afternoon back to Yuendumu.

'First contact at Yuendumu was in the 1980s,' Gloria tells us. 'So, relatively recent. It's small. We'll go to the store here so you can buy your food and supplies. Bring cash, tobacco if you need it. Sunscreen and sunglasses.'

'I am excited for my legionnaire's hat,' says Andreas.

The sun sets across the flat red as we drive north-west into the desert. The temperature drops. I ask Gloria about Yuendumu, how long she's been there, and about the questions I've been carrying from Melbourne and Canberra (pp.130-33). 'Just have common courtesy. Be gentle and patient,' she replies. I fall into a light sleep against the window.

We arrived to Yuendumu after dark last night. Cecilia Alfonso and Gloria Morales, who are hosting us at the artists' collective they run, direct us to the Yuendumu school to meet Wendy Baarda, one of the teachers who also works in the school's Bilingual Resource Development Unit (BRDU), making books about Warlpiri culture in both Warlpiri and English for the children.

'Insects, yes, we have made a few books,' says Wendy, a kind, soft-spoken Englishwoman who has lived in Yuendumu with her husband Frank for decades, speaks Warlpiri and has become part of the community. 'Honey ants, sugarbag' – the honey of a stingless bee – 'lerps. I don't know – Tess, are there more?'

Tess, Wendy's Warlpiri colleague in the BRDU, shakes her head.

'We will find out,' says Wendy. 'Let's go meet the ladies at Warlukurlangu.'

She leads us out of the air-conditioned building and across the schoolyard. We pass through a side gate, and Wendy leads us over to a tree, a tall eucalyptus. 'Ah, not ready,' she says, inspecting the leaves. She brushes off a couple of small white dots, and gives them to us to taste. They have almost no flavour. 'You see these – they are *yapuralyi* or *yimampi*. Lerp in English. In a few weeks, they will grow and be ready to harvest. The bugs [*Glycaspis brimblecombei*] produce a sweet nectar that dries on the leaf. Warlpiri people would rub it off and roll it into a ball, to take with.'

The Warlukurlangu artists' collective is a few minutes' walk away. 'The name is Warlpiri, and means "belonging to – *kurlangu* – fire – *warlu*".' Cecilia is the head of the collective, and has agreed to host us while we are here and let us hang out, help mix paints and talk with the artists. And maybe, if they want to, they will take us on a walk.

'So, you've arrived,' Cecilia says. 'I'll introduce you.' Outside, the artists – mostly elderly women, and a handful of men – are painting in groups of three and four, in the shade on the concrete. Cecilia takes us around to the groups to introduce us and why we're here. We linger with a few of them, then they return to painting.

'Midday is hottest, and we usually want to stay in the shade,' Sara Diana explains. Sara works with the artists to get them what they need and give feedback. 'In the afternoon when it gets a bit less hot, you might find more willingness to take you hunting.'

So we don aprons and begin our apprenticeship by mixing cobalt blue in multiple values. I work on washing brushes. Some of the women and men glance at us when they come in to get some more paint or a new brush. After a while, we exchange a couple of smiles, and later we sit together, cleaning brushes and talking about life in Yuendumu.

We end up spending time with a group of women, Tess, Ruth and Coral, who agree to take us to search for honey ants (pp.137–41). Our trip was successful. After returning, I spend time talking with Frank, Wendy's husband, to learn a bit more about the dreaming and Warlpiri skin names.

'The *jukurrpa*, often translated as 'dreaming' or 'dreamings', are fascinating. The sacredness of a certain creature at a specific site creates a positive feedback loop of population abundance: the organisms multiply in numbers, and their prominence in a place reinforces their sacrality. Grasshoppers, pythons, what have you.

'"Dreaming" doesn't really get at the idea, of course. It is quite the opposite of dreaming, which relegates the understanding of reality to an unconscious, mysterious state, when in fact it is a rich,

intricate and highly ordered system of interconnected stories, used to understand the world and transmit knowledge across space and generations. A closer translation of the word might be something like "cosmology".'

Frank's understanding of the *jukurrpa* reminds me of Rod, Gloria's boyfriend, whom we met in Alice Springs. He told me a story of one of his Arrernte friends who, when they were eating together, pointed to a grain of rice on Rod's beard and said, 'That's my Chambers Pillar,' referring to a notable sandstone rock formation south of Alice Springs, in Arrernte land. 'It's like the identification is complete,' Rod told me. 'This ridge *is* the caterpillar.' Forms and scales collapse into each other; it may be the ultimate poetic sensibility, systematized, making and made by the landscape.

'And then, there are the skin names,' Frank explains. 'They are given by an individual to fit a newcomer into the social system, to place them. There are eight skin names in Warlpiri, with two gender variations of each – female names begin with N, and male with J – in a cyclical arrangement. So, the son of a Napurrula will always be a Japangardi, for example, who will always have to marry a Nampijinpa, who in turn will always give birth to a Japanangka or Napanangka.'

He pulls out a sheet of paper with a diagram mapping out the flows of maternal, paternal and conjugal relations between skin names. Again I think of a story from Rod, who was given a skin name from another of his Arrernte friends: 'It is both a connection and an obligation, like with family. You don't refuse. One night – we're in the desert, it gets cold – I was walking back to my car with my Arrernte brother. He asks for my shirt, and I give it to him without thinking. You give literally the shirt off your back. The Arrernte call it *utyerre*, a string or tie.'

'These cycles are built into their cosmology, and their social structure,' Frank says, bringing me back to the present. 'It is a completely different conception of family, time, genealogy, past and future.' I wonder how long Frank lived here before the Warlpiri in Yuendumu shared this knowledge with him. Is this part of my own process of figuring it out?

In the evening, I sit with Sara on the porch of our house down the road, owned by the collective, where Sara lives and we are staying. She has a background in art history and worked in the art industry before moving here. She tells me more about Warlukurlangu.

'Well, it's a not-for-profit. It's funny, you know, all the dot painting – people think it's some ancient thing, but it really started as a painting style in the 1970s, with the modern aboriginal-art movement, which evolved as a response to some aboriginal artists doing representational paintings of ceremonies and other sacred things that other aboriginal artists thought should not be put out into the world, especially in that form. Evidence of ancient dot paintings has been found in the northern and western areas of the continent, but these cultures and styles are in any case different from contemporary practice – especially in the central part, where we are now.

'The focus of much of the art has become a way of expressing personal *jukurrpa* in an abstract, iconographic way. "Dreaming" is an inappropriate metaphor; it is more about embodiment, and mutual, cyclical, scaleless identifications.'

'"The ridge is the caterpillar", for example,' I venture.

'Right.'

I ask her a question that's been nagging at me: how she navigates the issues of a white person telling an aboriginal person how to make aboriginal art. 'I think about it, for sure. But at some point you just have to do it and get on with it. They know that, I know that. I work with them differently according to their goals. Some paint for the craft, others for the money. Both are fine with me.'

After a pause Sara finishes the thought. 'Overall, I think the collective is a good thing for the town, for everybody here. I don't think I know or have heard of anyone who disagrees. It's complicated, but it's better than if it wasn't here at all.'

Some weeks after we return from the field, I receive a yellow paper envelope in the mail. The note reads, 'Dear Josh. Greetings from us in Yuendumu. Here are your *yapuralyi*. I froze them before sending them to make sure. I also sent some books for you from the BRDU. Hope you're well. Enjoy. Wendy.'

I pull a light bundle from the package. Inside are some of the eucalyptus leaves with large white dots on them – the crystallized honeydew produced by psyllid larvae as a protective cover. I brush one off and taste it. Gently sweet. I spend the last hour of the day reading children's books, in Warlpiri and English, in the weak sun.

— Fieldwork Team: Josh Evans, Andreas Johnsen, Ben Reade. Guide: Wendy Baarda. Written by Josh Evans.

MAY 2014 Copenhagen, Denmark

YURRAMPI

I am already less than sure of the way back. Once you get beyond the sounds of the four elderly ladies and their crowbars in the dirt, and out of range of their colourful dresses, the outback, at least to my uninitiated eyes, looks the same in every direction: flat, scrubby, semi-arid, the earth cracked and full, for now, of new green after the recent rain. And no sign of a road or car.

I grasp for a blind, intuitive compass, which eventually reveals Wendy's white car through a gap in the acacias off to the left. The doors and trunk are unlocked and open. I rummage for a plastic can and set off back towards the others.

I am enjoying the mild discomfort of not quite knowing where to go. I can feel my senses open, taking in the broken branches and crushed nightshades where we set out, the angle of the sun, the direction of the dry riverbed. There is time. I come across the *yawakiyi* tree Ruth showed me on the way out. It is late in its season, but there are still a few black berries on it, warm in the sun, each with one big seed, thick, pasty flesh, and a sweet green taste like wheatgrass and raw cane sugar. From here, the desert fuchsias, also known as *miinypa* or *yanyirlingi* (*Eremophila gilesii*), spread out in wayward curves and lines. Their crimson blooms last for a brief time after rain, holding a drop of clear, fragrant nectar in the small bulb at the base of the petals below the ovary. Coral, whom I've caught up to, picks the flowers and sucks on them as we walk.

'They usually build a nest near the *manja* or the *miinypa* where the branches curve down, because when the rains come and the flowers come out, that's where they get food,' she says.

'As we do,' I respond. I follow Coral's lead, picking the tender blossoms and sucking out the nectar. I stop to take notes and a picture. Andreas comes up behind. 'Taste this,' I say, plucking him one, intact. We stand, mouths agape, stupefied at the taste. Coral is already back on the hunt – she wanders with a purpose, then sits, observes, waits, then stands, and resumes.

None of these women, nor anyone in their community, gets lost. Orientation to the land and each other is, as Frank had told me, 'core for their existence'. In general, I am wary of mysticizing traditional knowledge; here, it is in no way an overstatement. Embodied knowledge of cardinal directions seems cultured into Warlpiri people from birth, just as I gained 'left' and 'right'.

Now, I stand alone, still entranced by the single drops, and the mild vegetal flavour and springy texture of the flower.

After picking my way through the *miinypa*, I catch sight of Ruth's pink and blue clothes in the scrub off to the left, and hear Tess' cackle above the sounds of digging. What a group we've found: Coral Kelake, Ruth Napaljarri Stewart and Tess Napaljarri Ross, all between their sixties and nineties. Coral, the eldest, is a great-grandmother.

'I got it,' I say to Tess, coming up to the camp, holding out the plastic container.

'Yeah, that's good, we found another too,' she says. There is now a decently sized hole in the ground, and next to it, a pile of red dirt. Ben and Coral sit on the other side of the hole, observing; Andreas is up filming; Ruth has found a shady spot not far off. I sit with Wendy next to a *manja* – a type of acacia also called *mulga* (*Acacia aneura*).

'Do you think we should find some soon?' Wendy asks Tess, who has taken charge of the digging, methodically loosening shards of earth with her long iron crowbar – what seems to be the local multitool of choice.

'Oh yes, there are some here, we will find them,' says Tess, switching out her crowbar for the bucket to lift up excess earth. I get in there on my knees and scoop out the rest with my hands. Tess found this site by tracking some of the worker ants with yellow stripes on their abdomens to their nest, right next to a small desert fuchsia.

I'm thinking of all the flavours we have tasted in the desert today. 'What do the honey ants taste like to you, Tess?'

'They taste like different things. If they eat *manja*, the honey is light. If they eat *miinypa*, the honey is darker. But they are all sweet!' We have seen some of the yellow flowers of the *manja* today, but the desert fuchsia is really out in bloom.

CLOCKWISE FROM TOP LEFT: 1. Honey ant dreaming 2. The desert fuchsia 3. Newly dug honey ants
4. Honey ant mural in Yuendumur

'Aha! *Yurrampi*!' shouts Tess, and the site is alive as she begins lifting the first specimens out of the hole. 'See Jangala,' she says, addressing me, 'I followed the *ngarna*, the tunnels, and found them in the *minki*, their special chambers. They are in the *nyinantu*, the top chambers, because of the rain. And see, there, *ngipiri* – their eggs.'

The honey ants (*yurrampi* or *yunkaranyi* in Warlpiri; likely a *Melophorus* or *Camponotus* sp.) are also known as 'repletes' or 'plerergates': designated worker ants that are fed nectar in times of plenty until their abdomens engorge and they become living larders. In times of scarcity, the workers induce them to regurgitate some of the concentrated energy stored in their swollen bodies. They hang in long chambers called galleries, tended to by other workers and moved up or down based on the moisture in the soil. This is also why it is easier to find them after a rain, because the workers move them higher in the hive to prevent them from being drowned in the rising groundwater – which means only about a one-metre (three-foot) dig instead of three metres (ten foot).

Tess and Ruth's skin names are both Napaljarri; their kin are associated with the *ngapa jukurrpa*, or the raincloud/water dreaming. It seemed appropriate to me then that they were skilled at finding the honey ants just after the rain.

And whence my new skin name, Jangala? It is afterwards, from Frank, that I learn more about the intricate Warlpiri systems of skin names, the cyclical designations for kin. It is thus that I find myself a 'Jangala' – indicating, as far as I will be able to learn, a maternal relation of reciprocal obligation with the Napaljarris. I do not mind. 'Do be aware,' Frank advises me later, 'that the skin name is not a cuddly mark of kinship. Often it is much more about relations of mutual responsibility, and the name situates you within this system.'

Once we have a few honey ants, we ask Tess to show us how she eats them. She lifts up her hand and the sun catches the small amber orbs in her palm. She takes one gently but swiftly by the head, and sucks out the dark liquid from the back. She puts the body with its collapsed abdomen back down on the soil and the ant starts to scramble back down into the hole. It is unclear how long after, or even whether, it will survive the ordeal, though it seems to be quite vigorous as it returns to the earth.

Ben and I each take one up. The moment I touch the end of the abdomen to my tongue, I am struck with a mildly electric, numbing sensation, even before rupturing the golden orb. I do not know why this might be, but it is exciting. Then I suck. It takes a surprising amount of force to break, but once this threshold is met, the membrane bursts and the contents rush in and coat the inside of my mouth. It is indeed like a dark honey, sweet but also sour, with a lingering flavour like wild strawberries, semi-dried in the sun.

Tess keeps hauling them up. Ruth has come over, Wendy is getting in there and even Andreas puts the camera aside for a taste. We find maybe twenty-five in all, and this, Tess assures, is a small harvest. Sometimes, they will fill a whole pail, especially if the children are not along for the trip. What I keep thinking about is the connection between the clear, delicate, floral nectar of the desert fuchsia and the dark, rich, sour honey it becomes through the ants' life process.

We make our way back to Wendy's car to continue the hunt. We head to another area, a place called *Yurrampi Jukurrpa* – 'Honey Ant Dreaming'. Huge round boulders form hills that rise abruptly out of the flat landscape. Here we find bushes full of *marnikiji*, small oval berries deep purple in colour with small white speckles. They are brighter than the *yawakiyi*, springy and fruity when fresh. I also find some that have begun to shrivel on the plant, almost like raisins, with an intense, guava-like taste.

I collect with Tess. She tells me how her mother taught her how to gather fruits like the *yawakiyi* (*Psydrax latifolia*, sometimes called the native currant) and *marnikiji* (*Carissa spinarum*, sometimes called the conkerberry), insects like the honey ants and many other plants and animals. She is trying to keep these foods in her children's diets too. But it is increasingly difficult. 'They are trying to take our land from us, and our foods too. But we still do it,' says Tess. 'Some things, like the honey ants, are hard to get – it takes work. We don't do it for sustenance. But we do it together. We do it because we like it.' It reminds me of a book Wendy showed me that morning at the Yuendumu school called *Yanurnalu Kakarrara Yunkaranyiki*, or *We Went East Looking for Honey Ants* – one of a series of children's books the school has made to strengthen and diversify how people pass on their knowledge and their language to the next generations.

As we head back towards the car and the sun dips lower towards the honey ants, I am still mulling over the repletes and the fuchsia. They make so much sense together, and I want to bring them together on a plate. How beautiful and simple a dessert: the clear, light sweetness of the nectar, the deep round sweetness of the ant honey, tempered by its own acidity, and the fragrance and vegetal bitterness

of the flower. Maybe a few of the berries we found as a garnish, or maybe not. I am kicking myself for not making this connection earlier, when the ingredients were available and plentiful. Who knows if we will ever have them again, let alone together?

I look back towards the bouldered hills falling into their own shadow, the honey-ant monoliths stalking the horizon. Earlier, Tess told me these *are* the honey ants. It was not a gesture of likeness, but a confirmation of identity: metaphor, not simile. They are the same ones we dug up and ate. It does not matter that the ants are small and the boulders large, the first liquid and the second solid, or that they are forty-five minutes' drive apart. Their matters differ, as do their scales, but their essential form connects them inextricably in time and place. Tess taps into these relationships through stories learned from her parents and grandparents, filled in with her own experience.

Something clicks as we come back into town, and I start to notice the *yurrampi* on murals and signs where I didn't before. We drop off the ladies and hang out with their children and grandchildren and great-grandchildren as the sun hovers low above the flatness. At some point we say goodbye and begin our walk home. I stare into the sideways light and what Tess shared with me unlocks a cascade of possibilities.

I have in fact already eaten the dish I so desperately dream of making and am frustrated I cannot. Maybe the concept of culinary 'elaboration' here is not about 'making a dish' as a mixture of ingredients brought together on a plate; maybe it is a different type of gastronomic context altogether. The honey ants are never cooked – they are eaten immediately, or saved for later feasting, but always eaten live and on their own. And what could be done to make them better than they already are? For any cook to try to improve on how those ants tasted right there, in that form – warm out of your own dusty, ruddy hands – would not only be a challenge, but would miss the point.

'Making a dish' here, like connecting the honey ants in the nest and the honey ants on the hills to the fuchsia and the *mulga* and the berries of the desert, involves eating in succession. Insofar as the 'dish' concept makes sense here, it seems to be about eating that happens over time, not what comes together at once in a hand or on a plate. If there is

ever a 'dish', it is not contemporaneous. This is different from how many of us today conceive of eating. Yet it seems part of how people have been eating on this continent for tens of thousands of years.

But still – I cannot help it, it haunts me – I dream of the honey ants and desert fuchsia together in time, the nectar and the replete that it feeds. I have eaten it already, and I never will.

— Fieldwork Team: Josh Evans, Andreas Johnsen, Ben Reade. Guide: Wendy Baarda. Written by Josh Evans.

WITJUTI

I do not know what signs they see, but they know which trees to visit. Liddy Napanganga Walker, Esther Nungarai Fry and Amelia Brown Napaljarri – our group of Warlpiri elder teachers for the day – have each already sat down by an acacia's base and are digging into the earth with crowbars, while Janelle Clare Wilson Napurrula walks about gathering dead wood for a fire. They have taken us to find witchetty, known in Warlpiri as *ngarlkirdi*.

It is not long before they come down to the roots, thick and gnarled. Amelia has exposed a nice thick one. 'There, pull that.' she says, pointing. I wrap my hand around it and pull. It comes away more easily than I expected, and crushes in my hands – hollow, riddled with holes and cavities. 'Old,' she mutters. 'No good.'

Esther, a few trees away, shouts over in Warlpiri. 'Go, go,' says Amelia, walking in an arc between the acacias to settle at the ground of another. Esther holds up a section of fresh root, showing small tunnels. 'Not ready,' she says, stowing the root back in the hole.

Meanwhile, Liddy, the eldest elder of the group, has been digging at her own tree. She waves us over. She has her mesh hat pulled down over her face to keep the flies away. Her crowbar rests across her zebra-print shirt. 'There – hit,' she says, pointing. Ben gives a few hard jabs at the exposed root with the flat end of the crowbar. It gives a satisfying sound, fresh enough to crunch and dry enough to yield. Liddy leans down and pulls a thick white grub from the root. '*Ngarlkirdi*!' she exclaims with a smile, holding it in the palm of her hand.

'Ohh, Liddy!' Ben sings.

It smells of dry grass and clover, and hothouse. A little like prickly pear cactus. We keep it in a cup.

Over the next little while, we find a few more. It is not quite the season, so we are glad for what we can get. 'There are more later, in June and July, the cooler months,' Janelle tells us. We take one as a sample; the other three are for cooking.

Janelle has already built up the fire and it has begun to yield ashes. She places the kangaroo tail we have brought from town over the coals to singe off the fur. Cosmo, Cecilia's daughter, standing nearby, watches. She turns to us. 'Are you going to eat them?' she asks. I nod. 'Oh, yes!' adds Ben.

'How do we cook these things?' Ben asks the ladies, who have gathered around the fire. Amelia responds in Warlpiri. 'Throw them in the ashes, for just a little while,' Janelle translates. She removes the singed tail from the embers, wraps it in tinfoil and places it at one edge of the fire. Then she throws some dead eucalypt branches, full with dry leaves, over the flames. The leaves pop and squeal as the fragrant oils vaporize. They quickly reduce to ash. Janelle rakes out the coals with a stick, covering the tail to cook and leaving a space to cook the grubs.

'We'll save one to make an experiment,' Ben says. 'What do we have, soy sauce? Sugar? Garlic? Chillies?'

'We also have some of the bush tomato Frank gave us.'

'We'll do it back at the house.' He packs the biggest larvae away. 'Right, here goes.' He pops the other two larvae into the ash and covers them.

Immediately they begin to expand and straighten from the heat, almost doubling in size. After about a minute, the skin has crisped and turned shiny, and the body is firm. We remove them from the ash with sticks, and dust off the excess with our hands. Andreas makes us each taste in turn while he films.

'Nutty, really nutty,' says Ben. 'Like a macadamia vibe.'

Mine is a bit smaller and looks slightly different from the other two. 'It's like when you confit garlic for a really long time, and it doesn't taste like garlic anymore, it's just really creamy and sweet and savoury,' I tell Andreas. 'It smells like roasted red pepper, and confit garlic and nuts pounded together. Like romesco sauce. That's what it tastes like to me. It's delicious.'

As we take notes and talk with the ladies, Janelle removes the kangaroo tail from beneath the dying fire. She lets it cool for a moment, then unwraps the foil, revealing a gorgeous, glistening length of cartilage, fat and long fibres of meat.

ABOVE: A *ngarlkirdi* in the root of a wattle tree

She breaks it into pieces and passes them around. Soon our faces too are glistening.

On our walk back to the dirt road, we pass the carcass of a cow, partially decomposed. The flesh has collapsed; the hide has dried to the bone.

I ask Janelle where the witchetty grubs come from. 'Before, a snake buried a *ngarlkirdi* and it turned into many,' she says. 'Then he scattered them all over the land and they grew into *ngarlkirdi* trees. That is where they come from.'

Later that evening, back at the house, we marinate the *ngarlkirdi* in soy sauce and honey and leave it in the fridge.

That night, I read. The witchetty grub (from *witjuti*, in the Adnyamathanha language) is the larvae of a cossid moth, most often *Endoxyla leucomochla*, and sometimes others. The bush in which it lives and feeds is known as the wanderrie wattle (*Acacia kempeana*), and also, appropriately, as the witchetty tree.

Sixteen hours have passed. The grub doesn't seem to marinate. At all. Its skin is very hydrophobic, and the liquid just runs off.

'Well, let's try it anyway,' Ben says, heating a pan and melting a pat of butter. He places the grub into the sizzling butter and it expands, expectedly. Basting also only partly works; it helps cook the skin, but the butter itself runs off like rain from a leaf. We pour in some of the marinade and reduce it with the butter. Still it does not stick.

We plate it with some watermelon, lime, a bit of the marinade and salt. Ben cuts the grub into three portions, and places each piece on a thin slice of watermelon. It looks like popcorn, and has a dry and drying texture, like overcooked chicken. It is not unpleasant, nor anything special.

'Well, I think it's wholly unremarkable,' says Ben.

It is hard for me to respond. Why was this experiment unsuccessful? Firstly, there is probably a reason they are cooked in ash, with a softer, even heat – they need to be treated gently and cooked just lightly. Secondly, the experiment had no connection to the grub or the place. We used what we had around, in the house, but not what we truly had around, in the landscape. Experimenting is how we learn about what works and what doesn't. But any failure, in this case – especially when we have tasted the grub already and it was good – cannot be an intrinsic failure of the insect. It is a result of how it is cooked: with what, where, with whom.

That night, I write in my notebook: '"Sampling technique" goes beyond data collection – it extends into how we draw conclusions, whether and to what extent we take misdirections and "failures" into account. The blinkered pursuit of "the tastiest morsel" is not research; it is television.' No offence to television.

— Fieldwork Team: Josh Evans, Andreas Johnsen, Ben Reade. Guide: Janelle Clare Wilson Napurrula. Written by Josh Evans.

KANTA

When we came to Australia, we had heard or read about bogong moths (pp.130–33), lerps (pp.134–6), honey ants (pp.137–41), witchetty (witjuti) grubs (pp.142–4) and a few other species. We had never heard of the bush coconut.

This morning, at the Yuendumu school, Wendy mentions bush coconut in passing, though no one is sure exactly what it is, biologically. 'Kanta in Warlpiri,' she says. 'It's like a round nest that grows on the bloodwood. There is a grub inside, a small larva. You need to find the ones that have a black nose – then it is fresh and good to eat.'

It sounded like a riddle. If I didn't already have such a true impression of Wendy, I might even think it a ruse.

'You can get them down with a hooked stick, or stones,' she adds. 'Kids will climb the tree to get them.'

A couple of days later, after our comical attempt to marinate the witchetty (p.144), Andreas, Ben and I go for a walk in the afternoon. The house is at the edge of town, and the airstrip, a flat, grassy, wide space, is a few hundred metres away. We walk its length and mull. On the return, we spy a eucalypt with conspicuous black objects hanging in its branches. Are they a fruit? But the tree also has seedpods, now dry. Are they a parasite? A disease?

I have difficulty passing up a good tree-climb and need little invitation to clamber up the slender branches.

Up close, the objects look like knobbly quinces, almost tumorous and dark brown to black. I pull at a few and toss them down to the guys. On the descent, one branch proves slightly too slender and dry for my weight, and I slide – I like to think with somewhat of an air of grace, though I doubt it – to the ground. Dirt!

To take a proper photograph, Ben hoists me up on his shoulders.

We gather up the 'coconuts' and return to the house. Some are darker and seem dried out. When we crack them with the hatchet, they have nothing inside. They smell like the blackberry canes and dry grass at summer's end, where I grew up. An old dry one that lay on the ground near the tree is open, and we find some kind of grasshopper living inside. Others have a lighter exterior: rough grey to white, mottled with green underneath. They feel denser and are harder to open. We don't do a very good job, but when we do manage to open one of the few fresh ones, we are surprised and bewildered. It has a hollow inside, in which lies a yellow, juicy thing that tastes to me like white melon and Chinese egg custard. 'And maybe a bit of almond?' Ben proposes. 'Yes!' I say. The inner 'flesh' is white, smells like resin and looks and tastes a bit like coconut (aha!), with the texture of fresh nut – like a green almond, or green hazelnut.

'Is this an insect?' we ask each other.

Later on, when the others finish work at the artists' collective, we drive together to a nearby site. 'Jukka Jukka,' Sara tells us. 'It's a water *jukurrpa*. Lies on a songline, an oral map, east–west. It is a man's site.'

In the middle of the flatland rise prisms of red rock – some leaning against each other, some split from older wholes, some orthogonal, stalwart. Teardrops to climb on. The slight elevation is all one needs to see for miles. As the sun dips, the shadows of everything – the stones, the shrubs, each blade of grass – extend further towards the vanishing point, as if all their forms drain from the landscape with the light, and only with the light the following day will they return to take their posts. We recline like lizards on the day-warmed rocks, until and past the moment when the last drop of sun drains from the horizon line, which we watch.

We are back at the house for half an hour when there is a knock. 'I was driving home from the next town and I saw a whole tree of them and I thought, *I have to bring them back for you*,' Wendy says, as she enters with Frank and hands us a cardboard box. Originally packed with apples, it is now bursting with wayward eucalypt branches. We place it on the table and open it up – dozens of *kanta*! 'And I found some more info in Latz's book,' says Frank, offering an opened

CLOCKWISE FROM TOP LEFT: 1. Whole *kanta* **2.** *Kanta* with young adults **3.** Old *kanta* with a new tenant **4.** *Kanta* with juicy mother and larvae

page from *Bushfires and Bushtucker* (see References, p.328).

'Thank you! This is amazing! Do you think the ladies will show us how to open and eat them tomorrow?' I ask.

'I think they'll be very happy to have a big box of *kanta*,' Wendy says, smiling.

The next morning, we ask around at the artists' collective for the person who knows the most about *kanta*. 'Rahab, Rahab,' everyone says. They point beyond the back gate and across the street to a green cement-brick house.

We walk over and ask for Rahab Spencer. 'Yes, that's me!' says the woman in charge, a sunset-coloured scarf wrapped around her head.

'Rahab, we have this big box of *kanta* and we want to learn how to open them, how you eat them, and which ones you like best,' Ben says. 'The others at Warlukurlangu said you know the most. Will you help us?'

'Yeah, sit down, sit down, let's eat some *kanta*!' says Rahab.

So we all sit on the floor of the porch, with Rahab's mother, her sister Ruth, her daughter Cheryl, Cheryl's husband and the kids (Tyler, Cory and Leyla, who provide the distractions and entertainment), and we open dozens of *kanta*.

Rahab shows us the best way to open them. She stands the *kanta* on one end, finds the right spot and hits the top firmly and squarely with the blunt end of the hatchet. 'Ah, the blunt end,' Ben says to me. Yesterday we were having a fiasco with the sharp end, with *kanta* flying across the table.

Rahab cracks open the first few. They are all different inside. The first is a cavity with just the plump yellow thing. 'This is *kuyu*, the mother,' Rahab says. It is juicy, fresh, melony, flavourful. The second spills over with tiny, iridescent-winged things. '*Wangarla*,' says Ruth. Wendy later tells me this word also means 'crow'. These are a little savoury. The third looks fresh on the outside, and the inside is filled with nothing. '*Lawa*!' Rahab shouts. '*Lawa! Lawa!*' the children chant while circling.

'What does it mean?' I ask. '*Jampijinpa*!' Ruth calls me to attention. '*Lawa* means "nothing".' *Jampijinpa* is a skin name. I do not mention Jangala.

The inside of the fourth *kanta* is breathtakingly beautiful. The inner cavity has a pristine mother, and is lined all around the inner surface with tiny, pink, teardrop-shaped larvae. It looks like a living geode, or a micrograph of intestinal villi, or the individual cells of citrus fruits. The larvae have the subtle taste of raw champignons or button mushrooms, and, occasionally, an almost truffle-like depth. They are slightly astringent and creamy. We scoop them out with a finger. '*Warnparnpi*,' Rahab tells us the name.

In the fifth, the tiny larvae seem to have pupated, are lighter in colour and are no longer attached to the wall. They look almost like tiny tadpoles, with elongated tails. They are savoury, like the hatched ones.

Yet another yields an intact mother, hatched adults and a light-brown dust that almost looks like tiny eggs: soft granules that clump in the mouth, then melt and coat it. 'Yes, *ngipiri*,' Rahab says, citing the name.

The inner flesh of some is soft, in others dry. Overall, it bears a striking resemblance to coconut flesh in texture, yet with flavours of pine resin and, sometimes, celeriac (celery root). 'We call it *miyi*,' Rahab tells me, scooping it out with a metal spoon.

At some point, we all start swapping *kanta*, mixing different parts together, giving each other tastes of our concoctions in the half-empty shells, as if it were a cocktail jam session. '*Muku muru pingi*!' shouts Rahab – swallow the whole lot!

We also find another gall that has been taken over by another insect. '*Pukulyu*,' Rahab says as she opens it, yielding a decomposed interior with a white grub inside – not part of the *kanta*. 'Rotten.'

We pass around the hatchet, improving our opening skills, learning to use little but directed force and, once it's cracked, a gentle hand to open the hard shells without damaging what may or may not be inside. To me it feels like a big, intricate puzzle, collecting more and more pieces of corroborating evidence that begin to sort themselves into some kind of viable chronology. Of course, this is all already known to others, but I enjoy the thrill. And Rahab indulges me.

'Frank and Wendy said it was a kind of wasp, right?' I say to her and Ben. 'And the gall is the tree's response to the invasion in its tissue. So, suppose the mother wasp burrows into the tree branch. The tree begins to grow a gall around it, and the mother turns into this juicy, yellow thing. She lays eggs, which grow into larvae, and then pupate. These hatch into adults, which eat the mother, and then leave through the small hole left by the "black nose", now open, to start the cycle again.'

'*Milpa*, the "eye" – the little dot where the mother came in,' corrects Rahab.

'Go to Wendy, she will know it,' says Ruth. 'She is a professional Warlpiri!' The sisters laugh.

Back at the house, Ben and I consider what to do with our remaining six or seven *kanta*. 'Well, let's open them up and see what we have,' he says. We are lucky: five have mothers, and three have the delicate, mushroomy larvae. 'I'd like to make some eggs with them – you know, really slowly scrambled in a bain-marie, the larvae folded in at the end, the mothers lightly warmed,' Ben says.

'Sounds good. I'll use the gall flesh.' We have a whole bag of nice limes and the pun is too good to pass up. I cut the fresher galls into wedges of 'coconut', each with a wedge of lime. I even put a slice of lime into half an unused coconut. Harry Nilsson would be proud. With the leftovers, I scoop out the flesh and dress it with lime juice, lime zest, chopped red chilli and salt.

Ben's eggs are tasty, mainly because the eggs are cooked with care and butter. We agree that the beguiling taste of raw mushroom from the larvae doesn't come through, and the freshness of the mother is gone. It might be one of those things, like the honey ants, that just doesn't get better with cooking or 'elaboration'.

After we clean up, I have a spare moment and finally consult Peter Latz's pages on the bloodwood, also known as *yurrkali* or *Corymbia terminalis*:

> The gall is formed by a female coccid (*Cystococcus pomiformis*) which burrows into the plant tissue and, in some way, causes it to become 'cancerous'. She then produces young: winged males first and much smaller, wingless females later. When the mother grub dies, five or so females climb onto a male which then transports them to the next tree. He then dies – his sole purpose in life is to be a taxi! This parasitic growth may, however, itself be 'parasitised' by other insects, which spoil its food value.

Further in the section, he mentions how the gall flesh is eaten; that one may also find lerps on the tree's leaves; that the bloodwood is one of the most likely trees to be inhabited by the stingless bee (*Trigona* spp.), whose honey is called 'sugarbag' and is 'probably the most sought-after delicacy in central Australia.' He tells how the flowers of the tree are soaked in water and the sweet liquid drunk; and how the gum of the tree, *kino*, is diluted and used as a topical medicine for eyes, lips, wounds, burns, sores and sore throats. He tells how the red sap is also used to tan kangaroo-skin water bags, and how the tree's boles (swellings on the trunk) are often chopped off and hollowed out to make bowls to carry water. He tells how 'the living wood is used for certain implements and the dead wood is one of the most favoured firewoods, burning with a steady, hot flame.' He tells of the fruit capsules being fastened into hair for decoration, or strung together into necklaces, or used as children's toys. He tells of its role in ceremony and mythology.

Tomorrow we leave for Alice Springs. This night is our last in Yuendumu. We take our new friends, our remaining food, some firewood and water out into the desert, where we cook, eat and lie out under the moon.

— Fieldwork Team: Josh Evans, Andreas Johnsen, Ben Reade. Written by Josh Evans.

ESCAMOLES

———

After heating a sheen of oil in a pan, sorting through the *escamoles* on a metal tray, separating the whole ones from the broken, sautéeing minced white onion, adding the larvae to heat through and plump them, receiving off the *comal* – a smooth, flat griddle – a hot masa tortilla onto the plate from his comrade across the stove, scooping the larvae from the pan gently into the taco and garnishing with a cream of leek whites and kohlrabi, thin slices of green serrano chillies, small leaves of *epazote* and a powder of dried chilhuacle chillies, the line cook Eric Guerrero deftly proffers the plate to us, slanted towards Andreas' camera, and intones, briskly, '*Para ti.*'

I now understand why they call *escamoles* 'Mexican caviar'.

'You can't make people eat insects because we want them to eat insects,' says chef Enrique Olvera, from across the kitchen at his restaurant Pujol. 'But if it tastes good, it doesn't matter. Like this *taco de escamoles con colinabo y poro.*'

'Right, let's let the boys get set up for lunch service,' Enrique says, shifting gears. 'And you boys, get yourselves into the dining room.'

'Yes chef!'

There were many delicious things at lunch. I am still haunted by the *mole madre*, which had been made and used and remade with new ingredients for 323 days: dark and acetic, like a solid-state vinegar self-nursed, like an ascetic, to wisdom, garnished with a smaller daub of a lighter, nuttier, spicier,

fresh mole in the middle; as well as by a herbal tea at the end of the meal, made from cacao and corn silk. But the dishes with insects were what we were paying closest attention to. How was Enrique using the insects? How was he thinking with them? What ideas about how to eat them best were being communicated on the plate?

Baby *elote* (*elotito*), with a mayonnaise of coffee and *chicatanas* (*Atta mexicana*), a kind of leafcutter ant, served in a gourd filled with smoking corn husk.

Avocado with chia seeds soaked in *aguachile* (a mixture of water, chilli and lime), garnished with jalapeño and coriander (cilantro) flower, and seasoned with *sal de gusano de maguey* – salt mixed with dried maguey worm.

'We sometimes serve the *escamoles* on a tostada, a toasted or fried tortilla, or in an *infladita*, a puffed tortilla, with similar garnish: spring (green) onion, chilli, *epazote*,' says Joaquin Cardoso, Enrique's sous-chef, as he leads us upstairs after lunch service to the private dining room.

'Everyone eats them in the mayonnaise.' Enrique is already there, relaxed, with a bit of time. 'Plus, it's better for the flavour. That's what interests me: focusing on flavour. Using them like a spice. I think *chicatanas* are one of the most amazing flavours of my life.

'We get them from Oaxaca, from a coffee farm. The dish happened because I tasted them there, with the other things growing there, and the ingredients just fit together: the strong, mulchy flavour of the ants; the coffee; the smells of the undergrowth and the smoke. The young corn from the early planting. The *chicatanas* can really stand up to other strong flavours – big, umami flavours, meaty flavours, spicy flavours.

'We sometimes get them from Guerrero, where they also call them *hormigas culonas* – "big-assed ants". And we use the *cocopanche* in a similar way, but we blanch it three times first, because otherwise, it tastes too strongly, like urine.'

'Everything in its proper dose,' I offer.

'Exactly. Others, like the *gusanos de maguey*, work well with acid. The *chapulines* [grasshoppers; *Sphenarium*

spp.], and the *escamoles*, we use whole. The *escamoles* we can use lightly frozen, but not for too long, because then they really collapse – and they do not puff up like they should, which is important.

'Some insects are more rare, so I see them as more luxurious. In general I see insects as something special. For many, the season is short, they have to be found in the wild and it takes hard labour and knowledge.

'The *escamoles* are the true example. I love them. And JC here' – he points to José Carlos Redon, our guide while we are in Mexico City and around – 'brings me the best ones. I always think they

CLOCKWISE FROM TOP LEFT: 1. Prickly pear cactus **2.** Harvesting the *escamoles* **3.** Cooking up lunch on the *comal* **4.** Raw *escamoles* on a hand-pressed tortilla

go so well with white vegetables: leeks, parsnip, kohlrabi. To me, the kohlrabi and the *escamoles* have the same profile. Another dish I love is the *tuétano*, where we serve them with bone marrow. We always cook the *escamoles*, because a lot of people are allergic to something in the raw *escamol*.

'Think about all the weird things we actually eat,' Enrique points out. 'Honey is bee vomit. "Insects" are often only the ones we *don't* eat – when they are delicious, we instead say they are "delicacies".'

We talk until it's time to prepare for dinner service. Enrique wishes us well and walks down with us to the door.

We're up with the sun and driving north to Hidalgo. José Carlos, who goes by JC, and his brother Alessandro are taking us to the farm and educational space they run with their uncle, Armando.

'My grandfather was the one who gave them to me first,' JC tells us. 'He ate them all his life. In fact, later he got a kind of aversion – like the allergy Enrique was talking about yesterday. It happens more with older people. I don't know why.

'Most often he cooked them the "old" way – the Hispanic way, rather than the pre-Hispanic: in butter, with onion, serrano chillies, *epazote* and salt at the end. A kind of sofrito. Enrique's version is rooted in that. The pre-Hispanic way was to eat them raw, or cooked on the fire.

'I like them cooked with olive oil – a Mexican one, mild, from the Baja. Everything is good with butter, but to bring out the flavour, maybe olive oil is better. My favourite is perhaps with avocado oil: it burns higher, and has a milder flavour. Sauté them lightly, because they change abruptly in colour and lucency. Put them in a soft taco, fresh, handmade

masa, from the *comal* – that's the way. That's how we'll do it today.'

The *atole* is very sweet. The air is not yet warm.

The truck climbs a steep road to a stone building above the town of Puerto México. A large stone terrace overlooks the land, with curved, rock-lined beds and paths that wind among a stark jungle of cacti, some in bloom. The morning is quiet but for a neighbour's chickens and, the more I attend to them, the myriad sounds of smaller life.

'Welcome to Teotlacualli,' JC says.

We explore a bit while JC makes coffee. Trees with graceful draping leaves, in a line just below the terrace, swarm with curious creatures – black and spindly with orange dots. JC comes out from the kitchen in the stone house.

'What are they?' I ask.

'They are called *xahue*, or in this region's ethnic dialect of Nahuatl, *ñhañhu*. They have a high iodine content, part of which goes away when cooked. They taste nutty and earthy. And they love these mesquite trees.'

We sit next to the trees, in the sun as it rises. I stare at at the *xahue*.

'We have about one acre,' JC tells us. 'It's a non-profit farm I set up with my uncle Armando. We work on sustainable agriculture with a focus on plants and insects. All the profit goes back into the farm, as a mixed project for producing food, teaching students and community members and hosting visitors. We made the house from all recycled materials, built an anaerobic compost toilet, and underneath us is a reservoir that fills in the rainy season, from May to September, and can hold 100,000 litres of water.

'You might have heard of the "three sisters": the corn, beans and squash that grow synergistically. We call it *la milpa*. It is a Nahuatl word, and also refers to the whole system of growing things together – the specific species can vary regionally.

'The *escamoles* [*Liometopum apiculatum*] are part of our *milpa* here. We have three nests on the farm, which we can study more closely. We want to learn more about how the ants work, how they behave and respond to different conditions. But it is very difficult to move a nest or set one up. If they are not comfortable they will move. So we work around the ants – we work better where the nests already are. But if we can learn more about how they thrive, how they interact with the things living around them, maybe we can develop a system and then move it to other places. For example, we know the ants feed on maguey leaves, and they often build their nest under a maguey plant. They seem to like building around the plant roots, and into hillsides – maybe for the drainage.

'We monitor the nests to protect them. A nest usually matures at three years old; once mature, we can take around 40 to 50 per cent of the queen eggs – between 1 and 3 kilograms – over the whole season, which is one and a half months in March and April. If it is not ready, we will wait until it is. We tend to harvest three times, waiting two weeks in between. Sometimes, in a good season, we can do four. Only about one in 100 eggs will become a successful queen who founds a nest, if left to hatch. Some of them, instead, become food for us – royal caviar.

'Some nests are over 100 years old, tended by generations of *escamoleros*. There are twenty families that work on farms in Puerto México, and around a hundred nests in total on the *ejidos*, the owned lands. There are also some nests on the *tierras comunales*, the communal land. Traditionally, only local farmers collect from the communal land, but now sometimes others come. It is not illegal, per se, but the locals do not like it, and those others do so at their own risk. The worst part is that the thieves do not know the land, and they come and take everything – they ruin the balance of the system, not only for the ecology but also for the local economy.

'And then there are the middlemen, the "coyotes". They buy at very low prices and resell for much more. Some locals try to sell on the highway, but it is not very reliable. We are setting up a cooperative organization for the local *escamoleros*, to get a better price, get access to better restaurants who pay upon receiving, shorten the supply chain and cut out the coyotes. Our normal retail price is 1,300 to 1,500 pesos [approx. US$69 to 79] per kilo. That's fairly good for a producer to earn.'

A lithe man in a weathered straw hat walks the stone steps. 'Here is my uncle, Armando Soria Castañela,' says JC. 'Armando, meet Ben, Josh, Andreas.'

'*Cómo están*, boys? Welcome. You,' he points to me, 'need a hat.' He goes into the older, stone part of the building and returns with an extra one, of straw, with a blue chin string and a frayed rim.

A few minutes later, a woman walks up the slate slabs, wearing a tunic in shades of crimson. The colours remind me of the cochineal farm we visited in Oaxaca: the farmer raised the females of the *cochinilla* scale insect (*Dactylopius coccus* or *Dactylopius indicus*) on varieties of nopal, dried and crushed their bodies to make a pigment and adjusted the hue with citric acid and potassium hydroxide.

'*Hola*,' she says.

'This is Amelia Copca Cortés. She lives here in Puerto México,' JC explains. 'We are going to cook together today.

She has brought the corn for masa. Before we go, we will begin the nixtamalization.'

Amelia leads us over to a stone ledge of a raised bed dominated by an immense *garambullo* cactus. Nearby are a few metal *comales* and a large stone firepit built into the terrace. She pulls out a ceramic bowl, and places a few pieces of quicklime into it – '*la cal*'. She pours over some water. It immediately gives off some smoke and heat. She leaves it on the ledge, and pours a basket of corn kernels into a pot of water heating over the fire. She picks up the ceramic dish. '*La calidra*', Amelia says, watching us watch the slaked lime, making sure we are absorbing every step, and pours the limewater into the pot, withholding the stones. The opaque liquid swirls into the water, partially obscuring the grains. She stirs it with a wooden spoon, and already the kernels reveal a bit more yellow. 'Not too much, you see, so that it doesn't taste like calcium' JC says from the side. The water starts to simmer.

Armando comes over. 'Boys, let's go collect some – it's getting warmer and they'll be resting.'

We hop in the back of his pickup and drive down the hill, along another road.

'They are most active in the morning and evening, when it's cooler. So we harvest around midday, so that we don't disturb them when they work.'

Armando leads us among spines, overgrown maguey and dry branches that grasp at our hands and faces.

'You see here,' he says, kneeling down. 'This is called *caminito* – "little way".' A small groove, set just below earth level and shaded by scrub, is alive with shiny black. 'There are three or four ways, in any direction. It is the sign that takes them to the nest.'

He leads us further. Sometimes it feels like there is a path; other times not. He kneels near a large, gnarled maguey and pulls debris, the dried skeletal matrices of old nopal pads, from a hole that materialized but moments ago. He peers in, confers with his friend Enedino Peña Peña who has joined us on the hunt, and passes a word to JC. 'It's been harvested recently,' JC tells us.

We visit two more in the area, both in a similar state. 'How does it work?' Ben asks JC. 'Do people take care of certain nests, or is it a free-for-all? How do you control harvesting on public land of semi-private property?'

'That's the difficulty – it's a very grey area. That's why we want to make the cooperative, to strengthen the community and coordinate our work.'

We drive a little way to another area. Armando walks a few dozen metres and stops, standing by an enormous maguey, prehistorically large. He points to the leaves where there is a black residue, the same that is on his hands.

'We dig.' It does not have a hidden opening. It has not yet been dug.

It does not take long before Armando's body is covered in tiny black specks, up and down his arms and back and neck. They move and leave their mark on skin where it's exposed.

The hole angles down underneath the maguey. Armando calls to JC, who slices a piece of maguey, trims off the spines and hands it to his uncle. Armando's upper half disappears again into the hole. After some shuffling, he reemerges with a tangle of living things. Dark ants crawl in every direction over large, plump, white larvae, all enmeshed in an intricate structure that looks as if it's been CAD-designed and 3D-printed.

'This is the reticulum. We call it *trabecula*. They build it out of earth and twigs and spit. It is beautiful, no?' Armando says, handing it to us to admire.

'They can move the eggs to different chambers depending on the time of season and the developmental stage. This one's egg chamber is full.'

'Can I try?' I ask.

'Yes. Take this maguey leaf, as a plate, and use this dry nopal to brush them onto it.' Armando scrapes a piece of dry nopal fibre with a rock, abrading the end into a brush. 'Remember – gently, very gently.'

'Pull your socks over your trouser cuffs,' JC advises. 'Otherwise, lots of ants in your pants.'

The first thing is the smell: it feels like another atmosphere on, and in, my face. It smells like a young, blue, goat's cheese, delicate yet always on the verge of pungency. The eggs are mixed with the reticulum, the ants swarming on every surface. I brush the mixture of ants, larvae, reticulum and dirt onto the maguey plate with the nopal broom, and when it is full, I lift it carefully out of the hole. Armando takes it to inspect as I extricate myself and brush the ants from my arms. Tiny dots of black speckle my skin. Armando lets everything slide into a pail.

Ben lies down on his belly with his head down the hole. 'Oh, they're biting! Wow, what a smell. It's clean, fresh, sexy. How do you describe the smell of a truffle? It's like that.'

We take a few more platefuls and then fill in the newly made tunnel with the same dried nopal bones, and cover the lot with big rocks. '*Palcahuite*,' Armando says. 'The substitute. It lets us be as little invasive as possible for future harvests.'

We cover the pail with a tree frond to shade the larvae from the noonday sun,

and trek back to the road. Under a tree, Ben and I take a larva (what the locals call the 'egg') and a pupa each to taste.

'It has such a distinct flavour. What is that flavour?' I say.

'It's sort of reminiscent of avocado. And has a green, nutty thing, like – a fresh almond?' Ben ventures.

The larvae are like the cream layer of a small, young goat's cheese: vegetal, flowery, milky. The pupae are sweeter, more strong and more firm.

'Not sure about how the skin sticks in your mouth,' Ben says, removing the membrane with a finger. 'But the juice that goes everywhere is absolutely divine.'

We take another way back, and stop by Armando's friend who makes pulque. It is an alcoholic drink made from fermented maguey sap. When the maguey matures, after six or seven years, it produces a large flower bud at its centre. Before the cactus goes to seed and sends the flower up on a stalk several metres into the sky, the *pulquero* cuts off the flower bud and begins to hollow out the core of the cactus. She scrapes a little bit deeper into the core each day, and overnight the growing cavity fills with sap (*aguamiel*). In the morning, she harvests it with a calabash or siphon, and adds to it, the bit of active seed from the previous day, which has been left to strengthen – becoming more microbially powerful as it does unpalatable to drink. It takes a few hours for the whole to ferment, and must be consumed that day. In this sense it almost reminds me of milk – but also completely not. Sap from one maguey can be harvested every day in this way for about two months.

We stand around for a while, drinking pulque from a passed-around gourd. At some point, we clamber back into the pickup, with plastic bottles of the opaque elixir and a bit of added psychic lightness. Dogs prance. The car is fast.

When we return, Amelia has already pulled the pot off the fire, let it sit, drained the grains, rinsed them and begun to grind them on the *metate* with the *metlapil* – a flat mortar and pestle of volcanic rock, with a curved lip at the far end. Batch by batch, the ceramic bowl fills with fresh masa. It takes work to get it smooth.

Meanwhile, Enedino begins to clean the *escamoles*. He spreads them all out on a netted nylon sack, to loosen the larvae from pieces of reticulum, and brushes them with the fronds we used to cover the pail from the sun, helping the adults disperse. Then he places some of the mixture into a plastic strainer and dips it into a bucket of water, and the larvae float to the top. As he pulls it back up, the larvae pool together in the centre, and he deftly scoops them out into another sieve with a cupped hand. 'Can I try?' I ask him. It is difficult and takes some coordination. After a few amusing failures, I manage to catch more than just a few. 'Finally,' I say, smiling at my friend, and he grins.

JC is going through the cleaned larvae and picking out the ones that have begun to pupate and darken. 'Some people like the *negritos* best, once they start to mature into adults. But we don't tend to sell them.' They are stronger, with a firmer texture.

Amelia first shows us how to make tortillas by hand before we use the press to do the rest: only on the tips of the fingers, not with the palm. The men have begun tending the *comal*, scooping embers and burning logs from the firepit into its flat metal drum. The surface is already searing. Our tortillas cook quickly. Amelia sprinkles a few *escamoles*, raw, onto our warm tortillas – the surface

crackled, the edges rough like a coastline and having just begun to darken. 'The closest to the pre-Hispanic way we know,' says JC, taking a bite of his own. Three simple elements: corn, fire, larvae – some transformed, some, after the moment of harvest, not at all.

Now things really get going. Amelia's daughter Maria Ester del Valle Copca, also Enedino's wife, is busting out tortillas with the press, which she cooks on one half of the *comal*; the men have begun slicing fresh, acidic nopales and white onions onto the other half and turning them over with their machetes. Amelia is toasting *jitomate* (red tomato), coriander (cilantro), onion, garlic and serrano chillies on the *comal*, and grinding them in the *molcajete*, a bowl-like mortar and pestle made of the same porous, igneous rock as the metate and metlapil. JC takes me over to the mesquite trees, and takes off his hat. 'Time to collect some *xahue*.' He begins to pluck the clusters of spindly black insects off the thin branches and motions for me to do the same. We place them in his hat.

When we've gathered a few ('They are potent, so we don't need too many'), we upend the hat over the *comal*. We toast them briefly, put them into the *molcajete*, and grind to incorporate. They do bring a certain iodine note; once toasted, they also take on a distinct taste, reminiscent of roasted pistachio.

'A little bit of this jazz,' Ben says, filling a tortilla with the mixture of nopales, onions and *escamoles*. 'A little bit of this jazz,' he says as he adds some of the charred salsa. He bites and grunts in pleasure. 'Sweet, bitter, sour – this is the most real taco I've ever tasted,' he proclaims to the sky. The flavours stretch my palate taut, and singe away loose or lazy tasting. The heat of the *comal* has made the larvae plump up without making them collapse or overcook; they combine with the slithery nopales and barely softened onions into a robust, coherent whole, each providing what the others miss. The salsa adds bitterness, pungency and aroma that lifts the taco by its bootstraps.

Armando has returned from a little walk in the farm and plops a whole purslane plant onto the *comal*. '*Verdolaga*,' he says, turning it so it wilts evenly.

'So,' JC says, gathering our attention. 'I would like to show you the *ximbo*, a key culinary tradition of Hidalgo. We will come back and make it tomorrow, but we need to start today.'

He and Ben walk down the drive to the neighbour's house and ask to buy a cockerel. They return with the dead bird hanging in their hands. Amelia plucks it swiftly, drains the blood from the neck and eviscerates it. JC and Ben separate the giblets (to keep) from the stomach, intestines, head and feet (to bury), while Amelia singes the carcass, feet attached, on the *comal*. Ben breaks the body down after JC's directions. We marinate the halved crown, limbs, heart, lungs, liver, gizzards, neck and comb in pulque, and leave it overnight.

We return to Teotlacualli before the sunrise, at Andreas' request. He has a fixation on filming sunrises and sunsets, and he has already obtained both from within *La Ciudad*.

The valley is held in mist, grey gradually turning to mauve and dusty blue. We set off for the crest of the ridge above the farm, racing the sky as it colours the air. Dotting the surrounding slopes are mature magueys gone to seed, silhouetted, some flower stalks tall yet unopened, like enormous asparagus spears; others are crowned with clusters of flowers, bending outward in baroque ornament.

From the top, the ridgeline to the east begins to divest itself of its mist, with that line of surreal clarity that comes only in those moments just before a sun is imminent. Andreas extends the tripod's legs and sets the camera, daring the first drops of sun to spill.

We arrived sooner than we thought we had. Then, oranges and yellows enter the fray, rays pour and the world again has shadows. Andreas and I stay. JC and Ben walk back down the stony road to the farm, to build the day's first fire.

'It's *ximbo* day!' JC exclaims as Andreas and I return. The pulque has firmed the softer pieces of cockerel flesh and made the tougher ones more tender. We start the fire. While it grows, JC leads us into the grove of *garambullos*, their thorned arms widening out above our heads.

'I thought I would show you another of my favourite *escamol* recipes today, because it is the perfect season for the cactus flowers. It is simple and I love it. My mother would make it for me.' JC begins to pluck a few white flowers from the arms of *garambullo*. They have a delicate texture and a spring aroma, with bare, unoppressive echoes of jasmine.

After we have gathered a bowlful, we move to another area of the garden more dominated by maguey. In between them are smaller cacti with the same whorl of spiked, tapered blades, tinged purple. Some have sent up flower stalks, younger cousins to the giants on the hillsides. Yet these stalks are profuse with orange buds, a few just beginning to open from their pale, green tips, but most still held fast. I pick off a bud to taste: it is firm and vegetal and bitter, like cucumber skin. Armando slices off a few stalks with his machete, low on the stem. '*Sábila*.' A variety of aloe vera.

Next, a younger maguey nearby takes Armando's attention. He leads us over, and he and JC select and slice off a suitable, particularly spry blade. Armando shows us how to trim the tines off both edges, and thin the thicker central spine so it can be folded over itself lengthwise.

Back at the firepit, the flames have burned down the first wood, and embers are starting to accumulate. Armando places the maguey across the fire. It starts to sweat. He flips it over. Once it has softened to a suitable pliancy, he moves it over to a long wooden table brought from inside. We fill half of the gently concave side with the pieces of cockerel, sliced onions, garlic cloves, nopales, *quelites* (a general term for wild greens), and a healthy showering of *escamoles*. We add small amounts of *cenizo* (Texas sage, *Leucophyllum frutescens*) and *alcamfór* (a local species of Artemisia) for their herbal aromas. We fold the other half over the filled one, curve the sides into each other and tie with metal wire. We dig a pit into the fire's remains, into which we place the *ximbo*, and cover it over with embers.

Then JC takes us into the kitchen in the stone house. 'And now we make the eggs with eggs.' First, he has me pluck the individual aloe buds from the stalks and remove any debris from them and the *garambullo* flowers. He heats a large pan on the gas, melting a knob of butter, and cracks ten chicken eggs into a bowl and beats them with a bit of salt. He pours them into the pan, stirring slowly as they begin to coagulate. When they are half-coagulated, he adds the aloe buds and *garambullo* flowers, stirring gently to incorporate. As soon as the egg comes together he adds a couple of handfuls of *escamoles*, and stirs so they warm through and plump. '*Huevos revueltos con escamoles y flores de sábila y garambullo.*' He spoons some onto a few plates, hands three to us and takes the others outside. It seems simple, but the flavours are complex and the textures beautiful: staccato aloe buds; *garambullo* flowers with wilted outer petals and a still-crisp, fragrant core; plump *escamoles* that burst – all enrobed in chicken eggs ennobled with a bit of fat and heat. The ingredients share some affinity, but also each retains its character. Unassuming and effective cooking.

'My mother would also sometimes make us *tortitas de nopal* – a nopal pad, sliced in half, with cheese, jam and fried bacon in between like a sandwich, and baked for ten minutes,' he says.

About an hour after burying the *ximbo* – which works out almost exactly to when we are ready for a meal after our morning snack – it is ready to be exhumed. It is dug up with a shovel and transferred to the table. The maguey leaf is unfolded with succinct ceremony, revealing a succulent mess, its aromas rising in tangles of fragrant steam. We eat it with our hands, together with the neighbours.

A friend of Armando's climbs down the hill from above the farm. In his hand he carries a dry, discoloured nopal leaf. He comes over to the *ximbo*, and has us peer into a hole in the nopal. There are some pale worms within. He shakes them out into a ceramic dish, and takes them over to the *comal*, heats a bit of oil on the metal surface while pressing a tortilla, and cooks them both until crisp. '*Gusanos de nopal*,' he says, passing the simple taco around the circle. They taste of the cactus, vegetal and slightly sour. He finishes the last bite, rolls up his sleeves and dives with us back into the *ximbo*'s midst.

— Fieldwork Team: Josh Evans, Andreas Johnsen, Ben Reade. Guide: José Carlos Redon. Written by Josh Evans.

TORITOS

We meet Guillermina Muñoz Maldonado, a friend of our guide Ivan, in her neighbour's backyard. Enclosed with cinderblock walls, the lot is empty but for a large tree dominating one end. '*Aguacate, aguacate*,' she says, walking over to the avocado tree, carrying a large, green pail of water. We do not yet know what we are here to find.

She places the pail near the trunk, and dips in a hand before raising her eyes to the branches. She shifts her gaze with purposeful adjustments, until reaching up to a lower branch with her wetted hand and grasping across its top. When she brings her hand down, it is filled with small bugs that share the same mottled grey-green of the leaves.

'*Toritos*,' she says. And now, when we all look back up, patches that before looked like lichen or leaves now appear as clusters of insects along the branches. We spread out and begin scooping them into our wet hands. There also seem to be some with yellow heads and whiter wings. None of them seem to fly, or walk far.

'You could say the name, literally, means "little bulls",' Ivan explains. Later, I learn their English name, avocado lace bug; in Latin, *Pseudacysta perseae*.

I smell a handful before dipping them into the pail. They smell like green pepper; raw, they taste like it too. 'Very much like a pea pod,' suggests Andreas. He is right.

'They come in October to November, and February to March,' Guillermina tells us, translated by Ivan. 'And the avocados grow from March to September, so there are only a couple of months where we can't get something from this tree. One can find especially many in Michoacán, where they grow a lot of avocados. But I think we eat more of the insects here in Tlaxcala. And I find many in this tree here,' she says, smiling at her neighbour across the yard, who watches us from the doorway. 'Let's go back to my house, and I will show you how we cook them.' Guillermina picks up the pail, now with a sheet of toritos floating on the surface, and leads us up the street by the hand.

We cook in her courtyard. Plants in pots cover all surfaces. She fans the coals in a metal box to revive them, and places a *cazuela*, a wide ceramic dish, on top. We scoop the *toritos* out of the water, drain them through our fingers, shake off the excess water and put them into another smaller *cazuela*.

First, Guillermina scoops a bit of pork fat ('*manteca*') into the *cazuela*, which she tilts slightly to let the melting fat pool at one edge. At the other edge, she places some *toritos*, to let the water evaporate, before scooping them, once dry, into the fat and re-evening the dish. The *toritos* fry gently for five to seven minutes, turning a yellow-brown and becoming more generally savoury, but losing much of their distinctive flavour.

She removes the *cazuela* from the heat and replaces it with a flatter, wider, earthenware *comal*. She lets it heat, and when it is ready, she scoops some *toritos* alone onto the blackened surface. She stirs them, the heat still low. They dry slightly, keeping their green colour and clean, vegetal taste. Their legs straighten. They are removed.

'This is the more traditional, pre-Hispanic way,' she tells us. '*Tostado.*'

Then there is another way. She takes a corn husk, nestles some *toritos* into its base, closes it around itself and places it onto the *comal*. While the small package warms, she adds two whole tomatoes, turning them on the hot ceramic as their skin blisters and their flesh softens. When the tomatoes are ready, she reserves them, removes the *comal* and places the corn husk directly onto the coals. The court-yard fills with the scent of charring corn leaf. After a few final minutes, the husk has browned and the edges have blackened, but it has retained its shape. She takes it off, and unfurls it like an old scroll. Inside, the *toritos* have steamed in their own aromas with the added smells of the corn husk as it went from fresh to charred. They are plump and viridian. '*Tatemado,*' says Guillermina.

I like this way best. The *toritos*' distinctive taste – now strongly reminiscent of avocado – is revealed most clearly.

Guillermina has already moved on to the next preparation. She crushes a *chile de árbol* in the *molcajete*, adds a bit of

CLOCKWISE FROM TOP LEFT: 1. Holding the *toritos* in water 2. *Toritos tatemados*, steamed in a corn husk on the coals 3. A *torito* and grilled tomato taco 4. Guillermina's loom

water and the two grilled tomatoes, and crushes them into a salsa. Then she adds some of the *toritos tostados*, and crushes them through lightly. 'You can use these in salsa instead of avocado, especially when it's not avocado season.' She spoons the salsa into some tortillas, and sprinkles on some of the *toritos* fried in pork fat.

As we taste and compare the different preparations, discuss and take photographs and make notes, Guillermina goes into her kitchen and returns with a deeper ceramic pot, which she places onto the coals. After some minutes, the courtyard is filled with a new smell – a deeper, richer one. She lifts the lid, spoons some into more bowls and adds them to our already full table. 'Pork shoulder in adobo sauce,' she says, placing some just-steamed tamales onto the centre of the table. This morning, the research has, as it not infrequently does, morphed into a meal. We insist she sit with us, and together we eat. The sauce is thick and complex: multiple kinds of chillies, garlic, cumin, and other things that have mostly given up their individual identities in favour of the collective, assenting silently that they are better off for it.

Mexico's landscapes and cuisines are bewilderingly diverse. There are so many kinds of insects, only a fraction of which we have tasted, but already the list is long:

toasted *ahuautle*, the eggs of aquatic bugs; *gusanos de maguey*, maguey worms, fresh from the leaf, which are a little sour and fatty with notes of cashew and chicken; *gusanos azotadores*, from three different plants – *nogal*, with woody notes of hickory, *capulin*, herbal and grassy, *tejocote*, mushroomy and spicy with the aroma of cream; *xamoe*; *calpulalpan*; the *chicatanas* and *escamoles*, of course; and the *xahue* and *gusanos de nopal* at Teotlacualli. *Chapulines* from different places and with different preparations. Salts with *chicatanas*, *chapulines* and *chinicuiles* (red maguey worms) added for their flavours. *Gusanos de mantequilla*. Wasps cooked whole in the hive on the *comal*. And we cannot forget the honey ants (pp.162–4).

But of all of these, the *toritos* are, for me, quite remarkable. It is an effective exercise in how the mode of preparation can refract an organism's flavour in multiple directions. To ask what *toritos* taste like is not sufficient. We must also ask, at the same time, 'How are they prepared?'

— Fieldwork Team: Ben Reade, Josh Evans, Andreas Johnsen Guide: Ivan Fernando del Razo. Written by Josh Evans.

BINGUINAS

Somehow a crowd has sprouted. The entourage has swollen to include friends, friends of friends and local culinary students. Even Guillermina, who showed us the *toritos* in the morning (pp.159–61), wanted to come along for the afternoon. And to be honest, it makes me a bit anxious – there is already enough unpredictability in fieldwork, and a large group rarely makes it easier to focus on learning as much as possible in moments that may never come again.

Nor is the weather particularly encouraging. Amorphous grey hangs close and verges on darkening into a wetter density. The dry scrubland might like the rain, at least; the fields around us are dusty as we pick our way by the trees above the banks of a dry riverbed. The particular smell of pre-storm suffuses our arid nostrils.

Leading our party is Don Serafino, the owner of this land in rural Tlaxcala, where he produces nopales and *tunas* (the edible pads and fruits, respectively, of the prickly pear cactus), and, among other things, hunts for *binguinas* (honey ants; *Myrmecocystus mexicanus*), which he has done with his mother and brothers since he was two years old. It is the *binguinas* that have brought us to him.

It was just under two weeks ago that we first tasted honey ants in the Australian outback (pp.137–41). Now we are presented with the opportunity to try to find and taste some here. I wonder how they will compare.

Similarly to what we learned in Australia, here it is also considered ideal to search for *binguinas* just after or even during rain. Don Serafino leads us through and around his fields, telling us at points to spread out to look for trails of red ants. 'Sometimes, people will burn the brush to make them easier to spot,' he tells us. So far, we have spotted few ants, and a couple of likely holes in the earth end up empty. There are more than a few creatures, it seems, who build their homes in the ground. Don Serafino then picks his way down the embankment to the side of the stone riverbed. A few more attempts here yield anticipation, distracted interest, crowded bodies and dust in the tepid air. Our efforts seem to gain a kind of dramatic futility, a solemn significance bestowed by the superfluous quorum of followers. The situation would be excellent for literature; for research, it feels slightly less than useful.

At some point, Don Serafino pulls us on and up out of the riverbed, looping back around to the soccer field/car park where we began. There are some main lines painted in white on the silty earth. Somehow it seems appropriate that only after our wandering, in the play's final act, does the protagonist appear: just in front of one soccer goal, there is a hole with small but certain activity. Don Serafino immediately gets down to his knees and begins to dig.

At barely 50 cm (20 inches) down, he finds the first galleries. At first, there is only one, then two – but these are enough for joyous, even raucous, celebration. Everyone is laughing and joking and somehow Don Serafino manages to keep digging with the requisite care while also grinning wildly. Guillermina conjures a dish to hold the ants. Now using a twig to excavate, Don Serafino finds more – and as the set grows, gradations of amber begin to emerge. 'We call the lighter ones *savino*, and the darker ones *encino*. Different colours come from different food.' A recurring theme. 'And the deeper you go, the more sweet they become.' This is new – could it be due to the more constant temperature? The moister soil? Is the pattern robust?

It is not a huge harvest today – only twelve – but there are just enough for every member of the party to try one, with one remaining to take as a sample. Some have never tried them before. With this news, and buoyed by the afternoon's small triumph, Ben and I propose that we conduct an informal sensory analysis here on the pitch. With a bit of help, we are able to explain the idea: each taster will walk a few dozen metres from the others, to Ben, Andreas and me. The taster will choose an ant from the bowl, taste it and describe the taste with as many descriptors as they like, out of earshot of the rest of the group, and we will note them down. We will repeat until all have tasted. The group is game. We begin.

CLOCKWISE FROM TOP LEFT: 1. The *binguinas* hunting party **2.** Don Serafino finds the first *binguina* **3.** Collected *binguinas* **4.** Digging up the football pitch

Tasting notes (3–9 and 11 are translated from Spanish):

1. Ben: meat stock, umami
2. Josh: Sauternes, kiwi
3. Mimi (first time trying): tamarind, lemon, chilli
4. Ivan: honey, strong, bitter, fermented, intense, wine
5. Angel (first time trying): lime, lemon, honey with lemon drunk for coughs, aged white wine
6. Margarita: fermented pulque, vegetal, sweet, Tokaji wine, aguamiel (sap or juice) of maguey, white-wine yeast, beer yeast, honey
7. Don Serafino: wine, a little bitter, delicious wine
8. Irad: very sweet, red fruit, coats the mouth, Madeira wine, ripe fruit, blackberries
9. Guillermina: honey, cider, wine, bitter
10. Andreas: wine thing, honey, thicker, bitter, bitter honey, wine, Sauternes
11. Fabian: citrus, mandarin, lemon, white wine – different from the other time he tried them and it was bigger, darker, red fruits, red wine, fermented

Quite a satisfying day. We thank Don Serafino, pile into our caravan of cars and head back towards town, to prepare for the next.

— Fieldwork Team: Josh Evans, Andreas Johnsen, Ben Reade. Guide: Ivan Fernando del Razo. Written by Josh Evans.

AMAZONAS

⎯

From Lima, we fly to Cuzco, and on to Puerto Maldonado. From there, we travel by boat up the Madre de Dios River into Tambopata National Reserve. Our party on this leg consists of Ben, Andreas, me and our friends and colleagues: Palmiro Ocampo, chef of restaurants Hana y Sumi and 1087 Bistro in Lima, and Malena Martinez, director of Mater Iniciativa, based out of Restaurant Central in Lima, which conducts research to document indigenous Peruvian ingredients and the cultural knowledge that surrounds them. We stay at a midway camp overnight.

The river is wide and light brown and opaque; its repetition, accompanied by the outboard motor, hypnotic. We continue upriver to the research station.

Some hours later, when we arrive, we clamber up the steep, muddy bank and, happy to regain our legs, squelch our way along the slick path a few hundred metres into the forest to the wooden building of the research station. It is all open-air and raised on wooden pylons, with an enormous roof of thatched palm fronds rising out of the clearing. We drop our things.

The National Reserve, which has permitted us to enter, has also arranged for a local man to introduce us to some of the local insects. He is Xenon Yojaje, in Castilian, or Wojaje'e, in Ese'eja, the regional indigenous language. Xenon lives in Palma Real on Madre de Dios, about two hours downriver from Puerto Maldonado, in the opposite direction from us; such is the scale of the landscape that he is considered local. We stay together at the research station.

The afternoon finds us trekking through the forest around the station, getting acquainted with the land and with each other. Xenon is serene, and offers notes on things he knows as we encounter them. We communicate through Malena and Palmiro.

'I am sure we will find some kind of *suri* around here – the larvae that live in the palm. We make traps for them. When a palm is dying or it needs to fall, we cut it down and leave it. We know the beetle will come and lay its eggs. Then, we return a few weeks later, and the larvae are grown and fill the tree. Many people eat them raw – they are good against bronchitis and coughs.'

We transition suddenly into a bamboo grove. Xenon looks through the tall grass, finding sections with bumpy disruptions on their otherwise smooth outer surface, and makes shallow slices into the stems with his machete. He pulls some small *suri* from their bores. 'There are many kinds of *suri* in these forests, and they live in different trees. This kind lives in bamboo. We cook the larvae and adults together, sometimes. There are not so many of these right after the rain, like now. The water floods the bamboo chambers and drowns the larvae, and the beetles can't lay eggs.

'Sometimes, we find bamboo worms inside the bamboo chamber,' he says, slicing through a few stalks that seem likely houses. He shakes the cloven sections and a few translucent larvae fall out.

'I like the palm weevils more,' he says. 'They have a nice texture, more fatty.'

Later, Xenon stops us by a tree. A closer look reveals the trunk and surrounding ground to be active with very large ants. '*Izula*,' he says – the giant hunter ant, or bullet ant (*Paraponera clavata*). 'We feed the eggs to children so they grow big, strong and determined. *Asadito* – lightly grilled. The same with the larvae of the wasp. Years ago, people used to eat the adult ants also, to become stronger. The warriors ate them. That's why they were mean people. If the ants bite you, it can give you a fever. Some people don't care.' We find a few adults carrying larvae, and take them. The larvae have a velvety exterior, thick skin, a robust pop and a bitter taste.

What light does filter down through the canopy to the forest floor is starting to fade. 'We will return tomorrow, and go further,' says Xenon. We get back to the station, and by a dim lamp at a wooden table we eat and talk further with Xenon.

'Well, I grew up poor, so I guess that's why I became a creative eater,' he says. 'I would set bamboo traps for *grillos*, crickets to use for fishing bait,

CLOCKWISE FROM TOP LEFT: 1. *Callampa* mushrooms 2. Fresh heart of palm 3. *Suri juanesitos* 4. Amazonian stingless bee hive

and before baiting, I would take off the legs and eat them. That was strange, even for the people who eat *suri*. Crickets are food for fish.' He laughs gently.

'I have two daughters, twelve and five. They won't try any insect – well, sometimes the five-year-old will, but she barely dares. The TV brings them closer to the city life, and that doesn't really encourage the forest foods. So what should we do? Become an island? I don't know, I am not sure.'

'What is your family's favourite dish, then, Xenon?' I ask him.

'Our family's favourite – and that of our community – is *tacacho*: smashed plantain fried in pork fat. And the pork skin from the jowls. We also like *cecina*, salted dried pork.'

'And the names you gave us before, these were in Castilian?' I ask.

'Yes.'

'What are the names in Ese'eja?'

'The *suri* we call *soso*; the *izula* we call *shemé*; the *grillo* we call *sa'*. Though few people use these names now.'

I awake to a pair of red macaws on the wooden sill, each standing on one leg. In the other they clutch a piece of white bread, which they tear into with their beak. There are crumbs.

We set out and find a ripe palm trap immediately behind the research station. What luck! Xenon's machete bites into the trunk, revealing a criss-cross of tunnels similar to those we saw in Uganda (p.127). The smell is familiar: fruity, then cheesy, with white pepper. The *suri* are large. We collect them into a plastic container with some pulp from inside the tree, and keep them with us for later. The sound, when one puts an ear up to the trunk, is like a pail

gurgling up through mud at the bottom of a deep well.

Five minutes down the path from behind the station, leading inland from the river, Xenon shows us a termite nest built on the trunk of a tree. The termites (*termitas*, or *pachichi* in Ese'eja) are smaller than those we saw in Kenya and Uganda (pp.95–109), including the queen (the *reina* or *pachichiha*). 'The queen's fat is good for coughs,' Xenon says. 'It has a belly alive with fat.'

Within the termite-nest structure, in a clear echo of Tom's termite mound in Uganda (p.108), is a harder core which, when Xenon removes and cuts it open, turns out to be a hive of an Amazonian stingless bee (*bishawajoso* in Ese'eja). The larvae (*ebakua* or *ejá* in Ese'eja) are bitter and not so tasty, but the pollen (*chicha* or *i'áli*) is fermented and sour, and the honey (*miel* or *widi*) is runny, very sweet, fruity and lightly acidic. We take some of the pollen and honey with us as part of our roving pantry.

Today the jungle reveals even more smells. Suddenly we are enveloped in air that smells of garlic. 'The *ajosquiro* tree!' Palmiro exclaims, excited. 'I know this flavour – my father showed me first when I was a child. I have never seen the tree itself before,' he says, looking around. Xenon walks quietly over to a thick trunk and pats it to identify it to us: '*Yopa*.' The wood, in addition to its wet wood smell, bears the strong fragrance of crushed garlic, as do the broad, green, waxy leaves.

Later, we become wrapped in the raunchy, rank, androstenone smell of wild pig. The muddy ground here is particularly turned up. A few minutes later, we hear some grunts and squeals far off.

And, throughout, there are variations in the smells of earth and mud; a brief punctuation of unripe guava skin;

and, at one point, a taste of *cordoncillo* (*Piper aduncum*), known in English as the spiked pepper, which causes our tongues to numb.

Xenon harvests the core of a *paca* palm – the *palmito* – for a snack. It is mildly sweet and crunchy. From another, the *pona*, he harvests the feathery shoot called *chonta*. It is delicate, with an ethereal texture.

Back near the river, we stumble upon a log covered in white, lacy mushrooms, luminous in the dim brush. '*Callampa*, a mushroom; in Ese'eja, it is called *hidei*,' Xenon says, gathering them into a banana leaf. There is also another type on the log, denser ones with a lightly speckled brown cap.

What a rich pantry. Now that we are near the mooring post on the river, Xenon persuades a ranger from the station to take us to an island upriver, where we will be able to light a fire and cook.

We disembark, and pick our way into the island's forest. At an appropriate clearing, we begin collecting dry wood (as dry as we can find), and lay out our pantry on banana leaves: palm *suri* (*Rhynchophorus palmarum*); stingless bee honey and pollen; *ajosquiro* wood and leaf (*Gallesia integrifolia*); *callampas*, the white lacy ones and the thicker brown ones; *sacha culantro*, or 'jungle coriander' (*Eryngium fœtidum*), unrelated but somewhat similar in taste to coriander (cilantro). Palmiro has also brought along some salt, butter, oil and palm sugar from the kitchen at the station, and now sits whittling palm wood into long skewers. Xenon has dragged together some dry brush and begun a fire.

'Xenon, can you show us how you cook the *suri*?' I ask him.

Xenon takes one of Palmiro's skewers, slides it through two of the *suri*, whole, and begins to grill them neat over the flame-lapped wood.

'Can you tell us how you usually use these mushrooms?' I ask.

'The *hidei* are better fried with fat, and the brown ones are better steamed in a leaf. We use them like meat – either alone, or sometimes in a *juane*, with rice together in a leaf package. We can make them *juanesito*!' Xenon's eyes light up.

'In Peru, we add *-ito* to everything. Everything becomes cute, diminuitive,' Malena offers in explanation, a smile playing around her mouth. 'So a *juanesito* is to make in the style of a little *juane*.'

Palmiro takes some *suri*, rubs them with the stingless bee honey and sour pollen, skewers them and grills them with care. I take up Xenon's proposition for *juanesitos*. I pierce the *suri*'s body just above the neck, as we learned to do from Paul on Kalangala Island, Uganda (p.128), and lift out the brown digestive tract. The skin of these palm weevils seems tougher than that of the Ugandan ones; though the same white, fatty flesh spills out of them. I place one each in a broad *ajosquiro* leaf with a few of the white mushrooms and some salt, wrap them up, tie them with grass and nestle them into the ashes at the edge of the fire.

Our clearing has taken on a concentrated layer of smells: sugars and amino acids browning together, smoking woods, dripping fats, herbs exhaling their volatile breath from the heat. Xenon's *suri* roast from their own fat. They are substantial, with a good chew. Palmiro's have a skin that crackles from the extra glaze, the acidity of the pollen cutting through the fat. I retrieve the *juanesitos* from the ash. The outer layers of wrapped leaf have charred; the inner ones are intact. I open them. The smell is lovely, the fresh garlic-tree scent mingling with the mushroom and the fat pooling from the *suri*. The main challenge is the skin. 'They *are* tougher than the Ugandan ones, aren't they?' notes Ben. Palmiro and I get an idea. 'What if we squeeze out the fat, and use it to cook the mushrooms?' We place some more of the white mushrooms into an *ajosquiro* leaf, slice a hole in the *suri*, remove the digestive tract and squeeze the rest onto the mushrooms, tossing them with a bit of salt. We wrap and tie the leaf like the others and place it into the embers. After some minutes, when we can smell the fat and the scent of charring leaf, we pull it out. They are beautiful. The texture of the skin: something to work on more when we return to Lima.

'Hey, you know Josh, we should try out Paul's technique from Kalangala to share with Xenon,' suggests Ben.

'That's a great idea.'

We take the remaining *suri*, gut them, rinse them in a bit of water and toss them in a pot on the fire. The fat begins to render. They stew down. Then comes the magic point where enough moisture has evaporated and enough fat has rendered that they start to sizzle. They begin to brown and crisp.

We remove them from the heat. They continue to sizzle in the pot, which we pass to Xenon. He takes one with an index finger and thumb, smells and eats. A wide, true grin breaks across his face. We all eat them – even Malena, who has been generally hesitant about the whole insect thing, tries a small crispy bit and proclaims it tasty.

It is a good moment. And in some small way, I like to think that we may not only be receiving knowledge, but that we are also able sometimes to share it, bringing with us what we learn and seeing what cross-pollinations may take in different places. I do not presume us to be

causing any significant structural change overnight. But if, when we leave, a part of Paul Mugerwa from Kalangala Island in Lake Victoria, Uganda, stays with Xenon Wojaje'e in Palma Real in Madre de Dios, Peru – in the form of a new way to cook palm weevils, adding a technique to his arsenal, perhaps even one that makes it more likely for his daughters to try and like and develop an edible relationship with them – then maybe I can be naïve enough also to hope that our relationship with Xenon and this place and its community is not simply extractive, reproducing the same neocolonial dynamics we want to address and try to dismantle. In moments like these, where we are all picking caramelized grubs from the same pot with grubby fingers and smiling faces, I let myself believe that new histories may be made, face to face, dyad by dyad, taste by taste.

The hard, gourd-like bowl of the stingless beehive still holds a shallow pool of honey. It comes to close our meal: we pass the bowl around in turn, and the only way to eat it is to drink from it, and the only way to drink from it involves its complete envelopment of one's olfaction. The smell is full, sour, fruity, acetic; the honey is so sweet, warming, almost burning the throat as it goes down.

This is the furthest point on our journey into the Amazon. Every step from here is one back towards the city, towards other places. The other places, like the river in front of us, bearing us back, shrouding us in mist, have also already changed.

— Fieldwork Team: Josh Evans, Andreas Johnsen, Ben Reade. Guide: Malena Martinez, Palmiro Ocampo. Written by Josh Evans

LIMA JAM

———

Whereas some menus list the provenance of their ingredients primarily by place – which is to say, coordinates on the X–Y plane – the menu at Restaurant Central is indexed by altitude. 'Verticality,' chef Virgilio Martinez tells us when we arrive, 'is what defines the geography – and therefore the food – of Peru. So it is also how I think about Peruvian cooking.'

Some of the items on the menu I recognize from our travels; many more I do not. *Huarango. Sacha inchi. Chaco. Choclo, chulpi* and *kculli* corn. Wild *muña. Yacón. Pijuayo* hearts of palm. *Macambo. Aracatha, ayango, maras* salt. *Cañihua, tumbo. Arapaima, huito, airampo.* Tree tomato, *kiwicha. Cushuro, mullaca. Bahuaja* nut, *camu camu, huampo.* Cherimoya, coca leaf, *theobromas.* Stevia, *culen,* sisal. *Algarrobo.* I am thrilled and saturated just to roll their sounds around in my mouth.

There are vegetables, animals, minerals of all kinds; fungi and protists; cyanobacteria that grow into small spheres in pools on plains over 4,000 metres (13,000 feet) above sea level. It is the fruit of much more work than even the labour that takes place in their glass-walled kitchen, of receiving, organizing, processing, storing, preparing and serving the food. There is evidence of many months of research behind these plates, of travel across the country, and most importantly, of many people – holders of knowledge who have chosen to entrust it to Virgilio and his sister, Malena, who document it not just as notes, but as materials arranged on the plate. I get a sense of the meal as a series of field notes, impressions and lessons in ecology, sublimated by pleasure so that one may not even realize one is learning. But the knowledge is there regardless, running in the background.

After the meal, Malena, and Virgilio's wife and head chef of the kitchen, Pía, lead us through the kitchen, the office of Mater Iniciativa, where they document their research, and the rooftop garden where they are growing some of their own plant varieties. There are no insects on the menu; there do not need to be.

Today is our last in Peru, and we spend it cooking with Palmiro, at his restaurant 1087 Bistro in the Miraflores neighbourhood. We have some ideas we want to try out with the *suri,* while we can.

We start at the market, as one must. We encounter a few of the ingredients from Central last night. Many fruits: *Theobroma bicolor (macambo),* in addition to *Theobroma cacao; guanábana,* also known as cherimoya, soursop or custard apple; *aguaje,* a palm fruit; *sapote,* or sapodilla; *pan de árbol,* or breadfruit; *cocona; charapitas,* tiny orange chillies; *cucurma,* or fresh turmeric; *tumbo,* or banana passionfruit. And some herbs: *huacatay (Tagetes minuta,* also known as black mint or southern marigold), like a saucier, more brazen marigold; *chíncho,* related to *huacatay* but more subdued; and *muña (Minthostachys mollis),* also known as Andean mint, with a fittingly minty profile. We get some of everything.

Back at Palmiro's place, he has also secured some *ajosquiro* wood and leaves from one of his star suppliers, some dried *callampas* from the Amazon and *porcón* mushrooms from the Andes, as well as a crate filled with decomposed palm pith and dozens of live *suri*.

'Right! Let's get cooking!' Palmiro says, handing us some whites and aprons. 'What should we make?'

'I want to work on these stuffed *suri* I was trying in Tambopata,' says Ben. 'I have some ideas for it.'

'Great.'

'And Palmiro, I'd love to work with you on some things, if you like,' I say.

'Sure!'

We work throughout the morning and afternoon, inviting Palmiro's parents, brother, wife and daughter to come and taste what we manage to make by 3:00 p.m. Here is what we serve:

Suri panée

Ben's classic French treatment of the *suri*. He cleans and guts them in the Ugandan style, stuffs them with nasturtium flowers, chopped garlic, *muña*, salt and pepper, then breads them in a mixture of boiled and dried red quinoa, breadcrumbs, paprika and fresh thyme leaves. He makes

CLOCKWISE FROM TOP LEFT: **1.** Palm pith, solar infusion and lime **2.** Mushrooms ready for stuffing into *ajosquiro* leaves **3.** Amazon mushroom, *suri* fat and *ajosquiro* leaf **4.** *Suri chicharrones* with *charapita* chilli

a *cocona* salsa, chopping *cocona* fruit, *charapita* chilli and *huacatay*, and mixing them together with a bit of salt. He makes tiny onion rings, battered and deep-fried, then adds crushed garlic and thyme to the neutral frying oil, deep-fries the *suri panée* until golden, and drains them on a paper towel. He plates it with the *cocona* salsa, stacks the onion rings in a small tower that calls to mind the ribbed skin of the *suri*, and garnishes the plate with blanched, dried and deep-fried corn silk; watercress; romaine hearts brushed with a dressing of neutral oil, honey and lime juice; *ajosquiro* wood cream; and borage flowers.

Palm pith, solar infusion and lime

Palmiro and I make a small snack to refresh the palate. In addition to using the *suri*, we want to try using the fresh pith of the palms in which they live, which has a very particular, sweet, resinous scent, and a porous, crunchy texture. Palmiro already has a solar infusion of cacao fruit and saffron on hand. This is how he made it: he cut open the *Theobroma* pod, scooped out the beans and rubbed the fruity flesh off each one. He then mixed 20 grams of the flesh, 1 gram of saffron and 380 grams of filtered water into a clear glass bottle, covered the opening with a cloth, and left it in direct sunlight for two and a half weeks. Then he strained the infusion into another bottle and kept it in the refrigerator. We cut small, thin squares of the palm pith and seal them on full vacuum with the solar infusion, more fresh cacao fruit flesh, honey, salt, lime flesh and zest. We only manage to infuse them for a few hours; next time, we would like to do it for much longer – at least twenty-four hours – to allow them to really take up the flavour.

To serve, we cut small slices of lime flesh and place one on top of each square of pith, leaning against the cacao beans and sprinkled with some lime zest.

Suri chicharrones with *charapita* chilli

This is an attempt to take the chewy *suri* skins in a new direction. We gut and clean the *suri* in the Ugandan style, and remove the heads. We scrape out the fatty inner flesh and reserve it for another dish. Then, with a small sharp knife, we turn the *suri* skins so that they unravel into a long coil, blanch them in salted water and seal in a vacuum bag with chopped fresh turmeric. (Again, we are only able to marinate them for a few hours, and next time we would hope to do it for a day, so that they really take on the flavour and the gorgeous turmeric colour.) Then we remove them, stretch them out into their coils and dehydrate them for a few hours.

Once dry, we remove the skins from the dehydrator and deep-fry them in neutral oil heated to 180°C (350°F). They puff quickly, like *chicharrón* made with pork skin – the dish's inspiration. We remove them from the oil and let them drain on paper towels.

Then we remove the seeds and stems from a few of the *charapita* chillies, and cut them into thin, curved slices. To serve, we lay down a few flat pieces of *ajosquiro* wood, char them with a blowtorch until they smoke, and scatter the '*suricharrones*' and the thin slices of chilli across the aromatic, burning wood.

With a bit more time, we could also have made a simple emulsion with a purée of the chillies and an egg yolk blended with a neutral oil, to dip the *suricharrones* into. It did help to turn the chewy skins into a crunchy snack, and even more marinating and drying time would make them even better.

Amazon mushrooms, *suri* fat and *ajosquiro* leaf

This is our chance to recreate the mushrooms steamed with *suri* fat in the *ajosquiro* leaf we tested in Tambopata, now with a bit more precision. In preparation, Palmiro has already cold-infused some *ajosquiro* bark into cow's cream in a vacuum bag in the refrigerator for forty-eight hours. We strain the cream and whip it cold, until thick. This is also the cream Ben uses to garnish his *suri panée*.

Then we heat the *suri* fat, reserved from the *suricharrones*, so that it renders, then strain it and let it cool to room temperature. We rehydrate some of the Amazonian *callampas* and Andean *porcónes*, drain them, chop them finely, mix them with the rendered *suri* fat and salt, wrap the mixture in fresh *ajosquiro* leaves, tie them with string and steam them briefly. We serve them warm, untied, the leaf forming a bowl, garnished with the *ajosquiro* cream and small leaves of *huacatay* and *chíncho*.

Ajosquiro cream, Amazon mushroom and *suri* crumble

The mushroom dish above is simple and rustic. Palmiro plates up a more refined version, with a few extra components:

We use the same *ajosquiro* wood cream, but whip it a little more, into a thick foam. Palmiro also remixes the Ugandan stew-till-crisp method into another way to use the *suri*: he removes the heads and intestines, separates the fat from the skin, seals them together in a vacuum bag and confits them at 78°C (172°F) for three hours. Afterwards, he decants off the fat (to use for cooking the mushrooms), slices the skins into pieces and fries them in the remaining fat, removing them when brown and crisp. He seasons them with salt and places them in the dehydrator until crunchy.

We use some of the rehydrated mushrooms, and braise them in the remaining *suri* fat. And then a few extra garnishes. Palmiro quick-pickles some *charapita* chillies whole in a basic, sweetened vinegar brine, then strains out the chillies, removes the stems and seeds, slices them into curved pieces and lets the excess moisture dry off at room temperature.

The dried *callampa* mushrooms he dehydrates until completely dry and brittle, blends into a fine powder and sifts through a small sieve, to remove any larger bits.

And one of my favourites of the day: 'queso' of *pan de* árbol. Palmiro washes the *pan de* árbol with cold water, dries them with a cloth and roasts them in the oven at 170°C (338°F) for at least forty minutes. Once he removes them from the oven, he lets them cool and peels them – at which point he can grate the concentrated flesh, which comes to look and taste quite like a hard cheese.

To assemble the dish, he spoons a small amount of the *ajosquiro* cream onto a plate, and lets it spread into a circle. He places small pieces of the braised mushrooms, curved triangles of the pickled *charapita* chillies and the smallest *huacatay* leaves onto the cream, followed by the smallest petals of bougainvillea flowers and a dusting of the *callampa* powder. To one side of the cream, he sprinkles a line of *suri* crumble and grated *queso de pan de* árbol from one edge of the plate to the other – a chord of salt and fat and crunch.

Suri skins with soursop, herbs and flowers

A dessert inspired by the herbs, fruits and flowers of Peru's many landscapes. We run out of time to make this one properly, but with a bit more work it would be great.

We gut and clean the *suri*, remove the heads and reserve the fat for the mushroom dishes. We splay the skins, then blanch, dry, deep-fry and drain them.

We juice the *tumbo* fruit, strain and thicken it lightly with a touch of xanthan gum, then brush the interior of the empty cacao pod, whose fruit we use for the solar infusion, with the thickened, orange juice.

We purée the *guanábana*, strain and thicken it lightly with a touch of xanthan, then fill the deep-fried *suri* skins with the white, thickened purée. We place the filled *suri* skins around the hollow *Theobroma* pod and garnish with *muña* leaves and flowers, *clavelina* flowers and grated *pan de* árbol.

When we make this dish again, we will seal the blanched, splayed skins in a vacuum bag with dried hibiscus flowers, honey and a small amount of water, cook at 60°C (140°F) for one hour then let them rest at room temperature to infuse for a few more hours, then strain out the skins and dehydrate them before deep-frying – for a better texture, a brighter, fruitier flavour and a nicer colour.

After our little tasting – and useful feedback from Palmiro's family, on further ways to deal with the skin (could we ferment it somehow? Break it down enzymatically? Soften it in its own potent digestive juices?) – Palmiro makes us sit down to lunch. He cooks for us for hours, serving us dishes from his menu and ideas he is still working on, and only lets us leave, after weighing us down with gifts, when our flight departure grows imminent.

'*Muchas gracias* for this time, my friends,' he says. 'I learned much with you, and I hope you made good research and enjoyed your time in Peru. Until we meet again!'

— Fieldwork Team: Josh Evans, Andreas Johnsen, Ben Reade. Guide: Palmiro Ocampo. Written by Josh Evans.

INSECTS TO FEED THE WORLD

Marieke Calis picks us up at the station and drives us to her family home.

'Our company name, Kreca, comes from *krekels*, the Dutch for "cricket", and "Calis", our family name,' Marieke's mother Margot tells us, as she lays out bread, butter, cheese and cold cuts on the kitchen table. Marieke brews tea. 'I started rearing crickets thirty-five years ago, mainly for pet food,' Margot continues. 'The government has become more and more interested in helping us grow. Now, we work with many kinds: mealworms, morio worms [superworms], buffalo worms, house crickets, bandit crickets, African field crickets – oh, I don't like them, monkeys do though, it's the smell of chimpanzee – a couple types of cockroach, fruit flies – a wingless GM one and another called 'curlyflies', bred to have curly wings – wax-moth larvae, sun beetles. We have reared migratory locusts in the past, but we don't breed them in-house. Of all these kinds, we now produce, in total, several tonnes a week.

'We are interested now in focusing on insects for human food. I think there are lots of people who want to eat them, but are scared to prepare them. I don't think the whole world will eat insects and normal meat will go away. But insects will be a part of it.

'We have started freeze-drying them when we have many; they keep a long time – for one year, for pet food. For human consumption, we blanch them in boiling water beforehand, to get rid of any potential unwanted microbes.

Though with freeze-drying for human food, oxidation of lipids is more of a problem.

'A challenge is still the legislation. There are a few countries that allow insects for human consumption – Belgium allows ten species, and the Netherlands four – but in the EU in general, it is a grey area. No one knows exactly where to put it. So every country sort of has its own approach. We hope the conference [Insects to Feed the World, hosted by Wageningen University and the United Nations Food and Agriculture Organization (FAO) in Ede, which we went to the Netherlands to attend] will push things further.

'The longer I do this, the more I appreciate that an insect is not an insect. Not everyone raises a cricket the same way, and it makes a difference. We are trying for a higher level for humans; there are stricter rules for hygiene, for example, but it is worth it.'

'What about insect welfare?' Ben asks.

'We contacted Dutch welfare groups and they said, "What's the problem?"' says Margot. 'It's hard to know, I think. Right now we freeze them, which is like in nature here – that is how they die when winter comes. And they have cold blood, so I don't think it causes pain. But it is hard to know for sure.

'How about Marieke shows you the farm?' she concludes.

Behind the house was a series of buildings, semicircular in cross-section.

'So, I will show you some of our

operation. There are some parts that are open, and some other parts I can't show, of course,' Marieke says to us.

'That is fine,' we assure her.

'Here you see the crickets – we have designed a special water dispenser for them. I can let you see it, but no pictures please.'

The rearing boxes are kept in vertical racks when in use, and are stackable when not. The ones in use are each filled with corrugated-cardboard egg cartons or collapsible cardboard packing grids, some dry feed, a fresh carrot and the special water dispenser. The chirping is deafening. The sides of the boxes are smooth so that the crickets cannot climb out.

'Can you ever shut them up?' Ben asks.

'No … if they are too cold they don't chirp, though. But then, we would make them warmer.

'The insects go to each other – they naturally congregate. So we have to pay attention to it. Concentration affects size and growth rate. Too high a concentration makes a greater variety of sizes, and it takes them longer to grow. Though mealworms always grow up with different sizes, we find. Maybe the eggs are not laid at the same time.'

'And what do you feed them all?' Ben asks.

'Different things. All breeders have their own feed, both from different suppliers and their own blends. For some we use cornmeal, also used for chicken feed. We used to use wheat bran, but it is no longer suitable for livestock – the nutrients are not available enough. For some, like the crickets, we can use the carbon in waste paper. The wax-moth larvae we feed only honey, with some cornmeal.'

The more we have worked with different insects from different breeders and rearers, the more what Margot said has become clear: a cricket is not a cricket is not a cricket. In principle, this is somewhat obvious; one would be hard-pressed to say that industrially farmed Danish pork tastes and cooks the same as an organically or biodynamically raised pig, even of the same breed. But in practice, we also have to get to know the range of tastes – those that exist and those that are possible – of these organisms in particular. We gain visceral knowledge of these differences by tasting, and understanding how these differences in taste arise is of great importance for bringing farmed insects to a high level of quality – if that is the goal.

'Have you worked at all on using different feeds to enhance the flavour?' I ask Marieke.

'Well, we did a bit of work in 2002 on gut-loading insects to get nutrients into larger animals via the insects' feed. But it is hard, because one must control for the age and variety of insect, whether and how it has been purged [kept without food before killing to empty the digestive tract], and so on. No one is really focusing on it.'

'Do you breed your own crickets?' Ben asks her.

'Yes – we have a breeding stock and a sale stock. After they've laid eggs, they have used energy, so are lower quality, with less protein. So we make sure to sell them before they lay.'

'And do you breed selectively?'

'No, it takes time. That is its own project. There needs to be more knowledge about it, like there is for pigs and chickens.'

Marieke takes us to another room, where a woman is using a large machine to sort morio worms from the soil they live in. 'Even with mechanization, there will have to be people who regulate, watch, maintain, control. Currently we employ ten people full time, and fifteen part-time students. Three of the full-timers are mentally handicapped, and the government gives us a benefit as a social enterprise.' The woman using the machine empties a tray into a square funnel that sifts the finer dirt from the larvae, which then travel down a metal chute and into a crate, which has a grate at the bottom that filters out any larger debris. Most of the larvae are yellow with brown stripes, punctuated by a few that are near-white. 'These are ones that are moulting,' Marieke says, following my eyes. 'Their new skin is soft and white.'

We go into another room, warm and stuffy. 'This is where we grow and rear many of our species,' Marieke says 'We keep it at 30°C [80°F]. Then, for holding and selling, we transfer them to the 15°C [59°F] room, one day before or the day of sale – any more, and they lose fluid and weight. These temperatures are published knowledge. The mealworms we keep at 6°C [43°F] as they keep better cooler.'

There are all sorts of smells throughout the rooms. A long tunnel of morio worms (*Zophobas morio*) smells like old whole-wheat-bread crusts; the room of sun beetles (*Pachnoda butana*) smells musky and alluring, like castoreum (an extract from beavers' castor sacs used in perfumery) and rose. The sun-beetle larvae are curious creatures: placed on a flat surface, they skittle around on their sides in wide, wiggling loops. 'These ones, the adults, are mainly for big lizards and big birds – so far,' Marieke tells me.

'Have you ever had any problems with diseases?' Ben asks.

'There was one time, almost twenty years ago, when our crickets got a virus. There was no cure. The only thing we could do was kill them all, clean everything down very, very well, wait a bit and start again, with a new breeding stock with the most resistance. Vets didn't know about insect pathogens – most still don't really know as much as they do with other animals. But we are starting to get vets who specialize in insect pathogens and diseases. As for parasites, reared insects rarely have any, as long as they are raised well.

'We don't use any hormones or antibiotics here, though. Some other breeders, for example, rear giant mealworms by using growth and anti-pupation hormones on regular *Tenebrio molitor*. We tried it once, but the growth hormones prevented full development to adults in other species as well, which of course interfered with breeding and rearing!'

In another room, Marieke shows us the cockroaches. 'There are two species – you can see the differences – but we just can't keep them apart! They seem to prefer it that way, though, so even if it's a bit of chaos in the system, we're OK with it. They do have a very fascinating way of laying eggs: they have an 'egg tray', a growth that they extend out the back of their body. They let it dry out, then take it back into their body. Then the eggs hatch inside and they give birth to live cockroach babies.

'The children love to see the cockroaches with the egg tray. We work with children's programmes and they can come visit and see. You have to teach children that milk comes from a cow, and not from the supermarket, you know? You have to teach them where food comes from, whether it is milk or a cabbage or a cricket. Teach them what the cycles are. We need to show how it works – that it's an insect and not just proteins. The people who have already been buying many of our insects in the past for their pets, even they don't know where their live insects come from. So education is very important, and keeping our minds open to different people's needs.'

What Marieke says makes me think of a certain tension at play here. On the one hand, we want eaters to have closer, more direct relationships with where their food comes from; we want to encourage people to see not just 'protein', but the whole insect. On the other hand, one could say that the entire rationale of the kitchen is to transform organisms into forms that are deemed more appetizing, more edible, and often these processes involve changing the form of the organism into something else: abstracting and moving away from the whole organism. Is it possible to do both?

We loop back around to the house. Margot comes back into the kitchen.

'So, Margot, Marieke,' Ben says. 'Your operation is thriving. You are expanding. Where do you think all this can go from here? Is it mass production, global export?'

'It might happen, but we are so busy that I'm not busy with that kind of thought,' Margot responds.

'I suppose it is a possibility, with something that's emerging so fast, that one could very easily design a system that is completely unsustainable with a very sustainable insect,' Ben continues.

'Are people not more conscious of the fact that we can't go on as we are now?' Margot poses to the rest of us.

'The people in power at many companies are often more conscious of their ability to make huge amounts of money and manipulate the situation,' Ben replies.

There is a reflective silence at the table.

'What are you going to cook with?' Margot asks us.

'I would really like to cook with some of the sun beetles,' Ben says.

'Do you like to cook with it?'

'I have never cooked with it. And I'd like to cook with all of these things,' Ben continues, pointing at some containers of insects on the kitchen counter.

'Oh, it's OK, you are welcome to. We will bring you some tomorrow,' Margot says.

'Thank you very much for today, Margot and Marieke,' Ben concludes, 'for being such kind hosts and for showing us your farm.'

It is the day before the conference begins. Ben and I take over Foodcase, a research kitchen at Wageningen University, where they develop recipes for aeroplane food. We are going to cook some dishes with the insects Margot and Marieke have given us, and we invite some friends to come over later to serve as our tasting panel: Paul Rozin, a psychologist known as the 'grandfather of disgust', who will be speaking at the conference and who is also on our advisory board for this project; Chris Münke, a German friend from Copenhagen who worked with the FAO's Non-wood forest products section that published the 2013 'Edible insects' report; and Emily Anthes, an American journalist who is writing a long-form piece about the state of the art of insect-eating.

We lay out our ingredients and start prepping. 'Check this out,' Ben says from the stove. 'It was just released onto the animal-feed market last week. It's the fractioned fat from black soldier fly larvae. I think they'll be the first people in the history of the world to eat this.'

We cook for a few hours and set a few aeroplane-meal trays with the food in small rectangular dishes. Once our guests arrive, we put on some spare flight stewardess uniforms (skirts in royal-blue polyester with white trim, and hats to match) and wheel out the meals in a tall, narrow aeroplane-meal dispensary.

'So,' Ben begins, 'we have a selection of aeroplane meals for you all. We've got chicken here with garlic-saffron sauce, that's been crumbed with buffalo worms.'

'The drink is based on chia seeds,' I continue. 'It has cucumber, basil and a salt made from two different developmental stages of locust.'

'And then here is dung grub stew, made with the larvae of sun beetles and served with plantain chips.'

'There are two salads: one with tomatoes, sliced shallots and ground crickets, and the other, an endive filled with avocado and crispy mealworms.'

'We have some surf 'n' turf arthropod tempura – shrimp with house crickets in the batter – served with grasshopper-garum dipping sauce.'

'And a tabbouleh with freeze-dried desert locusts.'

'And soy milk, of course.'

'And finally, noodles fried in black-soldier-fly-larvae fat. I believe you're the first human beings on the planet to have ever been served anything cooked with this.'

'Please eat.'

The meal becomes the background for a lively discussion. Different eaters tackle the aeroplane meal differently. It is fascinating to observe.

'To be honest,' Ben declares, after some of the plates begin to empty and others are passed around, 'after travelling all around the world eating insects everywhere, I think all the farmed insects lack *flavour*. So, I think all of this has been more an exercise in how we can slip them into cooking, rather than how can we utilize their actual characteristics.'

I agree that this has been the primary exercise. Though I wonder about farming more generally. Surely we have

tasted some flavourful farmed insects – Monica's crickets in Kenya come to mind (pp.113–5), and Mzee's semi-cultivated tobacco crickets (pp.116–19). Insect-farming practices right now may not be focused much on flavour, but what if they were? What would it take to make a truly tasty farmed insect, and which species would be most viable? If we can farm delicious vegetables and fruits and fungi and raise delicious mammals, it seems suspect to think it would not also be possible with these smaller animals.

'What's in here, again?' Paul asks, pointing to the dung grub stew.

'These are sun-beetle larvae. You make a hole in their tail end and then squidge out all the black stuff.'

'Each larva?'

'Out of each larva, painstakingly –'

'They're good,' Paul interjects 'I like this texture. They're chewy, but they have a little … the chitin … I like these. And, you know, if Pepsi-Cola or someone like that gets into this business, they'll find a way to de-dirt them automatically.'

'And would that be your hope?' Ben follows up immediately.

'My hope here is that … I'm actually talking with some people at Pepsi-Cola,' Paul continues.

'Really?'

'Because they make Fritos. If you could replace ten per cent of the corn flour in Fritos with insect flour, nobody would even notice.'

'Who would it benefit?' Ben asks pointedly.

'Everyone will be better off if we eat a fair amount of insects in our lives,' says Paul. 'I mean, except the insects maybe – but even them, because there'll be more of them.'

Over these past three days we have attended the Insects to Feed the World conference, hosted by Wageningen University and the FAO in Ede. The conference has brought together more than 500 people from academia, industry and other sectors, to discuss and identify further directions for work on insects for food and feed.

We attended a range of talks that touch on interactions between scientific and indigenous knowledges, opportunities and challenges in mass production, medicinal values of insects, children and insect consumption, taxonomy problems, semi-cultivation and agro-ecology, zoonosis and genetic diversity in insect diseases, critical approaches to food security, fractionating insects into products for different industries, colonialism and cultural imperialism, and some surprises of sensory science. Needless to say, it has been fascinating to observe and interact with so many different people with different priorities, goals and hopes for edible insects.

One of these people was a student named Charlotte Payne who is doing research in Japan. She was helping her colleagues in the Japanese Vespula Society present tastes of *hobazushi* – rice with Japanese wasps, shiitake mushrooms and bamboo shoots, wrapped in a magnolia leaf (*hoba* in Japanese). We started talking, and she invited us to come and do fieldwork with her (pp.187–93).

Ben and I also had the opportunity to give an oral presentation on some of our fieldwork, entitled 'Taste first: Deliciousness as an argument for entomophagy', and during the evening cocktail hour on 15 May we also gave a short introduction to our work by serving tasters of Grasshopper Garum (pp.214–15) and Bee Larvae Ceviche (pp.240–41) to the

more than 500 conference participants. A favourite quip from our short talk, from Ben: 'If the food we're feeding people tastes like cardboard, we've got a real serious problem. What we need to do is make sure that everyone has the right not only to food, but to good-tasting, culturally appropriate and available food.'

But one of our most telling exchanges happened on the last day. During the lunch break, there were some stands around the perimeter of the room, and Ben struck up a conversation with a man at one of them who was presenting a company developing insect feed for animals – the same one from which he obtained the black soldier fly larvae fat we used at Foodcase.

'So at the moment it's mined purely for animals?' Ben asked.

'Yeah, yeah,' the man replied genially.

'OK.'

'At the moment.'

'But do you have a vision for human consumption?'

'Of course, of course, why not? But it's not allowed by European legislation at the moment.'

'So, like a tin of cat food, you might try to stick some black soldier-fly fat in it?'

'Yeah, why not?' The man started to look a little uncomfortable.

'Yeah, why not? I mean, if the cats like it, you know.' Ben started to grin. 'If it's good for the cat, it's good for the fly – ah, no, it's not good for the fly.'

The man laughed in a way that could be called nervous. 'No, no, no.'

'How does it smell? Can I smell it?' Ben grabbed a plastic container of the black soldier fly protein powder.

'No, it doesn't smell.'

Ben took a good whiff. 'Yeah, it smells.'

'Yeah …'

'Yeah, it smells.'

'I smell money.'

'Sorry? You smell money.' Now it was Ben's turn to laugh nervously. Each of them smiled, looking down, past each other.

'Smells like money,' Ben repeated.

Later that afternoon, during a poster session (at which attendees presented their research on posters hung up around the room), one poster in particular caught our eye. Its title was 'Entomophagy and Capitalism', in black text emblazoned on a gold background, with a silhouette of a grasshopper filled with euro coins. The author, Andrew Müller, was standing next to it, answering questions.

'And what do you like? Which insects?' Andrew asked Ben.

'Honey ants, termite queens, palm weevils ... but farmed insects, I'm not really into them,' said Ben.

'OK,' Andrew replied.

'There seems to be a little bit of a risk of people using the publicly perceived sustainability aspect or low carbon footprint or however we'd like to put it in order to just make mass amounts of money.'

'In the worst case, maybe, yeah,' Andrew said thoughtfully. 'I stayed in Laos and Thailand for about ten months, and my main aim at the beginning was just to see how it tasted and how it was collected and prepared and everything. But during this time I also noticed entomophagy is not always a good thing. Some people told me that 100 tonnes per day are being sold at this market' – he pointed to a photo on his poster – 'and there are people actually earning a lot of money. But it's not these people.' He pointed to the photo next to it, of many people huddled over woven baskets, tearing off wings and legs.

'No,' Ben concurred.

'And that's why I'm sort of very ambivalent about what's happening here,' Andrew continued. 'Because on the one hand, there is attention and people are thinking about the whole thing, but of course there are big companies present here as well. I heard that Nestlé is.'

'I'm sure they're not the only ones,' said Ben.

'I don't know if they're really interested in these people,' Andrew said.

'I don't think they're interested in these people,' Ben affirmed. 'I think they're smelling money.'

— Lab Team: Josh Evans, Andreas Johnsen, Ben Reade. Written by Josh Evans.

LIVØ

Today I meet with a BSc student, Annette Hjorthøj Jensen, who has done work for her bachelor's thesis on managing the cockchafer (*Melolontha melolontha*) as an agricultural pest with fungal biocontrol on the island of Livø in Limfjorden, in north-west Denmark. We sit on the deck of the boat and she gives me some background on the island and the insects, to prepare me before we go ourselves. After all our fieldwork around the world, it makes sense that we try to further investigate viable insects to eat in Denmark, beyond the bee brood from Copenhagen (pp.84–6) and the ants we forage from nearby forests (pp.87–9).

'The island is 320 hectares, and has been organic for fifty years,' Annette tells me. 'It is currently under the control of the Nature Agency, under the Ministry of the Environment, and is run as a research site for organic agriculture, because of its isolated location in the fjord. Karsten Kjærgaard is the farmer who lives on the island with his family. He runs the farm and has been there for ten years.

'The *oldenborrer* – how do you say in English?'

'Cockchafers.'

'Right – they have only really been a problem at all since the island went organic. Before that, they were kept away by the pesticides. But it's especially in the last five years that their population has increased significantly. Two years ago, 50 per cent of the grain yield was lost.'

'That's pretty serious!'

'Yes. The larvae live in the topsoil for three years, and they eat the roots of the grain grasses. The adult beetle lives in the trees that surround the fields, eating the leaves. They lay their eggs in May and June, and the larvae hatch and begin to grow. They dig down into the soil and hibernate over the winter, then grow more during the second and third summers. They pupate in the fourth summer, and hatch as adults the following spring, and the cycle begins again. Normally with the cockchafer, you see a *flyvår* – the year where the local population all emerge together – but on Livø, there are multiple populations, so some emerge every year.

'The larvae tend to be more of a problem in central Europe, where there is a lot of cereal cultivation. They might have become a problem on Livø because they have no natural predators there, like moles. When are you going?'

'Mid-June.'

'I'm sure you'll find some,' Annette affirms. 'Try digging close to the hedgerows – the beetles tend not to fly too far from the trees. The adults are most active at dawn and dusk, but during the day they stay in the trees. You can try to find some of them also!'

It is a pretty trip to Livø from Copenhagen. Ben, Roberto, Andreas and I meet at the rental car at 6:00 a.m. and drive up to Rønbjerg, where we will catch the ferry over to Livø. In the meantime we eat lunch, smoked fish from a shack on the wharf. Andreas has also brought his six-year-old son Midas and Midas' mother, Ranee Udtumthisarn, along for the trip. Ranee is from northeast Thailand and is chef of her own Thai restaurant in Copenhagen. In addition to being a good friend, she is coming so we can cook some bugs together. She arrives at the car with woven baskets for steaming sticky rice, a bag of ingredients and a very excited Midas hanging off her arm.

The trip comes at a transitional moment: Ben is about to leave the lab at the end of this month. He's been here for two years, and he's ready to go back to Edinburgh to start his own project, Edinburgh Food Studio. Roberto, meanwhile, came to the lab as an intern in February (after we met in Sardinia, pp.92–4), and has stayed since. When Ben announced he was leaving, we thought Roberto would make a fine head chef. So it is a significant trip, and our only chance to all work together in the field.

We are the ferry's only passengers. Once on Livø, we walk from the dock down a narrow paved road to a central cluster of buildings. The road is unimaginably aromatic: beach roses, St John's wort, mugwort, elderflower – a riot of everything in bloom. We drop our things at the island's guest house and set off further down the road towards the farm.

CLOCKWISE FROM TOP LEFT: 1. A cockchafer larva 2. Bente's bees 3. Lovage flutes and a bowl of *nam prik maeng da* 4. The steaming pot

The farm lies at the end of the road. The farm buildings and house enclose a wide, cobbled courtyard, with large linden trees that fill the space.

The only person home is Emilie, the daughter of Karsten and his wife, Bente. She takes us out to the back garden and opens some home-brewed beer. It has notes of wax and honey, little sweetness and a lingering flavour of lovage. We tell her what we're doing, while we pick white strawberries from the garden, ripe and soft, with an intense aroma of tropical fruits. She tells us a myth of how Livø was formed: two young trolls in love, throwing stones to each other across the fjord.

After a little while, Karsten returns. 'Shall we go out to the fields, and I can show you where to dig?' he asks. He leads us to the barn. We grab some shovels and follow him down a dirt road, cutting through the fields. Emilie comes along.

'In addition to being a public, organic, agricultural research station, we also use the island as a demonstration farm for old varieties of cereals,' Karsten tells us. 'These fields on the left are all old kinds of barley, and on the right is a kind of rye called *svedjerug*.

'It is a small island, but it has all the Danish nature types: dunes, forest, fields, beach, swamp. But this also means that Livø has the perfect conditions if you are a cockchafer – the adults like the oak trees in the hedgerows, and the larvae like roots of cereal crops. Livø has just the right mix.'

'And no moles,' I say.

'Right, no moles. There is 20–40 cm (8–16 inches) of topsoil in most places though, with clay underneath. During the winter, they tend to stay around the soil–clay barrier, but now that it is warmer, they have probably moved up. So we should find a few at least.'

Just before another road leads off to the right, Karsten brings us into the field. 'You can see in these recently planted fields that the grass is shorter in some patches. This is often where the larvae are most active. The more they eat the roots, the more it stunts the growth of the grass.' He digs his shovel into the field, levers up a block of soil and tips it onto its side. We start looking through the tangled roots for signs of the larvae. Karsten does a few more. 'Here's one,' he says, holding out his palm. The larva has an orange head and arms and a curious hooked shape, the end of its abdomen exaggerated, brown beneath the translucent skin.

We dig some more, but we only find a couple. We replace the soil and Karsten leads us back to the road. 'I will take you down to the south field, where last year there were the most. This year it is laying fallow, but you may find some still.'

At the end of the road, we curve to the left down a path cut in the grass between trees and a field of mature *svedjerug*. The rye is tall, sometimes almost as tall as Ben and me. We glimpse the water of the fjord over the swelling heads of the grass. The path curves to the left, cutting through the hedgerow, and we find ourselves at the edge of another field – much wider and without crops, sloping all the way down to the water.

We begin to dig. 'Make sure you replace any soil you dig up. So it doesn't wreck the tractor,' says Karsten.

'Thanks, we will!' I assure him.

Karsten and Emilie walk back across the field towards the lane. We spend the rest of the afternoon digging. Any larvae we unearth we keep in a plastic container with soil. By the time the sun has begun to shine we have found seventeen. We make sure our divots are replaced and head back towards the farmhouse.

This morning, serendipitously, Bente harvests drone brood (pp.87–9) from some of the island's beehives. She gives it to us to use.

Karsten has let us make a firepit in a field just beyond the fence near the farmhouse, which we dig right near a large stump – a perfect pre-existing work surface. Roberto and I gather flowers to use from around the field, and together with Ranee, we lay out the ingredients we have brought. Roberto gets the fire going.

After taking one cockchafer larva as a sample, we have sixteen left. 'Well, shall we split them evenly?' says Ben.

'You two can use them if you like – I'll work with the bee larvae,' I say.

'Right then, eight each,' Ben says, nodding to Roberto.

The taste of the beer Emilie served us yesterday stayed with me. It was particular and very tasty. That, and the fresh drone brood Bente has given us, make me think of the white, jasmine-like flowers blooming everywhere, and the enormous lovage plant in the garden.

On one side of the fire, Ranee is grilling small fish, marinated pork and giant water bugs (*Lethocerus indicus*) she has brought along. On the other, Roberto has got a pot of water simmering, and is blending sweetcorn, breadcrumbs, nasturtium and the gutted cockchafers in a small food processor powered by a pull-crank.

'Cool tool. What are you doing with that?' I ask.

'You will see,' he says, smiling.

We also try wrapping small pieces of brood comb in fig leaves from the Kjærgaards' garden, steaming them over the pot and cooking them in the ash, which reminds me of our Amazon cookout (p.168). The smell as they char is lovely, but the wax melts, as we suspected it might. The few that we can pick out are very flavourful, but most collapse into a molten mess and aren't so edible after that.

Meanwhile, Roberto has moulded his corn mixture back into the corn husk, closed it and tied it with a bit of husk. It looks very much like an unwrapped ear of corn. He places it on a bed of field flowers, lovage leaves and halved red onions, shovels smouldering embers from the fire overtop and buries the lot under dirt. 'Now we wait,' he says. Ranee is making *nam prik maeng da*, chilli paste with Thai giant water bug, and we take turns helping her pound the mixture of garlic, ginger, galangal, chillies and grilled fish with her pestle and mortar.

Ben has made two tastes with the cockchafers, both miniatures – single bites on small spoons. 'The cockchafers reminded me of the dung-beetle larvae we tasted in Kenya, where they squidged out the brown bit at the end and toasted them till crisp,' he explains. 'They tasted grassy. The lady who showed us had thistles growing in her garden; I remember showing her how one can peel off the skin and eat the stems. So, this first one is toasted cockchafer with thistles, brown cheese and cornflower.'

'The second one is more fun: fried cockchafer with pineapple, *gochujang* I made, and a reduction of Irn-Bru, often known as Scotland's other national drink – after whisky of course. That's just from stuff I like that I had on hand.'

The thistle one especially brings out the particular texture of the cockchafer larvae, both crunchy and chewy, with the dense thistle and the thick brown cheese – a Nordic favourite made by reducing vast amounts of whey until it caramelizes and gets dark and potent.

Roberto digs up his corn. The trompe l'oeil effect is achieved, but we agree that the larvae flavour, already mild, is buried.

It could be nice to try with more of them. The idea is good though: cooking them in the ground whence they came.

We sit around the stump, eating sticky rice and *nam prik*, grilled pork and winged beans with our hands. The *nam prik* is so aromatic and so flavourful, the giant water bug adding an unmistakable chord of something like concentrated watermelon candy. Or, of giant water bug.

We take the ferry back late that afternoon. Only seventeen larvae. It is not the first time we have had challenges of small amounts on fieldwork – so much depends on season, weather, and being in the right place at the right time, and one cannot get abundance every time. But our short time on Livø had me thinking all the drive home about a question with which we started this whole project: why don't we already eat insects in Denmark, or even, shall we say, in 'the West'?

Many people have proposed answers to this question, and increasingly many are interested in them. But it strikes me that one of the biggest reasons might be because nowadays, there really aren't that many insects (p.30). One of our collab-orators, Jørgen Eilenberg, professor of insect pathology and biological control at the University of Copenhagen, tells us that there is still quite high species diversity in Denmark; there just aren't such high numbers, even if there used to be. We chose high-seed-yielding grasses over the insects that compete with us for them. Could we make a system where we can have both?

Asking why Danes or Europeans or Westerners do not eat insects is a good question, but maybe not because it can or should help make everyone change their eating habits overnight. It need not lead to us newcomers all eating insects – but if it starts a conversation about the kinds of landscapes we make and the kinds we want to make, the kinds of agriculture we practice and the kinds we want to practice, then I think it will have achieved something much deeper and, in the short run and the long, much more important.

— Fieldwork Team: Ben Reade, Josh Evans, Roberto Flore, Andreas Johnsen. Written by Josh Evans

HEBO

We arrive in Kushihara after dark and a couple of hours' drive north-east from Nagoya, up into the mountains. Charlotte Payne, an English researcher based in Kushihara and our host while we are here, has us meet her at her kabuki practice at the village community centre. The kabuki club insists we share a break. They make us sencha and we eat rice crackers and mandarin oranges.

When they resume, Charlotte ducks out and shows us, in our rental car, to where we're staying. 'Daisuke and Shoko are really excited to have you,' she tells us, pointing us through the winding roads until we arrive at a wooden house surrounded by tall pines, with lights on in the windows.

'Welcome, welcome!' Shoko Miyake says, beckoning to us from the door. Daisuke Miyake comes out, shakes our hands with a big smile and helps us carry in our bags.

The first order of business is a shot of hornet liquor. Daisuke leads us to the back of the kitchen, where he pulls two large plastic drums from underneath a couch. They are both full of a yellow liquid: one lighter, one darker. Adult hornets, their bodies the length of my thumb and their wingspans the breadth of my palm, rest, entangled and preserved, at the bottom. Daisuke pours us each a small glassful of both kinds. 'This one,' he says, pointing to the lighter one, 'new. This one' – he points to the darker one – 'seven years. Welcome to Kushihara. *Kanpai!*' The taste of both liquors is deep and musky; I am reminded

I am drinking an animal. The new one is rough, with almost a note of young sloe-berry schnaps; the older one is mellowed and more integrated, with added layers of hazelnuts, bitter almond and pollen. But the animal musk is what prevails.

Daisuke and Shoko are a young couple with three young daughters. Daisuke, a forester, manages the local forest. In recent years, there has been a strong push towards growing forests for species diversity, rather than just for timber, and he is trying to implement these practices in the local forestry industry. Insects, especially the wasps, are one part of this effort. He pulls a few layers of a recently harvested wasp nest from the freezer to show us how they look. Soon we are gathered around the kitchen table spread with newspaper, helping to remove the larvae, pupae and adults with tweezers or fingers, one at a time, from the papery combs.

'Many insects have been consumed in most areas of Japan for a long while,' Charlotte tells us. 'Most of these traditions have lessened severely or died out entirely, because of changing perceptions, post-war pesticide-heavy agricultural practices, or habitat destruction. In some cases, such as with these wasps – known as *suzumebachi* in Japanese and *hebo* in the local Kushihara dialect; their binomial is *Vespula flaviceps* – in the rural regions of central Japan, their population is thought to be in decline, exacerbated by overharvesting of wild nests from the forested mountain landscape, or the *yama*, as it is known.

'At the same time, especially over the last few decades, the tradition of keeping wasps has survived and even developed in new ways. Some people in this region, especially older men, go out into the *yama* in the spring and attract adult wasps with bait – usually raw squid or small river fish. Once a wasp lands on the bait, they will give it a tiny ball of it, with a tiny white marker attached to it, and let it fly. They then try to follow it through the forest, until it returns to its nest. When they find the nest, which is still small at this early point in the season, they dig it up, put it into a small wooden box and take it home. At home, the collectors have any number of *hebo* houses – purpose-built wooden hives, into which they place the young nests. These are called *subako* – literally, 'hive box'. They care for them over the summer and fall, leaving food out for them – raw chicken breast and liver are popular choices, and sugar water or rock sugar – and watch the nest grow. With humans caring for the nests over the season in this way, they become much larger than they would otherwise grow in the *yama*.

'Then, in the late fall, when the nest is at its largest, people harvest them, separate the layers of comb and pluck out all the wasps, like we are doing now. They

CLOCKWISE FROM TOP LEFT: 1. *Hebo* houses **2.** Harvesting *hebo* nests **3.** Rice shaped for making *gohei mochi* **4.** Grilling *gohei mochi*

eat them and freeze them for later use. They are often given as gifts to family members and friends. They are a true delicacy, very highly valued.

'So, that is why I suggested you come now!' Charlotte concludes. 'Because all the keepers are about to harvest their nests. Many towns in the region have a big festival to celebrate the wasp harvest around this time. Kushihara's is one of the biggest and is in a few days, on the 3rd. It's been going since 1994 and has been becoming more popular. So it's great you'll be here for that.'

After we process a few layers of comb, Charlotte leaves us for the evening and we settle in. Shoko shows us her many food projects. 'My daughters have some different food allergies, so I just thought I would change my kitchen for the whole family,' she tells us in a mixture of English and Japanese. 'For example, we can't use sugar, but I use a special root from Hokkaido called *tensai daikon* – it is a type of daikon that is very sweet! I also make my own *amazake* – it is a sweet rice porridge that gets sweet from *kōji* [p.21].' She gives me the recipe.

'And I make our own miso – red miso and white miso, different ones with barley and with wheat.' She takes us into a closet to show us and so we can taste. 'It's fun! I love making all these things. And the wasps we just picked – let us make them into *tsukudani*! We will make it together now.'

She takes us over to the stovetop, and pours the wasp larvae and pupae into a heavy enamel pot. She adds soy sauce, some of the *tensai daikon* sugar and a bit of mirin and sake, until they are just covered. Then she heats them, brings the liquid to a simmer and lets it reduce. In the meantime, we talk. When the liquid has reduced and thickened, she turns off the heat. 'You can have them for breakfast tomorrow morning,' she smiles. '*Oyasumi nasai* – goodnight, *Joshu*.'

I am up early. Daisuke has already gone to the woods. The house is silent, but the kitchen table has been set. There is boiled rice in the rice cooker, miso soup on the stove and an assortment of condiments: *kuritake*, cooked chestnut mushrooms; *umeboshi*, pickled plums; and a mixture of *natto* (soybeans fermented by the bacterium *Bacillus subtilis* until slimy and pungent – 'I make it myself!' Shoko told me last night), rice *kōji*, sliced carrots and *kombu*. And the pot of *tsukudani* wasp brood. They have a rich taste: umami, salt, sweet and, afterwards, the distinctly foresty taste of oak moss (*Evernia prunastri*), often used as a green note in perfume. It is an aroma Ben taught me. I sit and enjoy the nourishment.

Soon Andreas joins, then Roberto. Today we hunt the giant hornet (pp. 194–9).

Today the whole village is in preparation for tomorrow's festival. We join a group – mainly ladies, with some men – at the community centre, who are preparing *gohei mochi*. Charlotte introduces us, and we get to work.

The large kitchen smells of rice and cedar. A pair of men are lightly pounding a huge pot of boiled rice, stopping after it holds together and before it becomes pasty. A group of elder women stand around a worktable, pressing the rice into specific wooden moulds. They show me how to fill the cracks and align the cedar slat so that it holds straight through the middle of the tapered shape of the pressed rice. We rest the moulded mochi into grooves in special flat wooden boxes, so that the rice is in contact with nothing but air. Each box holds twenty-five and tables in the large social room next door are covered with boxes. It seems we are preparing for quite a crowd.

Another woman is mixing the glaze in a large bucket. First, she simmers 2 kilograms of wasp brood and 200 grams of fresh ginger root with 7 litres (237 fl oz) of soy sauce. While it heats up, she grinds 7 kilograms of toasted peanuts in a food processor, and finishes them in a large ceramic bowl with a grooved pattern on the unglazed inside for roughness, called a *suribachi* – a kind of Japanese mortar and pestle. When the soy-sauce mixture simmers, she adds the peanuts with 7 kilograms of caster sugar and 1 kilograms of miso, stirring it all together and removing from the heat when it is thickened. This is the *tare*, the sauce that will be used to glaze the mochi tomorrow as they are grilled. 'It is also delicious with *kurumi*, Japanese walnut,' she tells me.

Outside it is damp and grey. For lunch, we head to a traditional Japanese house nearby, owned and maintained by a local non-profit organization in the village for the community to use. When we arrive, the Japanese-style hearth – a long grill pit lowered into the tatami floor – and the Western-style kitchen annex at the back are full of activity: three or four men sort wasps with long chopsticks onto plates of larvae, pupae and adults, which cover a long table; others prepare vegetables, tend the embers, and grill deer meat and shiitake mushrooms.

We eat adult *hebo* many ways: cooked in butter; as *tempura*, held together with batter; as *karaage*, deep-fried loose. The larvae we eat as sashimi – raw with their perfume, with rice, cooked spinach and sesame, pickled daikon and smoked Japanese sweet potato. It is a continuous meal, with some people leaving and more arriving. A group of new arrivals presents a huge platter of ripe persimmon, cottage cheese and fried wasps. For dessert, there is grilled mochi with yuzu and *kokutō*, black sugar.

Today is the wasp festival. This is the first year that Daisuke is running the show. The elders of the town passed responsibility for the festival down to him after last year, encouraging him to do as he and his friends wanted. 'We are keeping the tradition by making it new,' he told us on our first night.

We arrive just before 10:00 a.m. and the parking lot of the town hall is already beginning to fill with people, colourful tents and tables. Daisuke is setting up a stage with a sound system and his DJ friend in front of the building's entrance, with a big couch and many folding chairs for people to hang out on.

Caramelizing smells fill the breeze. A sizeable line has already formed for *gohei mochi*. We join it. We see some of our friends from yesterday. They grill the mochi, the surface now slightly drier; they then brush them all over with the *tare*, and return them to the grill until the glaze adheres and the surface starts to blister and take colour. They smile at us and give us a package of freshly grilled ones. It is perfect festival food: sweet, salty, umami, sharp, rich, generous, chewy and crunchy – and that refined wasp aroma hanging in the background, observing. My favourite part, perhaps, is the perfume of the cedar wood pervading the rice from within as it cooks.

In the neighbouring grass field, a long structure that looks like a hoop house for growing covered crops has been set up. A queue of white trucks already fills the inside, and more trucks are lined up to enter. We watch as every few minutes, a white-veil-clad wasp-keeper will come over to a table near to where we stand, with a few men sitting on one side with a large scale, and hand them a whole nest in a thick plastic bag. The men weigh the bag and write the weight on an attached paper. The keeper takes the nest over to another covered tent and deposits it onto one of a few raised platforms, according to its weight class. So far, they range between 2 and 5 kilograms.

We go over to the long structure to investigate. Charlotte finds us a few beekeeping veils. We pull them on over our clothes and enter through the clear plastic flap.

Wasps fill the air inside. Men in white clamber everywhere on white trucks. Wasp houses of all sizes and configurations fill the backs. The men help each other in clusters, readying *hachitori* – a small canister of zinc chloride, the smoke of which is used to sedate the wasps – and opening up the wooden houses. Some have mosses and ferns and other plants growing on their tops; some have holes on top, others have entrance slits at the side. Some are utterly unornamented and, if not for the festival context, I would have difficulty guessing they contained many thousands of organisms.

We join a cluster of men whom Charlotte knows. This is her second wasp festival, and she jumps right into the activity. One man lifts the lid slightly, and another drops in a smoking *hachitori*. After a minute, they tilt the lid up out of the box and onto the rim. The colony has built the nest down from the underside of the lid: it is covered in what almost look like curved, brown scales, with distinct layers in different shades. Charlotte sloughs off this papery outer layer, exposing the harder layers of comb underneath. She and another man use flat, metal implements to separate the nest from the wood. Once it is free, they place it into a plastic bag. 'Here, take this to the table with this piece of paper' – she hands me one like those I saw before – 'and have it weighed. Make sure the paper and the bag stay together!' Without missing a beat they move to the next hive box in the truck, calm and efficient as the others; the undercurrent in the tent, though, is palpably one of excitement.

All around, similar harvests are taking place. I spy an enormous hive being harvested from a huge clay pot, perhaps rather designed to house a tree.

We continue this way until all the hives are harvested and all the trucks have pulled out the other end of the tunnel. Now the tunnel lies empty, but for adult wasps that rest on the inner walls. Others, escapees, fly the festival.

The main crowd has now gathered beneath the nest tent, where the platforms have filled with bags. Most nests will be taken home by their carers, who will share them with friends and family; the others will be auctioned off.

Daisuke takes the stage to announce the carers with the largest nests, who become the winners of the festival.

'First, weighing in at 6.04 kilograms, Kanada Sumio-san! Kanada-san, please come up and accept your prize!' he says.

Kanada-san weaves politely through the crowd.

'We, the festival committee, on this day, 3 November 2014, name you the 2014 Kushihara *hebo* contest winner. Please accept the first prize, and also, a gift voucher from our sponsor. Please, a few words.'

'Thank you.'

The next fifteen or so winners are announced, with much applause and similarly succinct exchanges of thanks. There are a couple more brief speeches, and the official part of the festival is done. Some collectors and vendors begin to pack up shortly after, while others stay. The rest of the afternoon is spent with food, live then DJ-ed music, and a large, heated pail filled with bottles of warm sake and shochu. We stay until the very end and help Daisuke pack up the final equipment.

Later in the evening, we cook a big dinner for the community members who organized the festival.

After midnight, the day's work done, Charlotte proposes a trip to the *onsen*. We drive to the village's hot spring and climb up the slope behind it. Charlotte and Daisuke show us where to slip around the wooden fence, and we glide into the shallow pools, wisps of steam still rising to the moon as the heat dissipates into the fall night.

Today is our last in Kushihara. Charlotte takes us to visit a wasp-collector and carer named Yabushita-san who lives in Kushihara, through the forest on the other side of a mountain.

He and his wife are working in the garden when we arrive. He greets us at the step. Next to him sit two empty *hebo* houses, taken apart. We bow and shake hands. He and Charlotte exchange a few words, and he smiles and leads us around the corner of his wooden house. In the narrow space between the house and a small shed, semi-covered by the house's eaves and closed at the end by a rock wall, stand two wooden hive houses. Wasps still enter and exit through a slot on the front. 'You have not yet harvested these?'

I ask. He shakes his head. The wasps gather in dishes holding rock sugar in front of each slot, and harvest from small pieces of raw chicken attached to a row of metal wires, suspended at head height, pointing down.

Through Charlotte, Yabushita-san tells us more. 'Sometimes, the hives fall apart when we take them from the *yama*. They are small and delicate. But we can put them back together in a wire frame, and usually they are OK.

'I only feed them rock sugar, and the breast and heart of chicken. No honey, no sugar cubes. Of these two, that one is probably 2 kilograms, and the other is smaller, maybe half a kilogram.'

'How does he know?' I ask Charlotte.

'Based on their activity, and from experience, I estimate,' Yabushita-san responds. 'Keeping them this way allows them to grow bigger than in the wild. It is a lot of work, time, energy, money. But I like it. It is a hobby. Like how some people like fishing, I chase, collect and keep wasps.

'I had two nests in the festival. One was 2180 grams. I found it in mid-July. The other was 2450 grams. It started from a smaller nest, and I found it in early July. Last year I kept ten nests; this year, only four. This past spring, a lot of the nests in the mountains went bad – it was a wet spring, and the rainwater gets into the nest and sometimes it can get ruined. That's why we cover the boxes. These two boxes, and the two empty ones you saw by the step, I made myself about ten years ago.'

'And when did you start building the hives?' I ask.

'Oh, I made the first ones about thirty years ago, when I was forty-five years old. I started keeping wasps before that.

'As the head of the Kushihara Wasp-Loving Society, I encourage and support more people to keep wasps. It is enjoyable. It is also becoming more important: the wild populations have been decreasing in these last years, and we have to go further into the forest to find the new nests in the spring. So, some years ago, I started keeping a couple of hives – not for harvesting, but to propagate new queens. I stop giving them extra food in September, like the ones for harvest, so they will eat from nature to be strong, and more ready to hatch good queens that will hibernate well over the winter and build more good colonies for the next year. I do it for everybody – for the wasps, too.

'Then, a few years ago I guess, I also started keeping the queens myself, while they hibernate. In late November and December, the nest hatches all the new queens and males. They mate, the males die, and the queens hibernate before beginning new nests in the spring. So I place small pieces of bamboo in the eaves around the hives. The new queens like them; they are a perfect spot to hibernate – sheltered, dry. Every morning during the queen time, I check the bamboo pieces, shake out any hibernating queens, count them and put them into a small box with dry leaves and a cabbage leaf for moisture. When it is full, I stack the boxes and put blankets over them, to keep them warm over the winter. Then, when they wake up, they fly away into the woods, and begin their nests.

'It takes a lot of time to keep and store the queens. I used to do more. Maybe I will stop soon. But I hope more people start doing it. It is a good thing to practise.'

We drive back to the main part of Kushihara through the winding forest road. The *yama* that surrounds us, it strikes me, is not 'wild' in the sense of utter apartness from human activity; these forests have been largely replanted with cedar and cypress during the twentieth century, and are actively managed for logging and, increasingly, for biodiversity.

In a similar way, there is something different, hybrid, and interesting about the overwintering practice Yabushita-san described to us. It means that the practices of chasing wasps can't be described simply as a kind of 'wild-harvesting'. It means that collecting and keeping wasps entails a certain degree of entanglement with humans, such that the practices of each change the other. With overwintering queens, it becomes possible that these changes may even spill over across generations, leading to differences in behaviour not only as a result of relocating and feeding, but through selection. Differences that change wasp behaviour and ecology as a result of vespiculture may even, at some point, become heritable, inscribed in genetic code.

I may know more than when we came; though I am also aware of much more that I do not know. The wasps' oak-moss taste will stay, in the space in-between.

— Fieldwork Team: Josh Evans, Roberto Flore, Andreas Johnsen. Guide: Charlotte Payne. Written by Josh Evans.

KUMABACHI

We drive to Charlotte's house to pick her up. She needs a few more minutes. The garden outside her house is filled with gingko trees, the amber fruits dripping in the rain. I gather some and put them in the trunk. The car quickly gains the scent of baby vomit.

After a short drive, we meet Daisuke at his workspace and he lets us in. It's a space he shares with other men in the village, where they keep extra tools, equipment and time. Charlotte pulls full-body suits out of a closet. They are made of some thick, plastic material, and have a face hole covered with metal mesh – heavy duty. We pull them on over our clothes. Charlotte helps us tape the gaps at our boots and gloves. We approach the limit of becoming bodies hermetically sealed.

After another short drive, we park on the side of the road, on a slope over a small field. Daisuke's truck is already there. He is in his own white hermetic suit, talking with another man.

'That is Tetsuo Nakagaki,' Charlotte says, nodding to him from the car. 'He owns the plot of land where the hornets have built their nest. He has agreed to let us harvest it today. And later, we'll cook them together at his house just up there.' She points up the road.

We get out of the car and into the light rain. 'Nakagaki-san, please meet Josh, Roberto and Andreas.'

'*Yoroshiku.*' Nice to meet you.

We bind our taped gauntlets and greaves a bit tighter, and carry our tools down to the field. In addition to Daisuke's tools for harvesting hornet nests, we have a large plastic drum filled halfway with 40 per cent alcohol, another filled with whiskey and a smaller plastic bottle of honey.

We pick our way across the vegetable field to an embankment at the end near a small pool, its surface speckled with raindrops. We stand and survey the terrain. Daisuke has made some preliminary excavations into the exposed earth of the embankment, around the nest entrance. The fall has begun to colour the deciduous patches of the forest against the dark coniferous green; they are shrouded by cloud moving silently, transversing the slopes and the rest of the village beyond.

'So, we're going to be kneeling down, trying to swat them in,' I confirm with Charlotte.

'Yes. So once Daisuke starts digging out the hive, all of the adults are going to come out really fast trying to sting you, and when they do that, that's when you put them in the alcohol. Josh, you're going to be on that ledge there, right above the hive, and Roberto, you're going to be on that flat bit right below. Andreas will stand nearby filming.'

'Right, let's do it.'

We carry our drums of alcohol and kneel in position. Daisuke begins digging deeper into the embankment around the outline of the nest. The air soon swarms with aggressively defensive wasps. They look even bigger in flight than they did in the alcohol – at least as long as my thumb from head to sting. The sting itself is 5 mm (¼ inch), and can cause some serious damage if it gets into one's skin: it can cause whole limbs to swell up, and multiple stings can cause death. Hence the plastic armour.

But I'm not thinking about that as they dive-bomb my head and make indignant contact. I think about drumming. They are attracted to movement, and the best place to attract them is the mouth of the plastic drum, the portal of their doom. When I drum on the opening, they begin to hurtle at my hands, and when they do, I scoop them into the alcohol. In their death throes they excrete their venom and pheromones, a kind of final breath, spirits fixed in spirit that give it its yellow tint and alluring smell. It smells sour and nice, like the body odour of someone you like.

As their density begins to subside, I also scoop a few into the smaller bottle of honey. (The whisky and honey are Charlotte's experiments.)

Daisuke has lifted the hive whole into a large blue plastic crate. He separates the thick combs layer by layer, laying them each onto a tarpaulin to ensure all the adults have left. We make a final sweep to make sure all adults in the area have been safely stored in alcohol, using a net and our hands to pick any last ones out of the sky. Then, at a point, the ambient

CLOCKWISE FROM TOP LEFT: 1. Almost mature *imagos* 2. Giant hornet brood, in the comb 3. Removing the brood from the comb 4. Hornets, gingko fruits, and *mitsuba*, for a chawanmushi experiment

buzzing ceases. We gather our spoils and bring them back up to the cars and to Tetsuo, waiting above, watching.

The rain has strengthened. We sit around the Nakagakis' *kotatsu*, a low table heated from underneath with a blanket over the edge, inviting one's lower half. The slightly concave combs are spread on newspaper across its surface. They are remarkable: around the centre of each layer, each cell is covered with a white, papery dome. Around the edge of each comb layer, the larvae rear back and forth, surprisingly audible – a kind of rhythmic scratching. We take a few samples and dispatch any *imagos* (adults) that have developed the ability to walk. Charlotte holds one around the thorax with tweezers and shows us how a hornet-chaser threads the long white marker onto its body, in order to follow it back to the nest. Then, she bisects its head with scissors. One cannot be too careful with these creatures; they are magnificent and fearsome.

'When we hunt these, as with the wasps, there are different roles in the group. Some people attract them with the bait; some people attach the marker like this; some people dig out the nest. Different people are known to excel at different roles. Everyone usually runs to chase them at some point, though!' she laughs. 'Both the hornets and the wasps are part of the autumn wild harvest, along with mushrooms. Insects often have important roles in ecosystems, right – the hornets often have significant effects on the populations of other, smaller insects that are also agricultural pests, for example – and insect populations are often indicators for healthy ecosystems in general. People here are starting to notice the effects of changing farming methods, increasing

pesticide and fungicide use, and decreasing diversity. There are fewer hornets to harvest. And unlike the wasps, people do not keep the hornets – can you imagine why? Ha! So habitat conservation is even more important for these ones.'

We begin to remove the white paper domes with our fingers. Beneath the domed cells are developing pupae. As we work, a pattern reveals itself: each comb layer is a temporal snapshot of the brood's development. Some layers are almost all larvae; others are almost empty, save for an outer ring of imminent *imagos*. One layer has all stages, spiralling outward, back in time: near-adults with fully developed morphology in the centre, or even an empty cell or two where one used to be; then pupae with purple eyes and clear features; younger pupae, all white, with faces, antennae and legs emerging; and then, beyond the dome line, the active larvae, heaving their bodies back and forth, always the same movement, each oriented in its own way and somehow, despite being ordered by the hexagonal structure of the comb, strangely alone.

'They're called *kumabachi* – literally, "bear hornet". *Vespa mandarinia*. The adults bring back meat for the larvae, and the larvae give nectar to the adults. The adults cannot eat the flesh they gather – it is only for feeding the larvae. They only ingest liquids: larvae nectar, tree sap.'

A couple of Charlotte's friends come over. We sit around the *kotatsu* and process the brood, separating larvae, pupae and near-*imagos* onto plates. When the combs are empty, we cook.

Tetsuo's wife, Sayoko, shows us her method for hornet *tsukudani*. First she takes *tsuyu*, a versatile mixture of dashi (p.21), soy sauce, and sugar, which she has already made in a large amount. She adds some to a pot with a bit more sugar, mirin and gutted hornet larvae, covers it and lets it simmer for ten minutes. 'I also use this technique for other small animals, seaweed and shiso seedpods. It is very useful. Sometimes I will use dried persimmon skins for sweetness instead of sugar, or a bit of extra soy sauce, or ginger. But I don't have any ginger right now.'

'It's a shame there is no ginger!' I say – in a coincidental, irresistible chance for wordplay, the situation gives sense to the Japanese sentence '*shōga nai to shō ga nai*' (*shōga* means ginger and *shō ga nai*' is a phrase that means roughly 'it's a shame'). Sayoko laughs politely. Charlotte sniggers.

The *tsukudani* hornets are certainly more substantial than the wasps. They are sticky, meaty; they pop and chew like a cut from a larger animal. Very tasty, and strong – one cannot eat so many.

Roberto stews some white onion, spring (green) onion and sesame oil, adds a sauce of *katsuobushi* and soy sauce, and the steamed drone. With the *imagos*, he marinates them in soy sauce and sugar, then grills them on skewers, slowly, over the fire in the fireplace.

Meanwhile, Sayoko has steamed some *shungiku* – a green vegetable (*Glebionis coronaria*), the name of which translates directly as 'spring chrysanthemum' – with some *tsuyu*. The table starts to fill with dishes. Tetsuo shows me one of his favourite ways to eat the hornets. 'Sashimi,' he says, placing a whole, raw pupa into a small dish of soy sauce, and daubing on a small amount of *yuzukoshō*, a fermented paste of yuzu peel, chilli peppers and salt. The *yuzukoshō* helps temper the powerful animal taste of the hornet, and the strong aromatics of the yuzu and chilli dance with the flavours of the juicy, raw hornet. The pupae may be best for sashimi, I imagine, because it has no active digestive tract and therefore needs no gutting.

'We eat this with sake,' Tetsuo says, pouring us each a glass.

'The *kumabachi* can also be a medicine,' he tells us. 'When I was a child, there were not so many medicines as there are now; we would mix a hornet with hot water and drink it. Some would also use it on the skin, as long as there were no open wounds, so it didn't go directly into the bloodstream.'

We still have a lot of hornet brood left. We give some to Tetsuo and Sayoko, some to their friends, and pack some to bring to Shoko and Daisuke. Charlotte and I also make a few preparations to pursue further later: we marinate some in sake and shiso salt and start curing some in salt and sugar, hoping to smoke some over cypress wood at some point over the coming days. A final idea comes to me: they are quite proteinous, and very soft inside – could we blend them and set them into a chawanmushi, a kind of savoury custard usually made with dashi and chicken egg? They are, after all, an egg of another kind.

We sit, eating and drinking leisurely as the rain outside abates. Daisuke arrives and tries some of the dishes we have made together. Tetsuo tells us one more story before we go: 'Sometimes, I take a few days from work and go to Shizuoka [Prefecture] to hunt wasps and hornets. They have them there, but they don't eat them. There was one time where I was chasing a hornet back to its nest with my friend, and it took us running through a mandarin orchard. The owner thought we were stealing his fruits! We tried to explain to him that we were chasing giant hornets. But it might have been easier just to agree.'

It is the day after the wasp festival (pp.187–93). We return to the community's traditional house to cook. A group of elderly women who make regional food products remove wasp brood from the comb together, around the *kotatsu*. I get a chance to make a first try at a giant-hornet chawanmushi.

The equipment in the kitchen is fairly rudimentary, as are my skills in Japanese cuisine. But I try my best. Chawanmushi usually has certain seasonal delicacies inside, so I use a few bright-green gingko nuts (*ginnan*), halved; a small smear of gingko-fruit flesh, tangerine-coloured and astringent; and a leaf or two of *mitsuba* (Japanese wild parsley, *Cryptotaenia japonica*) in the bottom of the ceramic bowls. I blend some hornet larvae and wasp larvae, to make a version of each, and strain the mixtures through a sieve to remove any pieces of head and skin. The wasp mixture begins to oxidize and turn grey, while the hornet one does not. Curious. Will need to look into that later. I pour each mixture into a ceramic bowl, place them into a makeshift steamer I've cobbled together over simmering water in a pot and set the lid. I steam them for a few minutes until the mixtures have set.

They cook too long and at too vigorous a steam – the water boils faster than it should, and the ramshackle steaming tray doesn't help matters. Nonetheless, the ladies do me the service of tasting and offering feedback. The group agrees that the hornet is pretty challenging: it tastes like the skim-off from stock, or overboiled chicken. The wasp has a deep flavour, perhaps too strong. They suggest it may be better as a seasoning or garnish, rather than as the substance of the chawanmushi itself; or it could be diluted somewhat to a more appropriate intensity. This makes sense, as they do have quite a strong flavour. Also, the gingko fruit is just too astringent. There is clearly a reason only the nut is eaten.

Roberto makes lunch, a lovely blend of his Italian heritage and local Japanese ingredients: udon noodles made like pasta, with a creamy sauce of hornet-larvae purée, seasoned with soy sauce, green garlic and chilli and cooked low and slow so the proteins just barely set – dare I say like the egg in carbonara? It is garnished with fried adult wasps. The women too seem to enjoy it.

Charlotte has a surprise for us for dinner. We have been invited by the Japanese Vespula Society, based in Asuke in Aichi, the next prefecture over from Gifu, where Kushihara is, for a feast of autumn delicacies.

We arrive to a long table laid with two hotpots, tea, large bottles of sake and beautiful displays of autumn in the *yama*: bowls of whole *matsutake* mushrooms nestled on cedar fronds; thick slices of wild-deer-fillet sashimi; *yamaimo*, or Japanese mountain yam; large dishes of giant-hornet brood and adults; and many more ingredients line the table. A dozen or so men fill the room. Charlotte is the only woman. They welcome us. We toast with hornet liquor.

There are too many tasty things at once. Keiji Ando (known most simply as 'Ando'), the head of the society and the host of the evening, shows us how one pounds the wild mountain yam with a bit of water in a *suribachi*, a Japanese mortar and pestle, into a frothy slime, which, seasoned with a few drops of soy sauce and sake, is the ideal accompaniment to the deer sashimi – he picks up a slice with his chopsticks, places it into a bowl and pours a thin stream of the yam mixture onto it from a small spoon.

The textures are lovely, and together they're divine. The raw meat is slippery, firm and yielding; the pounded yam, even a small amount, coats the mouth smoothly and is surprisingly aromatic – foresty but clean, almost resinous and slightly sweet.

Another member has heated up oil in a portable fryer and has begun making *karaage* with the hornet adults. The adults are large already, and when deep-fried they puff up out of their exoskeletons to become enormous. Lightly salted, the wings and carapace gone glassy, they are an excellent accompaniment to Asahi beer.

Others have pulled the *matsutake* into long, thick strands. Someone hands me a strand raw. It tastes distinctly of pine (its arboreal associate), with a kind of horseradish-like pungency at the end that fills the nose and sinus.

Everyone lifts large dishes of raw vegetables, noodles, sausages and other ingredients onto the table, and begins arranging them into the savoury-smelling, simmering *tsuyu* in the hotpots: Chinese cabbage, spring (green) onion, hornet larvae and pupae, tofu, small sausages, *matsutake* mushrooms and dark noodles. 'Sukiyaki!' the men exclaim, imploring us to repeat the dish's name. '*Sukiyaki!*'

The rest of the night comprises arguments over the proper ratio of hornets to infusing liquor (three per 100 ml [3½ fl oz] is a popular one, but others insist the number of hornets should be much higher); a long discussion of virile foods in Japanese culture (incidentally, the hornets, hornet alcohol, *matsutake* and *yamaimo* are all prime examples); a spontaneous degustation of Nordic Food Lab's grasshopper garum (unanimously deemed '*umai!*' – delicious); the intercultural sharing of mildly lewd gestures; and unhurried, continuous eating and drinking. At some point, we get home to Kushihara, our individual and collective virility bolstered for a good long while.

— Fieldwork Team: Josh Evans, Roberto Flore, Andreas Johnsen Guide: Charlotte Payne. Written by Josh Evans.

KAISEKI IN AUTUMN

It is our last night in Kushihara. We invite Charlotte, Shoko, Daisuke and a few other friends for dinner at a local *kaiseki* restaurant. (*Kaiseki* is a traditional, multi-course dinner in Japan that follows a certain structure and is closely tied with the current season for its ingredients and imagery.) The restaurant is called Chikara, which means 'power'. The chef, Hiroyuki Ozeki, takes up the suggestion to make a menu highlighting the giant hornet and the wasp. Here is what he serves.

Magnolia leaf with miso, spring (green) onion, shiitake, ginger and enoki mushrooms. The large leaf is placed over a small flame; as the leaf is heated over the course of the meal, it causes the miso to sizzle and start to caramelize, at which point we stir the mixture and eat it, hot.

Sake. It is sometimes served this way, Ozeki-san tells us: warm, with a piece of blowfish. Here, instead, it is served with a single, adult giant hornet. The warmth brings out its strong, animal flavours.

Small appetizers. A cube of fresh tofu with a condiment of pounded wasp larvae and soybeans; a salad of chrysanthemum flowers, leaves and stems, with tiny giant hornet larvae and the herb *mitsuba*; *tamagoyaki*, sweetened egg, fried recursively in thin layers and rolled around *tsukudani* wasp larvae; a dashi jelly, with a single adult wasp suspended in the middle; and *tsukudani* wasp larvae on rice.

Dobinmushi. *Matsutake* mushroom broth with gingko nut, roasted hornet larvae and pupae, and *mitsuba*, self-seasoned with a slice of fresh *sudachi*, a small citrus, somewhere between yuzu and lime. Powerful, complex, refined, both satisfying and appetizing. A favourite.

Grilled *fu* with *satoimo* (a Japanese variety of taro), lightly grilled hornet larvae and pupae, and teriyaki sauce. *Fu*, also known as *seitan*, is wheat gluten. This is a substantial dish, yet somehow retains its lightness.

Vinegar dashi jelly made with *kuzu* (arrowroot) powder, okra, fig, persimmon, hornet larvae and pupae and shiso flowers. Lovely and refreshing after the *fu*. Perhaps it did not even need the hornets?

Chawanmushi. The expert tries his hand, and the result resonates. Made with a mix of dashi and blended, strained hornet larvae, with a thin layer of thickened dashi on top and a small, inset spoonful of grated ginger. The dashi helps dilute and round out the flavour of the hornet, and the ginger lifts its brooding character and tempers its musk. Beautiful.

Tempura larvae, pupae and adults, two of each, served with *sudachi* and *yukishio* (literally 'snow salt'), a bright-white, ultra-fine sea salt from Ishigakijima, one of the furthest south-west islands of the Okinawa archipelago. It is almost spicy in its high mineral content.

Soba. Buckwheat noodles, with hornet larvae in the *tsuyu*, or dipping broth.

Vanilla ice cream with lentils and tapioca in a simple syrup, garnished with mandarin, pineapple and kiwi.

As the tea is served, Ozeki-san comes out to talk through the meal with us. It is commendable how many ways he was able to incorporate the hornets into the *kaiseki* menu structure. For our purposes, it was great – though given their strong, distinctive flavour, for a normal meal it would be a bit much. Ozeki-san laughed and said, 'You asked for it.' Indeed we did.

His restaurant is open year-round but is most popular in the autumn, when many Japanese travel to the mountains to experience the changing colours, or *momijigari*, a practice of seasonal appreciation similar to cherry-blossom-viewing in the spring.

A light rain begins to fall as we drive home. Ours has been quite a special *momijigari*: dense and, I suspect, lasting.

— Fieldwork Team: Josh Evans, Roberto Flore, Andreas Johnsen Guide: Charlotte Payne. Written by Josh Evans.

CLOCKWISE FROM TOP LEFT: 1. Vinegar dashi jelly **2.** Chawanmushi **3.** Magnolia leaf with miso
4. Various small appetizers

SAKURA FRASS

——

Our last evening in Japan somehow ends up aligning with a meeting of the *Nihon-konshū-ryōri-kenkyū-kai*, the Japanese Insect Cuisine Research Association. We can't not go.

We arrive at the address, a cozy bar tucked into a side street twenty minutes' train ride from Shibuya station. Many people, mainly younger ones, fill every seat. Shoichi Uchiyama, the leader of the group, greets us as we enter. He tells us how his grandfather used to make *donburi* with silkworm pupae in Nagano, and how he tried some grasshoppers with some friends and liked them. Then he started getting more into it, and discovered that there are many different kinds and that many are delicacies. He organized a global edible-insects event at a zoo in Tokyo sixteen years ago, and the group has been growing ever since. Soon the meetings began to be held once a month; now, they are held twice a month, including extra events for collecting insects, mainly grasshoppers and cicadas, during their seasons.

'The image of insects for many Japanese people is negative – but this comes from a certain generation, an older idea from wartime subsistence,' Uchiyama-san explains to us. 'Though eating insects has been around in Japan for much longer than that. And nowadays, for many young people, it is novel and interesting.'

The group makes a few dishes: cricket tempura with crushed-cricket salt, miso soup and rice steamed with cherry-caterpillar frass (the excrement of insect larvae), with the caterpillar on top. The caterpillar is unnotable, but the rice is remarkable.

'Yes, this is an insect that is not traditionally eaten in Japan, actually. It is called *sakura kemushi* in Japanese, *Phalera flavescens* in Latin. *Sakura* means cherry tree. This caterpillar only feeds on the leaves of the cherry tree. So its frass is purely digested cherry leaves.' Uchiyama-san opens the plastic container for us to smell. Our noses are engulfed in a heady fragrance of cherry blossom and cherry wood. Such a powerful, beautiful smell, from tiny brown caterpillar droppings.

'In China, there is a tradition of using certain insects' frass as medicine – in tea, or directly. So we brew the *sakura kemushi* frass into tea, and then use the tea to cook the rice. That's where it gets the nice smell, and the light pink colour.

'Some years there are many, some years not, and no one really knows why. So I am trying to rear them myself.'

He gives us a few grains to put into alcohol as a sample. They quickly dissolve, turning the ethanol a deep, dark green. For years to come, neither the colour nor the incredible smell fade.

— Fieldwork Team: Josh Evans, Roberto Flore, Andreas Johnsen Guide: Charlotte Payne. Written by Josh Evans.

THAILAND FIELDWORK

'Show us the contents of your bag, please.'

When leaving for fieldwork, I always await the moment when I have to perform the small ritual that accompanies every airport security check.

'What's *that*?' asks the police officer, pointing at a plastic bag brimming with plastic vials, small amber glass bottles, pipettes and a bunch of small kitchen tools. My chef's travel kit has captured the attention of yet another security guard. Grasshoper garum, bee bread, Anty Gin (p.222), some tinctures, Japanese giant killer hornets *(Vespa mandarinia japonica)* preserved in alcohol and *kōji* spores *(Aspergillus oryzae)* are spilled onto the sleek, metal examination table.

I attempt to explain the bottle of fermented grasshopper garum and the gin infused with ants to the officer, but instead he just places everything back in the bag, dumbfounded. I carefully pack the precious contents back into my backpack.

We leave the perplexed Copenhagen airport-security officer behind, looking forward to travelling to a place where insects are well-known as an ingredient rather than as a pest. Perhaps.

Thailand is our destination. Together with food-systems researcher Afton Halloran from the University of Copenhagen, I have been invited to Le Cordon Bleu Culinary School in Bangkok, to collaborate with a team of French and Thai chefs and present a workshop on insects in a gastronomic context.

The plan is to spend seven days in Bangkok meeting the different faces behind the enormous Bangkok food scene, exploring the vibrant markets and jamming in the teaching kitchen at Le Cordon Bleu with some brave chefs. On the final day in the city, we will meet up with Afton's colleagues and fellow researchers from Kenya, Uganda, Cambodia, Italy, the Netherlands, Denmark and Thailand, for a study trip organized by Professor Yupa Hanboonsong of the GREEiNSECT research group. After visiting the United Nations Food and Agriculture Organization's (FAO) regional office and the sufficiency-economy projects of King Bhumibol Adulyadej, we will head to Isan, the north-eastern region of Thailand.

Upon our arrival at Le Cordon Bleu, we are met with a mixed reception of blatant scepticism and enthusiasm, and are ensured that we are, without a doubt, the first ever to cook with insects here, at an institution that dates back to 1895. After the introduction, a French cuisine chef exclaims with a sense of pride, 'I have been in Thailand for almost twelve years now, and I have never tried an insect … and I am married to a Thai woman!' Another just shakes his head disapprovingly and says, 'I am not ready for this.' We are off to a pretty rough start.

Probably one of the greatest challenges that I have experienced during the past few years that I've worked on this project is trying to make people feel comfortable working with out-of-the-ordinary ingredients like insects.

I explain to French chefs Christian Ham and Willy Deraude that, as with every other ingredient they might approach for the first time, insects will require some time if they want to unlock their potential. 'There are over 250 edible species of insects in Thailand alone – each insect celebrated in different regions of the country for its unique properties,' I note, studying my fellow organisers' faces. Their eyes start to flicker as I catch their attention with the image of entering a new territory of possibilities.

As we work on planning the event, Chef Rapeepat Boriboon (aka Chef A) colours my world with marvellous stories of his childhood, when he collected wild insects in the rice fields with his grandmother. His eyes smile as he recounts the numerous tales. He later confesses that, for him, serving insects at an important culinary institution like Le Cordon Bleu is about elevating a part of his own gastronomic culture – one that has not always been positively considered by chefs coming from outside – to another level. Even though Chef A is the chef of Thai cuisine at the institution, he has never had the opportunity to serve insects during his classes. For him, this event is a redemption of his heritage. I feel close to him in this moment.

CLOCKWISE FROM TOP LEFT: 1. Weaver ants at a Khon Kaen market 2. An Isan technique for steaming dishes similar to Lovage Flute (pp.302–4) 3. Frozen silkworm pupae at Talaad Thai market 4. Giant water bugs at Talaad Thai market

In our search for ingredients, Afton, Chef A, the academic manager, Christophe and I end up at Talaad Thai, South East Asia's largest market, where a whopping 12,000 tonnes of products are traded daily.

We wander past the green and red mountains of chillies and lemongrass, through the labyrinth of meticulously constructed pyramids of Kaffir limes, onwards to the stacks of ginger, galangal, buffalo skin and preserved rats from north-eastern Thailand, arriving at the fruits and vegetables. On the periphery of the market, vats of warm curries in varying shades of green, yellow and red are served to the market vendors. Everything is thoughtfully organized into rectangular sections. The omnipresent hum of the countless market-goers looms overhead. The air is impregnated with the pungent aromas of pandan leaves and the spicy chillies, which mingle ever so gently with the light, warm breeze. It is an orchestra of perfumes and the wind is its director.

I feel minuscule in front of this awesome diversity, considering the limited selection that we sometimes have in Denmark. Here it is evident that diverse food from all regions of Thailand is cherished, celebrated and highly integrated into people's everyday lives.

Finally we arrive at the insect section. Wholesalers hawk both wild and farmed insects, ranging from extraterrestrial-looking giant water bugs (*maeng da*, or *Lethocerus indicus*), to mole crickets (*maeng grachon*, or *Gryllotalpa africana*) with their shovel-like forelimbs. Christophe points to the frozen block of yellowish silkworm pupae, slowly melting in the February heat, and Afton ogles the bamboo borers (*non mai phai*, or *Omphisa fuscidentalis*). Faced with the difficult decision of choosing which ones to buy, Afton and I decide to buy a little bit of everything.

We proceed through the maze of rectangular stalls, guided by Chef A. He waves his hand over the rows of fresh wild herbs, suggesting that we purchase a few different kinds to experiment with. We turn left and hit an olfactory wall of garlic, each piece sorted by size and variety, some pre-peeled and some whole. Some of those will do, too.

We return to Le Cordon Bleu with our loot and quickly get down to work.

This is the moment that I have been waiting for! During our exploration in Livø, Ranee Udtumthisarn, a chef from northeast Thailand who has her own Thai restaurant in Copenhagen, showed Ben, Josh and I how to prepare *nam prik maeng da*, a popular condiment, using the male giant water bug (p.185). This is, by far, one of my favourite-smelling insects. During our research at the market, I find one small cart selling lychee stink bugs (*maeng khaeng*, or *Tessaratoma paillosa*), which have a very similar smell to the giant water bug. When I first taste it, the colour green immediately flashes in my mind. It is one of the most complex flavours I have ever experienced in an insect: Kaffir lime, coriander (cilantro) and apple skin, with sweet notes of banana and tropical fruit. Incredible.

Until today, I have only experienced that flavour in a savoury context; I can't wait to see how Chef Willy is going to deal with this unusual ingredient. I scoop some of the small lychee stink bugs out of one of the market bags, and Willy quickly becomes enthused with the idea of using their strong Kaffir-lime-leaf aroma the same way that vanilla would be used to flavour a cold infused cream. It is the beginning of something delicious. The guys are getting really excited.

The result is white-chocolate spheres filled with a stink-bug-infused cream, and the bamboo-borer biscuit topped with fermented bee bread. The combination of these ingredients is extremely successful. The intensity of the stink bug fits perfectly together with the sweet notes of the white chocolate. The acidity and the flavours of ripe tropical fruits from the bee bread give a boost that make me fall completely in love with this one-bite bonbon. In order to add a crunchy texture at the base of the sphere, Willy prepares pastry dough by mixing some flour with toasted bamboo borer. The fattiness and the combination between the nutty taste and sourness of the bamboo borer are exactly what we are looking to represent in this dish.

Christian finds pleasure in the nutty flavour of the cockchafer-like insect, taking inspiration from a previous bread project developed at the Lab. We create a crisp flatbread with herbs and the roasted exoskeleton of the beetle, topped with a buttercream made from its softer internal part.

Meanwhile, Chef A is completely concentrated on his preparation. With his incredible smile, he proudly calls us over to show off his creation. The result is a beautiful small bite made with chopped grasshopper cooked in a *miang khum* sauce made from tamarind, ginger, bird's-eye chillies, fish sauce, shallots and shrimp paste, thickened with freshly grated coconut. He shapes the mixture into a meatball-sized ball, then sprinkles crushed lotus seeds on top of it and serves it on a lotus petal. An authentic taste from Thailand.

After moving beyond the confines of comfort, our time is up. Four plates emerge as the fruits of our collective labour in the kitchen: a cricket-infused broth, cockchafer butter and herb crisp, bamboo borer and stink bug bite, and a grasshopper lotus-petal snack.

The desire to look beyond the most apparent conventional ingredients at hand for gastronomic innovation, and the push to further culinary frontiers, are strong driving forces for many involved with food. Looking to the undervalued, forgotten and underutilized is certainly a place to start. Insects represent major blind spots in our current Western culinary repertoire.

At the end of four intense days, we leave with a feeling of satisfaction, knowing that we have made a little bit of history and managed to educate a diverse group of people about why they should care about insects not just as ingredients, but also as an important part of our food systems.

The village of the cricket farmers

It is a hot, dry day. Afton and I feel guilty thinking that, halfway around the world, Copenhagen is dark, dreary and covered with snow.

We move from noisy Bangkok to Khon Kaen, one of the major urban centres of Isan, the region where we will be staying for the coming days. Khon Kaen is the birthplace, as well as the heart and soul, of the concept of small-scale cricket farming that was born nearly twenty years ago. It was in this region where Afton spent two months researching the environmental impacts of cricket farming. However, she quickly realized how important it was to return in order to investigate the dramatic impact that this farming technique had had on people's lives. I will soon realize this too.

Forty kilometres from Khon Kaen, our second destination is the small village of Baan Saento. The next days will be spent travelling and talking with the farmers, trying to understand the role that cricket farming plays in people's lives. Cricket farming started in Baan Saento in 2008, and now over half of the village has integrated small-scale cricket production into their farming activities.

We are first welcomed into the home of Khun Kamroi, an elder in the village. He beckons the group to follow him as he shuffles towards the backyard. Standing around the pen, I can't help but notice how few inputs there are: egg cartons, some round water containers and a couple of large, plastic bowls for collecting the crickets are the only tools he needs. Afton points over to a sea of grey egg cartons to our left, noting that the farmers leave everything under the intense sunlight to sanitize it, so it will be ready to be used again for the next cycle of crickets.

I am extremely fascinated, seeing how this simple technique has developed. First, a bunch of crickets are collected from the wild. They are then allowed to breed in small, rectangular pens, constructed out of concrete and lined with beautifully coloured tiles around the rim. I learn later that the tiles are mainly used for keeping the crickets from escaping the pen.

In order to put this all into perspective, we need to imagine a timeline of agricultural history. Between 10,000 and 13,000 years ago, human beings in the so-called Fertile Crescent began domesticating and farming wild animals. Nearly 7,000 years ago, honeybees (*Apis mellifera*) became the first insect species domesticated for human use. Staring at the small, black crickets as they scramble around in Khun Kamroi's concrete-block pens, it sinks in just how recent of a development cricket-farming

actually is. Enchanted by hearing about the farmers' challenges and the innovative spirit they used in overcoming them, I feel like I am witnessing another point being etched into the agricultural timeline.

With nothing more than some concrete blocks and mortar, egg trays, plastic containers, nylon netting, rice-husk ash and some tiles, a farmer can create a series of small pens in which to put cricket eggs. The eggs hatch after seven to nine days, and their short lives begin. After thirty-five to fifty days, depending on the species, the male crickets begin their sweet serenade. After mating, the females deposit eggs into moist soil or rice-husk ash, and the crickets are harvested and eaten or sold. Sometimes the eggs are even sold or exchanged, with other farmers in the surrounding village or further away.

Investing in the materials to carry out this small operation is very manageable for Khun Kamroi, and the short life cycles of the crickets suit his modest lifestyle. For this eighty-year-old, cricket farming is light and easy work. His home is built in layers from different periods; the cricket pens are the newest addition.

Although he chooses to rear two different species, Khun Kamroi prefers the two-spotted cricket, *Gryllus bimaculatus* De Geer, because they take even less time to grow and fetch a higher price. Alternating between the two-spotted cricket and the common house cricket (*Acheta domesticus*) helps him to prevent any disease that might decimate the cricket population – a small trick he learned from one of his neighbours.

I can compare this to the similar way that we rear animals and grow vegetables in Sardinia – a sort of lightly regulated means of home production, where products are mostly self-consumed and sold in an informal way to the same community. In that moment, the image of my sister with her small, organic-egg production flashes in my mind; I laugh to myself at the resemblance. Here I am in Thailand, witnessing a similar experience, but with tiny crickets replacing my sister's flock of hens.

The history of how cricket farming began in Thailand is equally interesting. According to Afton's research[1], cricket farming was developed as a response to the 1997 Asian economic crisis. Domestic migrants, mostly those from north-eastern Thailand, were one of the most vulnerable groups during the crisis, suffering from the highest overall job losses in industries situated in Bangkok and other urban centres. Shortly after, researchers began promoting low-technology farming methods to assist these unemployed workers when they returned to their villages in the poorest region of the country, Thailand's north-east. Because these migrants were mostly temporary or seasonal workers, they still had land back in their home villages. By integrating cricket farming into their farms, families and communities vulnerable to the shock of rice prices and yield fluctuations were now able to have an additional income.

At the same time, Thailand's large-scale economic transition increased levels of industrial and agricultural pollution, as well as significant shifts in land use, making wild insects more difficult to access. This rapid industrial growth encouraged the use of even more powerful herbicides and pesticides to boost agricultural production and efficiency, meaning that some insect species that had previously been a part of human diets were now unsafe to eat. Domestication of wild insect species was proposed to relieve pressure on the hunting and collecting

of wild populations, as well as to create safer food. Farming insects also led to the opportunity to produce much larger quantities of insects, in a concentrated manner, than can usually be collected from the wild. This could possibly translate into specialization, and consequentially to larger revenues and economies of scale for rural farmers.

Before heading to visit the final farmer, we are diverted down a small footpath to the farm of Khun Petch Wongtam. High up in the canopy of a kusum tree, hanging down from the branches, are tens of bunches of straw. Inside these bunches are lac insects (*Kerria lacca*). The multifunctional resin created by these insects can be used as wood finish, cosmetics or dye for wool and silk.

Crickets are only one small part of the patchwork comprising Khun Petch's self-sufficient garden empire. The landscape is dotted with cassava, bananas, traditional leafy vegetables, chillies, tomatoes, starfruit and jackfruit trees, herbs and a fish pond.

We head back into the village for lunch. As I go to wash my hands, a group of men beckons me to their corner. They are huddled snugly together around a concrete cylinder that Khun Petch uses to keep wild crickets, which he often introduces to his stock. One of the oldest men unveils a bottle of home-made rum and invites me to take a swig. The intense flavour of the distilled sugar cane catches me off-guard – then I remember that I have a surprise for them, too! I run back over to my backpack and grab some small vials of the Anty Gin that I always carry with me for special moments like these. Our mischief quickly comes to an end when Khun Petch's wife calls us to come see what she and her neighbours are cooking in the kitchen.

A group of elderly women are standing by a huge wok full of cooking oil. The ladies, all dressed identically in pink, flowery shirts, direct me to add to the oil the hundreds of two-spotted field crickets and house crickets that have just been collected fresh from the pens in front of the house. They are sizzled together with garlic, then drained and mixed with some freshly chopped pandan leaves and lemongrass.

The lunch is laid out on colourful, handwoven mats, which the group is ushered over to sit on. Together the group feasts on *pla pao*, grilled red tilapia stuffed with lemongrass and pandan leaves; *gai yang*, Isan-style grilled chicken, accompanied by two spicy dipping sauces; and Khun Petch's family's own *khao neo*, sticky rice. This perfect balance between tastes, smells and textures transmits a clear message: grab more! Though I have had the chance to work with crickets farmed in Europe before, the taste of these fresh crickets is far different from anything that I have experienced.

After dancing and singing with our new friends on the mat that has acted as our lunch table, we return to Khon Kaen for the night. As I watch Baan Saento become a speck in the distance, I realize how different insect farming is there. Like Afton, I have witnessed the way that crickets have positively impacted people's lives. I have also witnessed how crickets have been added to the endless bounty of agricultural diversity that sustains the lives of this small village.

At this moment, a common misconception about why people would eat insects is quashed for me: despite what people might think in Europe, in cultures where the consumption of edible insects is commonplace, they are not used as a substitute for meat or fish; rather, they are used as an additional ingredient in an everyday diet.

Experiencing this beautiful cross-pollination of cultures, knowledge and the aspirations of my new Thai friends makes me reflect on how many times the omission of small but essential details can completely change the perception of the entire reality, and the future development, of successful projects like this one in Thailand. This moment significantly influences my subsequent work at the Lab; I begin to develop recipes and concepts that are more oriented towards storytelling, rather than just pure pleasure and taste.

— Fieldwork Team: Roberto Flore and Afton Halloran. Hosts: Professor Yupa Hanboonsong, Professor Tasanee Jamjanya and the GREEiNSECT research group. Written by Roberto Flore with Afton Halloran.

EUROPEAN PARLIAMENT

During the summer of 2015, I am delighted to receive an email from the European Parliament Media Services and Monitoring Unit in Brussels. It is an invitation to present some of the research that we had been doing, at a press seminar on novel foods.

After getting the official confirmation for the event, I run into the kitchen and start to jot down ideas for the dishes that I am going to serve. A long list of concepts, experiences, travels and landscapes spread across the paper: two years of work at the Lab summed up in a very long list. But throughout this process, the same images constantly re-emerge in my mind: the faces of incredible people. People who opened their homes and hearts to us; people who treated us as special guests, and shared their cultures, lives and dreams with us. It is clear that, whatever I am going to prepare, these stories are going to be the core of the messages I wish to transmit through the food.

The seminar, entitled 'What Will We Be Eating in 2025?', merges discussions of a mix of ingredients and materials that may legally become a part of European diets in the future, such as food obtained from cellular cultures, foods containing 'engineered nanomaterials', insects and microalgae. My first impression of this is of a messy desk that needs to be put in order; the EU is intending to create clearer legislation on an argument which had been confusing Europe since 1997.

I am initially afraid to present our work at a seminar where insects, together with nanomaterials, are being called 'novel' components of European food. But the opportunity to disseminate our work to a large group of people who are responsible for developing future policies regarding food eliminates every doubt in my mind. This is the opportunity of a lifetime.

I call Afton to inform her of this amazing opportunity, and tell her that I have decided to share the stage with her. After all, Afton had previously worked with the UN's Food and Agriculture Organization (FAO) on the topic of valorizing traditional diets containing insects, and she is now conducting important research related to the evaluation of insects as a component of sustainable food systems. This is the best moment to bring attention to this topic and potentially influence policy at a regional level.

The event attracts a lot of attention, as it is the first time that someone has ever been invited to do a cooking demonstration in the confines of the European Parliament. As we will be presenting ingredients that are not legally recognized as food, a letter allowing the conditional serving of food which contains insects is written by Martin Schulz, the president of the European Parliament himself. I am baffled by the fact that while I have to obey strict regulations, I am able to cook with ingredients which are not even considered legal!

After months of tinkering with different ingredients and ideas, I managed to refine and solidify the recipes for the event.

Afton, former lab intern Santiago Lastra and I develop a comprehensive one-and-a-half-hour workshop for seventy journalists from twenty-three European nations, Members of Parliament and other stakeholders.

To start, we serve two species of ants (*Formica rufa* and *Lasius fuliginosus*) on a spoon. I often use these tiny ants as a warm-up exercise for the audience, so they can move beyond the preconception that we should only eat insects because they might be a more environmentally sustainable source of protein. But ants are not interesting because of their protein content; they are interesting because they offer something so powerful and concentrated in a small bite, making them a superb ingredient for demonstrating that we are not exploring the full potential of our surrounding landscapes. Such flavour is encapsulated in these minuscule and unassuming beings! Even if they are not considered to be valuable by most people, ants play an important role in keeping forest ecosystems alive.

The ants are followed by a bite-sized, nixtamalized-Øland-wheat taco with bee larvae (pp.258–60). I create the taco to deliver a specific message: it is designed to look and taste like Mexican food, but is developed with 100 per cent Nordic ingredients. This is the perfect platform for discussing the importance of valorizing the knowledge of other cultures.

I think it is unfortunate how the argument for edible insects has been developing in the Western world. Discussing the introduction of a new ingredient, and then, consciously or unconsciously, ignoring or underestimating the cultural background and value of that ingredient, is a major mistake if we really do want to introduce insects into our everyday diets. We also need to facilitate possibilities for learning what we can from other cultures.

For example, having learned about the *escamoles* in Mexico, we can apply this cultural knowledge to Scandinavia, but using bee larvae instead. Creating a dish that tastes Mexican but uses only Nordic ingredients was a way to demonstrate this similarity. Through the valorization of Mexican know-how, it was possible to create something delicious with local ingredients found in Denmark. Eating insects does not necessarily mean importing them from other places; there is little sense in eating insects if we do not address the aspect of culture, and look to our own to unlock the secrets of nature.

After the taco, the journalists and Members of Parliament are treated to a tempeh and cricket broth (pp.274–6). In many gastronomic cultures in Asia, protein is handled in a very different way than it has been traditionally in Europe: the fermentation of many non-animal-source proteins is the key to unleashing the sixth taste, umami. My dish represents a way to discuss protein from a different perspective: not through using the whole insect, but through using its flavour. The tempeh also offers itself as a means of talking about other kinds of protein substitutes that are non-animal in origin, and about the significance this has in promoting diversified diets.

It is an incredible workshop, one that both the organizers and those invited to the event highly appreciate. It feels like we leave a piece of ourselves in the Parliament that day. In fact, for nearly a year after the event, a larger-than-life image of me was projected onto a big screen surrounding the European Parliament entrance near Place du Luxembourg.

—Written by Roberto Flore
with Afton Halloran

RECIPES FROM THE LAB

INSECT GARUMS

Makes 300–350 g

ORIGINAL GRASSHOPPER
GARUM
400 g whole grasshoppers
  (*Locusta migratoria*)
600 g greater wax moth larvae
  (*Galleria mellonella*)
225 g pearl barley *kōji* (p.21)
300 g filtered water
240 g salt

This is the first insect garum recipe, developed by Lars Williams, head of research and development at the lab from 2009 to June 2011. This technique began as a general exploration into fermentation for umami taste, starting with fish sauces inspired by those of South East Asia and ancient Rome (hence garum, one type of ancient Roman fish sauce). It branched out from there, into squid guts, beef trimmings, pheasant, hare and many different kinds of insects. Fermenting them not only harnesses their protein for umami power, but makes their tastes familiar while easing the psychological hurdle of consuming the insect whole.

ORIGINAL GRASSHOPPER GARUM

Blend the insects in a blender or food processor until broken up, but not smooth. Put the purée into a bowl, add the barley *kōji*, water and salt and mix together until combined and the salt has dissolved. Transfer the mixture to a non-reactive container, such as glass, and cover the surface of the mixture with clingfilm (plastic wrap). Keep the container at 40°C/104°F (in an incubator or other equally warm area) and leave for at least 10 weeks to ferment. The liquid garum will separate out to the bottom of the container. Decant or siphon off the liquid with an appropriate pipette or tube, then filter it through a funnel lined with coffee filter paper. The fermented garum has the faint aroma of oyster sauce, a distinct nuttiness and an underlying smell of roasted fermented cacao. It can be kept in the refrigerator, where it will continue to evolve slowly, or it can be transferred to sterilized jars or bottles and pasteurized (in an oven with a temperature probe, for example) at 72°C/162°F for 15 seconds, after which it will be indefinitely shelf-stable.

NOTE

The paste left over after filtering the liquid is also excellent, and should be passed through a fine mesh sieve (strainer).

Yield varies depending on the insect used, but usually ranges from 20–40% for the first fraction garum and from 10–20% for the second fraction.

SINGLE-INSECT GARUM
1 kg insects (55.9% by composition)
240 g salt (13.4% by composition)
300 g filtered water (16.8% by composition)
250 g pearl barley *kōji* grains (14% by composition), p.21

Recipe image p.216

After the Original Grasshopper Garum, we began making single-species garums to highlight the particular taste of each insect: grasshopper (*Locusta migratoria*), house cricket (*Acheta domesticus*), greater wax moth larvae (*Galleria mellonella*), honeybee brood (*Apis mellifera*) and mealworm (*Tenebrio molitor*). The mealworm was the only unsuccessful one – its trials were rather thin and one-note in taste. The rest are superb, complex and versatile. In principle, any insect could work, though more protein-rich ones will likely work better than more fat-rich ones, as the proteins will be broken down into amino acids (= umami), while the fats will oxidize. We have provided amounts here but also given per cent by composition so you can scale the recipe up or down.

SINGLE-INSECT GARUM

Blend the insects, salt and water in a blender or food processor until it is a rough purée. Add the *kōji* grains and mix to combine. Place the mixture in clean glass containers (we use 1-litre cylindrical flasks) and cover the surface with clingfilm (plastic wrap). Keep the container at 40°C/104°F (in an incubator or other equally warm area) and leave for at least 10 weeks to ferment. The liquid garum will separate out to the bottom of the container. Decant or siphon off the liquid with an appropriate pipette or tube, then filter it through a funnel lined with coffee filter paper. We call the filtered liquid 'first fraction garum'. The smooth paste left on the filter paper may also be used, after being passed through a fine mesh sieve; we call it 'first fraction paste'. The remaining solids from the fermentation may be squeezed through a Superbag; the resulting liquid (usable, but with more impurities than the first fraction) may be filtered through filter paper in the same fashion as above, yielding 'second fraction garum' and 'second fraction paste'.

Transfer the garums into sterilized glass jars or bottles with lids that seal, and pasteurize (in an oven with a temperature probe, for example) at 72°C/162°F for 15 seconds, after which they will be indefinitely shelf-stable. The pastes can be sealed in vacuum bags or sterilized glass jars with lids and kept in the refrigerator.

—Written by Josh Evans

Insect Garums

Moth Mousse

MOTH MOUSSE

Serves 4

SMOKED HAZELNUT MILK
250 g hazelnuts, skins removed
500 g filtered water
0.5 g xanthan gum
5 g juniper wood shavings

CHICKEN PURÉE
1 chicken breast, skinned
  and deboned

MOTH MOUSSE
200 g wax moth larvae
  (*Galleria mellonella*)
200 g smoked hazelnut milk
  (made earlier)
75 g chicken purée (made earlier)
2 g sea salt
5 g faux foie (optional, but
  recommended)

Nurdin Topham, a chef and friend of the Lab, headed up this dish, for an event called Pestival at the Wellcome Collection in London in spring 2013. We lightened the wax moth larvae into a classic mousseline, serving it with morels and hazelnut cream to play off the larvae's nuttiness.

SMOKED HAZELNUT MILK
Put the hazelnuts and water into a Thermomix and blend on high power for 2 minutes. Pour into a plastic container with a lid and leave in the refrigerator overnight. The next day, squeeze the liquid through a fine Superbag into a bowl to separate the milk from the pulp. You should be left with 550–560 g of milk. Discard the pulp.

Pour the hazelnut milk into the Thermomix, add the xanthan gum and blend on high power until the xanthan gum is incorporated. Pour the milk into a large bowl and cover with clingfilm (plastic wrap). Using a smoke gun (a handheld food smoker) and the juniper wood shavings, fill the bowl with juniper smoke and infuse, covered, for 10 minutes. Repeat until the milk has a distinct smoky flavour. Set aside.

CHICKEN PURÉE
Chill the Thermomix jug in the freezer. Dice the chicken breast, place in the Thermomix and blend on full power for 45 seconds until smooth. Chill the jug with the purée for 10 minutes, then blend again to create a fine purée. Pass through a fine tamis to remove any sinew and set aside.

MOTH MOUSSE
Chill the Thermomix jug. Prepare a bowl of iced water. Bring a pot of water to a boil, blanch the wax moth larvae for 5 seconds, then remove with a slotted spoon and plunge into the iced water. Drain and pat dry with paper towels. Transfer the larvae to the Thermomix jug with 100 g of the smoked hazelnut milk and blend on full power for 1 minute. Scrape down the sides of the blender jug and repeat 3 times. Pass through a very fine mesh sieve. It should yield 140 g. Reserve in a metal bowl, on ice.

MOREL AND HAZELNUT CREAM

60 g dry mead
60 g unsalted butter
600 g chestnut (cremini)
  mushrooms, very
  thinly sliced
100 g dried morel mushrooms,
  soaked overnight
60 g shallots, very
  thinly sliced
300 g smoked hazelnut milk
  (made earlier)
3 g fresh lemon verbena sprig
10 g faux foie (optional,
  but recommended)

TO FINISH

20 g unsalted butter
150 g small fresh or rehydrated
  morels, well washed and dried
15 g dry mead
3 g fresh lemon verbena sprig
faux foie, to taste (optional,
  but recommended)
4 hazelnuts, roasted, skins
  removed and halved
8 small ramson flowers
  (*Allium ursinum*) or
  garlic flowers
sea salt, to taste

Recipe image p.217

Clean and chill the Thermomix jug. Add the passed larvae purée, chicken purée, 100 g of the smoked hazelnut milk and seasonings to the jug and blend on full power until it is a silky smooth mousse. As a test, wrap 30 g of the mousse mix in a clingfilm 'boudin' (like a small sausage) and poach in an immersion circulator or water bath at 65°C/149°F for 10 minutes. Season to taste. The mousse should be light and delicate with a gentle smoky flavour. Place in a metal bowl, wrap in clingfilm and reserve on ice.

MOREL AND HAZELNUT CREAM
Boil the mead in a pan for 30 seconds, then set aside.

For the mushroom stock, melt half the butter in a large frying pan and caramelize half the chestnut (cremini) mushrooms until golden and crisp. Cook the remaining chestnut mushrooms in a dry pan until soft. Strain the morels, reserve the soaking liquid and pass through a fine mesh sieve. Add the caramelized mushrooms and morel soaking liquid to the softened mushrooms and simmer for 20 minutes. Skim, remove from the heat and then let rest for 20 minutes. Press and pass the stock through a chinois.

For the sauce, melt the remaining butter in a pan over low heat and cook the shallots for 8 minutes until translucent, with no colour. Stir in the morels and cook for 5 minutes. Add the hazelnut milk, boiled mead and mushroom stock and simmer for 15 minutes. Remove from the heat and add the lemon verbena sprig, cover with a lid and let infuse for 20 minutes. Using a hand-held blender, blitz the mixture for 10 seconds, then pass through a fine sieve. Season to taste and add the faux foie, if using.

TO FINISH
Poach the moth mousse 'boudins' as above. Heat the butter in a pan over medium heat, add the morels, mead and a little sea salt and and sauté briefly. Remove from the heat, add the lemon verbena sprig, faux foie to taste, if using, and cover with a lid. Reheat the morel and hazelnut cream in a saucepan and blend with a hand-held blender to emulsify. Lift the 'boudins' from the water bath, slice and place in warmed bowls. Spoon the cream around the moth mousse and top with morels. Garnish with the nuts and flowers.

—Written by Josh Evans with Nurdin Topham

BEE BROOD GRANOLA

—

Makes about 850 g

WET MIXTURE
250 g bee brood (frozen,
    or fresh if available)
100 g honey (any kind, as desired)
2 g salt

DRY MIXTURE
375 g whole rolled oats
150 g sesame seeds
150 g sunflower seeds
75 g pumpkin seeds

OPTIONAL ADDITIONS
fennel seeds, to taste
crushed juniper berries,
    to taste
birch sap, to taste

TO SERVE
dehydrated whole bee
    larvae, to taste
yogurt or milk, to taste
    (optional)

This dish was developed early on in the project as a simple way to introduce newcomers to eating insects in a familiar context (p.49). The savouriness of the brood comes through strong, but there are no whole insects to be seen.

WET MIXTURE
Let the bee brood thaw if using frozen, then blend in a blender or food processor with the honey and salt.

DRY MIXTURE
Preheat the oven to 160°C (325°F). Put the dry ingredients (including fennel seeds and/or juniper berries, if using) onto a baking sheet, add the wet mixture and stir until thoroughly mixed. Spread the mixture thinly over the base of the sheet and bake for 16 minutes, or until golden, stirring after 5, 10, 13 and 16 minutes to make sure it cooks evenly. If desired, stir some birch sap through the mixture around minute 13, for added sweetness and bigger clusters, then spread back out and continue to cook until golden. Remove, let cool and store in an airtight container.

TO SERVE
For an extra 'bee' effect, mix some dehydrated bee larvae into the cooled granola for more texture. Serve with yogurt or milk or as desired.

NOTE
This recipe uses bee brood – the larvae and pupae together, in whatever ratio the comb gives.

—Written by Josh Evans

Bee Brood Granola

ANTY GIN AND TONIC

---

ice cubes
2 parts Anty Gin
3 parts high-quality tonic water
1 drop of carmine (liquid
  cochineal), per glass
dried whole cochineal, to
  decorate (optional)

This cocktail was developed by Ben and the team, as part of a menu for an event we did called Pestival at the Wellcome Collection in London in the spring of 2013. For this event we designed and distilled our own Anty Gin in collaboration with The Cambridge Distillery, which in addition to the requisite juniper and a few supporting botanicals of wood avens (*Geum urbanum*), alexander seed (*Smyrnium olusatrum*) and stinging nettle (*Urtica dioica*), features red wood ants (*Formica rufa*) as the aromatic star. The result is a complex, well-balanced gin; the ants bring key citrus notes and, for me, a distinct tingling on the tongue, similar to the feeling a few minutes after eating a nasturtium seed.

We coloured our G&T with a drop of carmine, which is derived from the scale insect cochineal, to begin the event festively and to illustrate, with the first taste, already two different ways of using insects for their sensory properties that do not involve consuming one whole.

Half-fill a tumbler or highball glass with ice cubes, then add the gin, carmine and tonic water. Stir lightly, decorate with dried whole cochineal, if using, and serve.

—Written by Josh Evans

Anty Gin and Tonic

THE WHOLE HIVE

Serves 4

PROPOLIS TINCTURE
200 g 60% ethanol
20 g propolis powder

HONEY KOMBUCHA
1 kg water
50 g honey (any kind, as desired)
100 g live kombucha (from
   a previous batch)

BEESWAX ICE CREAM
70 g beeswax
400 g double (heavy) cow's
   cream (38% fat)
255 g whole (full-fat) cow's
   milk (3.5% fat)
200 g cow's milk yogurt
3 g guar gum
1.3 g salt
93 g trimoline

One of our researchers, Guillemette Barthouil, was the mastermind behind this dish, made for the Pestival event at the Wellcome Collection in London in 2013. Her concept was to develop a dessert based on all the elements of the beehive beyond honey: propolis, beeswax, bee bread and some blossoms. The only thing we didn't manage to incorporate this time was royal jelly – our next challenge…

PROPOLIS TINCTURE
Put the ingredients into a sealed container and let infuse for at least 1 week. Strain and store in an atomizer.

HONEY KOMBUCHA
Put all the ingredients for the honey kombucha into a large jar and mix together until the honey is dissolved. Cover the opening with a clean cloth, tie with string and leave at room temperature for 4–5 days to ferment. Taste the mixture every day until the desired balance of sourness and sweetness has been reached, then refrigerate to make sure the mixture doesn't keep fermenting.

BEESWAX ICE CREAM
Freeze 20 g of the beeswax, grind it in a Thermomix and mix with 50 g of the cream. Leave in a refrigerator at 4°C/39°F for 18 hours (the cold infusion, for the fragrant, waxy top notes).

The next day, freeze the remaining beeswax, grind it in the Thermomix and mix with the remaining 350 g of the cream. Seal the mixture in a vacuum bag on full seal, and keep it in an immersion circulator or water bath at 80°C/176°F for 1 hour (the hot infusion, for the deep, structured mouthfeel).

Meanwhile, put the cold infusion into a 250-micron Superbag and squeeze it over a bowl to pass. Set aside 30 g of the cold-infused cream.

Mix the milk, yogurt, guar gum and salt in a large bowl. Put the trimoline into a small saucepan and melt over low

HONEY KOMBUCHA SAUCE
190 g honey kombucha
   (made earlier)
10 g bee bread
1.2 g agar agar

HONEY CRISPS
100 g crumiel

TO FINISH
crumiel, to sprinkle
4 chambers bee bread
4 cherry or apple blossoms
   and sepals

Recipe image p.226

heat (it should not become hot, just liquid). Remove from the heat, add to the milk mixture and stir to combine.

When the hot infusion is done, place it in the freezer or a blast chiller until the cream reaches 37°C/98.6°F. The beeswax should solidify into a block – discard it and pass the rest of the cream through a Superbag. Weigh 270 g of the hot-infused cream, add the reserved 30 g cold-infused cream, mix with the other ingredients in a Paco container, blend in the Pacojet then freeze in a freezer. When it is frozen thoroughly, blend it again in the Pacojet.

HONEY KOMBUCHA SAUCE
Put the honey kombucha and bee bread into a bowl and stir together to combine. Infuse in a refrigerator at 4°C/39°F for 18 hours, stirring occasionally. Don't stir for the last 2 hours, so the bee bread sediments remain at the bottom. Decant the liquid through a Superbag into a pan. Add the agar and mix thoroughly. Bring to a boil, hold for 30 seconds, then remove from the heat and let cool until it sets. Put the mixture into a Thermomix and blitz until smooth, then pour into a squeeze bottle and set aside.

HONEY CRISPS
To reproduce the hexagonal beeswax shape, we made our own moulds by pressing beeswax into silicone. Preheat the oven to 150°C/300°F. Dust a thin layer of crumiel on the moulds, then put them into the oven for 3 minutes. Remove from the oven, press beneath a silicone sheet and return to the oven for 30 seconds. Remove from the oven, wait until the caramel has reached body temperature (37°C/98.6°F) and peel the crisps carefully from the moulds. Just before serving, spray with some of the propolis tincture.

TO FINISH
Chill the serving plates. Sprinkle a little of the crumiel just off-centre on each plate. Make a rocher (one-handed quenelle) of the beeswax ice cream and spoon onto the crumiel. Squeeze a small amount of the honey kombucha sauce near one end of the rocher. Place a honey crisp upright, nestled between the ice cream and the sauce. Finish the plate with a sprinkle of crumiel, broken pieces of bee bread and cherry or apple blossom petals and sepals.

—Written by Josh Evans with Guillemette Barthouil

The Whole Hive

Rhubarb and Roseroot

RHUBARB AND ROSEROOT

Serves 4

ROSEROOT TINCTURE
100 g roseroot (*Rhodiola rosea*)
200 g alcohol (min 60% abv)

RHUBARB ROOT OIL
45 g dried rhubarb root
150 g sunflower oil

RHUBARB JELLY
600 g rhubarb, trimmed of leaves
  and thinly sliced (for syrup)
90 g caster (superfine) sugar
5 g leaf gelatine

This dish is from Bug Jam, a collaboration with chefs Josh Pollen and Nurdin Topham in May 2016. Josh took the lead on this dish. Here's his description: 'Receiving the last pink rhubarb of the spring offered us a chance to make a simple, beautifully coloured jelly. Cooking the rhubarb with sugar at a low temperature drew out an extremely clear red juice, which we set with gelatine (gelatine giving the best wobble – what good is jelly if it doesn't wobble?).

'We added aromatic accents to the jelly with bee bread, water mint – an especially pungent wild variety – and wood ants, which added tiny bursts of lemon-like acidity. The rhubarb root oil rounded out the flavour of the rhubarb stalk and provided an unctuous texture. A tincture of roseroot (*Rhodiola rosea*) is sprayed over the plate as it is served, so the first interaction the guest has is with a spicy, alluring, rose-like aroma.'

ROSEROOT TINCTURE
Coarsely grind the roseroot in a Thermomix, add it to a sealable dark glass jar and pour in the alcohol, making sure to cover the roots completely. Seal and let macerate for at least 6 weeks in a cool, dark place. When fully aromatic, strain a small amount of the tincture through a fine mesh sieve and store in an atomizer (mist spray bottle).

RHUBARB ROOT OIL
Put the dried rhubarb root and oil in a Thermomix heated to 80°C/176°F and blend at high speed for 5 minutes. Transfer to a plastic tub and macerate for 8 hours, or overnight. The next day, strain the mixture through a funnel lined with filter paper, collecting the oil in another plastic tub that has a lid. When all the oil has filtered through, close and store in the refrigerator.

RHUBARB JELLY
Toss the rhubarb and sugar in a bowl, then add to a vacuum bag and close on a full seal. Put the bag into an immersion circulator or water bath at 40°C/104°F and then leave for

TO FINISH
4 chambers bee bread
36 red wood ants (*Formica rufa*)
16 water mint (*Mentha aquatica*)
  leaves

Recipe image p.227

45 minutes. The heat will be enough to soften the rhubarb without breaking it down (otherwise the juice will be cloudy) and the sugars will draw the juice out of the slices, without being heated enough to acquire any caramel flavours.

Remove the bag from the water after 45 minutes and put the rhubarb and syrup into a Superbag or a very fine sieve, collecting the syrup as it drips through into a bowl. Weigh the amount of syrup (you should have roughly two-thirds of the weight of the total rhubarb, about 400 g). Pour the rhubarb syrup into a saucepan. (The remaining fruit pulp can be made into a second batch of syrup, albeit somewhat diminished in flavour, if cooked gently with equal measures of water and sugar and strained – save this for another recipe.)

Soak the gelatine in a small bowl of cold water for 5 minutes. Add to the rhubarb syrup in the pan over very low heat and stir until the gelatine has clearly dissolved. Pour the mixture through a fine mesh sieve into a plastic tub and cool for 30 minutes at room temperature. Transfer the jelly to the refrigerator and chill for at least 6 hours, or overnight, until it has set.

TO FINISH
Remove any residual wax from the bee bread and break into 8 rough chunks. Sort the ants, removing any dirt or twigs. Wash the water mint, blot dry on paper towels and store in the refrigerator in a closed tub with a damp paper towel until ready to serve.

When ready to serve, break up the jelly with a fork – not so much as to lose definition, but enough to loosen its structure. In the centre of a small, white, round-bottomed bowl, place a tablespoon of the jelly, levelling it slightly with the spoon. Create a few small depressions in the surface of the jelly into which some of the rhubarb root oil will pool. Pour a drizzle of rhubarb root oil over the jelly, finding the little dips and using enough so that a ring of bright yellow oil gathers around the red jelly. Place 8 pieces of bee bread and 4 leaves of water mint onto the jelly, add the ants and finish with a small spritz of tincture from the atomizer over the dish.

—Written by Josh Evans with Josh Pollen

CHIMP STICK

—

Serves 4

5 pieces juniper wood (see photo
  for rough size)
200 g clear, light honey
150 g buckwheat groats, soaked
  in water overnight
butter, for frying
4 liquorice roots
1 kg rice or another grain
50 g yellow linseed (flaxseed)
20 red wood ants (*Formica rufa*),
  frozen within 1 hour
  of harvesting
24 smelling carpenter ants
  (*Lasius fuliginosus*), frozen
  within 1 hour of harvesting
24 freeze-dried raspberry pieces
20 small purple shiso cress leaves
20 small lemon verbena leaves
20 small cherry blossoms

This dish was the brainchild of chef Josh Pollen, who helped develop the menu for the Pestival event at the Wellcome Collection in London in 2013. It was inspired by chimpanzees' ingenuity in using sticks to fish ants and termites from their mounds. Guests could choose whether to suck all the edible parts off the stick or pick at it and taste the flavours individually. Our hope was to evoke the flavours and textures that surround the ants in their field or forest habitat, and to use their sour taste to brighten the palate for the menu to come.

Toast a piece of the juniper wood with a blowtorch until its surface is blackened. Place the blackened wood in the honey and let infuse overnight.

The next day, strain the honey and set aside. Drain the buckwheat and spread out to dry. Melt some butter in a frying pan over medium heat and toast the buckwheat until golden brown. Remove from the heat, cool, then wrap in cloth and crack into coarse pieces using a rolling pin.

With a small knife, whittle the liquorice roots, removing all the rough skin and thinning them to a more slender shape. Leave a section at one end unwhittled as a handle. Brush the liquorice roots on all the whittled sides with a light coating of the honey, just enough to make things stick but not drip. Place the liquorice roots, handle-side down, into a bowl of rice to hold the roots upright for assembly. Begin to stick the ingredients onto the liquorice roots. Start with the buckwheat and lindseed (flaxseeds), then the ants, raspberries, herbs and cherry blossoms.

TO SERVE
Place the 4 remaining pieces of juniper wood on 4 separate plates. Char with the blowtorch until blackened. Remove the chimp sticks from the rice and rest on the smouldering wood, handle-side on the plate. Serve immediately.

—Written by Josh Evans with Josh Pollen

Chimp Stick

BEE BREAD BUTTER

—

Makes: about 50% yield

**1 kg full-fat (heavy)
  unhomogenized cream
1 chamber bee bread
fine salt, to taste**

When we learned at the Lab that bee bread is chock-full of lactic acid bacteria, we thought to use it to inoculate cream to make cultured butter. The result was potent.

Pour the cream into a non-reactive container and add the bee bread. Leave for 1 hour at room temperature, then strain through a sieve to remove the bee bread. Cover the cream with a lid or clingfilm (plastic wrap) and leave the inoculated cream at room temperature for 24 hours.

After 24 hours, put the cream into the refrigerator for at least a few days until it is thick and flavoursome, to taste. Culturing at room temperature for the whole period, especially with the potency of the bee bread, can sometimes yield an overly rapid fermentation and putrid flavours.

When the cream has reached your desired thickness, acidity and flavour, pour it into the chilled metal bowl of a stand mixer, and whip until the butterfat and buttermilk separate out. Alternatively, whip the cream by hand: pour it into a chilled metal bowl, wrap well with clingfilm, and shake in circles until the butterfat and buttermilk separate out. Drain the excess buttermilk and reserve for another purpose. Press the butterfat together into a mass, then throw it against a hard surface like a chopping (cutting) board and/or wash it under cold running water to remove any remaining buttermilk and season with salt as desired. Put the butter into a ramekin, and serve with grilled bread, blanched vegetables or with other dishes. It may be kept for at least a few days at room temperature or longer in the refrigerator – if it lasts.

—Written by Josh Evans

Bee Bread Butter

OATCHI

Serves 4

BIRCH BUD SALT
fresh birch buds
salt

OAT MILK
200 g whole pressed or
    rolled oats
600 g filtered water
4 g sea salt

OAT FLOUR
80 g whole pressed or
    rolled oats

OATCHI
65 g oat flour (made earlier)
400 g oat milk (made earlier)
3 g birch bud salt (made earlier)

Chef Nurdin Topham created this dish at Bug Jam, a collaboration he, Josh Pollen and I made in May 2016. It was partly inspired by the *gohei mochi* we encountered on our fieldwork at the annual wasp festival in Kushihara, Japan (pp.187–93). The idea was to recreate the soft, gelatinous texture of the glutinous rice *mochi* with a Nordic grain, and contrast this texture with a crispy glazed exterior – a platform for the roasted caramelized bee pupae. This recipe also uses a Nordic Food Lab icon, a few-years-old fermented deer leg – 'deer bushi' or 'shikabushi' as we like to call it. It is modelled after the traditional Japanese *kastuobushi*, a fermented, smoked and dried fillet of skipjack tuna, which when thinly shaved is used in many preparations as a basic condiment, and may be used in place of deer bushi here, if one does not happen to have a fermented deer leg on hand.

BIRCH BUD SALT
Put equal weights foraged birch buds and salt into a mortar and crush together with a pestle until well combined and the desired fineness is reached. Store in an airtight container.

OAT MILK
Preheat the oven to 160°C/325°F. Spread the oats for both the oat milk and the oat flour on a baking sheet and roast in the oven for 10 minutes until toasted. Stir if necessary to ensure they toast evenly. To make the oat milk, put 200 g of the toasted oats into a Thermomix with the filtered water and salt, then blend on full power for 45 seconds. Pour the mixture into a 250-micron Superbag and squeeze it into a bowl. Set aside.

OAT FLOUR
Put the remaining toasted oats into the Thermomix and blend until finely ground.

OATCHI
To make the oatchi, put 65 g of the oat flour into a large bowl, add 400 g of the toasted oat milk and stir to make

DEER TARE
120 g mead
80 g birch syrup
60 g bee larvae garum (p.215)
8 g deer bushi (p.21), finely shaved

FRIED BEE PUPAE
50 g sunflower oil
100 g bee pupae
1 g birch bud salt

TO FINISH
8 birch twigs
birchwood pieces, for grilling
50 g neutral oil, for frying
  (optional)

TO SERVE
4 g deer bushi, finely shaved
40 g spring (green) onions,
  finely sliced
4 ramson flowers (*Allium ursinum*)
8 chive blossoms
  (*Allium schoenoprasum*)

Recipe image p.236

a smooth, thick batter. Season with the birch bud salt and pour into a 325 × 176 mm (12.8 × 7 inch) pan (⅓ size Gastro-tray). Cover with foil and pierce the foil with a small knife. Steam for 25 minutes in the combination oven on 100 per cent steam or in a steamer. Remove and cool for 30 minutes, then refrigerate for 2 hours, or for 30 minutes in a blast chiller. Spread the remaining toasted oat flour out on a plate. Once the oatchi is cold, cut out 8 oval shapes with a 6 cm (2¼ inch) circular cutter or ring mould. Coat in the oat flour and set aside.

DEER TARE
Put the mead into a small saucepan, add the birch syrup and bee larvae garum and simmer gently until reduced by one-fifth of its total volume. Remove from the heat, add the deer bushi, cover and infuse for 5 minutes. Pass through a fine sieve into another small pan and set aside.

FRIED BEE PUPAE
Heat the oil in a frying pan or skillet over high heat. Add the bee pupae and shallow-fry, shaking the pan gently to keep the pupae moving, until they are a rich golden brown. Drain, season lightly with birch bud salt and set aside.

TO FINISH
Prepare the birch twigs by removing the leaves, then at one end scrape away the bark with a small knife and whittle the end to a point. Carefully skewer the oatchi cakes onto the prepared birch twigs. Grill over hot birchwood embers until the surfaces are blistered and the edges just begin to char, or, alternatively, fry in a pan in hot neutral oil until the surfaces are golden and crispy.

TO SERVE
Place the oatchi on serving plates and with a pastry brush generously glaze with the deer *tare*. Top with the roasted bee pupae, some deer bushi shavings, finely sliced spring (green) onion, the ramson flowers and chive blossoms.

NOTES
Tare is a Japanese word for a sauce or glaze.

—Written by Josh Evans with Nurdin Topham

Oatchi

Chawanmushi

CHAWANMUSHI

Serves 4

DEER DASHI
20 g kombu
500 g filtered water
20 g deer bushi (p.21),
  finely shaved
10 g bee larvae garum (p.215),
  plus extra if needed
1 g potato starch
a little birch syrup (optional)

CHAWANMUSHI
250 g fresh or frozen bee larvae,
  thawed if frozen
250 g deer dashi (made earlier
  and cooled)
0.5 g xanthan gum

Here is another dish of Nurdin's from our Bug Jam collaboration in May 2016. Chicken eggs and wasp eggs share some physical properties, which in the field made us think that the latter might be useful in contexts more familiar to the former. I made a very rough attempt at a chawanmushi (pp.197–8), and we also ended up encountering one made with giant hornet larvae as part of a kaiseki dinner during our fieldwork in Japan (pp.200–1). Here is our recreation of this weepingly soft savoury Japanese custard with Danish bee larvae. The initial trials were inspired by the flavour combination of the savoury bee larvae custard with a condiment made from a paste of large bitter cress leaves, which had a close resemblance to fresh wasabi root. To round out and balance the bee larvae flavour, we made a dashi with aged kombu and the deer bushi (see 'Oatchi', pp.234–5; *katsuobushi* may be used here instead, if necessary). Garnished with asparagus tips and grilled girolles, it made a fitting tribute to the moment when spring gives way to summer.

DEER DASHI
Put the kombu and the water into a vacuum bag and rehydrate for 30 minutes. Preheat the sous vide machine or water bath to 60°C/140°F. Place the kombu and water still in the bag in the preheated water bath for 1 hour. Remove and cool, then open the bag and strain through a fine sieve into a saucepan. Bring the kombu stock to a boil, add the finely shaved deer bushi and bee larvae garum, cover with a lid and remove from the heat. Let infuse for 5 minutes before passing through a fine sieve into a bowl.

Set aside 250 g of the deer dashi to cool for the chawanmushi. Pour the remaining 250 g of deer dashi into a small saucepan. Pour a spoonful of the dashi into a small bowl, add the potato starch and stir until it has dissolved. Whisk this mixture back into the dashi in the pan over medium heat for 1–2 minutes, or until it has thickened. Taste and adjust the seasoning if necessary with a little birch syrup and/or a drop of bee larvae garum. Set aside.

BARBECUED GIROLLES
15 g dried ceps (porcini)
300 g warm filtered water
200 g girolle mushrooms
20 g grapeseed oil
35 g shallots, cut into 2-mm
  (⅛-inch) slices

BITTERCRESS CONDIMENT
20 g large bittercress
  (*Cardamine amara*) leaves
2 g sea salt

TO FINISH
8 asparagus tips (4 white, 4 green)
8 small bittercress leaves
8 garden cress (*Lepidium sativum*)
  blossoms

Recipe image p.237

CHAWANMUSHI
Put the bee larvae into a Thermomix, add the 250 g cooled deer dashi and the xanthan gum and blend on full power for 1 minute. Pass through a fine Superbag and decant into 4 bowls suitable for steaming and serving. Cover loosely with foil, prick the foil with a small knife and steam in a combination oven at 80°C/176°F or in a steamer for 8 minutes. Set aside.

BARBECUED GIROLLES
Put the dried ceps (porcini) into a heatproof bowl, pour in the warm filtered water and leave until rehydrated. Meanwhile, clean the girolles, reserving the trimmings. Begin to make the glaze by heating the grapeseed oil in a pan over low heat, adding the shallots and cooking for 5 minutes until soft but with no colour. When they are rehydrated, drain the ceps and reserve the soaking liquid. Add 30 g of the reserved girolle trimmings, the ceps and cep soaking liquid to the pan and simmer until it is reduced by half. Pass the mixture through a sieve into the pan and simmer again until it has reduced to a glaze consistency.

Put the girolles into a frying pan or skillet and torch them with a blowtorch, turning them evenly until they have a light char all over. Pour less than 1 cm (½ inch) of the mushroom glaze into a small saucepan, set over medium heat, add the mushrooms and toss them in the glaze for a couple of minutes, just until they are coated and warmed through. Set aside.

BITTERCRESS CONDIMENT
Put the bittercress leaves and salt into a mortar and pulverize with the pestle to a fine purée, then set aside.

TO FINISH
Have a bowl of iced water ready. Bring a pot of salted water to a boil, add the asparagus tips and blanch for 2 minutes. Remove with a slotted spoon and plunge them into the iced water to refresh, then drain. Place the asparagus tips and barbecued girolles on top of the set chawanmushi, then garnish with a small spoonful of the bittercress condiment, bittercress leaves and garden cress blossoms. Finally, spoon a little of the thickened deer dashi over the top of the dish.

—Written by Josh Evans with Nurdin Topham

BEE LARVAE CEVICHE

Serves 4

RHUBARB VINEGAR
1 kg fresh rhubarb
lab-grade ethanol (96% abv)
live vinegar (our go-to is a raw
  apple balsamic vinegar, but
  any raw vinegar will work; the
  more neutral the flavour, the
  better the rhubarb flavour
  will come through)

SØL SALT
20 g dried dulse (*Palmaria
  palmata*; *søl* in Danish)
100 g sea salt

TO FINISH
28 fresh or frozen bee larvae
100 g rhubarb vinegar
  (made earlier)
2 g *søl* salt (made earlier)
10 g red oxalis (*Oxalis corniculata*)
  stems, very thinly sliced
20 fresh redcurrants
20 red oxalis (*Oxalis
  corniculata*) leaves
12 sections of lemon
  thyme leaves

This dish is based on a series of ceviche experiments made by Sebastian Moreno Henao, a chef from Colombia who interned with us in the summer of 2013. He arrived at this preparation for whole young bee larvae, a true celebration of their delicate texture.

RHUBARB VINEGAR
Juice the rhubarb. Whatever the yield, add ethanol until it is 7 per cent by weight of the total mixture. Add 20 per cent by weight of the live vinegar, put into a non-reactive container, cover with a cloth and tie it down with kitchen string (twine) or a rubber band. Let ferment until all the alcohol has turned to acetic acid. You will be able to smell when there is no longer any alcohol. Alternatively, use an aquarium bubbler (found in any pet shop) to rapidly aerate the mixture, which will yield a finished vinegar in 5–7 days. The slow version, however, will likely be more flavourful.

SØL SALT
Dry the dulse in a dehydrator until brittle. Blend to a powder in a Thermomix (or other powerful blender or food processor), then add the salt and blend further to a fine powder. Keep in an airtight container.

TO FINISH
Choose the most pristine bee larvae, and if using frozen larvae, let them thaw for 3 minutes at room temperature. Pour the vinegar into a small bowl, add the bee larvae and season with the salt to taste. Leave for another 3 minutes.

Remove the bee larvae from the vinegar and place 7 in the middle of each serving bowl. Add the sliced oxalis stems to the vinegar left in the mixing bowl, and dress each plate with a little of the vinegar. Place the redcurrants, oxalis leaves and lemon thyme leaves around the bee larvae and serve immediately.

—Written by Josh Evans with
Sebastian Moreno Henao

Bee Larvae Ceviche

TSUKUDANI BEE LARVAE

—

Makes about 120 g

100 g bee larvae garum (p.215)
30 g honey
50 g bee larvae

In Japan, *tsukudani* – simmering with soy sauce, sugar and sometimes dashi, *tsuyu*, mirin and/or ginger – is a common technique for preparing different types of insects (pp.189, 196–7). I wanted to try this technique with some of our Danish insects, and bee larvae seemed like the obvious choice because they bear a close physical resemblance to *hebo*, or the larvae of the Japanese wasp (*Vespula flaviceps*).

Put the bee larvae garum into a small saucepan and warm over low heat for a couple of minutes. Add the honey and stir to dissolve. Cook very gently until it has reduced to half of its original volume. Do not allow the sauce to reduce too quickly, otherwise it will gain a bitter flavour.

Once the sauce has reduced, add the bee larvae and mix gently to coat them in the sauce. Cook gently for a few minutes until the larvae become firm. Remove the pan from the heat before they shrivel, and serve.

If you would like to preserve the larvae for a longer time (as is the tradition), cook them a little more so that they lose more of their moisture – though their texture is best when they retain some of their plumpness.

NOTES
Serve as a condiment with rice, other cooked grains or cooked vegetables. It can also be stored in the refrigerator for at least a week, depending on how much liquid has been removed.

—Written by Josh Evans

Tsukudani Bee Larvae

ANTS ON A LOG

———

Serves 4

LOG
400 g celeriac (celery root)
40 g butter
2 g birch bud salt (p.234)

BARK CRUMB
50 g celeriac (celery root) skin
  (reserved from the log)
50 g sweet dark rye bread, dried
1 g ground coffee

ROASTED SUNFLOWER
SEED CREAM
250 g sunflower seeds
about 250 g filtered water
50 g cold-pressed sunflower oil
1 g fine sea salt

Nurdin, Josh and I made this dish at Bug Jam. Ants on a log is a classic North American kids' snack originating from the 1950s. The basic version involves spreading peanut butter into a celery stalk (the 'log') and sticking raisins into it (the 'ants'). The metaphor was too tempting not to make literal.

LOG
Peel the celeriac (celery root), reserving the outer skin for the bark crumb. Slice the celeriac into 3-cm (⅛-inch) thick slices and cut the slices into long batons. Shape the batons into bent cylinders so that they resemble logs. Slight imperfections are desirable. Heat the butter in a pan until the milk solids caramelize to a golden brown colour, then remove from the heat and let cool slightly. Add the brown butter to a sous vide bag with the celeriac logs and season with the birch bud salt. Seal and cook in an immersion circulator or water bath at 85°C/185°F for 30–40 minutes, or until soft and melting but still retaining texture.

BARK CRUMB
Preheat the oven to 300°C/572°F. Put the reserved celeriac skin onto a baking sheet and cook in the oven for about 10 minutes, or until charred. Cool, then blend in the Thermomix or food processor and pass through a fine sieve over a bowl to yield a fine ash. Clean the Thermomix or food processor, then blend the dry rye bread until finely ground. Transfer to a bowl, add some of the celeriac ash and the ground coffee until the desired colour and flavour balance is reached, and mix together to create a bark for the celeriac log. Set aside.

SUNFLOWER SEED CREAM
Preheat the oven to 160°C/325°F. Spread the sunflower seeds out on a baking sheet and roast in the oven for 10 minutes until golden. Remove from the oven, place in a bowl and pour in enough water to cover. Let soak in the refrigerator overnight. The next day, drain the seeds through a sieve set over a bowl, reserving 100 g of the

TO FINISH
16 small lovage leaves
40 small sweet cicely leaves
160 smelling carpenter ants
(*Lasius fuliginosus*)

Recipe image p.246

soaking liquid. Put the seeds, the reserved soaking liquid, the sunflower oil and salt into a Pacoject container and blast freeze in a blast freezer until completely frozen. When frozen, remove from the freezer, put the container into the Pacojet and blend. Re-freeze in the blast freezer until completely solid again, then blend again until the mixture is a smooth cream. Taste and adjust the seasoning if necessary.

TO FINISH
Pick the youngest, smallest lovage and sweet cicely leaves and set aside. Spread the bark crumb out on a plate, roll the celeriac log in it until it is completely coated, and shake off the excess. Trim the ends of the log flat to reveal the clean white wood. Place on a serving plate, and place at least 40 ants on the log, or more if you can manage. There should not be any on the plate. Spoon a small mound of roasted sunflower seed cream near the log, then arrange the sweet cicely and lovage leaves overlapping all around it so that it resembles a small fern.

—Written by Josh Evans with
Nurdin Topham

Ants on a Log

WHEAD AND WEED

Serves 4

CLOVE ROOT OIL
150 g sunflower oil
45 g wood avens (*Geum urbanum*) roots

REDUCED YOGURT WHEY
1 kg cow's milk plain (natural) yogurt (3.5% fat)

Another Bug Jam creation led by Josh Pollen: 'After discovering that a decent simulacrum of the flavour of mead could be achieved by reducing clear yogurt whey with honey (thus "whead"), we built a dish around it, including beeswax to add another layer of bee-related flavour.

'The dish is designed as a bridge between savoury and sweet, the bee larvae being delicately savoury, and the broth tart, complex, aromatic and slightly sweet. After a number of trials of blanching the larvae in water with different levels of salinity and for different amounts of time, we alighted on a process that plumps the bee larvae but leaves them soft and creamy inside.

To accompany the main elements of the dish we chose three aromatic components: tiny field pansies, shoots of hemp plants and an oil infused with the gentle clove-like flavour of the roots of wood avens (*Geum urbanum*). The pansies, although small, add a gentle floral aroma and a tiny hit of nectar, adding to the list of tastes related to the bees' work.'

CLOVE ROOT OIL
Put the sunflower oil and wood avens roots into a Thermomix heated to 80°C/176°F and blend at high speed for 5 minutes. Pour the mixture into a container, cover and let macerate in a dark, cool place for 8 hours, or overnight. Strain the mixture through a coffee filter paper set inside a funnel, then, once all the oil has filtered through, discard the filter paper, and fill a pipette with the filtered oil. Set aside.

REDUCED YOGURT WHEY
Set a clean piece of muslin (cheesecloth) over a fine sieve in a bowl. Pour the yogurt into the centre of the muslin and tie the 4 corners together to make a tight parcel. Add a weight to the top of the bag and put it in the refrigerator for 8 hours, or overnight. After 8 hours (or overnight) you should have about 500 g of clear, bright yellow whey. Save the strained yogurt for another use.

'WHEAD' SAUCE
250 g reduced yogurt whey
  (made earlier)
15 g beeswax
25 g wildflower honey
0.4 g xanthan gum

TO FINISH
12 hemp shoots (*Cannabis sativa*)
20 field pansies (*Viola arvensis*)
40 g bee larvae, frozen
fine sea salt, to taste

Recipe image p.247

Pour the yogurt whey into a medium pot and simmer slowly over low heat until it is reduced by a quarter of its volume. Its colour will turn from a greenish, electric yellow to a slightly more orangey yellow as it caramelizes.

'WHEAD' SAUCE

Remove the reduced whey from the heat, measure out 250 g and add the pieces of beeswax to it to infuse. Cool for about 1 hour to room temperature, then chill until the wax resolidifies. Strain the sauce through a sieve into a pan, add the honey and very gently heat while stirring, just to melt the honey and allow it to dissolve. Check the seasoning – you are looking to balance the sourness of the whey with the sweetness and slight bitterness of the honey. Add the xanthan gum to the broth – its job is to thicken the broth very lightly so it clings to the garnishes and has a just-perceptible unctuousness. Disperse the xanthan gum into the broth by blending it at high speed with a hand-held blender. Stop the blender and leave the sauce for 2 minutes for the gum to hydrate, then blend at high speed again. Strain slowly through a very fine sieve to remove any air bubbles. Set aside.

TO FINISH

Pick individual leaves from the hemp shoots, wash and blot dry on paper towels. Pick the stems from the field pansies, leaving just the flower heads. Set a small pot of salted water over medium heat to blanch the bee larvae.

Select the most plump and pristine bee larvae and add to the pot when the water has reached 75°C/167°F. Blanch them for 8 seconds, then quickly remove them with a slotted spoon and use paper towels to blot off any excess water. In the bottom of a deep-curved bowl, arrange the bees in a layered array. Add 3 tablespoons of the sauce, carefully to avoid disturbing the larvae, followed by 3 hemp leaves, 5 pansies and 5 drops of clove root oil.

NOTE

A chamber vacuum can be used to de-aerate liquids – place the liquid in an open container, close the chamber and run it on a full seal cycle. The vacuum will cause any air bubbles to expand and pop, leaving the liquid bubble-free.

—Written by Josh Evans with Josh Pollen

HORNET HIGHBALL

—

Serves 1

ice cubes
2 g Japanese giant hornet liquor
60 g whisky of choice
150 g soda water (club soda)
   or sparkling water
1 twist of lemon peel

This drink is how Nurdin, Josh and I took our nightcap with our nightly debriefs during Bug Jam. Nurdin had just arrived to the Lab from Hong Kong after three weeks travelling in Japan. Among the many goodies he brought with him was a bottle of Nikka whisky. Our other in-house Japanese spirit was the liquor of the giant hornet, obtained during our fieldwork in Gifu prefecture in central Japan (pp.198–9). The rest is history.

Half-fill a highball glass with the ice cubes and add the hornet liquor with a pipette. Pour in the whisky of your choice, followed by the soda water (club soda) or sparkling water and a twist of lemon peel. Stir and serve immediately.

—Written by Josh Evans

Hornet Highball

PORRIDGE AND LABRADOR TEA

Serves 4

PORRIDGE
20 g buckwheat
10 g kamut wheat
20 g purple (PurPur) wheat
15 g babushka wheat
100 g cow's yogurt whey (reserved
   from Whead and Weed, p.248)
25 g butter
1 g birch bud salt (p.234)
15 g rolled oats
50 g cow's milk
5 g honey
2 g bee larvae garum (p.215)
5 g apple balsamic vinegar or
   apple cider vinegar

LABRADOR TEA OIL
30 g northern Labrador tea
   (*Rhododendron tomentosum*)
   leaves
150 g sunflower oil

A very Josh Pollen dish, from our Bug Jam collaboration: 'Owing to a surfeit of brilliantly coloured varieties of Scandinavian grains, we wanted to make a savoury porridge seasoned with bee larvae garum, honey and birch bud salt. It is flanked in a bowl by accompaniments to be added to each bite: the leaves and flowering tops of garlic mustard (*Alliaria petiolata*), an oil infused with northern Labrador tea (*Rhododendron tomentosum*), an aromatic evergreen shrub, and several rows of bee larvae, lightly blanched and painted with an emulsion of yogurt whey and butter.'

PORRIDGE
Soak each variety of grain separately, except the oats, in the yogurt whey for 24 hours until the husks are softened. Drain, reserving the whey, then rinse the grains under cold running water and blot dry with paper towels. Set aside.

Heat 10 g of the butter in a pan over medium heat, add the buckwheat and fry for some minutes until the grains are an amber colour, then season with half the birch bud salt. Drain on paper towels and set aside.

Put all the wheat grains and the reserved yogurt whey into a pot, top up with water to cover the grains, season with the remaining birch bud salt and cook for 1½–2 hours, or until they are cooked through. Drain and set aside.

LABRADOR TEA OIL
Blend the Labrador tea leaves with the oil in a Thermomix set to 60°C/140°F. Transfer to a container with a lid and let macerate overnight. The next day, strain the mixture through a coffee filter paper into a small container with a lid and set aside.

PORRIDGE CONTINUED
Toast the oats gently in a dry saucepan over medium heat until they are fragrant and just beginning to colour, a few minutes. Add the milk and honey and cook the oats gently until they have thickened and hydrated, but are still fairly

TO FINISH

64 bee larvae, frozen
sea salt, to taste
1 tsp butter
1 tsp yogurt whey
honey, to taste
birch bud salt (p.234), to taste
20 small garlic mustard
    (*Alliaria petiolata*) leaves
12 garlic mustard flower
    head tips

Recipe image p.254

loose. Add the whole cooked grains, reserving a tablespoon of fried buckwheat to garnish. Stir the remaining butter, the bee larvae garum and apple balsamic vinegar or apple cider vinegar into the grains, then reduce the heat to the lowest possible setting and cook very gently for 5 minutes.

TO FINISH

Set a small pot of water over medium heat to blanch the bee larvae. Season the water with the salt to taste. Select the most plump and pristine bee larvae and add them to the pot when the water has reached 75°C/167°F. Blanch them for 8 seconds, then quickly remove them from the water with a slotted spoon and use paper towels to blot off any excess water.

Melt the butter with the yogurt whey in a small pot over medium-low heat and stir to emulsify. Arrange the bee larvae to one side in a bowl, overlapping each other slightly. Stir honey, to taste, into the porridge, and adjust the seasoning with a pinch of birch bud salt. Place 1 tablespoon of porridge in a quenelle next to the bee larvae. Flank the bee larvae and porridge with garlic mustard leaves on one end and flowers on the other, then using a pastry brush daub the bee larvae and porridge with the butter-whey emulsion. Spoon 3 tablespoons of the Labrador tea oil into the centre of the bowl and serve.

NOTE

Kamut, purple (PurPur) and babushka wheat are all varieties of ancient grains. As its name suggests, purple wheat is a striking purple-coloured variety.

—Written by Josh Evans with Josh Pollen

Porridge and Labrador Tea

Sheep Heart Tartare

SHEEP HEART TARTARE

—

Serves 2

BRINE
200 g water
10 g salt
ice cubes

TARTARE
50 g fresh sheep heart
10 g extra-virgin olive oil
100 g birch wood
100 g juniper branches
4 green juniper berries, crushed
10 g dried figs
8 g Anty Gin (p.222)
2 g pure essence of ants from
   The Cambridge Distillery
0.2 g black pepper
10 g clover honey
3 g salt

I love to use heart as an ingredient. For many people, the heart represents a difficult organ to cook because it requires specific knowledge in order to prepare it correctly or because, psychologically, it is not accepted as a food. Sadly, the heart is an often undervalued ingredient. This pulsing centre is a constant source of fascination for me; there is only one heart in every body. It's the only organ that makes a sound – constantly beating the rhythm of life, it signals its presence.

Every time I use sheep meat – especially intestines – in a recipe, it reminds me of my childhood and my grandfather who was a shepherd. In this particular recipe, I use the figs from the tree that my grandfather planted over eighty years ago. Bound to the emotions of family traditions, the beats of a heart signify more than just food, but memories and traditions passed down from generation to generation.

On several occasions, the sheep heart tartare was paired with a shot of Anty Gin. I developed this recipe at the Lab for Tavole Academiche at the University of Gastronomic Science in Italy.

BRINE
Combine the water with the salt and stir until the salt dissolves, then add the ice cubes. Set aside.

TARTARE
Wash the heart in the iced brine, then remove the hard parts and the fat with a sharp knife. Dry the heart with a clean cloth, then brush the heart with olive oil. In a smoker, cold smoke the heart using a mix of birch wood and fresh juniper branches. Five minutes of smoking will be enough to give the meat a mild, smoky flavour.

Put the smoked heart into a vacuum bag with the crushed juniper berries, seal and put into the refrigerator overnight.

TO SERVE
2 pieces birch bark
15 g Anty Gin (p.222)

Recipe image p.255

The next day, using a very sharpe knife chop the heart into irregular sized pieces, then chop the figs in the same manner and put both into a bowl. Pour in the Anty Gin and add a few drops of olive oil, to taste. Add the ant essence and black pepper and mix well. Add the crushed juniper berries, the honey and salt and mix. Put the mixture into a vacuum bag, seal and place in the refrigerator for 1 hour.

TO SERVE
Open the bag and mix together with a spoon to give an airy consistency before plating. Serve the tartare on top of a birch bark. Add a little Anty Gin on top and set fire to the bark before serving.

—Written by Roberto Flore

BEE LARVAE TACO

—

Makes lots of tacos!

MASA
1 kg water
10 g calcium hydroxide
  (slaked lime), p.316
100 g Øland wheat
2 g salt
neutral oil, for spraying

This dish is connected to the 'What Will We Be Eating in 2025?' seminar that I was involved with at the European Parliament with Afton Halloran and Santiago Lastra in late September 2015 (pp.210–11).

For me, the larvae represent a connecting point between many cultures (Sardinia, Japan, Mexico and so on) despite their differences in taste. I love to create dishes that bridge gastronomic traditions. This dish tells the story of the research that I conducted at the Lab with Santiago, using the Mexican technique of nixtamalization on Nordic grain.

The taco was cooked on an artisanal basalt plate from Sardinia, which is similar in form and use to the Mexican *comal*. The taco is then served on Oaxacan tiles from my trip to Mexico in 2016.

MASA
Mix the water and calcium hydroxide (slaked lime) together in a pot until the calcium hydroxide dissolves. Bring to a simmer over medium heat, add the wheat and cook for 45 minutes. Remove from the heat and leave the cooked wheat in the calcium hydroxide solution for 6 hours.

Wash the cooked grains under cold running water a few times until they no longer produce bubbles when rinsed. Strain with a sieve and grind in a Thermomix (or a *molcajete*, if you have one), until it forms a smooth dough. Put the masa into a bowl and season with the salt. Spray 2 sheets of baking parchment with neutral oil. Weigh out 6-g balls and press between the 2 sheets of baking parchment using a tortilla press. Heat a frying pan over medium heat. Add 1 tortilla and cook for 45 seconds on each side, then turn to the first side again and cook for a final 45 seconds until the tortilla is cooked but not dry or brittle. Remove and set aside on a damp towel. Repeat with the rest of the dough.

FILLING

12 g pork fat
60 g salad onions
20 g spring (green) onions
5 g garlic, chopped
8 g bee larvae garum (p.215)
60 g water
3 g salt
3 g lime juice
10 g wood sorrel stalks
3 g smoked mild chilli powder
3 g coriander seeds
500 g filtered water
200 g bee larvae

TO FINISH

20 wood sorrel leaves
20 coriander (cilantro) leaves
20 marigold flowers, petals
   separated

Recipe image p.260

FILLING

Heat the pork fat in a large pan over medium heat, add the onions and chopped garlic and gently sauté until cooked. Increase the heat to high, stir and be careful not to burn or over-caramelize the vegetables. Add the garum and tap water and cook for another 2–3 minutes. Season with the salt, then put the mixture into a large bowl, add the lime juice and a few wood sorrel stalks, the smoked chilli powder and coriander seeds. Cover with clingfilm (plastic wrap) and leave the filling to rest for 1 hour to allow the flavours to mix together.

In a small pan, bring the filtered water to a boil and blanch the larvae for 2 minutes. Drain the larvae and mix gently into the vegetable mixture.

TO FINISH

Spoon equal portions of the filling down the centre of the tortillas. Top with wood sorrel leaves, coriander (cilantro) leaves and marigold petals, to taste.

VARIATION: TOSTADA

Instead of using a soft taco, you can fry the masa in pork fat until golden and serve as a crunchy tostada.

NOTE

Celebrating biodiversity also means promoting diversity. In the case of this taco, the larvae are the main ingredient, but eating insects doesn't always mean that every meal needs to be made up of 100 per cent insects. If you fry the larvae, they can become a crunchy topping for other dishes, such as a taco.

—Written by Roberto Flore

Bee Larvae Taco

Spicy Cricket and Asparagus

SPICY CRICKET AND ASPARAGUS

Serves 4

ASPARAGUS
80 g white asparagus

LACTOFERMENTED
PEA WATER
100 g whole fresh peas, washed
2 g salt

In May 2016, Afton Halloran and I travelled to Mexico. The sights, smells, colours and people of the markets of Mexico City were a warm welcome to a new place, leaving us with an everlasting impression of this vibrant nation. At the famous Mercado de San Juan a number of insect products from all over the country can be found. One of them is *gusano de maguey* (agave worms), a species of moth that has been consumed in Mexico since pre-Hispanic times. In Mexico it is possible to eat *gusano de maguey*, for example, in mixiotes, tamales and salsas. *Sal de gusano* (agave worm salt) is a slightly smoky, savoury condiment. Gusanos are harvested from the agave, dried and then crushed with chilli and sea salt. The salt is also delicious with a nice glass of mezcal. In fact, during Expo 2015 in Milano, Santiago Lastra, Afton and I snuck into the Mexico Pavilion, ate some amazing Mexican cuisine from different parts of the country and drank mezcal (with *sal de gusano*) in good company. Encapsulating these memories in the flavours and form of this dish is my way of thanking all of my friends from Mexico for opening their hearts and sharing their unique cultures.

Back at the Lab and inspired by the *sal de gusano*, I wanted to recreate this spicy salt and combine it with two delicious, seasonal ingredients: white asparagus from Lammefjord and peas from Saarupgård, an organic farm close to Copenhagen. In this dish, the spicy salt is used on asparagus, but it would also pair well with a shot of mezcal.

ASPARAGUS
Using a vegetable peeler, peel the asparagus, then cut them into long strips, keeping the original shape. Set aside.

LACTOFERMENTED PEA WATER
Using a juicer or extractor, juice the peas, then weigh the quantity of the liquid and add the salt. Transfer to a vacuum bag, place in the vacuum machine and keep at 25°C/77°F until the liquid reaches pH 4.6 (this takes about 4 days). (Use litmus paper to test the pH.) In case the pH has not

SPICY CRICKETS
50 g live house crickets
  (*Acheta domestica*)
500 g water
1 g salt
10 g mildly smoked chillies
1 g freeze-dried lime pulp or citric
  acid, to taste

SOUR KOMBUCHA BUTTER
100 g fresh butter
6 g coriander seeds
120 g dry kombucha
0.2 g xanthan gum

TO FINISH
24 sea purslane leaves

Recipe image p.261

reached pH 4.6, keep fermenting until it does. Strain the pea water through fine filter paper into a bowl and store in the refrigerator until you need to use it for plating.

SPICY CRICKETS
Put the crickets in the blast chiller for about 30 minutes, or until frozen. Bring the water and salt to a boil in a pot. Add the crickets and blanch for 1 minute, then remove with a slotted spoon and place in a dry frying pan or skillet set over high heat and toast until lightly browned and dry. Put the crickets in the dehydrator set at 65°C/149°F overnight. The next day, put the dehydrated crickets with the remaining ingredients into a mortar and grind together using a pestle until it is a powder. Set aside.

SOUR KOMBUCHA BUTTER
Melt the butter in a pan over medium heat and add the coriander seeds. Transfer to a vacuum bag, seal and place in the refrigerator to infuse overnight. The next day, bring the butter back to room temperature, then pass through a chinois into a bowl to eliminate the seeds. Add the dry kombucha to the butter, then, using a hand-held blender, blend to create an emulsion with a liquid consistency. Add the xanthan gum and blend for another 30 seconds, then spoon the kombucha butter into a steel bowl or heavy-duty plastic container that can be put into a vacuum machine and compress in the vacuum machine. Processing the kombucha in this way will remove all the air bubbles that were created when blending. Set aside.

TO FINISH
Lay a piece of baking parchment on the work surface, then arrange the asparagus side by side on top of the paper. Sprinkle the asparagus with the cricket powder, then place on the dish. Add dots of the kombucha butter around the asparagus, then carefully add the pea water without pouring it over the top of the asparagus. Add 6 sea purslane leaves on top of the asparagus in a decorative pattern.

NOTE
Many edible larvae are incorrectly called worms. Agave worms are actually the larval stage of the moth *Comadia redtenbacheri*.

—Written by Roberto Flore

ANT TEARS

—

Makes 9

TEARS
100 g water
1 g agar agar
150 g Anty Gin (p.222)

TO FINISH
9 wild Mexican coriander flowers
  (*Eryngium foetidum*)
9 red wood ants (*Formica rufa*)
1 g chilli powder

Ants are a great first ingredient to use when you want to introduce people to the unique flavours of insects. We served two species of ant – the common wood ant (*Formica rufa*) and the smelling carpenter ant (*Lasius fuliginosus*) – on a spoon at the European Parliament (pp.210–11) and later created a more refined version of the dish in the Lab. This refined version encapsulates the Anty Gin (p.222) in a delicious water mochi (*mizu shingen mochi*) sphere and is served with ants and fresh flowers.

TEARS

Off the heat, pour the water into a pot, then slowly add the agar agar and stir to dissolve. Mix slowly and thoroughly with a spoon. Place the pot on the stove, turn on the heat to medium and keep stirring the mixture until a gentle simmer is achieved. Simmer for 2 minutes, then remove the pot from the heat and leave until the mixture is at room temperature. Add the Anty Gin then carefully pour into a 9-hole spherical silicone mould and chill in the refrigerator for 5 hours, or until the spheres have a jelly-like texture.

TO FINISH

Arrange the Mexican coriander flowers around the water mochi spheres. Place one ant on top of each sphere and sprinkle a little chilli powder around it to decorate. Eat and enjoy the sensation of the formic acid tingling in your mouth.

—Written by Roberto Flore

Ant Tears

SMOKED LATUCA

—

Serves 4

SMOKING
500 g charcoal pieces
500 g juniper wood chips
50 g fresh birch and juniper leaves

SMOKED LATUCA
100 g lettuce
20 g Sardinian ivy honey,
   for brushing
fresh, seasonal wild herbs
   and flowers, such as nasturtium
   flowers, coriander (cilantro)
   flowers, wild carrot leaves
   and flowers, and sheep sorrel
   flower to taste
40 g red wood ants
   (*Formica rufa*)

I am proud of my Sardinian heritage. I know a lot about the dietary habits of the ancient Nuragic people of Sardinia. It is known for certain that hunting bees for honey during this era was a dangerous practice reserved only for men. The Nuragic people also collected wild herbs and evolved sophisticated gastronomic techniques such as smoking, baking and boiling. In areas of Sardinia, like Barbagia and Gallura, the dish *latuca e mele* (lettuce and honey) is still part of the common heritage, even after 3,000 or so years.

Ants, attracted by honey, faced their doom as they became trapped inside this sweet, sticky glue, so I can imagine how the people of this civilization became used to consuming the honey, wax, bee larvae and ants in one mouthful.

Many people believe that adding insects to our diets is the future of food. I prefer to reflect and put a dish from my ancestors under the spotlight. This dish is dedicated to Giovanni Fancello for his tireless effort to shed light on the ancient history of food, especially that of Sardinia.

SMOKING

In a large stainless steel bowl, light the charcoal with a blowtorch and allow it to burn for a few minutes, before covering it with the juniper chips and leaves. This will create the smoke but no large flame. Place a perforated rack onto the rim of the bowl, taking care to keep the fire alive by providing enough airflow. Alternatively, use a smoker.

SMOKED LATUCA

Wash the lettuce and collect the crunchiest, juiciest leaves from the interior of the lettuce. Using a pastry brush, brush the leaves with the honey and place on top of the rack. Cover with an equal sized stainless steel bowl and smoke for 1 minute, then place the leaves on a serving plate and tie them together in a bunch with butcher's string (twine). Scatter the herbs, flowers and ants over the lettuce.

—Written by Roberto Flore

Smoked Latuca

GELATO CLANDESTINO

—

Serves as many people as you can!

ICE CREAM
50 g double (heavy) cream
300 g whole (full-fat) sheep's milk
500 g fresh aromatic wood, such
   as mastic (*Pistacia lentiscus*)
   or myrtle (*Myrtus communis*),
   for smoking
13 g sorrel honey
200 g *casu marzu*
liquid nitrogen

In 2013, during the Lab's first visit to Sardinia, I suggested to Ben the idea of making the Gelato Clandestino while visiting Francesco Corrias's farm. At that time in the fieldwork, Ben and I only had a few tools and raw ingredients available for making this dish. The big luxury of that day was the tank of liquid nitrogen that Antonio Maria had in the back of his car … and my amazing friends singing *a cuntrattu* in the vineyard!

In August 2014, I celebrated my confirmed long-term position as head of culinary research and development at the Lab, and I decided to create a more refined version of this dish for the second advisory board meeting. Alex Atala was also fascinated to see and taste the *casu marzu* that day. Thanks to Nicola Chessa, a good friend of mine in Sardinia, who made the *casu marzu*, and my mother, Pina, who carefully packaged the cheese to send from Seneghe to Copenhagen, we succeeded in receiving an entire Casizolu *casu fattu a cazu* just in time for the meeting and for MAD4. I also managed to share some spoonfuls with the guests socializing around the MAD tent.

This recipe has undergone constant evolution: Gelato Clandestino inspired the *escamoles* ice cream that JC, Peter Gerard (Andreas' friend) and I made for the international premiere of the documentary film about our research, *Bugs,* at the Tribeca Film festival in New York in 2016. (It was impossible to bring a piece of living *cazu marzu* past US border control. It was also out of season at that time.) The ice cream was served on the High Line to passers-by.

ICE CREAM
Put the cream and milk into the stainless steel bowl of a stand mixer and mix to combine. Put the bowl into a cold smoker and lightly smoke for 10 minutes with the fresh aromatic wood. Remove from the smoker and then mix in the honey. Set aside.

Recipe image p.270

TO FINISH
40 seasonal flowers, leaves or
other garnish, such as wild
fennel, blackberry leaves
and grape skins

Cut open the top of the *casu marzu*. Spoon out 200 g of the softest, most weeping section of the cheese and add to the cream and milk mixture. Beat with a whisk until smooth but still thick.

Put this mixture into the bowl of a stand mixer (medium-high speed) and carefully start to pour the liquid nitrogen into the bowl as it mixes. Make sure you wear protective safety gloves and glasses and avoid spilling the liquid nitrogen on your body. Mix until the mixture has a soft ice-cream-like texture.

TO FINISH
Scoop out the ice cream and serve immediately garnished with seasonal flowers.

NOTE:
Casu marzu is a mix between a wild and artisanal product. Like all cheese made with unpasteurized milk by expert artisans, each piece will be unique and special. The dairy base is useful mostly to balance the strong flavours and give a more creamy texture. In this case, you can balance the taste by adding a bit more honey to the recipe.

During the photo shoot, we decided to recreate an environment similar to the one that we had when we first made Gelato Clandestino in Sardinia. We served the ice cream on a cactus paddle.

This is not a 'real' ice cream (you won't have the same texture of ice cream by using this recipe). However, the intention was to create a recipe similar to that day in Sardinia when we made Gelato Clandestino in the vineyard.

—Written by Roberto Flore

Gelato Clandestino

The Honeycomb

THE HONEYCOMB

Makes 20

ICE CREAM

20 g beeswax
100 ml liquid nitrogen
280 g fresh double (heavy)
    cream 38% fat
550 g fresh whole (full-fat) milk
    3.5% fat
20 g fresh wax moth larvae
    (*Galleria mellonella*)
90 g caster (superfine) sugar
24 g heather honey
30 g Thick & Easy instant
    food thickener
30 g trimoline

The balsamic quince vinegar that we have at the Lab is becoming more delicious by the year. In November 2015, Tobin and I were working on the development of a few dishes for the Lab's first birthday at the University of Copenhagen. That day we developed a beeswax panna cotta with quince and quince balsamic vinegar. Later, I refined the plate and used it for a lecture at the university on how gastronomic innovation can be inspired by nature. Initially, the dish was designed with bee larvae but here I have created a new version with wax moth larvae. Because wax moths are considered a pest for beekeepers, we wanted to find a way to valorize the gastronomic value of this insect.

ICE CREAM

Put the beeswax into a stainless steel bowl, then, wearing protective gloves, carefully pour the liquid nitrogen over the top and crush in a mortar using a pestle to make a powder. Transfer the powdered beeswax to a vacuum bag and add the cream. Seal in the vacuum machine. Fill a circulator with water up to the maximum amount. Leave the bag in the circulator at 60°C/140°F for 30 minutes. Increase the temperature to 65°C/149°F for another 20 minutes. Remove the bag and let cool on a work surface for 30 minutes. Cut open the bag, pour into a Superbag and strain into a bowl.

Heat 50 g of the milk in a small pot on the stove until nearly boiling, add the wax moth larvae and blanch for 30 seconds. This will make the taste milder, otherwise it will be really strong. Strain the larvae and place in a stainless steel bowl. Add the remaining milk and mix together using a hand-held blender, then pass through a chinois into another bowl. Transfer the mixture to a stainless steel pot and add the cream mixture, sugar, honey, food thickener and trimoline and blend with a hand-held blender. While stirring, heat the mixture gently to 86°C/186.8°F. Remove from the heat and let cool. Put into 2 steel Pacojet containers, freeze, Pacojet and freeze again.

QUINCE SPHERES
501 g water
7 g malic acid
150 g quince
1 g lemon balm leaves
100 g caster (superfine) sugar

GARNISH
a few drops quince balsamic
   vinegar

Recipe image p.271

QUINCE SPHERES

Fill a large bowl with 500 g of the water and add the malic acid. Using a small apple corer, cut out 30 small spheres of quince and put into the water.

Put the lemon balm leaves, the remaining 1 g of water and the sugar (2:1 ratio) into a stainless steel pot and stir to combine. Bring to a boil, then add the small quince spheres and boil for 1 minute. Remove from the heat and let the quince spheres rest in the warm syrup for 8 minutes, then remove and discard the lemon balm leaves. Close in a vacuum bag and seal at 100 per cent vacuum.

Remove the quince spheres from the syrup with a slotted spoon and lightly burn the surface of the spheres with a blowtorch.

TO FINISH

Remove the cold ice cream from the freezer, put it into a piping (pastry) bag and pipe it onto your chosen serving item. Arrange the quince spheres on the ice cream, drizzle with the quince balsamic vinegar and serve.

—Written by Roberto Flore

CRICKET AND ROSE INFUSION WITH FERMENTED BEANS

—

Serves 4

TEMPEH
100 g dried Öland brown beans
1 kg water
20 g apple cider vinegar
0.3 g *Rhizopus* spp. spores

This dish was served at the European Parliament in September during the seminar 'What We Will Be Eating in 2025?' The idea behind the design of the dish was to recreate the visual effect of a classic bean stew but with the surprise effect of an unexpected taste. I wanted to explain how creating umami flavours by breaking down proteins can offer a chef's approach to the current protein-centric (such as cricket powder) view of edible insects. For more information see pp.214–5.

Bernat Guixer Mañé, a former intern at the Lab, and I were working on tempeh during the summer of 2015. We had a few interesting discoveries about tempeh and found that there were different possibilities to use the enzymes that are produced during the post-fermentation of tempeh. When Bernat ended his internship, both he and I continued to work on this exciting project and we ended up with some very interesting results. Here is one of the first recipes developed with this new method.

TEMPEH
Perforate large ziplock bags with holes approximately 5 mm (¼ inch) in diameter spaced 1 cm (½ inch) apart to allow oxygen to penetrate the bean cake for proper fungal development. Set aside.

Put the dried beans into a large saucepan and then pour in 500 g of the water. Bring to a boil, then remove the pan from the heat. Leave the beans to soak in the water overnight in the saucepan at room temperature. The next day, strain the beans and hull them by separating the external part (hull) from the bean, either by hand or using a hulling machine.

Pour the remaining water into a pot and add enough vinegar until it reaches a pH of 4.8. (Test using a pH meter.) Bring the water and vinegar mixture to a boil, add the beans and cook for 12 minutes. Strain the beans

TEMPEH PASTE FOR THE BEANS
35 g Tempeh (made earlier)
50 g extra-virgin olive oil
0.3 g Icelandic salt
0.8 g dried morels
0.3 g smoked pimento
0.5 g bay leaves
2 g garlic
0.1 g ground black pepper

CRICKET INFUSION
100 g fresh crickets (*Acheta domesticus*)
200 g tap water
10 g walnut oil
1 × 30-g piece spring (green) onion
10 g dried ceps (porcini)
10 g cricket garum (p.215)
3 g rose root tincture
1 winter cress

TO FINISH
4 rose petals (*Rosa rugosa*), torn

Recipe image p.276

and spread them out on a dish towel to dry and cool for approximately 20 minutes. Inoculate the beans with the fungal spores by sprinkling the spores on top of the beans following the ratio indicated by the culture supplier. Put the inoculated beans into the prepared perforated ziplock bags. The thickness of the filled packages should not exceed 2 cm (¾ inch). Cook in an incubator set at 30°C/86°F for 24–30 hours. The humidity will largely self-regulate within the ziplock bag.

TEMPEH PASTE FOR THE BEANS
Once the tempeh is ready, cut it into small pieces and put into a Thermomix. Blend for 1½ minutes at maximum speed until it is a moist, thick and smooth paste. Scoop out the paste and form the mixture into 100 small 0.5 g balls shaped like a bean. Put all the remaining ingredients into a vacuum bag, add the tempeh-paste beans and seal at 96 per cent vacuum. Set a circulator to 60°C/140°F, place the sealed vacuum bag into the water and cook for 24 hours.

CRICKET INFUSION
Have a bowl filled with iced water ready nearby. Clean the crickets by removing any foreign material. Bring a saucepan of water to a boil, then add the crickets and blanch for 15 seconds. Plunge the crickets into the ice bath to cool down. Heat the walnut oil in a frying pan or skillet, add the crickets and roast until golden brown. Add the remaining ingredients for the cricket infusion to a vacuum bag, then add the crickets. Seal at 100 per cent vacuum and cook in the incubator set at 86°C/187°F for 45 minutes. Remove the bag and cool down in the blast freezer, then strain with a Superbag.

TO FINISH
Freeze-dry the rose petals on a tray in a freeze drier until completely dry (it will take a few hours). Store in a plastic container until needed. Pour the cricket infusion into 4 small bowls. Dot 12 tempeh-paste beans around and in the cricket infusion and top with the torn rose petals.

NOTE:
Rhizopus spp. spores are responsible for the fermentation of the beans used in the process of making tempeh.

—Written by Roberto Flore

Cricket and Rose Infusion with Fermented Beans

Bug Bao

BUG BAO

Makes 12

BAO
40 g caster (superfine) sugar
130 g warm water (25°C/77°F)
5 g fresh yeast
130 g plain (all-purpose) flour
90 g Chinese wheat starch
2 g baking powder
10 g grapeseed oil

STEAMED SPLIT PEAS
100 g dried yellow split peas

GRASSHOPPER FILLING
100 g live grasshoppers (*Locusta migratoria*)
6 g garlic cloves
10 g spring (green) onion
5 g mild red chilli
1 g coriander (cilantro) roots
12 g bee larvae garum (p.215)
8 g coriander (cilantro) honey
3 g salt
160 g water

Bao are steamed and filled buns found throughout Asia. Eating a well-made bao is like eating a tiny piece of a cloud because the dough is so soft and spongy. The bao were made to create an experience where people could enjoy the surprising deliciousness of a smooth and savoury grasshopper filling inspired by the traditional Chinese custard bun.

BAO

In a stainless steel bowl, dissolve the sugar in the warm water then add the yeast and mix thoroughly until smooth. Set aside. Sift the flour, wheat starch and baking powder into the bowl of a stand mixer. Start the mixer, slowly adding the yeast-water-sugar mix to the dough until it is all combined and the dough has become soft to touch. Add the grapeseed oil and mix until the dough is smooth and elastic. Put the dough into a stainless steel bowl and cover with clingfilm (plastic wrap). Let prove for 40 minutes or until it has doubled in size. Roll the dough out until 1 cm (½ inch) thick and cut it into 12 portions with a 7-cm (2¾-in) round pastry cutter.

STEAMED SPLIT PEAS

Preheat the oven to 100°C/212°F. Using the steamer option on the oven, steam the yellow split peas for 2 hours. Once tender, pass through a tamis to create a smooth consistency.

GRASSHOPPER FILLING

Put the live grasshoppers into a freezerproof box and freeze in a blast chiller for 30 minutes to kill them. Remove from the chiller and clean the grasshoppers in a tray by removing the wings and legs. Bring a pot of water to a boil, add the grasshoppers and blanch for 1 minute. Drain and let dry on a clean dish towel. Finely chop the garlic, spring (green) onion, chilli and coriander (cilantro) roots, then place in a frying pan or skillet with the grasshoppers and dry roast over medium heat for about 5 minutes, stirring occasionally until golden brown. Add the garum, honey and salt, pour in the water and bring to a gentle boil. Cook for about 5 minutes until the liquid has completely reduced. Remove the pan from the heat and place the grasshopper mixture in a Thermomix. Blend the mixture for about 30 seconds, then add the yellow split peas and blend for another 30 seconds. Remove the mixture from the Thermomix and pass through the tamis into a bowl. Set aside.

TO FINISH

To assemble the bao, line a bamboo steamer with baking parchment. Form the filling into small balls (6–10 g each) with your hands, then place them in the centre of the cut-out dough rounds. Now begin to pleat the edges of the bun, slightly stretching the corners of the dough to meet another side going around in a circular motion, pinching the dough together to seal the bun completely. (By pleating with your right hand, you are simultaneously twisting the bun with your left hand, resulting in a tightly encased ball.) Turn the pleated side onto to its bottom and place it in the prepared steamer. Repeat with the remaining filling and dough.

Half fill a pot with cold water, place the bamboo steamer on top of the pot and let the bao prove for 10 minutes. After 10 minutes turn the heat to high and as soon as the water is boiling, reduce the heat to medium and steam the bao for 5 minutes. Remove the steamer from the heat and let the bao stand inside the steamer for 10 minutes. (Don't open the lid of the steamer, even if you are very curious!) The dough should be soft and spongy when ready.

SOUR CHERRY POWDER

Remove the stones (pits) from the cherries. Freeze the cherries until frozen. Put in the freeze drier until ready, then blend to a powder in a Thermomix.

TO SERVE

Take a round brush, dip it in the sour cherry powder and make a dot on the top of the bun.

—Written by Roberto Flore

APPLES AND ANTS

—

Serves 4

APPLES
150 g water
2 g ascorbic acid
500 g apple juice
5 g Anty Gin (p.222)
3 fresh juniper berries
380 g apples

RHUBARB JUICE
800 g rhubarb
300 g filtered water
1 g liquorice powder
7 g liquorice syrup
3 g angelica seeds

TO FINISH
seasonal herbs and flowers, such
    as wood sorrel, lemon verbena
    and nasturtium flowers
15 red wood ants (*Formica rufa*)

In Denmark in July, the apples are beginning to form fruit and the rhubarb season is coming to an end. Apples, rhubarb and ants represent a broad spectrum of sourness that can be incorporated into a recipe. I created this dish with my friend Ruben Hernandez to explore these seasonal flavours.

APPLES
Pour the water, ascorbic acid, apple juice and Anty Gin into a stainless steel bowl that can be put into a vacuum machine. Add the juniper berries. Using an apple corer, cut the apples into 12 cylinders of different lengths, then use a knife to cut the ends to make them flat. Put the apple cylinders into the stainless steel bowl and compress in a vacuum machine in order to infuse the apples in the liquid. Keep the apples in the liquid and chill in the refrigerator for 2 hours.

RHUBARB JUICE
Wash and remove the leaves from the rhubarb stalks, then juice the stalks in a juicer. Put the juice into a stainless steel pot and bring to the boil, removing any foam with a small mesh sieve (strainer). Turn off the heat and strain the liquid through a Superbag into another stainless steel bowl. Add the liquorice powder, liquorice syrup and angelica seeds and mix together. Place in a plastic container with a lid and keep in the refrigerator until ready to serve.

TO FINISH
Using a small pasta cutter, cut the wood sorrel and lemon verbena leaves and the nasturtium flowers into small round confetti. Pour the rhubarb juice into each bowl. Place 3 apple cylinders of various heights into the middle of each bowl and top with different colours of the seasonal confetti and 1–2 ants.

—Written by Roberto Flore

CHOCOLATE COCHINEAL

—

Makes 4

CHOCOLATE LEAF
4 edible leaves from a plant of
your choice (see method)
20 g Oialla Bolivian chocolate
with 92% cocoa solids

We chose to use Oialla Bolivian chocolate with 92 per cent cocoa solids because of its high quality. Oialla follows the cocoa from harvest to the finished chocolate so every step of the supply chain is monitored. The company works closely with the indigenous communities living near the jungle where the wild cocoa fruits are harvested. While Peru is the main producer of cochineal (85 per cent of total global production), Bolivia is also an important global producer. Cochineal is a scale insect from which the naturally red dye carmine is derived. Carmine is often used as a natural food colouring. In Latin America, *flor de Jamaica* (hibiscus) is commonly consumed as *agua de Jamaica* (hibiscus tea). Together these ingredients form the base of this simple, but delicious, dessert inspired by the vibrant flavours and colours of Bolivia.

CHOCOLATE LEAF

Find a non-toxic leaf from a plant of your choice. We chose a very veiny leaf so that the fine lines would show up on the chocolate, revealing the intricate details of the leaf. Temper the chocolate by coarsely chopping three-quarters of it and placing it in a heatproof bowl. Finely chop the rest of the chocolate and set aside. Half-fill a saucepan with hot water, then set the bowl of coarsely chopped chocolate on top of the pan, making sure that the bottom of the bowl isn't touching the water and slowly heat the water. Don't let it boil. Stir the chocolate frequently so it melts evenly and smoothly. Check the temperature and when it reaches 55–58°C/131–136°F, remove the bowl from the pan. Set aside one-third of the melted chocolate in another bowl and keep warm, then stir in the finely chopped chocolate to the remaining two-thirds of the melted chocolate and return to the heat. Check the temperature, it should reach 28–29°C/82–84°F, then add the reserved melted chocolate and stir until the temperature reaches 31–32°C/88–90°F. Brush 2–3 layers of the chocolate onto your chosen leaves. Put the chocolate-coated leaves into the refrigerator over-night to set.

HIBISCUS
80 g warm water (80°C/176°F)
5 g dried hibiscus flowers
10 g honey

TO FINISH
2 g hibiscus powder
4 dried whole cochineal

Recipe image p.284

The next day, carefully peel each leaf off, revealing a beautiful imprint of the leaf in the chocolate. Store the chocolate leaves in an air-tight container in a cold and dry environment until ready to serve.

HIBISCUS
Pour the warm water into a heatproof bowl, add the hibiscus and leave for at least 3 hours until it is hydrated. Strain the hibiscus liquid into a pot and add the honey. Heat on the stove until the honey has dissolved. Pour the mixture into an open container and leave in the dehydrator set at 55°C/131°F for 12–24 hours, or until the mixture is the consistency of thick honey.

TO FINISH
Using a soft pastry brush, brush each leaf with hibiscus powder. Put the thick hibiscus mixture into a piping (pastry) bag and make a small dot on each chocolate leaf. Place a dried cochineal on each dot.

—Written by Roberto Flore

Chocolate Cochineal

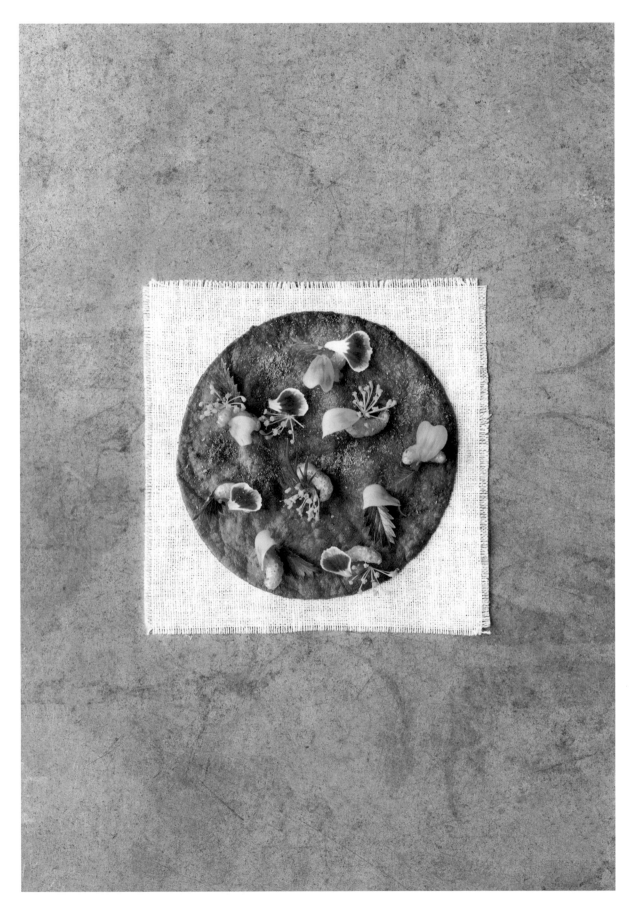

Bee Bite

BEE BITE

Serves 4

BEE LARVAE CRUNCH
90 g fresh bee larvae
3 g salt
10 g sunflower oil

CURED EGG WITH
GRASSHOPPER GARUM
40 g hen's egg yolk
5 g Grasshopper Garum (p.214)

In summer 2014, I started to research the possibility of creating a crunchy snack using only bee larvae as a main ingredient. I succeeded in creating the crunchy part, but this preparation never officially became a dish. In the Lab, projects are often temporarily parked in one of our big black cupboards where we store those projects that sooner or later will be developed. In July 2016, after coming back from a long period of travels and inspiring moments, I returned to the Lab to focus on the research and development of the dishes that were going to be a part of this book. Bee Bite is one of those dishes that I have perfected together with my friend, chef Ruben Hernandez.

BEE LARVAE CRUNCH
Cut out 8 rectangular pieces of baking parchment, about 6 × 6 cm (2½ × 2½ inches) in size. Heat a frying pan or skillet over medium-low heat, then put one sheet of baking parchment into the pan. Lightly brush some sunflower oil onto the baking parchment with a basting brush. Using a fork, crush the bee larvae on the baking parchment until they have a creamy texture, then lightly season with the salt. Place another piece of baking parchment on top and lightly squish the bee larvae with a uniform weight. Let the larvae gently coagulate for about 5 minutes, until they become crunchy and are golden brown. The final result must be a crunchy, flat disc. Set aside and repeat with the remaining baking parchment and bee larvae.

CURED EGG WITH GRASSHOPPER GARUM
Put the hen's egg yolk into a vacuum bag and add the garum. Close the bag at full vacuum and set aside. Add water to a circulator (each circulator has a minimum and maximum, fill to the max). Heat the water until it reaches 68°C/154°F. Place the bag in the water and leave for 50 minutes, then remove the bag and let cool in a bowl filled with cold water and ice cubes. Once cool, remove the egg yolk mixture from the bag and put into a piping (pastry) bag. Set aside.

LOVAGE LEAF POWDER
500 g lovage leaves

TO GARNISH
100 g sunflower oil, plus extra
  for brushing
30 g frozen bee larvae
salt

TO FINISH
40 seasonal aromatic herbs and
  flowers, such as salad burnet
  (*Poterium sanguisorba* L.),
  carnation petals, marigold
  petals, dill flowers and
  carrot leaves
0.5 g lovage leaf powder
  (made earlier)

Recipe image p.285

LOVAGE LEAF POWDER
Wash the lovage leaves, then spread them out on a dehydrator tray. Place the tray in the dehydrator set at 55°C/131°F and leave for about 6 hours until dried out. Once dry, mix in a Thermomix until a fine powder is achieved. Set aside.

TO GARNISH
Heat a frying pan or skillet over high heat until very hot. Pour in the sunflower oil, allowing it to heat but not smoke, then add the frozen bee larvae and fry for 2–3 minutes until golden, puffed and crispy. Remove the larvae from the pan and place on paper towels to remove any excess oil. Spread the larvae out on a dehydrator tray, then place the tray in in the dehydrator set at 65°C/149°F and let dry overnight until ready to use. Add salt, to taste, before serving.

TO FINISH
Place the bee larvae crunch on a plate. Pipe 8 dots of the cured egg on top of the larvae crunch, then place the 8 fried bee larvae garnish on the dots and add the seasonal aromatic herbs and flowers on and around the bee larvae. Sprinkle the lovage powder over the top and serve. Repeat for the remaining 3 bee bites.

—Written by Roberto Flore

PEAS 'N' BEES

Serves 4

PEA CREAM
1.5 kg fresh peas, in pod
  (about 500 g podded peas)
800 g water, for blanching
  and chilling
400 g cold filtered water
salt and freshly ground
  black pepper

BLANCHED BEE LARVAE
200 g water
4 g salt
2 g lovage leaves
28 frozen bee larvae

TO FINISH
28 blanched peas, skins removed
3 g fermented bee pollen
  (optional)

This dish emerged from several sources of inspiration. I was reminded of an Italian dish from 1500 BCE called *risi e bisi* – rice with peas – because the larvae reminded us of rice.

Bee larvae are often a waste product of organic beekeeping, since the drones are removed periodically in the summer months as a strategy to lower the Varroa mite population in the hive. They are also extremely nutritious – around 50 per cent protein and 20 per cent unsaturated fats – and their flavour can vary according to the local flora and season. This makes them an exciting product to work with in the kitchen. The bee larvae we used in this dish came from a beekeeper in Værløse, on the outskirts of Copenhagen.

PEA CREAM
Remove the peas from the pods and have a bowl of 400 g salted iced water ready nearby. Bring a pot of 400 g salted water to a boil and blanch the peas for 1 minute. Remove and cool in the iced water. Drain and place on a dish towel to remove any excess water. Reserve 40 peas for the garnish and put the remainder into a Thermomix with the cold filtered water. Season to taste and blend at high speed for 2 minutes. Pass through a chinois, put into a stainless steel bowl that can be put into a vacuum machine and vacuum to remove any bubbles. Set aside.

BLANCHED BEE LARVAE
Bring the water to a boil in a small pot, add the salt and lovage leaves and return to a boil. Once boiling, turn off the heat, add the frozen bee larvae and leave for 1½ minutes, allowing the heat of the water to cook the larvae. Remove the larvae with a small metal sieve and set aside.

TO FINISH
Warm the pea cream gently in a pan, making sure it doesn't boil. Pour into 4 bowls. Add 7 blanched larvae and 7 peas to each bowl. Serve with fermented bee pollen, if using.

—Written by Roberto Flore

Peas 'n' Bees

GRASSHOPPER AND BIRCH SYRUP DANGO

Makes 4

GLAZE
30 g birch syrup
100 g Grasshopper Garum (p.214)

DANGO
100 g rice flour
100 g *shiratamako* (see note p.291)
2 g caster (superfine) sugar
150 g water

Dango are savoury or sweet Japanese dumplings related to *mochi* and they are made from rice powder (*shiratamako*) and rice flour. They are often skewered on bamboo sticks with 3–5 *dango* together. For different seasons and occasions there are different methods of preparation, colours and flavours.

We wanted to pay homage to the *Mitarashi dango* from Kyoto, a type of *dango* covered with a thick sweet soy sauce glaze. Instead of using soy sauce we used our own delicious grasshopper garum (p.214) to create a similar level of umami. The birch syrup used in this recipe was tapped directly from forest trees in northern Sweden. The flavours of the garum and the elegant and intriguing flavours of the birch syrup together create a perfect marriage of the unique aromas laying on the soft pillows of the *dango mochi*.

Our grasshopper and birch syrup *dango* are shown here circling a charcoal fire where the *dango* are traditionally slow roasted. Close your eyes and let yourself be transported to the Japanese countryside.

GLAZE
Put the birch syrup and grasshopper garum to taste into a stainless steel bowl and mix well with a spoon until it is a homogenous sauce.

DANGO
Make the dough by putting the flour, *shiratamako*, sugar and water into a stand mixer and mix together well until the dough is glossy and elastic and doesn't stick to the sides of the bowl.

Using your hands, make tiny balls weighing 30 g each, press gently down to give them a flat shape. With your finger, press down in the centre to create a small hole. This is where the sauce will go.

TO FINISH
4 wooden twigs
10 g edible seasonal flowers
   and leaves

Recipe image p.292

Put the *dango* into a large pot of water, bring to a boil, then reduce the heat and simmer for about 3 minutes. The dango are ready when they float to the surface and appear puffy. Remove the *dango* from the water with a slotted spoon and let dry on a clean cloth.

TO FINISH
Light a charcoal grill. Using a small knife, whittle one end of the twigs, removing the rough bark and leave the other end unwhittled as a handle. Skewer 3 *dango* on each twig and gently grill on the charcoal grill for 2 minutes, or until slightly browned and toasted. Remove from the grill, brush the glaze on top and decorate with the edible seasonal flowers.

NOTE
Shiratamako is a type of Japanese sweet glutinous rice flour or rice powder used to make rice cakes and other sweet confectioneries.

—Written by Roberto Flore

Grasshopper and Birch Syrup Dango

Wax Moth Cured Egg Yolk

WAX MOTH CURED EGG YOLK

Serves 4

TAGLIOLINI
70 g black barley
180 g purple (PurPur) wheat
5 g hibiscus flowers
8 egg yolks

TERMITOMYCES
MUSHROOM DASHI
500 g water
4 g bancha tea
5 g termite mound mushroom
    (*Termitomyces schimperi*)
8 g badderlocks seaweed
    (*Alaria esculenta*)
2 g salt
8 g cricket garum (p.215)
8 g Kenyan lightly smoked honey

WAX MOTH FLAKES
100 g whole (full-fat) milk
100 g wax moth larvae (*Galleria
    mellonella*)
3 g salt
200 g sunflower oil

This dish plays with the texture that comes from the shapes of the skin of the wax moth larvae. In Japan, dashi can be made with a wide variety of ingredients. Tea is one of them. Here we use bancha tea, where tea leaves are harvested from the second flush of sencha between summer and autumn (fall). During the fieldwork in Japan, I was fascinated by the nuances of some of the different dashi that I tried.

TAGLIOLINI
Combine all the ingredients in the bowl of a stand mixer and mix with the dough hook for about 2 minutes to make a stiff pasta dough. Put the dough into a vacuum bag, seal and let rest for 1 hour in the refrigerator. Remove from the refrigerator and, using a rolling pin, roll out on a lightly floured work surface until the dough is thin. Pass the pasta dough through a pasta machine on the 0.3 mm setting. Cut the strands to be 30 cm (12 inches) long.

TERMITOMYCES MUSHROOM DASHI
Combine all the ingredients in a vacuum bag and seal in a vacuum machine. Using a circulator, heat a water bath at 60°C/140°F, then place the bag in the water and cook for 40 minutes. Remove the bag and cool to room temperature, then open and strain the liquid through a Superbag into a bowl and set aside.

WAX MOTH FLAKES
Bring the milk to a boil in a saucepan. Add the larvae and continue to boil the milk for 1 minute. Remove the larvae from the milk with a metal sieve and put into the container of a hand-held blender. Pulse until the larvae are coarsely crushed. Heat the oil in a frying pan or skillet, add the crushed larvae and fry until crunchy in texture. Spread the larvae flakes out on a dehydrator tray, place in a dehydrator set at 50°C/122°F and leave overnight.

CRUNCHY EGG
10 g wax moth garum (p.215)
10 g apple cider vinegar
20 g extra-virgin olive oil
salt, to taste
4 egg yolks

Recipe image p.293

CRUNCHY EGG

Preheat the oven to 68°C/154°F using the steaming function. Mix the garum, vinegar, oil and salt together in a small plastic container suitable for steaming, then slowly place all the egg yolks in the liquid without breaking them. Ensure that the yolks are fully covered by the oil. Close the lid and put into the oven for 40 minutes. Remove and leave to rest in the refridgerator overnight.

TO FINISH

Just before serving, gently roll each egg yolk in the crunchy wax moth flakes. Set aside.

Bring a pot of salted water to a boil. Add the pasta and cook for 30 seconds. Warm the dashi in another saucepan and pour into 4 small, deep dishes. Add the pasta to the dashi and add the crunchy egg as preferred.

—Written by Roberto Flore

WAX MOTH LARVAE COCOON

—

Serves 10–15

COCOON
40 g organic beeswax
20 g walnut oil
240 g white chocolate, broken
  into pieces

This recipe, along with the *casu marzu* Gelato Clandestino (pp.268–9), is one of the first insect-based desserts that I developed in relation to this project. When Ranee Udtumthisarn was teaching me, Ben and Josh how to make *nam prik maeng da* during the fieldwork in Livø (pp.182–6), I fell in love with the giant water bug (*Lethocerus indicus*) and its fragrance.

When Afton and I travelled to Thailand for the event at Le Cordon Bleu (pp.203–9), we developed the bamboo worm and stink bug bite together with chef Willy Daurade. One year later, when we were presenting at a conference in Italy, Professor Yupa Hanboonsong brought us a bag of giant water bugs from Thailand as a gift. With the fresh giant water bugs in hand, I returned to the Lab and began tinkering with the recipe that we created in Thailand. The result is a delicate and decadent sphere, radiating with the tropic perfumes of the giant water bug.

COCOON
Melt the beeswax in a stainless steel pot at 68°C/154°F on an induction stove. As soon as you can see that the beeswax has melted, reduce the heat to low and add the walnut oil, then the chocolate, and mix slowly for 1 minute (ensure that you are not forming air bubbles). Using tough silicone gloves, cut off the end of each glove finger to make small balloons (similar in size to those in the photo) by blowing hard into the detached fingers and tie the ends. Dip each balloon slowly into the chocolate-wax mixture, 3 times per balloon, to coat well. Remove from the mixture and hold in the air to dry for 10 seconds. Place each balloon (tied-side up) in an eggcup and chill in the refrigerator for 30 minutes. Pierce the balloons with a sharp needle and remove them very carefully from the chocolate coating. The result should be a white cocoon shape.

FILLING

1 giant water bug
   (Lethocerus indicus)
150 g whole (full-fat) milk
40 g double (heavy) cream
45 g caster (superfine) sugar
80 g mascarpone
35 g wax moth larvae
   (Galleria mellonella)
1.5 g agar agar

CHERRY REDUCTION
400 g juicy, overripe wild cherries,
   stoned (pitted)
50 g honey

TO FINISH
3 g fresh bee pollen

Recipe image p.298

FILLING

Lightly toast the giant water bug in a frying pan or skillet. Pour 100 g of the milk into a vacuum bag, add the toasted giant water bug and seal in the vacuum machine. Put the bag into a circulator at 85°C/185°F for 15 minutes. Cool down before placing in the refridgerator overnight. The following day, filter the milk through a piece of muslin (cheesecloth) or a Superbag. Set aside.

Put the cream and sugar into a bowl and partially whisk together. Add the mascarpone to the mixture. Heat the remaining milk in a small stainless steel pot until warm. Add the wax moth larvae and blanch for 30 seconds. Blend with a hand-held blender, then pass through a chinois into a bowl. Add to the cream and mascarpone mixture.

Heat the milk that was infused with the giant water bug, add the agar agar and stir until the agar agar has dissolved. Remove from the heat and vigorously whisk into the cream mixture. Leave for 1 minute, then transfer the cream mixture to a piping (pastry) bag and carefully pipe the cream into the cocoons. Place the cocoons in the refrigerator for 30 minutes to let the filling set.

CHERRY REDUCTION

Juice the cherries in a juicer, pass through a piece of muslin or a Superbag and put into a small plastic container. Add the honey. Put the container into a dehydrator at 50°C/122°F and leave to reduce until the liquid becomes the consistency of a thick syrup.

TO FINISH

Remove the wax moth cocoons from the refrigerator. Put the thick cherry reduction into a piping bag and make a small dot on each cocoon. Crush the bee pollen to a fine powder in a mortar using a pestle, sprinkle it over the cocoons and serve.

—Written by Roberto Flore

Wax Moth Larvae Cocoon

Fish and Crick

FISH AND CRICK

Serves 4

LETTUCE
200 g romaine lettuce
2 g salt

TEMPURA BATTER
10 g tapioca starch
35 g cornflour (cornstarch)
20 g rice flour
35 g water
1 kg sunflower oil

FRITTO MISTO
50 g small species fish (depends
    on the season and the place
    in the world; choose ones with
    with the smallest bones)
100 g fjord shrimp
100 g crickets (*Acheta domestica*)
70 g grasshoppers (*Locusta
    migratoria*)

MAYONNAISE
2 eggs
1 egg yolk
30 g vinegar
juice of ½ lemon
500 g sunflower oil

When I was travelling with Afton in northeastern Thailand (pp.203–9), I noticed that many street food carts served crickets with small shrimps and tiny grasshoppers. This was interesting because crickets are the terrestrial equivalent of shrimp. This recipe could help us to break the ice for someone who is approaching an insect for the first time.

During the recipe development for this book, I mostly tried to avoid using the whole insect in order to highlight the flavour and potential of insects from a different point of view. But it's important to remember that in some cultures, where insects are a common ingredient, insect textures and shapes are also appreciated.

LETTUCE
In a vacuum bag, lactoferment the lettuce by adding the salt. Seal the bag at 100 per cent in a vacuum machine. Let ferment for 10 days in a warm place. Spread the lettuce leaves out on a dehydrator tray. Place in the dehydrator set at 60°C/140°F and leave overnight.

TEMPURA BATTER
Mix all the batter ingredients, except the oil, in a stainless steel bowl that can be put into a vacuum machine. Put the bowl into a vacuum machine and compress 2 times. In a deep frying pan heat the oil to 180°C/350°F or until a cube of bread browns in 30 seconds.

FRITTO MISTO
To make the fritto misto, carefully dip the fish, shrimp and insects into the batter and deep fry one by one in the oil until they are crispy. Remove from the oil with a slotted spoon and drain on paper towels.

MAYONNAISE
Put all the ingredients (except the oil) into the narrow container of a hand-held blender. Begin to blend, then slowly start to add the oil to the mixture. Blend until a mayonnaise consistency has been achieved.

DIP

sunflower oil, for sweating
50 g onion, chopped
50 g carrot, chopped
180 g tomatoes, chopped
24 g dry chipotle chilli
15 g apple cider vinegar
25 g white wine vinegar
100 g water
20 g caster (superfine) sugar
2 g oregano
1 bay leaf
salt, to taste

Recipe image p.299

DIP

Place a stainless steel pot on the stove over medium heat. Pour in a little oil. When the oil is hot, add the onion and sweat. Add the carrots and tomatoes and cook for 30 minutes over low heat. Add the chilli and remaining ingredients and cook for 15 minutes. Remove from the heat, pour the mixture into a Thermomix and blend for 1 minute on high speed. Strain the contents though a Superbag and put into a stainless steel bowl. Mix with the mayonnaise (at a ratio of 3:1 sauce to mayonnaise) and season to taste with salt.

TO SERVE

Serve the fermented lettuce and fritto misto with the dip on the side.

NOTE:

It is important to select small crickets and grasshoppers for this recipe because their exoskeletons are still relatively soft. I prefer to use crickets that are less than 15 days old.

—Written by Roberto Flore

LOVAGE FLUTE

—

I created this dish in June 2014, when Ben, Josh and I visited the island of Livø in Limfjord, northern Jutland to conduct fieldwork. While investigating the European cockchafer on the island, we also obtained some fresh bee larvae from a local beekeeper, together with some very mature lovage stalks, from her garden. As part of an outdoor experimental cookout I prepared an aromatic stock with flowers and herbs and cooked the delicate, fatty larvae inside the lovage stalks along with jasmine flowers that at the time were riotously in bloom. The herbal and floral notes of the larvae were enhanced in this rustic and simple preparation.

For this book, I chose to stick with the original shape of the lovage flute, adding a few more elements to balance the flavour of this recipe. When I saw the enormous lovage stalks on Livø, it reminded me of Afton's recount of harvesting the new rice in Kujang Sain village in Sarawak, Borneo with her host family and cooking it together at their longhouse. The fresh hill rice is slowly steamed in a bamboo stem cavity over a fire. Bamboo stalk cavities are used throughout Asia for cooking and steaming different rice dishes.

A year after the Livø fieldwork, I met expert beekeeper Andrea Paternoster at the University of Gastronomic Sciences in Pollenzo, Italy. Over a glass of homemade mead, Andrea and I discussed the virtues of using bee larvae as an ingredient. Andrea produces 16 different kinds of monofloral honey and he gave me a few small pots of the most rare kinds as a gift. For this recipe, I decided to use the wild carrot flower honey, and I dedicate this dish to Andrea and his bees.

Makes 4

FLUTE
120 g fresh bee larvae
2 g salt
10 g wild carrot flower honey
20 jasmine petals
1 lovage stalk, cut into 5-cm
   (2-inch) long pieces
50 g beeswax

BROTH
50 g lovage leaves
500 g water

TO SERVE
8 coriander (cilantro) flowers
   and leaves

Recipe image p.304

FLUTE

Extract the live bee larvae from the honeycomb with a pair of tweezers. To make this easier, put the comb into a blast freezer for 4 hours to freeze the larvae. Once the larvae are frozen they will be easier to manipulate.

Sprinkle the larvae with the salt, honey and jasmine petals, then carefully stuff the larvae into the lovage pieces. In a small cast-iron pan, melt the beeswax to 68°C/154°F on an induction stove. Once it is liquid, dip the ends of the lovage pieces into the wax a few times until the hole at each end is fully sealed.

BROTH

Prepare an aromatic broth by putting the lovage leaves and water into a large pan and bringing to a boil. Once the boiling point has been reached, reduce the heat until it is simmering, then carefully lower the flutes into the water. Cook for 4 minutes.

TO SERVE

Remove the flutes from the water. Open the lovage by gently cutting away the top in a rectangular shape with a sharp knife. Sprinkle with the coriander (cilantro) flowers and leaves and serve immediately.

—Written by Roberto Flore

Lovage Flute

Ugali

UGALI

—

The International Conference on Legislation and Policy on the Use of Insects as Food and Feed in East Africa in Kisumu, Kenya was a real milestone event. It was my first time travelling to Africa. I'm sure that it's a similar experience for many people, but I was fascinated to observe how different Kenya was when compared to the one-sided image that we are constantly told of this vibrant and diverse place. I was happy to be travelling with Afton. This was her eighth time in Kenya, the place where part of her PhD fieldwork on cricket farming is being carried out. Her research is a part of the GREEiNSECT research group.

After visiting the cricket farm at Jaramogi Odinga Oginga University of Science and Technology in Bondo, I could see that things had changed immensely since Ben and Josh first visited in 2013 (p.102). Afton's close friend and research assistant, Jackline Oloo, has been a major part of developing small-scale cricket farming techniques for Kenyan farmers. Jackline also has a tremendous passion for cooking. While in Kenya, I learned so much about popular Kenyan cuisine and traditional Luo dishes from her. I left with a desire to create a dish dedicated to the Kenyans working tirelessly to celebrate their traditional cuisines.

I started to develop the first version of this dish during the field trip to Livø (pp.182–6). It was my first fieldwork trip as an official member of the Nordic Food Lab in 2014. Similar to the time when we developed the Gelato Clandestino in Sardinia (pp.92–4), the development of the dishes we made in Livø was related to what was available in the countryside that surrounded us. I found a shovel and started to dig a hole to build a primordial barbecue pit as we generally do in Sardinia to cook a suckling pig underground. As I travelled through Kenya, I found that the texture of *ugali* (a stiff corn staple that is similar to Mexican tamale) was really similar in taste and consistency to the dish I made for the first time in Livø. When I found the hand-crafted soapstone plate on which this dish was

CORN
156 g fresh corn kernels, reserve
   the cob, husk and silk
2 g salt
90 g cornflour (cornstarch)
40 g water
piri piri chillies, to taste
8 g cricket garum (p.215)
2 g lime
6 g toasted sesame oil
fresh, clean, moist soil,
   for covering
fresh, clean, moist sand,
   for covering
fresh aromatic leaves and flowers,
   for covering

TO FINISH
2 g corn silk (see method)
sunflower oil, for frying
5 g Grasshopper Garum (p.214)
0.3 g piri piri chilli
3 g toasted sesame oil

Recipe image p.305

plated in Kisumu, Kenya, I bought it with the vision of recreating a similar version of the dish in the Lab.

CORN
Lactoferment the corn kernels by adding 2 per cent salt of the weight of the corn and put in a sealed vacuum bag for a 10 days in the refrigerator at 5°C/41°F. After one week, put the corn into a Themomix, add the rest of the corn ingredients, except the soil, sand and leaves and flowers, and mix gently for 3 minutes, or until it is a smooth dough. Let rest in the Thermomix container for 30 minutes, then mould the lactofermented corn around the middle of the reserved cob. Set aside.

Arrange the reserved husk and silk on a dehydrator tray, place in the dehydrator, set at 50°C/122°F and dry overnight.

Preheat the oven to 120°C/250°F. Fill a deep gastro tray one-third full with clean, moist soil and sand, then top with aromatic leaves and flowers. Wrap the cob with the dried husks and place into the soil and sand mixture. Cover with more aromatic flowers and leaves, then cover again with soil and sand. Bake in the oven for at least 2 hours.

TO FINISH
Remove the baked cob from the soil, open and cut into 2-cm (¾-inch) thick slices around the cob. In a frying pan, fry the corn silk in a little sunflower oil. Before serving, mix the grasshopper garum, chilli and sesame oil together, put into a small spray bottle and spray the corn and corn silk with the mixture. Place the baked corn on a plate and arrange the fried corn silk alongside. Serve as a side dish to a vegetable stew or roast chicken.

—Written by Roberto Flore

FROM THE FIELD

Serves 1

ROSE PETAL VINEGAR
100 rose petals
300 g light apple cider vinegar

SAUCE
10 g Grasshopper Garum
    (p.215)
10 g birch syrup
20 g rose petal vinegar
    (made earlier)

BOUQUET
1 pigeon claw
185 g sunflower oil, for frying
½ pigeon breast, skin left on
3 yarrow leaves (*Achillea
    millefolium*)
2 wild garlic leaves
2 pea shoots
4 wild carrot leaves
3 wild horseradish leaves
3 tender wild asparagus shoots
2 small wild beetroot (beet) leaves
salt flakes, to taste

TO FINISH
5 g Grasshopper Garum
    (p.215)
salt flakes, to taste

At the basis of the argument as to why we should incorporate insects into our diets, Nordic Food Lab has always said that insects can bring a more complex understanding of the food and taste diversity connected to our surrounding ecosystems. They are a means of exploring the potential of the edible landscape.

ROSE PETAL VINEGAR

Infuse the rose petals in the vinegar in a sterilised glass bottle or jar for 2 months.

SAUCE

In a steel bowl, mix the grasshopper garum with the birch syrup. Add the rose petal vinegar and mix. Set aside.

BOUQUET

Bring a pot of water to a simmer, add the claw and cook for 45 minutes. Remove the claw with a slotted spoon and dry on a tray in the dehydrator at 65°C/149°F for a few hours. In a deep frying pan heat the oil to 180°C/350°F or until a cube of bread browns in 30 seconds. Deep-fry the claw.

Light a charcoal grill. Put the pigeon breast, the remaining rose petal vinegar and a pinch of salt into a vacuum bag. Seal at 100 per cent vacuum and marinate for 30 minutes at room temperature. Fill an immersion circulator with water and heat to 52°C/126°F. Put the breast (in the bag) into the circulator for 20 minutes. Remove and put the breast into a small metal tray. Grill for 1 minute on each side, brushing with the sauce. Remove from the grill and keep warm. Make a bouquet with the shoots and leaves and place on a serving plate. Slice the breast and hide tiny pieces in the bouquet. Decorate with the pigeon claw.

TO FINISH

Put the grasshopper garum into a spray bottle and spray onto the bouquet. Serve with salt flakes on the side.

—Written by Roberto Flore

What do we eat, what do we not eat, and why?

This project has been nominally about bugs; now, at its end, it seems to have evolved into something else. It has been about asking the question above repeatedly in different contexts – tracing the ways in which this simple and not-so-simple line reflects and sets our values, defines the possibilities of our food systems and shapes the landscape in profound ways.

Insects are a pretty good way to start these conversations for many of us newcomers. They make us pause; they cause us to take a step back, and to consider, in general, what and how we eat.

From the beginning, our goal was never to *promote* insects, per se – it was to investigate them and their gastronomic potential. And the Lab will continue to work with them in this pursuit. Our fieldwork, a brief overview of a fraction of all the world's insect-eating traditions, allowed us a glimpse of different ways insects are normal – a range of ways they can make sense in a place.

So what makes sense where we are? Who gets to decide, and how? No one decides a cuisine alone; but we have a few ideas about what we think makes sense here, in the Nordic region.

There is a peculiar sensation in coming back to where we started and choosing to work with the same bugs with which we began. Yet there is also a satisfaction in encountering them anew, learning and relearning our region. Local bee larvae seem even more special now: an abundant, overlooked, nourishing, versatile, tasty local resource that may hold some of this positive potential everyone is talking about – and which might even be realized, if we ensure that interest grows holistically, for and with the community. Local ants have an extra potency now: they may be another way to help valorize forests and other ecosystems, whose value is consistently and grossly underestimated – as long as we harvest them for the ecology, and not in spite of it. And there is a reason these ones taste best and compel us most strongly.

After the premiere of our documentary film in New York, an audience member began a great discussion by noting, 'So, in essence, the film is about polyculture'. Absolutely it is. And so too, we think, is this book, this project, and all the Lab's work. It is not a new idea; it's a really old one. Let's eat lots of different things. Let's grow and make and harvest lots of different things. Let's share our different things with each other. Let's be plural and eat plurally. That's the future. It's what tastes the best.

Wood sorrel (*Oxalis Acetosella*)

DATE	BINOMIAL	COMMON NAMES (Local language)	COMMON NAME (English)
2012–2016	*Formica rufa*	*Rød skovmyre* (Danish); *Rød skogmaur* (Norwegian)	Red wood ant
2012–2016	from *Apis mellifera*	*Biyngel* (Danish)	Bee brood
2013–2016	*Lasius fuliginosus*	*Orangemyre* (Danish)	Smelling carpenter ant
2013–2016	from *Apis mellifera*	*Bibrød* (Danish)	Bee bread
2013.10.12	from *Piophila casei*	*muschittu de su casu* (Sardo)	Cheese fly
2013.11.26–2013.12.14	*Macrotermes bellicosus / Macrotermes subhyalinus / Pseudocanthotermes sp. / Odontotermes kibarensis*	*Kongo* (Tuken); *Biye* (Luo); *Chisua* (Luhya); *Empawu, nsejere* (Luganda)	Termite
2013.12.3	*Chironomus* sp. / *Chaoborus* sp.	*Sam* (Luo)	Lake-fly / Lake-fly cake
2013.12.9	*Brachytrupes* sp.	*Jjenje* (singular), *mayenje* (plural – Luganda)	Giant cricket, tobacco cricket
2013.12.10	*Ruspolia differens*	*Nsenene* (Luganda)	Katydid
2013.12.11	*Rynchophorus phoenicis*	*Ssiinya* (singular), *masiinya* (plural – Luganda)	Palm-weevil larva
2013.12.14	*Trigona* sp.	*Kadoma* (Luganda)	Stingless bee
2014.3.10	from *Glycaspis brimblecombei*	*Yapuralyi, yimampi* (Warlpiri)	Psyllid lerp
2014.3.10	*Melophorus* sp. / *Camoponotus* sp.	*Yunkaranyi, yurrampi* (Warlpiri)	Honey ant
2014.3.11	Cossidae; generally *Endoxyla leucomochla*	*Ngarlkirdi* (Warlpiri)	Witchetty grub

LOCATION(S)	TASTE	RELATED STORIES AND RECIPES
Copenhagen, Denmark; Steigen, Norway	Intensely sour, lemon, caramelized lemon rind (best used raw/frozen)	Ants (pp.84–6); Anty Gin and Tonic (pp.222–3), Chimp Stick (pp.230–31), Rhubarb and Roseroot (pp.227–9)
Copenhagen and Livø, Denmark	Umami, fat, slightly sweet, raw nuts, avocado, honey-dew melon, green, herbaceous, milk, smooth (raw/fresh/blanched); umami, crispy, bacon, mushroom (fried/roasted)	Bee Brood (pp.87–9), Insects to Feed the World (pp.175–81); Insect Garums (pp.214–16), Bee Brood Granola (pp.220–21), Bee Larvae Ceviche (pp.240–41), Peas 'n' Bees (pp.288–9), Tsukudani Bee Larvae (pp.242–3), Lovage Flute (pp.302–4), Oatchi (pp.234–6), Chawan-mushi (pp.237–9), Porridge and Labrador Tea (pp.252–4), Whead and Weed (pp.247–9)
Copenhagen, Denmark	Mild acidity, Kaffir lime	Ants (pp.84–6); Chimp Stick (pp.230–31), Ants on a Log (pp.244–6)
Copenhagen, Denmark	Sour, bitter, moist, dense, floral, tropical fruits, mango, pollen	Bee Bread (pp.90–91); The Whole Hive (pp.224–226), Bee Bread Butter (pp.232–3), Peas 'n' Bees (pp.288–9), Rhubarb and Roseroot (pp.227–9)
Seneghe, Sardinia	Eaten in *casu marzu*, the cheese the flies form: spicy, strong, blue cheese, wild mountain herbs	From Sardinia to the Nordic Food Lab (pp.92–4); Gelato Clandestino (pp.268–70)
Chebarsiat, Elnuni, Epanga Valley, Rusinga Island, Bondo, Majiwa, Kakamega and Onyurnyur, Kenya; Banda Kyandazza, Uganda	Crunchy, nutty, fatty, savoury (soldiers/alates, toasted); fatty, soft, springy, sweetbreads, foie gras (queen, fried in own fat)	Termite Saga (pp.95–109)
Bondo, Kenya	Fishy, lightly bitter, strong (patted into cakes and dried)	Sam (pp.110–12)
Lukindu, Uganda	Chicken (thigh), fat, umami, juicy, lamb's brain (head), mild, creamy, sweet (abdomen)	Mayenje (pp.116–19)
Kiboobi, Uganda	Crisp, springy, savoury, shrimp minus the sea (fried/fresh)	Nsenene (pp.120–24)
Kalangala Island, Uganda	Fatty, tender, crispy bits of cooked fat, cheesy, white pepper (fried in own fat)	Masiinya (pp.125–9)
Banda Kyandazza, Uganda	Stingless-bee honey: wine, Sauternes, fruits, sourness, lemongrass	Termite Saga (pp.95–109)
Yuendumu, NT, Australia	Mild sweetness	Lerp (pp.134–6)
Yuendumu, NT, Australia	Sweet, sour, tingly/numbing, dark honey, sun-dried wild strawberries (raw, live)	Yurrampi (pp.137–41)
Yuendumu, NT, Australia	Nutty, macadamia nut, confit garlic, roasted red pepper, romesco sauce (cooked lightly in eucalyptus ashes of fire)	Witjuti (pp.142–4)

DATE	BINOMIAL	COMMON NAMES *(Local language)*	COMMON NAME *(English)*
2014.3.12	*Cystococcus pomiformis* and *Corymbia terminalis*	*Kanta* (Warlpiri)	Bush coconut
2014.3.18	*Atta mexicana*	*Chicatana, hormiga culona* (Spanish, Mexico)	Big-arsed ant
2014.3.19	*Pachilis gigas*	*Xahue* (Ñha-ñhu)	
2014.3.19	*Liometopum apiculatum*	*Escamoles* (Spanish, Mexico)	Queen-ant egg
2014.3.21	*Pseudacysta perseae*	*Toritos* (Spanish, Mexico)	Avocado lace bug
2014.3.21	*Myrmecocystus mexicanus*	*Binguinas* (Spanish, Mexico)	Honey ant
2014.3.23	*Dactylopius coccus / D. indicus*	*Cochinilla* (Spanish, Mexico)	Cochineal bug
2014.4.3	*Rynchophorus palmarum*	*Suri* (Spanish, Peru); *soso* (Ese'eja)	Palm-weevil larva
2014.4.3	*Trigona sp.*	*Abeja sin aguijón* (Spanish, Peru); *bishawajoso* (Ese'eja)	Stingless bee
2014.6.16	*Melolontha melolontha*	*Oldenborre* (Danish)	Cockchafer
2014.6.17	*Lethocerus indicus*	*Maeng da* (Thai)	Giant water bug
2014.10.31	*Vespula flaviceps*	*Hebo* (Japanese, Kushihara dialect); *kuro-suzumebachi* (Japanese)	Japanese wasp
2014.11.1	*Vespa mandarinia*	*Kumabachi* (Japanese, Kushihara dialect); *Ō-suzumebachi* (Japanese)	Giant hornet
2014.11.7	*Phalera flavescens*	*Sakura kemushi no fuu* (Japanese)	Cherry caterpillar
2015.02.14	*Omphisa fuscidentalis*	*non mai phai* (Thai)	Bamboo borer
2015.02.14	*Tessaratoma paillosa*	*maeng khaeng* (Thai)	Lychee stink bug
2015.02.21	*Acheta domesticus*	*sading* (Thai)	Common house cricket
2015.02.21	*Gryllus bimaculatus*	*tong dam* (Thai)	Two-spotted cricket

LOCATION(S)	TASTE	RELATED STORIES AND RECIPES
Yuendumu, NT, Australia	Juicy, fresh, melon (mother); raw button mushrooms, a bit truffly (larvae); savoury (pupae, hatched *imagos*); coconut flesh, resinous, celery root (gall flesh)	Kanta (pp.145–9)
Mexico City and Oaxaca, Mexico	Strong, mulchy, undergrowth	Escamoles (pp.150–58)
Puerto México, Hidalgo, Mexico	Strong, iodine (raw), roasted pistachio (toasted on comal)	Escamoles (pp.150–58)
Puerto México, Hidalgo, Mexico	Young blue goat's milk cheese (nest aroma); avocado, fresh almond, vegetal, flowery, milky (raw larvae)	Escamoles (pp.150–58)
Contla de Juan Cuamatzi, Tlaxcala, Mexico	Vegetal, avocado leaf, green pepper (fried in pork fat; toasted; steamed in corn husk)	Toritos (pp.159–61)
Jésus Huitznahuac, Tlaxcala, Mexico	meat stock, umami, Sauternes, kiwi, tamarind, lemon, chilli, honey, strong, fermented, bitter, intense, wine, lime, pulque, vegetal, sweet, Tokaj, yeast, red fruit, Madeira, cider, mandarin; usually eaten live and raw, often immediately	Binguinas (pp.162–4)
Oaxaca, Mexico	Mainly used as textile pigment, sometimes food colourant: cactus aroma, slightly bitter taste	Escamoles (pp.150–58)
Tambopata, Madre de Dios, Peru	Fruity, cheesy, white pepper, fatty	Amazonas (pp.165–9), Lima Jam (pp.170–4)
Tambopata, Madre de Dios, Peru	Amazonian stingless-bee honey: runny, very sweet, fruity, lightly acidic	Amazonas (pp.165–9)
Livø, Denmark	Crunchy, chewy, grassy	Livø (pp.182–6)
Livø, Denmark	Intensely aromatic, tropical fruits, citrus, watermelon candy	Livø (pp.182–6)
Kushihara, Gifu, Japan	Umami, forest, oak moss	Hebo (pp.187–93), Kaiseki in Autumn (pp.200–1)
Kushihara, Gifu, Japan	Strong, meaty, chewy, animal, pungent	Kumabachi (pp.194–9), Kaiseki in Autumn (pp.200–1); Hornet Highball (pp.250–51)
Tokyo, Japan	The smell of the frass: cherry leaf, cherry blossom, cherry stone, bitter almond	Sakura Frass (p.202)
Bangkok, Thailand	Candlenut; fermented bamboo shoots; fried, corn (blanched)	Thailand Fieldwork (pp.203–9)
Bangkok, Thailand	Kaffir lime, coriander, apple skin with sweet notes of banana and tropical fruits	Thailand Fieldwork (pp.203–9)
Baan Saento, Thailand	Slightly fishy, walnut (fried with pandan leaves)	Thailand Fieldwork (pp.203–9); Cricket and Rose Infusion with Fermented Beans (pp.274–6)
Baan Saento, Thailand	Nutty, umami (fried with pandan leaves)	Thailand Fieldwork (pp.203–9); Fish and Crick (pp.299–301)

5'-RIBONUCLEOTIDES:
Compounds that contribute to the taste of umami. Also known industrially as E635, when used as a flavour enhancer.

ACETIC FERMENTATION:
In vinegar production, the process by which alcohol is converted into acetic acid.

AGAR AGAR:
A gelling agent derived from seaweed, which retains its gelling properties up to a temperature of 80°C (176°F).

ALATES:
The winged form of insects such as ants or termites.

ANGELICA:
A wild edible plant (*Angelica archangelica*) with a strong, fragrant, almost soapy flavour. The stems, leaves and seeds can be preserved, cooked or eaten raw.

APIOLOGIST:
One who studies bees.

AUTOCHTHONOUS:
Emerging in to a place or locality.

BARLEY KOJI: See KOJI

BEE BREAD:
Honey or pollen used as food by bees.

BEE BROOD:
In a hive, the beeswax structure of cells where the queen bee lays eggs; also, the immature bees between being laid and hatching as adults.

BIRCH BUD SALT:
An aromatic seasoning made by pounding or blending the early buds of the birch tree with salt.

BIRCH SYRUP:
A syrup made by reducing the sap of birch trees. Can be found in some Scandinavian supermarkets.

BLAST CHILLER / BLAST FREEZER:
Equipment that chills or freezes food at a fast rate.

BUTABUSHI:
Pork inoculated with *Aspergillus glaucus* mould, then aged and dried to produce a flavourful, umami-rich product. Based on *katsuobushi*, a Japanese product using skipjack tuna.

CALCIUM HYDROXIDE:
A colourless crystal or white powder most commonly used for clarifying, binding and pickling as well as nixtamalization. Also known as slaked lime. Unprotected exposure can cause chemical burns so take extreme care when using and do not allow to come into contact with skin.

CHITINOUS:
Of or pertaining to chitin, the main structural component of the hard outer exoskeleton of insects, especially arachnids and crustaceans.

COLEOPTERA:
The order of beetles, from the Greek for 'sheathed wing'. The largest order in the animal kingdom.

COLONY COLLAPSE DISORDER:
The phenomenon that occurs when the majority of worker bees disappear and leave behind a queen and a few nurse bees to care for the remaining survivors.

COMBINATION OVEN:
An oven that can cook with dry heat (grill/broil, convection), wet heat (steam), or both in combination.

CRUMIEL:
A commercial product made from honey in its crystallized state. Can be used to add honey flavour to dishes in a dry or crisp form. Contains dried honey powder and maltodextrin.

DASHI:
A Japanese broth made from water, aged kelp (kombu) and preserved, fermented fish (*katsuobushi*).

DEER BUSHI:
A product similar to *butabushi* but made from deer meat. Also called *shikabushi*.

DEHYDRATOR:
A device that preserves food by drying it.

DIPTERA:
The order of true flies, containing more than one million species including the housefly, horsefly and mosquito.

ENFLEURAGE:
The extraction of essential oils and aromas from flowers using odourless animal or vegetable fats.

EPHEMEROPTERA:
The order of mayflies – aquatic insects with brief lifespans.

ETHANOL:
The principle type of alcohol found in alcoholic beverages, produced by fermentation of sugars by yeasts.

ETHNOENTOMOLOGY:
The study of insects in human cultures.

FAUX FOIE:
A plant-based fermented sauce developed at Nordic Food Lab, strongly reminiscent of foie gras in taste.

FORMIC ACID:
A chemical produced by ants for defense. It gives many ants a sour taste.

FORMICIDAE:
The taxonomic family of ants.

FRASS:
The excrement of insect larvae or the refuse produced by boring insects.

GARUM:
A fermented fish sauce used in the cuisines of ancient Greece, Rome and Byzantium.

GASTRONORM PANS: See GASTRO TRAYS

GASTRO TRAYS:
A deep metal tray used in professional kitchens for food storage and preparation.

GENERA:
Plural of 'genus', the major subdivision of a family or subfamily in biological taxonomy; usually consisting of more than one species.

GLUTAMATE:
A naturally occurring amino acid found in many different types of food. Contributes to umami taste.

GUAR GUM:
Powder used as a thickening, stabilizing, suspending and binding agent.

HAEMOLYMPH:
A fluid analogous to blood that circulates in the body cavities and tissues of invertebrates.

HEMIPTERA:
The order of insects that includes true bugs, cicadas and aphids, known for using their sucking and piercing mouthparts to extract plant sap.

HYDROPHILIA:
The ability of a chemical compound to combine with, or attract, water.

HYDROPHOBIC:
Of a chemical compound, having no affinity for, or having the ability to repel, water.

HYMENOPTERA:
The third-largest order of insects, comprising sawflies, wasps, bees and ants.

IMAGO:
The last stage of insect growth, in which it attains maturity. Also called the *imaginal* stage.

IMMERSION CIRCULATOR:
An electrically powered device that circulates and heats a warm fluid kept at a precise and stable temperature.

INCUBATOR:
An enclosed apparatus for keeping foods or other materials at a stable temperature.

INOCULUM:
A substance used to introduce a desired microbial culture into a substrate for fermentation.

INSTAR:
A phase between two periods of moulting in the development of an insect larva or other invertebrates.

KAMUT:
An ancient grain with a rich, nutty flavor.

KATSUOBUSHI:
Fermented, smoked and dried skipjack tuna.

KOJI:
Cooked rice, barley or soybeans that have been inoculated with the fungus *Aspergillus oryzae*.

KOJI EXTRACT:
A product developed at Nordic Food Lab by reducing koji-macerated water into a thick syrup.

KOMBUCHA:
Sweetened black tea or other liquids fermented with a Symbiotic Colony of Bacteria and Yeast (SCOBY) into a fizzy, sour beverage.

LACTIC ACID BACTERIA (LAB):
See LACTIC FERMENTATION.

LACTIC FERMENTATION:
The use of bacteria to convert sugar into lactic acid; used to make products such as yogurt or sauerkraut.

LEPIDOPTERA:
The order of butterflies and moths.

LIQUID COCHINEAL:
Bright purple-red food colouring made from the *Dactylopius coccus* insect.

LIQUID NITROGEN:
The gas nitrogen that has been cooled to -196°C/-320°F and become a liquid. Odourless, colourless and tasteless, it can be used for freezing foods. Exercise extreme caution when using and wear safety gloves and glasses.

LITMUS PAPER:
Paper used to indicate the acidity or alkalinity of a substance.

MAGUEY:
The agave or century plant, from which mescal, pulque and tequila can be made.

MALIC ACID:
A colourless, crystalline compound found in certain fruits and responsible for their sour taste. It is also used in the ageing of wine and as an additive.

MICROBIOTA:
The community of microorganisms that live within a plant, animal or human host.

MICROPLANE:
A high-quality grater used in professional kitchens.

NIXTAMALIZATION:
The process of cooking dried corn in alkali water to remove the kernels' skins and produce masa dough, which is the basis for corn tortillas, tamales and other corn-based foods.

ORTHOPTERA:
The order of insects that includes grasshoppers, crickets, katydids and locusts.

PACOJET:
A piece of kitchen equipment that can blend products very finely to produce smooth-textured sorbets and purées, as well as other creations such as frozen powders.

PACOJET CONTAINERS:
The receptacles used with a Pacojet.

PHYLOGENETICS:
The study of the evolutionary history of a group of organisms based on observing similarities and differences in their physical or genetic characteristics.

PHYLUM:
The second-highest taxon, below 'kingdom', in biological taxonomy.

POLYSACCHARIDE:
A chain of multiple carbohydrates, such as starch or glycogen, which help store energy in the body, or cellulose and chitin, which are used respectively in the structure of cell walls and exoskeletons.

PROPOLIS:
A resinous substance made by honeybees from resin and sap collected from tree buds, used to maintain the hive structure.

PULQUE:
A traditional, central Mexican alcoholic beverage made from the fermented sap of the maguey (agave) plant.

PURPUR WHEAT:
A striking purple-coloured variety of wheat.

RHIZOPUS SPP.:
A genus of fungi some of which are used in the production of *tempe*, a traditional Indonesian fermented cake of soybeans.

ROSE ROOT:
The root of a wild plant (*Rhodiola rosea*). Juicy and fibrous in texture and high in vitamins A and C, it has a powerful rose-like aroma and a slightly bitter taste.

SENSORY-SPECIFIC SATIETY:
A marked decrease in the hedonic response to a particular food or taste, as a consequence of consumption of enough of that certain type of food or taste.

SHIKABUSHI: See DEER BUSHI

SHISO:
A cultivated aromatic herb (*Perilla frutescens*, also known as Perilla) used in Asian cooking.

SILICA GEL / ANHYDROUS SALT PACKET:
A naturally occurring mineral that is used as a desiccant to control humidity and to avoid spoilage of foods.

SILPAT:
A non-stick silicone baking mat.

SØL SALT:
A seasoning made by pounding aged dulse (*Palmaria palmata*), an edible seaweed, with salt.

SUBPHYLUM/SUBPHYLA:
In the traditional Linnaean system of classification, the category that divides phylum into even more distinct groupings, above the taxon called 'class'.

SUPERBAG:
A fine-mesh, flexible bag through which ingredients can be sieved or strained.

TAMIS:
A kitchen utensil known as a drum sieve with a mesh base.

TAXON:
A level of traditional biological taxonomy. The seven primary taxa, in order of most general to most specific, are kingdom, phylum, class, order, family, genus and species.

TERMITARIUM:
A nest built by a colony of termites underground, above ground (as a mound or in a tree), or an artificial nest used to house termites in a laboratory.

TERMITOMYCES:
A genus of edible mushrooms found on termite mounds that have a symbiotic relationship with their hosts.

THERMO-CIRCULATOR: See IMMERSION CIRCULATOR

THERMOMIX:
Kitchen equipment that can blend ingredients at the same time as heating them.

TRIMOLINE:
Inverted sugar syrup, which includes both glucose and fructose. Used by many chefs for baking, it can also be stirred into sorbet mixture before processing, to keep it smooth.

UGALI:
A starchy East African food usually made from maize cooked with water to a thick, stiff porridge-like consistency.

VACUUM BAG:
The bag used in a vacuum sealer.

VACUUM SEALER:
Kitchen appliance that preserves food in a bag by removing the air around it and sealing it under vacuum.

WATER BATH:
In its simplest form, a vessel of hot water in which food can be cooked gently. Many professional kitchens use a thermo-circulator or immersion circulator, which can maintain temperatures precisely for long periods of time.

XANTHAN GUM:
A product derived from fermented starch, used as a thickening agent and to maintain solids in suspension within a liquid.

ØLAND WHEAT:
A heritage wheat that originated from Øland Island, Sweden.

REFERENCES AND FURTHER
READING

NORDIC FOOD LAB
PUBLICATIONS

Publications are listed chronologically, from most recent. All publications are available on the Nordic Food Lab website: nordicfoodlab.org/publications

Payne CLR, Evans J. Nested Houses: Domestication Dynamics of human–wasp relations in contemporary rural Japan. *Journal of Ethnobiology and Ethnomedicine.* (in revision)

Evans J. 2016. Les insectes comme mets. In: Motte-Florac E (ed.) *Savoureux Insectes.* Tours: Presses Universitaires François-Rabelais de Tours.

Evans J, Müller A, Jensen AB, Dahle B, Flore R, Eilenberg J, Frøst MB. 'A descriptive sensory analysis of honeybee drone brood from Denmark and Norway'. *Journal of Insects for Food and Feed* (2016): 277–283.

Müller A, Evans J, Payne C, Roberts R. 'Entomophagy and power'. *Journal of Insects for Food and Feed* 2 (2016): 121–36.

Halloran A, Roos N, Flore R, Hanboonsong Y. 'The development of the edible cricket industry in Thailand'. *Journal of Insects as Food and Feed* 2 (2016): 91–100.

Evans J, Alemu MH, Flore R, Frøst MB, Halloran A, Jensen AB, Maciel-Vergara G, Meyer-Rochow VB, Münke-Svendsen C, Olsen SB, Payne C, Roos N, Rozin P, Tan HSG, van Huis A, Vantomme P, Eilenberg J. '"Entomophagy": an evolving terminology in need of review'. *Journal of Insects for Food and Feed* 1 (2015): 293–305.

Evans J. 'Bee bread'. *Books, Health and History: The New York Academy of Medicine.* Published 1 October 2015. Accessed 29 June 2016. www.nyamcenterforhistory.org/2015/10/01/bee-bread.

Reade B, de Valicourt J, Evans J. 'Fermentation art and science at the Nordic Food Lab'. In Sloan P, Legrand W, Hindley C (eds.), *The Routledge Handbook of Sustainable Food and Gastronomy* (London and New York: Routledge, 2015): 228–41.

Münke C, Halloran A, Vantomme P, Reade B, Evans J, Flore R, Rittman R, Lindén A, Georgiadis P, Irving M. 'Wild ideas in food'. In Sloan P, Legrand W, Hindley C (eds.), *The Routledge Handbook of Sustainable Food and Gastronomy* (London and New York: Routledge, 2015): 206–13.

Halloran A, Münke C, Vantomme P, Reade B, Evans J. 'Broadening insect gastronomy'. In Sloan P, Legrand W, Hindley C (eds.), *The Routledge Handbook of Sustainable Food and Gastronomy* (London and New York: Routledge, 2015): 199–205.

Halloran A, Flore R, Mercier C. 'Notes from the "Insects in a gastronomic context" workshop in Bangkok, Thailand'. *Journal of Insects for Food and Feed* 1 (2015): 241–43.

Frøst MB, Giacalone D, Rasmussen KK. 'Alternative methods of sensory testing: working with chefs, culinary professionals and brewmasters'. In Delarue J, Ben Lawlor J, Rogeaux M (eds.), *Rapid Sensory Profiling Techniques and Related Methods: Applications in New Product Development and Consumer Research* (Cambridge, Massachusetts: Woodhead Publishing, 2015): 353–82.

Deroy O, Reade B, Spence C. 'The insectivore's dilemma, and how to take the West out of it'. *Food Quality and Preference* 44 (2015): 44–55.

Evans J, Flore R, Pedersen JA, Frøst MB. 'Place-based taste: geography as a starting point for deliciousness'. *Flavour Journal* 4, 7 (2015).

Evans J. 'Labre larver og lække insekter [Luscious larvae and delicious insects]'. Dansk Magisterforening. Published 12 January 2015. Accessed 29 June 2016. dm.dk/FagligtForum/NaturvidenskabSundhedMiljoe/Artikler/LabreLarver.

Evans J. 'Insects as a delicacy: the value of diversity in deliciousness'. *moMentum+* 4 (Copenhagen: Jordbrugs Akademikere, 2014): 30–34.

Evans J. 'Observations from the frontier of deliciousness'. *MAD Dispatches: What Is Cooking?* (Copenhagen: MAD, 2014): 80–91.

Barthouil G. 'The MADFeed guide to smoking foods' *The MADFeed.* Published 27 May 2014. Accessed 29 June 2016. www.madfeed.co/2015/the-madfeed-guide-to-smoking-foods.

Evans J. 'Dispatches from the Lab: on the hunt for honey ants in the Australian outback'. *The MADFeed.* Published 17 April 2014. Accessed 29 June 2016. www.madfeed.co/2015/nordic-food-lab-on-the-hunt-for-honey-ants-in-the-australian-outback.

Evans J. 'Dispatches from the Lab: exploring the deliciousness of insects in Africa'. *The MADFeed.* Published 19 February 2014. Accessed 29 June 2016. www.madfeed.co/2015/dispatches-from-the-lab-exploring-the-deliciousness-of-insects-in-africa.

Evans J. 2013. Нормы от "Номы", или красиво есть не запретишь. Новая Нордическая кухня (Nomas normer, eller der er intet forbud mod at spise smukt og sundt). Ankerhjerte I/S, 2013, 208 s.

Barthouil G. 'Spis flere af biernes produkter [Eat more of the bees' products]'. *Tidsskrift For Biavl* 8 (Denmark: Danmarks Biavlerforening, 2013).

Reade B. 'Bog butter'. *Proceedings of the Oxford Symposium on Food and Cookery 2012: Wrapped and Stuffed* (Totnes, Devon, England: Prospect Books, 2013).

319

Evans J. 'Insect gastronomy'. *Cereal Magazine* 3 (2013).

Evans J. 'Cereal killing'. *Wolf Magazine* 2. Published 10 June 2013. Accessed 29 June 2016. issuu.com/wolffoodjournal/docs/wolf_magazine_issue_2/17?e=7052941/3249800.

Risbo J, Mouritsen OG, Frøst MB, Evans J, Reade B. 'Culinary science in Denmark: molecular gastronomy and beyond'. *Journal of Culinary Science and Technology* 11, 2 (2013): 111–30.

Evans J. 2012. 'Non-trivial pursuit: new approaches to Nordic deliciousness'. *Anthropology of Food* Special Issue no.7. Published 10 January 2013. Accessed 29 June 2016. aof. revues.org/7262.

Hermansen ME. 'Creating terroir: an anthropological perspective on new Nordic cuisine as an expression of Nordic identity'. *Anthropology of Food* Special Issue no.7. Published 22 December 2012. Accessed 29 June 2016. aof.revues.org/7249.

Mouritsen OG, Williams L, Bjerregaard R, Duelund L. 'Seaweeds for umami flavour in the new Nordic cuisine'. *Flavour Journal* 1, 4 (2012).

KEY REFERENCES /
FURTHER READING
These are relevant to multiple sections of this book. Starred references are also recommended as further reading.

Belluco S, Losasso C, Maggioletti M, Alonzi CC, Paoletti MG, Ricci A. 'Edible insects in a food safety and nutritional perspective: a critical review'. *Comprehensive Reviews in Food Science and Food Safety* 12, 3 (2013): 296–313.

* Bodenheimer FS. *Insects as Human Food* (The Hague: W. Junk, 1951).

* Burlingame B, Dernini S. *Sustainable Diets and Biodiversity: Directions and Solutions for Policy, Research and Action* (Rome: Food and Agriculture Organization of the United Nations, 2010).

* DeFoliart GR. 'Insects as food: why the Western attitude is important'. *Annual Review of Entomology* 44 (1999): 21–55.

* Durst PB, Johnson DV, Leslie RN, Shono K. *Edible forest insects: humans bite back. Proceedings of a workshop on Asia-Pacific resources and their potential for development* (Chiang Mai, Thailand: Food and Agriculture Organization of the United Nations, Regional Office for Asia and the Pacific, 2010).

Gjerris M, Gamborg C, Röcklinsberg H. 'Ethical aspects of insect production for food and feed'. *Journal of Insects as Food and Feed* 2, 2 (2016): 101–10.

* Hanboonsong Y, Jamjanya T, Durst P. *Six-legged Livestock: Edible Insect Farming, Collecting and Marketing in Thailand* (Bangkok: Food and Agriculture Organization of the United Nations, Regional Office for Asia and the Pacific, 2013).

Haraway DJ. *When Species Meet* (Minneapolis: University of Minnesota Press, 2008).

Holt V. *Why Not Eat Insects?* (Whitstable, UK: Pryor Publications, 1885).

Jongema Y. 'List of edible insects of the world.' Wageningen UR. Published 1 June 2015. Accessed 29 June 2016. www. wageningenur.nl/en/Expertise-Services/Chair-groups/Plant-Sciences/Laboratory-of-Entomology/Edible-insects/Worldwide-species-list.htm.

* Kuhnlein HV, Erasmus B, Spigelski D (eds). *Indigenous peoples' food systems: the many dimensions of culture, diversity and environment for nutrition and health* (Rome: Food and Agricultural Organization of the United Nations, 2009).

Loo S, Sellbach U. 'Insect affects'. *Angelaki: Journal of the Theoretical Humanities* 20 (2016): 79–88.

Lundy ME, Parrella MP. 'Crickets are not a free lunch: protein capture from scalable organic side-streams via high-density populations of *Acheta domesticus*'. *PLOS One* 10 (2015): e0118785.

McGrew WC. 'The other faunivory: primate insectivory and early human diet'. In Stanford CB, Bunn HT (eds.), *Meat-Eating and Human Evolution* (Oxford: Oxford University Press, 2001): 160–78.

Meyer-Rochow VB. 'Can insects help to ease the problem of world food shortage?' *Search* 6 (1975): 261–62.

Oonincx DGAB, van Itterbeeck J, Heetkamp MJW, van den Brand H, van Loon JJA, van Huis A. 'An exploration on greenhouse gas and ammonia production by insect species suitable for animal or human consumption'. *PLOS ONE* 5, 12 (2010).

Price PW. *Insect Ecology: Behavior, Populations and Communities* (New York: Cambridge University Press, 2011).

Raubenheimer D, Rothman JM. 'Nutritional ecology of entomophagy in humans and other primates'. *Annual Review of Entomology* 58 (2013): 141–60.

Rozin P. 'Food is fundamental, fun, frightening, and far-reaching'. *Social Research* 66 (1999): 9–30.

Rumpold B, Schlüter O. 'Nutritional composition and safety aspects of edible insects'. *Molecular Nutrition and Food Research* 57 (2013): 802–23.

* Sen A. *Poverty and Famines: An Essay on Entitlement and Deprivation* (Oxford: Oxford University Press, 1981).

Tan HSG, Fischer ARH, Tinchan P, Stieger M, Steenbekkers LPA, van Trijp HCM. 'Insects as food: exploring cultural exposure and individual experience as determinants of acceptance'. *Food Quality and Preference* 42 (2015): 78–89.

* Tomlinson I. 'Doubling food production to feed the 9 billion: a critical perspective on a key discourse of food security in the UK'. *Journal of Rural Studies* 29 (2013): 81–90.

van Huis A. 'Edible insects contributing to food security?' *Agriculture & Food Security* 4, 20 (2015).

* van Huis A, van Itterbeeck J, Klunder H, Mertens E, Halloran A, Muir G, Vantomme P. *Edible Insects: Future Prospects for Food and Feed* (Rome: Food and Agriculture Organization of the United Nations, 2013).

* Yen AL. 'Entomophagy and insect conservation: some thoughts for digestion'. *Journal of Insect Conservation* 13 (2009): 667–70.

NORDIC FOOD LAB
(PP.17–23)
Sections of this text appear in their original form on the Nordic Food Lab website ('Who we are') and in 'Non-trivial pursuit: new approaches to Nordic deliciousness', for Anthropology of Food.

Brillat-Savarin JA. *The Physiology of Taste*. Originally published 1825, trans. Fisher MFK, 1949 (New York: Vintage, 2011).

Mouritsen OG. 'Seaweeds for flavour'. *Flavour Journal Launch*. Published 28 March 2012. Accessed 29 June 2016. www.slideshare.net/BioMedCentral/ole-g-flavour-launch.

O'Mahony M, Ishii R. 'A comparison of English and Japanese taste languages: taste descriptive methodology, codability and the umami taste'. *British Journal of Psychology* 77 (1986): 161–74.

WORKING WITH INSECTS
(PP.25–37)
Sections of this text appear in their original form on the Nordic Food Lab website ('Blog'), and in 'Insect gastronomy', for Cereal Magazine; *'Broadening insect gastronomy', for* The Routledge Handbook of Sustainable Food and Gastronomy; *'Observations from the frontier of deliciousness', for MAD Dispatches; and 'Insects as a delicacy', for* moMentum+.

Atala A. 'Insects and plants: together for life'. *MADFeed*. Published 28 August 2011. Accessed 29 June 2016. www.madfeed.co/video/insects-plants-together-for-life.

DeFoliart GR. 'An overview of the role of edible insects in preserving biodiversity'. *Ecology of Food and Nutrition* 36 (1996): 109–32.

Evans J. 'Video of our presentation at MAD: delineating the edible and inedible'. *Nordic Food Lab*. Published 12 September 2012. Accessed 29 June 2016. nordicfoodlab. org/blog/2012/9/video-of-our-presentation-at-mad-2-delineating-the-edible-and-inedible.

Gammage B. *The Biggest Estate on Earth* (Sydney, Australia: Allen & Unwin, 2011).

'How to feed the world in 2050'. Food and Agriculture Organization of the United Nations. n.d. Accessed 29 June 2016. www.fao.org/fileadmin/templates/wsfs/docs/expert_paper/How_to_Feed_the_World_in_2050.pdf.

Lévi-Strauss C. *Anthropologie structurale* (Paris: Plon, 1958).

Morgan DE. 'Chemical sorcery for sociality: exocrine secretions of ants (Hymenoptera: Formicidae)'. *Myrmecological News* 11 (2009): 79–90.

Morgan DE. 'Trail pheromones of ants'. *Physiological Entomology* 34, 1 (2009): 1–17.

Persic A, Martin G (eds.). *Links between biological and cultural diversity: concepts, methods and experiences. Report of an International Workshop* (Paris: UNESCO, 2008).

Tan HSG, Fischer ARH, van Trijp HCM, Stieger M. 'Tasty but nasty? Exploring the role of sensory-liking and food appropriateness in the willingness to eat unusual novel foods like insects'. *Food Quality and Preference* 48 (2016): 293–302.

'Soy facts & data'. WWF. n.d. Accessed 29 June 2016. wwf. panda.org/what_we_do/footprint/agriculture/soy/facts/.

'Soy, you & deforestation'. WWF. n.d. Accessed 29 June 2016. wwf.panda.org/what_we_do/footprint/agriculture/soy/consumers/.

'What causes hunger?' United Nations World Food Programme. 2014. Accessed 29 June 2016. www.wfp.org/hunger/causes.

INSECTS: AN ACQUIRED TASTE
(PP.39–51)

1 I use the term 'intentional' here for a number of reasons. Without a doubt, I must have eaten insects and insect parts before. According to EU legislation, cereals and categories of flour, groats and meal are allowed to contain a certain amount of 'miscellaneous impurities'. This means weed seeds, damaged grains, extraneous matter, husks, dead insects and fragments of insects. Not that it is a lot: for oats 1 per cent is allowed; for wheat and rye, 2 per cent. However, consider the diet rich in cereals that has characterized my upbringing and adult life – I'm a sucker for good bread, and my remaining vices include copious amounts of good Danish pastry – a low estimate is that I must have consumed at least 1.5 kilos of insects through wheat alone.

2 Although tedious, it is necessary to clarify a few concepts: familiarity in relation to a food or beverage is defined as the subjective feeling of recognition. A familiar food may also have features that are unfamiliar to the eater, yet at a superordinate level it is still perceived as familiar.

Atala A. 'Insects and plants: together for life'. *The MADFeed*. Published 28 August 2011. Accessed 29 June 2016. www.madfeed.co/video/insects-plants-together-for-life.

3 Novelty in relation to food is a bit more elusive in its definition. Novelty is both the property of being new, uncommon and previously unencountered by the eater. Again, this is at a superordinate level.

4 This is not limited to food; it applies to the majority of manufactured goods and consumer products. In 1951, the industrial designer Raymond Loewy coined the term the MAYA principle: Most Advanced Yet Acceptable. To be successful in the market, a new product has to be so advanced that it is novel when compared to what already

exists in that product category, but it must not be so deviant that it will not be accepted because it is unfamiliar.

5 A cold, liquid dessert made out of buttermilk, often thickened with egg yolks or with cultured dairy products such as *ymer*, A38 or plain yogurt. It is slightly sweetened, and flavoured with vanilla and lemon zest. It is served with *kammerjunkere*, a sweet and crumbly biscuit, and often seasonal red berries, such as strawberries and raspberries. The best *koldskål* I have ever had was created by Nordic Food Lab. It had a twist on the flavour, using lemon verbena. It was served with freeze-dried lingonberries, raspberries and cranberries, homemade *kammerjunkere* and was topped with lemon-thyme sugar.

6 nordicfoodlab.org/blog/2012/10/bee-larvae-granola

7 nordicfoodlab.org/blog/2014/2/a-side-of-bee-larva-with-your-afternoon-coffee

Bottero J. *The Oldest Cuisine in the World: Cooking in Mesopotamia* (Chicago: University of Chicago Press, 2004).

Chandrashekar J, Hoon MA, Ryba NJP, Zuker CS. 'The receptors and cells for mammalian taste'. *Nature* 444, 7117 (2006): 288–94.

Giacalone D. 'Consumers' perception of novel beers'. PhD thesis. University of Copenhagen, 2013.

Giacalone D, Duerlund M, Bøegh-Petersen J, Bredie WLP, Frøst MB. 'Stimulus collative properties and consumers' flavor preferences'. *Appetite* 77C (2014): 20–30.

Giacalone D, Frøst MB, Bredie WLP, Pineau B, Hunter DC, Paisley AG, Beresford MK, Jaeger SR. 'Situational appropriateness of beer is influenced by product familiarity'. *Food Quality and Preference* 39 (2015): 16–27.

Giacalone D, Jaeger SR. 'Better the devil you know? How product familiarity affects usage versatility of foods and beverages'. *Journal of Economic Psychology* 55 (2016): 120–38.

Loewy R. *Never Leave Well Enough Alone* (Baltimore: Johns Hopkins University Press, 2002).

Meyerhof W, Born S, Brockhoff A, Behrens M. 'Molecular biology of mammalian bitter taste receptors: a review'. *Flavour and Fragrance Journal* 26, 4 (2011): 260–68.

Mouritsen OG, Styrbæk K. *Umami: Unlocking the Secrets of the Fifth Taste* (New York: Columbia University Press, 2014).

Nielsen, LE. 'Danskernes Holdning Til Bilarvegranola - En Ny Insektbaseret Snack [Danish Consumers' Attitude to Bee Larvae Granola – a New Insect-Based Snack]'. Bachelor's Thesis. (University of Copenhagen, 2013).

Norman DA. *Emotional Design: Why We Love (or Hate) Everyday Things* (New York: Basic Books, 2004).

Ortiz Sanchez M. 'Welcoming insects at the table'. Master's thesis. Delft University of Technology, the Netherlands, 2014.

Pedersen JA. 'Disgusting or delicious: utilization of bee larvae as ingredient and consumer acceptance of the resulting food'.

Master's thesis. University of Copenhagen, 2014.

Prescott J. *Taste Matters* (London: Reaktion Books, 2013), first edition.

Rozin P. 'The selection of food by rats, humans and other animals'. In Hinde, J, Beer, RA and Shaw, E (eds.), *Advances in the Study of Behavior, Volume 6* (New York: Academic Press, 1976): 21–76.

Spence C, Piqueras-Fiszman B. *The Perfect Meal: The Multisensory Science of Food and Dining* (London: Wiley-Blackwell, 2014).

Szczesniak AS. 'Texture is a sensory property'. *Food Quality and Preference* 13, 4 (2002): 215–25.

Tan HSG, Fischer ARH, Tinchan P, Stieger M, Steenbekkers LPA, van Trijp HCM. 'Insects as food: exploring cultural exposure and individual experience as determinants of acceptance'. *Food Quality and Preference* 42 (2015): 78–89.

van Trijp HCM, Steenkamp JB. 'Consumers' variety seeking tendency with respect to foods: measurement and managerial implications'. *European Review of Agricultural Economics* 19 (1992): 181–95.

TERMS: BUGS, INSECTS AND ENTOMOPHAGY (PP.53–69)
Sections of this text appear in their original form in '"Entomophagy": an evolving terminology in need of review', published in the Journal of Insects for Food and Feed.

Aissaoui M, Valmalle P. 'Le Petit Larousse et le Petit Robert: les rivaux des mots nouveaux'. *Le Figaro*. Published 20 May 2015. Accessed 29 June 2016. www.lefigaro.fr/livres/2015/05/20/03005-20150520ARTFIG00360-le-petit-larousse-et-le-petit-robert-les-rivaux-des-mots-nouveaux.php>.

Anonymous. 'La entomofagia'. *Ibérica* 11 (1919): 278–89.

Aristotle. *History of Animals*, trans. DA Thompson. Internet Classics Archive. Accessed 29 June 2016. classics.mit.edu/Aristotle/history_anim.mb.txt.

Athenaeus. *Deipnosophistae*, trans. CB Gulick. Loeb Classical Library. Published 17 Feb 2011. Accessed 29 June 2016. penelope.uchicago.edu/Thayer/E/Roman/Texts/Athenaeus/4A*.html.

Barreteau D. 'Les Mofu-Gudur et leurs criquets'. In Baroin C, Boutrais J (eds.), *L'homme et l'animal dans le bassin du lac Tchad—Actes du colloque du reseau Mega-Tchad, Octobre 15–17, 1997, Orleans, France* (Paris: Editions IRD [Institut de Recherche pour le Developpement], Collection Colloques et Seminaires, Université Nanterre, no. 00/354, 1999): 133–69.

Bergier E. *Peuples entomophages et insects comestibles: Ètude sur les moeurs de l'homme et de l'insecte* (Avignon, France: Imprimerie Rulliere Frères, 1941).

Berlin B. *Ethnobiological Classification: Principles of Categorization of Plants and Animals in Traditional Societies* (Princeton, New Jersey: Princeton University Press, 1992). 'Bug'. Wikipedia. Accessed 29 June 2016. en.wikipedia.org/wiki/Bug.

Bukkens SG. 'The nutritional value of edible insects'. *Ecology of Food and Nutrition* 36 (1997): 287–319.

Caparros Megido R, Sablon L, Geuens M, Brostaux Y, Alabi T, Blecker C, Drugmand D, Haubruge E, Francis F. 'Edible insects' acceptance by Belgian consumers: promising attitude for entomophagy development'. *Journal of Sensory Studies* 29 (2014): 14–20.

'Category: English words suffixed with –phagy'. Wiktionary. Accessed 29 June 2016. en.wiktionary.org/wiki/Category: English_words_suffixed_with_-phagy.

Chakravorty J, Ghosh S, Meyer-Rochow VB. 'Comparative survey of entomophagy and entomotherapeutic practices in six tribes of eastern Arunachal Pradesh (India)'. *Journal of Ethnobiology and Ethnomedicine* 9 (2013): 1–12.

Chapman AD. 'Numbers of living species in Australia and the world' (Canberra, Australia: Australian Biological Resources Study, 2006).

Christensen D, Orech F, Mungai M, Larsen T, Friis H, Aagaard-Hansen J. 'Entomophagy among the Luo of Kenya: a potential mineral source?'. *International Journal of Food Sciences and Nutrition* 57 (2006): 198–203.

Costa-Neto EM. 'The significance of the category "insect" for folk biological classification systems'. *Journal of Ecological Anthropology* 4 (2000): 70–75.

DeFoliart GR. 'Insects as human food: Gene DeFoliart discusses some nutritional and economic aspects'. *Crop Protection* 11 (1992): 395–99.

Dictionnaire Le Petit Robert 2014 (Paris: Le Robert, 2013).

'Entomophagy'. Google Ngram Viewer. Accessed 21 May 2015. books.google.com/ngrams/graph?content=entomophagy&year_start=1800&year_end=2000&corpus=15&smoothing=3&share=&direct_url=t1%3B%2Centomophagy%3B%2Cc0.

'Entomophagy'. Oxford Dictionaries Online. Accessed 29 June 2016. www.oxforddictionaries.com/definition/english/entomophagy.

Gordh G, Headrick D. *A Dictionary of Entomology*. (Collingwood, Australia: CSIRO, 2011).

Halloran A. 'EU har taget et vigtigt skridt [The EU has taken an important step]'. *moMentum+* 4 (2014): 8–10.

Halloran A, Vantomme P, Hanboonsong Y, Ekesi S. 'Regulating edible insects: the challenge of addressing food security, nature conservation, and the erosion of traditional food culture'. *Food Security* 7 (2015): 739–46.

Harris M. *Good to Eat: Riddles of Food and Culture* (New York: Simon and Schuster, 1985).

Herodotus. *The Histories*, trans. Macauley GC. Project Gutenberg. Published 25 Jan 2013. Accessed 29 June 2016. www.gutenberg.org/files/2707/2707-h/2707-h.htm.

Hogue CL. 'Cultural entomology'. *Annual Review of Entomology* 32 (1987): 181–99.

Hooks B. 'Eating the Other: desire and resistance'. *Black Looks: Race and Representation* (Boston: South End Press, 1992).

Humle T, Matsuzawa T. 'Oil palm use by adjacent communities of chimpanzees at Bossou and Nimba Mountains, West Africa'. *International Journal of Primatology* 25 (2004): 551–81.

'Insect'. Oxford Dictionaries Online. Accessed 29 June 2016. www.oxforddictionaries.com/definition/english/insect.

Johnston J, Baumann S. 'Democracy versus distinction: a study of omnivorousness in gourmet food writing'. *American Journal of Sociology* 113 (2007): 165–204.

Kellert S. 'Values and perceptions of invertebrates'. *Conservation Biology* 7 (1993): 845–55.

Laurent E. 'Definition and cultural representation of the category *mushi* in Japanese culture'. *Society & Animals* 3 (1995): 61–77.

Leer J, Kjær KM. 'Strange culinary encounters: stranger fetishism in *Jamie's Italian Escape* and *Gordon's Great Escape*'. *Food, Culture & Society* 18 (2015): 309–27.

Lévy-Luxereau A. 'Note sur quelques criquets de la région de Maradi (Niger) et leur noms Hausa'. *Journal d'Agriculture Traditionelle et de Botanique Appliquée* 37 (1980): 263–72.

'List of Feeding Behaviours'. Wikipedia. Accessed 29 June 2016. en.wikipedia.org/wiki/List_of_feeding_behaviours.

Looy H, Dunkel FV, Wood JR. 'How then shall we eat? Insect-eating attitudes and sustainable foodways'. *Agriculture and Human Values* 31 (2014): 131–41.

Lycett SJ, Collard M, McGrew WC. 'Phylogenetic analyses of behavior support existence of culture among wild chimpanzees'. *Proceedings of the National Academy of Sciences* 104 (2007): 17,588–92.

Martins Y, Pliner P. 'Human food choices: an examination of the factors underlying acceptance/rejection of novel and familiar animal and nonanimal foods'. *Appetite* 45 (2005): 214–24.

McGrew WC, Linda F, Marchant C, Payne C, Webster T, Hunt KD. 'Chimpanzees at Semliki ignore oil palms'. *Folia Primatologica* 28 (2010): 109–21.

Menzel P, D'Aluisio F. *Man Eating Bugs: The Art and Science of Eating Insects* (New York: Random House, 1998).

Meyer-Rochow VB. 'Local taxonomy and terminology for some terrestrial arthropods in five different ethnic groups of Papua New Guinea and central Australia'. *Journal of the Royal Society of Western Australia* 58 (1975): 15–30.

Meyer-Rochow VB. 'Food taboos: their origins and purposes'. *Journal of Ethnobiology and Ethnomedicine* 5 (2009): 1–10.

Misof B. et al. 'Phylogenomics resolves the timing and pattern of insect evolution'. *Science* 346 (2014): 763–7.

Novotny V, Basset Y, Miller SE, Weiblen GD, Bremer B, Cizek L, Drozd P. 'Low host specificity of herbivorous insects in a tropical forest'. *Nature* 416 (2002): 841–44.

Obopile M, Seeletso TG. 'Eat or not eat: an analysis of the status of entomophagy in Botswana'. *Food security* 5 (2013): 817–24.

O'Malley R, McGrew WC. 'Primates and insect resources'. *Journal of Human Evolution* 71 (2014): 1–3.

Paoletti MF (ed). *Ecological Implications of Minilivestock: Potential of Insects, Rodents, Frogs, and Snails* (Enfield, New Hampshire: Science Publishers, 2005).

Pennisi E. 'All in the (bigger) family: revised arthropod tree marries crustacean and insect fields'. *Science of the Total Environment* 347 (2015): 220–21.

Pliny the Elder. *The Natural History*, trans. Bostock J. Perseus Digital Library. Accessed 29 June 2016. www.perseus.tutts/hopper/text?doc-Perseus%3A1999.02.0137%3Abook%3D1%1%3Achapter%3Ddedication.

Posey DA. 'Hierarchy and utility in a folk biological taxonomic system: patterns in classification of arthropods by the Kayapó Indians of Brazil'. *Journal of Ethnobiology* 4 (1984): 123–39.

Ramos-Elorduy J, Moreno JMP, Prado EE, Perez MA, Otero JL, De Guevara OL. 'Nutritional value of edible insects from the state of Oaxaca, Mexico'. *Journal of Food Composition and Analysis* 10 (1997): 142–57.

Riley CV. *Sixth Annual Report on the Noxious, Beneficial and Other Insects of the State of Missouri* (Jefferson City: Hegan & Carter, 1871): 144. books.google.fr/books?id=nwYdAQAAMAAJ&pg=RA2-PA144&dq=%22entomophagy%22&hl=en&sa=X&ei=AsJdVcnmMIq4UcnSgZAD&ved=0CCsQ6AEwAg#v=onepage&q=%22entomophagy%22&f=false.

Rozin E, Rozin P. 'Culinary Themes and Variations'. *Natural History* 90 (1981): 6–10.

Rozin P. 'Development in the food domain'. *Developmental Psychology* 26, 4 (1990): 555–62.

Rozin P, Fallon AE. 'A perspective on disgust'. *Psychological Review* 94 (1987): 23–41.

Schiefenhövel W, Blum P. 'Insects: forgotten and rediscovered as food'. In MacClancy J, Henry J, Macbeth H (eds.), *Consuming the Inedible: Neglected Dimensions of Food Choice* (New York: Berghahn Books, 2007): 163–76.

Schimitschek E. 1961. *Die Bedeutung der Insekten für die Kultur und Wirtschaft des Menschen in Vergangenheit und Gegenwart* (Boceklerin, insanligin geccmisteki ve bugunku kultur ve iktis hayattaki onemi). Übersetzung Uslu, S. Orman Fakiiltesi konferanslari 1959, Istanbul Universitesi 908: 1–48.

Schimitschek E. 'Insekten als Nahrung, in Brauchtum, Kult und Kultur'. In Helmcke JG, Stark D, Wermuth H (eds.), *Handbuch der Zoologie – eine Naturgeschichte der Stämme des Tierreichs*, vol. 4 (Berlin: Akademie Verlag, 1968): 1–62.

Simoons FJ. 'Rejection of fish as human food in Africa: a problem in history and ecology'. *Ecology of Food and Nutrition* 3 (1974): 89–105.

Simoons FJ. 'Traditional use and avoidance of foods of animal origin: a culture historical view'. *Cultural Food Patterns and Nutrition* 28 (1978): 178–84.

Tuorila HM, Meiselman HL, Cardello AV, Lesher LL. 'Effect of expectations and the definition of product category on the acceptance of unfamiliar foods'. *Food Quality and Preference* 9 (1998): 421–30.

Turner NJ, Łuczaj ŁJ, Migliorini P, Pieroni A, Dreon AL, Sacchetti LE, Paoletti MG. 'Edible and tended wild plants, traditional ecological knowledge and agroecology'. *Critical Reviews in Plant Sciences* 30 (2011): 198–225.

van Huis A. 'Insects as food in sub-Saharan Africa'. *Insect Science and Its Application* 23 (2003): 163–85.

van Huis A, Dicke M, van Loon JJA. 'Insects to feed the world'. *Journal of Insects as Food and Feed* 1 (2015): 3–5.

Virey JJ. 'De l'entomophagie ou de la nourriture tirée des insectes chez différentes peuples et de ses effets sur l'économie animale'. *Dictionnaire des Sciences Médicinale* (1810): t.15.

Wansink B. 'Changing eating habits on the home front: lost lessons from World War II research'. *Journal of Public Policy and Marketing* 21 (2002): 90–99.

Webster TH, McGrew WC, Marchant LF, Payne CL, Hunt KD. 'Selective insectivory at Toro-Semliki, Uganda: comparative analyses suggest no "savanna" chimpanzee pattern'. *Journal of Human Evolution* 71 (2014): 20–27.

Yates-Doerr E. 'Meeting the demand for meat?' *Anthropology Today* 28 (2012): 1.

POLITICS AND POWER (PP.71–81)
Sections of this text appear in their original form in 'Entomophagy and Power', written collaboratively with Andrew Müller, Charlotte Payne and Rebecca Roberts and published in the Journal of Insects for Food and Feed.

Bohnsack R. *Rekonstruktive Sozialforschung: Einführung in qualitative Methoden*. 9., überarbeitete und erweiterte Auflage (Opladen, Germany, and Toronto: Verlag Barbara Budrich, 2014).

Bourdieu P. *Distinction: A Social Critique of the Judgement of Taste* (Cambridge, Massachusetts: Harvard University Press, 1984).

Chaparro C, Oot L, Sethuraman K. 'Overview of the nutrition situation in seven countries in Southeast Asia'. FHI 360/FANTA-report (2014). Accessed 29 June 2016. www.fantaproject.org/sites/default/files/download/Southeast-Asia-Nutrition-Overview-Apr2014.pdf.

DeFoliart GR. 'Sky prawns and other dishes: food of the future'. *Insect Food Newsletter* 5 (1992): 8.

Dossey AT, Morales-Ramos J, Rojas G (eds.). *Insects As Sustainable Food Ingredients* (Saint Louis, Missouri: Elsevier, 2016).

Durst PB, Hanboonsong Y. 'Small-scale production of edible insects for enhanced food security and rural livelihoods: experience from Thailand and Lao People's Democratic Republic'. *Journal of Insects as Food and Feed* 1 (2015): 25–31.

Edelman M. 'Food sovereignty: forgotten genealogies and future regulatory challenges'. *Journal of Peasant Studies* 41 (2014): 959–78.

zu Ermgassen EK, Phalan B, Green RE, Balmford A. 'Reducing the land use of EU pork production: where there's swill, there's a way'. *Food Policy* 58 (2016): 35–48.

FairWild Standard Version 2.0 (August 2010). Accessed 29 June 2016. www.fairwild.org/documents/.

Foucault M. 'The subject and power'. *Critical Inquiry* 8 (1982): 777–95.

Foucault M. 'The subject and power'. In Dreyfus H, Rabinow P (eds.), *Michel Foucault: Beyond Structuralism and Hermeneutics* (Chicago: University of Chicago Press, 1983): 208–26.

Glaser BG, Strauss AL. *The Discovery of Grounded Theory: Strategies for Qualitative Research* (Chicago: Aldine, 1967).

Goodman D, DuPuis EM. 'Knowing food and growing food: beyond the production–consumption debate in the sociology of agriculture'. *Sociologia Ruralis* 42 (2002): 5–22.

Goodman D, Watts M (eds.). *Globalizing food: agrarian questions and global restructuring* (London/New York: Routledge, 1997).

Goodman MK. 'Reading fair trade: political ecological imaginary and the moral economy of fair trade foods'. *Political Geography* 23 (2004): 891–915.

Gramsci A, Hoare Q, Nowell-Smith G. *Selections from the Prison Notebooks of Antonio Gramsci* (New York: International, 1972).

Guthman J. 'Commodified meanings, meaningful commodities: re-thinking production–consumption links through the organic system of provision'. *Sociologia Ruralis* 42 (2002): 295–311.

Hudson I, Hudson M. 'Removing the veil? Commodity fetishism, fair trade, and the environment'. *Organization & Environment* 16 (2003): 413–30.

Kelemu S, Niassy S, Torto B, Fiaboe K, Affognon H, Tonnang H, Maniania NK, Ekesi S. 'African edible insects for food and feed: inventory, diversity, commonalities and contribution to food security'. *Journal of Insects as Food and Feed* 1 (2015): 103–19.

Kreutzberger S, Thurn V. *Harte Kost* (Munich: Ludwig Verlag, 2014).

Linnér BO. *The Return of Malthus: Environmentalism and Post-war Population-Resource Crises* (Strond, UK: White Horse Press, 2003).

Lueger M. *Grundlagen Qualitativer Feldforschung: Methodologie, Organisierung, Materialanalyse* (Vienna: WUV-Verlag, 2000).

Malthus TR. 1798. *An Essay on the Principle of Population, As it Affects the Future Improvement of Society*, vol. 2. Originally printed for J. Johnson in St. Paul's Churchyard, London. Accessed 29 June 2016. www.esp.org/books/malthus/population/malthus.pdf.

Mayring P. *Qualitative Inhaltsanalyse: Grundlagen und Techniken*. 11. vollständig überarbeitete Auflage (Weinheim, Germany: Beltz Pädagogik, 2010).

McMichael P. 'A food regime analysis of the "world food crisis"'. *Agriculture and Human Values* 26 (2009): 281–95.

Muthu SS (ed.). *Social Life Cycle Assessment: An Insight* (Singapore: Springer, 2015).

Müller A. 'Insects as food in Laos and Thailand – a case of "westernisation"?' In Kofahl D, David W (eds.), *Food Culture of South East Asia* (2016 – in press).

Payne CLR, Scarborough P, Rayner M, Nonaka K. 'Are edible insects more or less "healthy" than commonly consumed meats? A comparison using two nutrient profiling models developed to combat over- and undernutrition'. *European Journal of Clinical Nutrition* 70 (2015): 285–291.

Phillips L. 'Food and globalization'. *Annual Review of Anthropology* 35 (2006): 37–57.

Pollan M. *The Omnivore's Dilemma* (New York: Penguin Press, 2006).

Rigg J. 'Rural-urban interactions, agriculture and wealth: a Southeast Asian perspective'. *Progress in Human Geography* 22 (1998): 497–522.

Rumpold BA, Schlüter OK. 'Potential and challenges of insects as an innovative source for food and feed production'. *Innovative Food Science & Emerging Technologies* 17 (2013): 1–11.

Sankharat U. 'Cambodian child migrant workers in the Rong Kluea Market area in Thailand'. *Asian Social Science* 9 (2013): 24–32.

Smart B. 'The politics of truth and the problem of hegemony'. In Hoy DC (ed.), *Foucault: A Critical Reader* (Oxford: B. Blackwell, 1994): 208–21.

Stehfest E, Bouwman L, Van Vuuren D, Den Elzen M, Eickhout B, Kabat P. 'Climate benefits of changing diet'. *Climatic Change* 95 (2009): 83–102.

Steinfeld H. *Livestock's Long Shadow: Environmental Issues and Options* (Rome: Food and Agriculture Organization of the United Nations, 2006).

Tsing A. *The Mushroom at the End of the World: On the Possibility of Life in Capitalist Ruins.* (Princeton, New Jersey: Princeton University Press, 2015).

United Nations Development Programme. *Human Development Report 2015* (New York: United Nations, 2016). Accessed 29 June 2016. hdr.undp.org/sites/default/files/2015_human_development_report.pdf.

U.S. Food and Drug Administration. 'How to understand and use the nutrition facts label'. Updated 30 November 2015. Accessed 29 June 2016. www.fda.gov/Food/IngredientsPackagingLabeling/LabelingNutrition/ucm274593.htm.

van Huis A. 'Insects as food in sub-Saharan Africa'. *International Journal of Tropical Insect Science* 23, 3 (2003): 163–85.

van Huis A. 'Potential of insects as food and feed in assuring food security'. *Annual Review of Entomology* 58 (2013): 563–83.

Vantomme P, Münke C, van Huis A, van Itterbeeck J, Hakman A. 'Insects to feed the world conference: summary report'. Food and Agriculture Organization of the United Nations/Wageningen University (2014). Accessed 29 June 2016. www.wageningenur.nl/en/show/Insects-to-feed-the-world.htm.

Weber M. *Wirtschaft und Gesellschaft.* (Tübingen, Germany: JCB Mohr [P Siebeck], 1922).

Weis T. 'The meat of the global food crisis'. *The Journal of Peasant Studies* 40 (2013): 65–85.

Yates-Doerr E. 'The world in a box? Food security, edible insects, and "One World, One Health" collaboration'. *Social Science and Medicine* 129 (2015): 106–12.

Yen AL. 'Insects as food and feed in the Asia Pacific region: current perspectives and future directions'. *Journal of Insects as Food and Feed* 1 (2015): 33–55.

Yhoung-aree J, Chavasit V, Khunsanong S. 'House cricket farming and chain of distribution to consumers: preliminary identification of the quality, safety and critical points of hazard of the produces'. (Bangkok: Institute of Nutrition at Mahidol University, 2014).

Ziegler J, Kober H. *Wir Lassen Sie Verhungern* (Munich: Bertelsmann, 2012).

ANTS (PP.84–6)
Sections of this text appear in their original form on the Nordic Food Lab blog, 'Insect gastronomy', in Cereal Magazine, *and 'Insects as a delicacy' in* moMentum+.

Cengiz ZT, Yilmaz H, Dülger AC, Çiçek M. 'Human infection with *Dicrocoelium dendriticum* in Turkey'. *Annals of Saudi Medicine* 30, 2 (2010): 159–61.

Le Bailly M, Bouchet F. 'Ancient Dicrocoeliosis: occurrence, distribution and migration'. *Acta Tropica* 115, 3 (2010): 175–80.

Małagocka J. 'Viability of *Dicrocoelium dendriticum metacerkariae* in host ants after exposure to freezing, boiling and ethanol'. University of Copenhagen student report (2015).

Otranto D, Traversa D. 'Dicrocoeliosis of ruminants: a little known fluke disease'. *Trends in Parasitology* 19, 1 (2003): 12–15.

Schuster R. 'Infection patterns in the first intermediate host of *Dicrocoelium dendriticum*'. *Veterinary Parasitology* 47, 3–4 (1993): 235–43.

Theodoridis Y, Duncan JL, MacLean JM, Himonas CA. 'Pathophysiological studies on *Dicrocoelium dendriticum* infection in sheep'. *Veterinary Parasitology* 39, 1–2 (1991): 61–66.

BEE BROOD (PP.87–9)
Sections of this text appear in their original form on the Nordic Food Lab blog, in 'Cereal killing' in Wolf Magazine, *and in 'A descriptive sensory analysis of honeybee drone brood from Denmark and Norway', published in the* Journal of Insects for Food and Feed.

Calis JNM. 'Parasite-host interactions between the varroa mite and the honey bee: a contribution to sustainable varroa control'. Doctoral thesis, Wageningen University (2001).

Charriere JD, Imdorf A, Bachofen B, Tschan A. 'The removal of capped drone brood: an effective means of reducing the infestation of varroa in honeybee colonies'. *Bee World* 84 (2003): 117–24

Dietemann V, Pflugfelder J, Anderson D, Charrière JD, Chejanovsky N, Dainat B, de Miranda J, Delaplane K, Dillier FX, Fuch S, Gallmann P, Gauthier L, Imdorf A, Koeniger N, Kralj J, Meikle W, Pettis J, Rosenkranz P, Sammataro D, Smith D, Yañez O, Neumann P. '*Varroa destructor*: research avenues towards sustainable control'. *Journal of Apicultural Research* 51, 1 (2012): 125–32.

Foley K, Lecocq A, Jensen AB. 'Drone brood production in Danish apiaries and potential for drone brood for consumption' (in preparation).

Fuchs S, Langenbach K. 'Multiple infestation of *Apis mellifera* brood cells and reproduction in *Varroa jacobsoni* Oud'. *Apidologie* 20 (1989): 257–66.

Gade B, Theuerkauf R. *Biavl: bier, blomster og honning* [Beekeeping: bees, flowers and honey] (Denmark: Lindhardt og Ringhof, 2016).

Haydak MH. 'The food of the drone larvae'. *Annals of the Entomological Society of America* 50, 1 (1957): 73–75.

Hendriksma HP, Shafir S. 'Honey bee foragers balance colony nutritional deficiencies'. *Behavioral Ecology and Sociobiology* 70 (2016): 509–17.

Jensen AB, Evans J, Jonas-Levi A, Benjamin O, Martinez I, Dahle B, Roos N, Lecocq A, Foley K. (2017) 'Standard methods for *Apis mellifera* brood as human food'. In V Dietemann; J D Ellis; P Neumann; (Eds) The Coloss Beebook, Volume III: standard methods for *Apis mellifera* hive products research. Submitted May 2015 to *Journal of Apicultural Research* 56. www.tandfonline.com/doi/full/10.1080/00218839.2016.1226606

Jonas-Levi A, Benjamin O, Martinez JJI. 'Does a parasite infestation change the nutritional value of an insect? Varroa mites on honey bees as a model'. *Journal of Insects for Food and Feed* 1, 2 (2015.): 141–47.

Rosenkranz P, Aumeier P, Ziegelmann B. 'Biology and control of *Varroa destructor*'. *Journal of Invertebrate Pathology* 103 (2010): 96–119.

Ruttner F. 'Races of bees'. In *The Hive and the Honey Bee* (Hamilton, Illinois: Dadant & Sons, 1975): 19–38

Schulz AE. 'Reproduction and population-dynamics of the parasitic mite *Varroa jacobsoni* oud – and its dependence on the brood cycle of its host, *Apis mellifera*'. *Apidologie* 15, 4 (1984): 401–19.

Valentin D, Chollet S, Lelièvre M, Abdi H. 'Quick and dirty but still pretty good: a review of new descriptive methods in food science'. *International Journal of Food Science & Technology* 47, 8 (2012): 1,563–78.

Vejsnæs F, Jørgensen AS, Theuerkauf RT. 'Varroa og dens bekæmpelse [Varroa and its control]'. *Tidsskrift for Biavl* 8 (2005).

Wallberg A, Han F, Wellhagen G, Dahle B, Kawata M, Haddad N, Simões ZLP, Allsopp MH, Kandemir I, De la Rúa P, Pirk CW, Webster MT. 'A worldwide survey of genome sequence variation provides insight into the evolutionary history of the honeybee *Apis mellifera*'. *Nature Genetics* 46 (2014): 1,081–88.

Winston ML. *The Biology of the Honey Bee* (Cambridge, Massachusetts: Harvard University Press, 1991).

BEE BREAD (PP.90–91)
An earlier version of this text was published on the New York Academy of Medicine blog, and then on the Nordic Food Lab blog.

Akhmetova R, Sibgatullin J, Garmonov S, Akhmetova L. 'Technology for extraction of bee bread from the honeycomb'. *Procedia Engineering* 42 (2012): 1822–25.

Anderson KE, Carroll MJ, Sheehan T, Mott BM, Maes P, Corby-Harris V. 'Hive-stored pollen of honey bees: many lines of evidence are consistent with pollen preservation, not nutrient conversion'. *Molecular Ecology* 23 (2014): 5904–17.

Degrandi-Hoffman G, Eckholm BJ, Huang MH. 'A comparison of bee bread made by Africanized and European honey bees (*Apis mellifera*) and its effects on hemolymph protein titers'. *Apidologie* 44, 1 (2013): 52–63.

Gherman BI, Denner A, Bobiş O, Dezmirean DS, Mărghitaş LA, Schlüns H, Moritz RFA, Erler S. 'Pathogen-associated self-medication behavior in the honeybee *Apis mellifera*'. *Behavioural Ecology and Sociobiology* 68 (2014): 1777–84.

Gilliam M. 'Microbiology of pollen and bee bread: the genus Bacillus'. *Apidologie* 10, 3 (1979.): 269–74.

Gilliam M. 'Microbiology of pollen and bee bread: the yeasts'. *Apidologie* 10, 1 (1979): 43–53.

Gilliam M, Prest DB, Lorenz BJ. 'Microbiology of pollen and bee bread: taxonomy and enzymology of molds'. *Apidology* 20 (1989): 53–68.

Herbert EW, Shimanuki H. 'Chemical composition and nutritive value of bee-collected and bee-stored pollen'. *Apidologie* 9, 1 (1978.): 33–40.

Mattila HR, Rios D, Walker-Sperling VE, Roeselers G, Newton ILG. 'Characterization of the active microbiotas associated with honey bees reveals healthier and broader communities when colonies are genetically diverse'. *PLOS One* 7, 3 (2012).

Nagai T, Nagashima T, Myoda T, Inoue R. 'Preparation and functional properties of extracts from bee bread'. *Nahrung – Food* 48, 3 (2004): 226–29.

Vásquez A, Olofsson TC. 'The lactic acid bacteria involved in the production of bee pollen and bee bread'. *Journal of Apicultural Research* 48, 3 (2009): 189–95.

Yoder JA, Jajack AJ, Rosselot AE, Smith TJ, Yerke MC, Sammataro D. 'Fungicide contamination reduces beneficial fungi in bee bread based on an area-wide field study in honey bee, *Apis mellifera*, colonies'. *Journal of Toxicology and Environmental Health, Part A* 76, 10 (2013): 587–600.

TERMITE SAGA (PP.95–109)
Ayieko MA, Ndong'a MFO, Tamale A. 'Climate change and the abundance of edible insects in the Lake Victoria region'. *Journal of Cell and Animal Biology* 4, 7 (2010): 112–18.

Christensen DL, Orech FO, Mungai MN, Larsen T, Friis H, Aagaard-Hansen J. 'Entomophagy among the Luo of Kenya: a potential mineral source?' *International Journal of Food Sciences and Nutrition* 57, 3–4 (2006): 198–203.

Jouquet P, Traore S, Choosai C, Hartmann C, Bignell D. 'Influence of termites on ecosystem functioning. Ecosystem services provided by termites'. *European Journal of Soil Biology* 47, 4 (2011): 215–22.

Kinyuru JN, Kenji GM, Njoroge MS. 'Process development, nutrition and sensory qualities of wheat buns enriched with edible termites (*Macrotermes subhylanus*) from Lake Victoria region, Kenya'. *African Journal of Food, Agriculture, Nutrition and Development* 9, 8 (2009): 1,739–50.

Kinyuru JN, Konyole SO, Kenji GM, Onyango CA, Owino VO, Owuor BO, Estambale BB, Friis H, Roos N. 'Identification of traditional foods with public health potential for complementary feeding in western Kenya'. *Journal of Food Research* 1 (2012): 148–58.

Lesnik JJ. 'Termites in the hominin diet: a meta-analysis of termite genera, species and castes as a dietary supplement for South African robust australopithecines'. *Journal of Human Evolution* 71 (2014): 94–104.

Owuor Odula E. Badilisha. Accessed 13 July 2016. <www.badilishapermaculture.org>.

Sileshi GW, Nyeko P, Nkunika POY, Sekematte BM, Akinnifesi FK, Ajayi OC. 'Integrating ethno-ecological and scientific knowledge of termites for sustainable termite management and human welfare in Africa'. *Ecology and Society* 14 (2009): 48.

van Huis A. 'Insects as food in sub-Saharan Africa'. *International Journal of Tropical Insect Science* 23, 3 (2003): 163–85.

SAM (PP.110-12)

Ayieko MA, Kinyuru JN, Ndong'a MF, Kenji GM. 'Nutritional value and consumption of black ants (*Carebara vidua Smith*) from the Lake Victoria region in Kenya'. *Advance Journal of Food Science and Technology* 4, 1 (2012): 39-45.

Ayieko MA, Ndong'a MFO, Tamale A. 'Climate change and the abundance of edible insects in the Lake Victoria region'. *Journal of Cell and Animal Biology* 4, 7 (2010): 112-18.

Ayieko M, Oriaro V. 'Consumption, indigenous knowledge and cultural values of the lakefly species within the Lake Victoria region'. *African Journal of Environmental Science and Technology* 2, 10 (2008): 282-86.

Ayieko MA, Oriaro V, Nyambuga IA. 'Processed products of termites and lake flies: improving entomophagy for food security within the Lake Victoria region'. *African Journal of Food, Agriculture, Nutrition and Development* 10, 2 (2010): 2,085-98.

MAYENJE (PP.116-19)
This section was originally published in an earlier form in 'Dispatches from the Lab: exploring the deliciousness of insects in Africa', on the MADFeed website.

DA Ofori DA, Anjarwalla P, Mwaura L, Jamnadass R, Stevenson PC, Smith P. 'Pesticidal plant leaflet: *Tagetes minuta L*'. University of Greenwich Natural Resources Institute (2013). Accessed 10 June 2016. projects.nri.org/adappt/docs/Tagetes_factsheet.pdf.

BOGONG MOTH (PP.130-33)
Pettina L. 'Spatial and temporal characteristics of arsenic in the bogong moth (*Agrotis infusa*)'. PhD thesis. La Trobe University, Victoria, Australia (2010).

LERP (PP.134-6)
Kemarre Turner M. *Iwenhe Tyerrtye: What it Means to Be an Aboriginal Person* (Alice Springs, Australia: IAD Press, 2010).

YURRAMPI (PP.137-41)
This section was originally published in an earlier form in 'Dispatches from the Lab: on the hunt for honey ants in the Australian outback', on the MADFeed.

Latz P. *Bushfires and Bushtucker: Aboriginal Plant Use in Central Australia* (Alice Springs, Australia: IAD Press, 2004).

WITJUTI (PP.142-4)
Latz P. *The Flaming Desert: Arid Australia – A Fire Shaped Landscape* (Alice Springs, Australia: IAD Press, 2007).

KANTA (PP.145-9)
Sections of this text appear in their original form in 'Observations from the frontier of deliciousness', for MAD Dispatches.

INSECTS TO FEED THE WORLD (PP.175-81)
Nakagaki BJ, DeFoliart GR. 'Comparison of diets for mass-rearing *Acheta domesticus* (Orthoptera: Gryllidae) as a novelty food, and comparison of food conversion efficiency with values reported for livestock'. *Journal of Economic Entomology* 84, 3 (1991): 891-96.

LIVØ (PP.182-6)
Heyden B. *Kochbuch oder Gründliche Anweisung, einfache und feine Speisen mit möglichster Sparsamkeit zuzubereiten.* 16. Auflage. (Reutlingen, Germany: Enßlin und Laiblin, 1887): 40.

Massard JA. 'Maikäfer in Luxemburg: Historisches und Kurioses'. *Lëtzebuerger Journal* 60, 88 (2007): 26-27.

Schneider JJ. 'Maikäfersuppen, ein vortreffliches und kräftiges Nahrungsmittel'. *Magazin für die Staatsarzneikunde* 3 (1844): 403-5.

Krutz H. 'Maikäfersuppe – eklich oder köstlich?' aid. Published 27 April 2016. Accessed 26 June 2016. www.aid.de/inhalt/maikaefersuppe-eklig-oder-koestlich-6270.html.

'Maikäfersuppe'. Wikipedia. Last modified 12 February 2016. Accessed 26 June 2016. de.wikipedia.org/wiki/Maik%C3%A4fersuppe.

May H. 'Die Maikäfer sind wieder da'. NABU. Published 6 May 2008. Accessed 26 June 2016. www.nabu.de/tiere-und-pflanzen/insekten-und-spinnen/kaefer/01263.html.

Manoi. 'Maikäfersuppe'. Kochrezepte. Accessed 26 June 2016. http://www.kochrezepte.de/suppe-rezepte/maikaefersuppe-44460.html.

'Rezept für Maikäfersuppe'. Zukunft des Essens. Accessed 26 June 2016. www.zukunftsessen.de/rezepte/rezept-fur-maikafersuppe/.

HEBO (PP.187-93)
Cronon W. 'The trouble with wilderness: or, getting back to the wrong nature'. *Environmental History* 1 (1996): 7-28.

Lorimer J. *Wildlife in the Anthropocene: Conservation after Nature* (Minneapolis: University of Minnesota Press, 2015).

THAILAND FIELDWORK (PP.203-9)
1   Halloran A, Roos N, Hanboonsong Y. 'Cricket farming as a livelihood strategy in Thailand.' *Geographical Journal* (2016). onlinelibrary.wiley.com/doi/10.1111/geoj.12184/full.

SOME SPECIAL THANKS

To all our team members, past and present, who have made our work what it is:

Ni Lenette, Maya Hey, Liis Tuulberg, Jonas Astrup Pedersen, Marilyn Koitnurm, Anna Sigrithur, Yelena Montoya Rodríguez, Rebecca Roberts, Tobyn Excell, Andrew Müller, Rosemary Liss, Bernat Guixer, Santiago Lastra, Charlotte, Holm Brodersen, Meradith Hoddinott, Jason Ball, Johnny Drain, Avery McGuire, Anna Dabrowska, Peter Hartley Booth, Youngbin Kim, Alec Borsook, Ben Reade, Guillemette Barthouil, Edith Salminen, Kritika Suratkal, Justine de Valicourt, Alicynn Fink, Nick Phelps, Sarah Warren, Arielle Johnson, Emil Johansen, Elisabeth Paul, Kristen Rasmussen, Sebastian Moreno Henao, Richard Lam, Ana Caballero, Josh Pollen, Anne Overmark, Julius Schneider, Emil Glaser, Nurdin Topham, Mark Emil Tholstrup Hermansen, Rachele Elena, Ulla Kaja Radeloff, Lars Williams and Sarah Britton.

And particularly to those team members who contributed to our insect project in some way: Ni Lenette, Maya Hey, Jonas Astrup Pedersen, Anna Sigrithur, Rebecca Roberts, Andrew Müller, Bernat Guixer, Santiago Lastra, Meradith Hoddinott, Avery McGuire, Ben Reade, Guillemette Barthouil, Sebastian Moreno Henao, Ana Caballero, Josh Pollen and Nurdin Topham.

To Lars Williams, Mark Emil Hermansen and Arielle Johnson, for being crucial players in the very beginning, and to the entire team at Noma and MAD.

To René Redzepi, chef-patron of restaurant Noma and the one who planted the seed for our research.

To the Velux Foundation, for supporting our research and making this project possible.

To our Project Advisory Board:
Mark Bomford, director of the Yale Sustainable Food Project; Paul Rozin, professor of psychology, University of Pennsylvania; Arnold van Huis, professor emeritus of entomology, Wageningen University; and Alex Atala, chef-patron of Restaurant D.O.M., São Paulo.

To our project collaborators in the Insect Pathology and Biological Control Research Group at the University of Copenhagen, Professor Jørgen Eilenberg and Associate Professor Annette Bruun Jensen.

To Andreas Johnsen, *sine qua non*.

To the stellar team of publishers, editors, photographers and designers who worked through thick and thin to bring this book to life: especially Ellie Smith and Sophie Hodgkin, our editors at Phaidon; Chris Tonnesen, for the photographs; Michael Wallace for the artworking and Rich Stapleton and Rosa Park, for the design.

And to all those who helped us along the way by sharing their hearths and homes, their knowledge and skill and energy:

DENMARK
Oliver Maxwell and Bybi, Thomas Laursen, Søren Wiuff, Bente Qvist Kjærgaard, Karsten Kjærgaard, Kollektivet Maos Lyst, Emilie Kjærgaard, Knud Sørensen, Ida Hvid, Ranee Udtumthisarn and Midas Rosforth.

ITALY
Francesco Corrias, Antonio Maria Cubadda, Isidoro (Sidoe) Perria, The Flore family and Enrico Cirilli.

KENYA
Pamela Muyeshi, Kiran Jethwa, John 'Tito' Shikhu, John Kariuki, Jane Karanja, Donald Kipkoech Rotich, Beuton Kiprono Sang, Victor Kipkorin Taraiya, John K. Kemoi, John Koech, Sylvester Kipkebut, Kapkiyai Elijah, Chebii Cheptoo, John Ngugi, Thomson Oletenges, Caleb Kemboi, Philip Ochieng, Philip Barno, Onesmus Opande, Raphael Sumba Ochieng, F. M. E. Wanjala, Meliab Nasanibu, Ferdinand Wafula, Rechael Eyauma, The Epang'a Valley community, Evans Owuor Odula, Badilisha Eco Village, Michael Odula, Otieno Nundu, Monica Ayieko, Jackline Oloo, Florence Awuor, Beatrice Ngesa, Wilburforce Mate, Osewre Joseph Oketch, Patrick Onyango Puye, Shellan Omondi Onyango, Monica Ondiso, Gilbert Anyanda, Alex Ebosa, David Idewa, Benjamin Mwene and Jeremiah Odoi.

UGANDA
Edie Mukiibi, Mzee John Ssentongo, Gerald Gyagenda, Daniel Galabuzi, Paul Mugerwa, Benezet Alozias, Rogers Sserunjogi, Tom and Rita Lubeba and Philip Nyeko.

AUSTRALIA
Kelly Donati, Susan Lowish, Bill Gammage, Tyronne Bell, Wally Bell, Karen Williams, Warlukurlangu Artists of Yuendumu, Cecilia Alfonso, Gloria Morales, Wendy Baarda, Frank Baarda, Sara Diana, Coral Kelake, Ruth Napaljarri Stewart, Tess Napaljarri Ross, Liddy Napananga Walker, Esther Nungarai Fry, Amelia Brown Napaljarri, Janelle Clare, Wilson Napurrula, Ruth Spencer, Rahab Spencer, Cheryl Walker, James Viles, Kylie Kwong, Jock Zonfrillo, Duncan Welgemoed and Stewart Wesson.

MEXICO
José Carlos (JC) Redon, Enrique Olvera, Joaquin Cardoso, Armando Soria Castañeda, Amelia Copca Cortés, Enedino Peña Peña, Maria Ester del Valle Copca, Ivan Fernando Del Razo Carillo, Guillermina Muñoz Maldonado, Don Sefarino, Alejandro Ruíz and José Manuel Baños.

PERU
Palmiro Ocampo, Brisa Deneumostier, Reiser Tuanama Salas, Virgilio Martinez Veliz, Malena Martinez, Rodolpho Pesha and Xenon Yojaje.

THE NETHERLANDS
Margot and Marieke Calis, Andrew Müller, Emily Anthes, Christopher Münke and Grace Tan.